『中国式现代化的故事』丛书

张占斌 总主编

为什么是上海？

中国式现代化的上海故事

中共上海市委党校（上海行政学院） 编著

国家行政学院出版社
NATIONAL ACADEMY OF GOVERNANCE PRESS

中央党校出版社集团
国家行政学院出版社

图书在版编目（CIP）数据

为什么是上海？：中国式现代化的上海故事 / 中共
上海市委党校（上海行政学院）编著 . — 北京：国家行政
学院出版社，2023.11（2024.1 重印）

（"中国式现代化的故事"丛书 / 张占斌主编）

ISBN 978-7-5150-2829-3

Ⅰ . ①为… Ⅱ . ①中… Ⅲ . ①现代化建设－研究－上
海 Ⅳ . ①D675.1

中国版本图书馆 CIP 数据核字（2023）第 199888 号

书　　名　为什么是上海？——中国式现代化的上海故事
　　　　　WEISHENME SHI SHANGHAI ?—— ZHONGGUOSHI XIANDAIHUA DE SHANGHAI GUSHI
作　　者　中共上海市委党校（上海行政学院）　编著
统筹策划　胡　敏　刘韫劼　陈　科
责任编辑　陈　科　陆　夏
责任校对　许海利
责任印制　吴　霞
出版发行　国家行政学院出版社
　　　　　（北京市海淀区长春桥路 6 号　100089）
综 合 办　（010）68928887
发 行 部　（010）68928866
经　　销　新华书店
印　　刷　北京新视觉印刷有限公司
版　　次　2023 年 11 月北京第 1 版
印　　次　2024 年 1 月北京第 2 次印刷
开　　本　185 毫米 ×260 毫米　16 开
印　　张　25.5
字　　数　437 千字
定　　价　85.00 元

本书如有印装问题，可联系调换。联系电话：（010）68929022

出版说明

　　党的二十大报告指出，从现在起，中国共产党的中心任务就是团结带领全国各族人民全面建成社会主义现代化强国、实现第二个百年奋斗目标，以中国式现代化全面推进中华民族伟大复兴。习近平总书记在中央党校建校 90 周年庆祝大会暨 2023 年春季学期开学典礼上的讲话中首次创造性提出"为党育才、为党献策"的党校初心。紧扣党的中心任务，践行党校初心，中央党校出版集团国家行政学院出版社和中央党校（国家行政学院）中国式现代化研究中心特别策划"中国式现代化的故事"系列丛书，邀请地方党校（行政学院）、宣传部门、新闻媒体、行业企业等方面共同参与策划和组织编写，从不同层次、不同维度、不同视角讲述中国式现代化的地方故事、企业故事、产业故事，生动展示各个地区、各个领域在大力拓展中国式现代化新征程上的理念创新、实践创新、制度创新、文化创新等，精彩呈现当代中国以中国式现代化全面推进中华民族伟大复兴的宏大历史叙事，以讲好中国式现代化的故事来讲好中国故事。

　　该丛书力求体现这样几个突出特点：

　　其一，文风活泼，以白描手法代入鲜活场景。本丛书区别于一般学术论著或理论读物严肃刻板的面孔，以生动鲜活的题材、清新温暖的笔触、富有现场感的表达和丰富精美的图片，将各地方、企业推进中国式现代化建设的理论思考、战略规划、重要举措、实践路径等向读者娓娓道来，使读者在沉浸式的阅读体验中获得共鸣、引发思考、受到启迪。

其二，视野开阔，以小切口反映大主题。丛书中既有历史人文风貌、经济地理特质的纵深概述，也有改革创新举措、转型升级案例的细节剖解，既讲天下事，又讲身边事，以点带面、以小见大，用故事提炼经验，以案例支撑理论，从而兼顾理论厚度、思想深度、实践力度和情感温度。

其三，层次丰富，以一域之光映衬全域风采。丛书有开风气之先的上海气度，也有立开放潮头的南粤之声；有沉稳构筑首都经济圈的京津冀足音，也有聚力谱写东北全面振兴的黑吉辽篇章；有在长江三角洲区域一体化发展中厚积薄发的安徽样板，也有在成渝地区双城经济圈中走深走实的川渝实践；有生态高颜值、发展高质量齐头并进的云南画卷，也有以"数"为笔、逐浪蓝海的贵州答卷；有"强富美高"的南京路径，也有"七个新天堂"的杭州示范……丛书还将陆续推出各企业、各行业的现代化故事，带读者领略中国式现代化的深厚底蕴、辽阔风光和壮美前景。

"中国式现代化的故事"系列丛书既是各地方、企业推进中国式现代化建设充满生机活力的形象展示，也是以地方、企业发展缩影印证中国式现代化理论科学性的多维解码。希望本丛书的出版，能够为各地方、企业搭建学习交流平台，将一地一域的现代化建设融入全面建设社会主义现代化国家的大局，步伐一致奋力谱写中国式现代化的历史新篇章。

国家行政学院出版社

"中国式现代化的故事"丛书策划编辑组

总　序

　　党的二十大擘画了全面建成社会主义现代化强国、以中国式现代化全面推进中华民族伟大复兴的宏伟蓝图。中国式现代化是前无古人的开创性事业，是强国建设、民族复兴的康庄大道。回顾过去，中国共产党带领人民艰辛探索、铸就辉煌，用几十年时间走完西方发达国家几百年走过的工业化历程，创造了经济快速发展和社会长期稳定的两大奇迹，实践有力证明了中国式现代化走得通、行得稳；面向未来，在以习近平同志为核心的党中央坚强领导下，各地方各企业立足各自的资源禀赋、区位优势和产业基础、发展规划，精心谋划、奋勇争先，在推进中国式现代化过程中将展现出一系列生动场景，一步一个脚印地把美好蓝图变为现实形态。

　　中国式现代化，是中国共产党领导的社会主义现代化，既有各国现代化的共同特征，又有基于自己国情的中国特色。中国式现代化，是人口规模巨大的现代化，是全体人民共同富裕的现代化，是物质文明和精神文明相协调的现代化，是人与自然和谐共生的现代化，是走和平发展道路的现代化。这五个方面的中国特色，不仅深刻揭示了中国式现代化的科学内涵，也体现在不同地方、企业推进现代化建设可感可知可行的实际成果中。中国式现代化理论为地方、企业现代化的实践探索提供了不竭动力，地方、企业推进中国式现代化建设的成就也印证了中国式现代化道路行稳致远的时代必然。

　　为讲好中国式现代化的故事，更加全面、立体、直观地呈现中国式现代化的丰富内涵和万千气象，中央党校（国家行政学院）中国式现代化研究中心和中央党校出版集团国家行政学院出版社联合策划推出"中国式现代化的故事"系列丛书，展现各地方、企业等在着眼全国大局、立足地方实际、发挥自身优势，推进中国式现代化建设上的新突破新作为新担当，总结贯穿其中的完整准确全面贯彻新发展理念、构建新发展格局、推动高质量发展的新理念新方法新经验。我们希望该系列丛书一本一本地出下去，能够为各地更好推进中国式现代化建设以启迪和思考，为以中国式现代化全面推进中华民族伟大复兴凝聚更加巩固的思想基础，为进一步推进中国式现代化的新实践、书写中国式现代化的新篇章汇聚磅礴力量。

中央党校（国家行政学院）中国式现代化研究中心主任

2023 年 10 月

序 言

城市的兴衰与其所在国家的发展状况密切相联，一国所拥有的政治体制、所处的历史环境和所面临的现实任务，塑造、影响着城市的发展战略与具体路径；同时，城市的现代化故事既彰显了其所在国家现代化乃至世界现代化的共性特征，也书写了带有这座城市特质的现代化传奇。

正是在这个意义上，上海之于中国，之于世界，具有特殊意义。作为世界观察中国、中国走向世界的窗口与前沿，上海的故事不仅属于上海，还能辐射全国、影响世界。

20 世纪初，美国人玛丽·宁德·盖姆韦尔（Mary Ninde Gamewell）在其所著《中国之门：上海图景》（*The Gateway to China: Pictures of Shanghai*）一书中开篇就指出，要了解中国，就去上海。"上海宛如一个小小的世界，在这里可以近距离地研究整个中国的缩影。"她把上海与中国紧密联系起来，强调上海是了解中国的窗口。

确实，上海作为中国的窗口城市，在中国式现代化进程中具有独特的样本意义。若以百年为尺度，上海作为中国共产党的诞生地和初心始发地，一百多年的上海发展史，就是一部新旧中国的苦难史、抗争史、改革史、开放史；可以说，上海就是中华民族从站起来、富起来到强起来的缩影。

20 世纪 30 年代，上海成为亚洲的国际金融中心，被誉为"东方巴黎"，称得上当时中国"最现代化的城市"。但这样的辉煌只持续了很短一段时间。实际上，近 100 多年来，上海也并不是一直领先，其发展几经沉浮，甚至到了 20 世纪 80

年代改革开放的春潮在中华大地涌动时，上海还扮演着改革"后卫"的角色。那时，上海尽管占有 10 个全国第一的经济指标，如工业总产值、上缴国家税利、出口创汇等，同时也有人口密度最大、人均道路面积最少、缺房户比重最高、车辆事故及癌症发病率居全国城市之最等 5 个"倒数第一"。

上海真正的繁华复兴，是从改革开放后开始的。中国改革开放的总设计师邓小平曾说过，"上海是我们的王牌，把上海搞起来是一条捷径"。20 世纪 90 年代初，浦东开发开放，上海被赋予了改革开放排头兵的重任。如今，上海国际经济、金融、贸易、航运中心基本建成，正在形成具有全球影响力的科技创新中心基本框架，全面提升城市能级和核心竞争力。短短几十年时间，中国走过了发达国家数百年的工业化历程。作为国家战略的承载地、改革开放排头兵、创新发展先行者，上海正走出一条超大城市治理现代化新路。现在，上海的浦东新区已成为社会主义现代化建设的引领区，继续扮演着开路先锋、继续发挥着示范引领作用。

衡量一个城市发展的尺度很多，定量的指标更有说服力。2012 年到 2022 年这 10 年间，上海全市生产总值从 2.13 万亿元跃升到 4.47 万亿元，经济总量稳居全国中心城市首位；近 10 年来，上海着力保障和改善民生，全市居民人均可支配收入从 3.86 万元提高到 7.8 万元，人均期望寿命从 82.41 岁提高到 84.11 岁；上海正努力践行"人民城市"理念，坚持把最好的资源留给人民，全面推动滨水公共空间的改造提升，先后实现了黄浦江核心段 45 千米岸线、苏州河中心城区 42 千米岸线贯通，还江于民、还岸于民，昔日的"工业锈带"逐步蜕变为今天水清、岸美、宜游的"生活秀带"。从 2022 年这一年来看：上海港集装箱吞吐量突破4730 万国际标准箱，连续 13 年位居世界第一；上海市工业战略性新兴产业产值占规模以上工业总产值的比重提高到 43%，集成电路、生物医药、人工智能三大先导产业规模达到 1.5 万亿元；上海的金融业增加值达到 8626.31 亿元，比上年增长 5.2%，占上海地区生产总值比重的 19.3%……

上面我们所列举的这些数据比较客观地展示上海这座城市的发展活力、魅力与潜力。同时，这些客观的数据是城市现代化程度的重要指标，它们也是引发人们包括国际友人关注中国、品味上海的现实动因。

总之，上海在包容并蓄中厚积薄发，在创新发展中破茧成蝶。中国式现代化是有目标、有规划、有战略的，其在上海的图景不是虚无缥缈的，而是可感可及的，这幅美丽的画卷无疑是向世界诠释中国式现代化的最生动样本。正如2020年11月12日，习近平主席在浦东开发开放30周年庆祝大会上指出的："浦东开发开放30年取得的显著成就，为中国特色社会主义制度优势提供了最鲜活的现实明证，为改革开放和社会主义现代化建设提供了最生动的实践写照！"

上海作为一个拥有常住人口2500万人左右的超大城市，正在加快推进中国式现代化建设。上海的现代化实践主要聚焦高质量发展、高品质生活、高效能治理和高水平开放等方面，涵盖了包括经济、政治、社会、文化和生态等方面的具体内容，这些生动诠释了中国式现代化的本质特征和原则要求。上海的现代化发展，其直接影响不囿于上海，还包括国内、国际。就上海的国际影响力来说，其影响力与吸引力与日俱增。近年来，上海利用外资呈现逆势增长态势。2023年第一季度，实际使用外资达78亿美元，同比增长28.1%；总部经济集聚发展，跨国公司地区总部、外资研发中心累计分别达到907家、538家。

当人们漫步在上海街头，感受到上海的建筑可阅读、街区宜漫步、公园可休憩，如果再叠加上对上述发展数据的知晓，可能很多人就会自觉不自觉地发出这样的疑问：为什么是上海？上海为什么能？这个问题不仅是国内外学者、治国理政者常会思考的问题，也是上海市委党校（上海行政学院）在涉外交往过程中，尤其是许多外国政党、政要，以及不少来自港澳台的同胞，来沪交流访问时不断被问及和引发他们思考的热点问题。我们编写这本书，正是想解答他们心中的这个疑问。这些来校访问、交流的外国友人、港澳台同胞来沪的时间有限，他们参观访问的地点有限，听到的课程次数有限，因而对上海、上海故事的了解也有限。为了消除这些"有限"，我们组织我校从事涉外教学的相关老师编写了这本中英文资料，以期对他们认识、了解上海进而认识、了解中国有所裨益。

习近平主席指出，中国式现代化既有各国现代化的共同特征，更有基于自己国情的中国特色。所以，我们在讲述中国式现代化的上海故事时，尽管立足于上海的历史、实践与案例，但切入的问题都是各国在推进现代化过程中的共性问题，如发展的问题、增进民生福祉问题、城市治理问题、贫困治理问题和开放共赢问题等，这些问题是引发大家一起讨论、对话和共鸣的前提。同时，我们在讲述上海在破解这些现代化过程中共性问题的案例时，注重归纳操作层面的解决路径或政策举措，并在最后尝试着从学理层面阐释这些具体做法背后的理论依据。

全书共分五章。第一章"百年巨变：中国式现代化的亮丽名片"作为全书的"总论"，在交代上海经济社会发展整体概貌及特点基础上，着重就上海作为中国共产党的诞生地和改革开放的前沿阵地作了阐述。红色基因与改革开放两者相辅相成，成就了上海开放、创新、包容的城市品格，这也是理解"为什么是上海"的关键之处，是上海不断创造发展新奇迹的勇气、智慧和力量源泉之所在。第二章、第三章、第四章重点聚焦10多年来上海经济社会发展新举措、新思路、新做法，分别围绕"高质量发展""高品质生活""高效能治理"展开。第五章"共享开放：为中国和世界贡献上海智慧"，重点介绍了上海在服务全国中发展自身、在面向全球中推进高水平对外开放，跳出上海看上海、立足全国看上海、瞄准世界看上海，展现上海建设具有世界影响力的社会主义现代化国际大都市的格局、胸襟、情怀。

在每章的写作安排上，包含共性问题、案例演绎和总结提炼三部分。陆家嘴金融城的兴起、张江科学城的战略承载、中国宝武集团（上海）传统企业的低碳绿色转型、衡复历史文化风貌区保护和开发、15分钟社区生活圈的美好生活打造、中心城区"嵌入式"养老服务、老旧小区城市更新、"一网通办"城市数字化转型、重大议题中的公众参与、东西部协作中的上海力量、国际航运中心洋山深水港建设、中国国际进口博览会……这些案例绘成了一幅中国式现代化的上海画卷。

这幅美丽的画卷，融鲜活的案例、翔实的数据、温情的画面和理性的启迪于一体，见人、见物、见情、见理，特别是"见情""见理"，这既是城市发展的价值指向，也是其进一步发展的深层力量。习近平主席指出："中国式现代化，是中国共产党领导的社会主义现代化"，"党的领导决定中国式现代化的根本性质"，"人民城市"重要理念来源于中国共产党的本质属性，是对中国城市发展的准确价值定位。上海从以前的"十里洋场"、"冒险家的乐园"到今天的"人民城市"理念下的活力四射、诗意栖居、共建共享等，实际上就是把"人民城市人民建，人民城市为人民"重要理念贯彻到城市发展的全过程和城市工作的各个方面，实现以资本增值为中心向以人民为中心的主旨回归，把为人民谋幸福、让生活更美好作为城市工作的鲜明主题。本书的十几个案例尽管主题不同，但是背后的价值理念是一致的，可以说都是对"人民"概念及其利益诉求的具体展现、有效回应。

本书由中共上海市委党校（上海行政学院）组织编写。多年来，中共上海市委党校（上海行政学院）坚持"现代化、综合性、研究型、开放式"办学理念，积极开展以外国政党干部为主体的国（境）外人士来校或线上考察交流活动，获得了广泛认可和普遍好评。

希望这本书作为辅助读物，能给读者进一步认识上海、深度了解中国提供一种新的视角或者引发其对中国问题进一步思考，从而为增进友谊、扩大共识和加强合作贡献我们的绵薄之力。

中共上海市委党校（上海行政学院）教育长、教授　罗峰

2023 年 9 月

目 录

第一章 百年巨变：

中国式现代化的亮丽名片

后　记

百年巨变：
中国式现代化的亮丽名片

外国朋友如果来中国旅行，通常会被告知"要看一百年的中国，就来上海"。2015年9月23日，习近平主席访问美国华盛顿州塔科马市，在参观林肯中学时对课堂上的学生们说："要看千年的中国去西安，看五百年的中国去北京，看一百年的中国去上海。"

为何了解百年中国的发展历史，要来上海？上海这一百多年究竟发生了哪些惊人的变化？何以产生这些变化？让我们带着这些问题走进这座城市——上海。

上海对于中国而言，是一座年轻而独特的城市。180多年前，上海是中国东海岸边、长江出海口旁的小县城。1840年鸦片战争之后，中国遭遇"三千年未有之变局"，外国殖民者用坚船利炮叩开了中国的大门，上海自此开启了自己跌宕起伏的风云历程。百年沧桑，上海不仅仅见证了中华民族的风风雨雨，更见证了神州大地的磅礴巨变，从曾经的"十里洋场"到如今的"人民城市"，从新中国建立前的百废待兴到如今国际化大都市的欣欣向荣，上海就是中国现代化进程的缩影，是中国式现代化的亮丽名片。

领导中国式现代化的力量源头也诞生在上海，那就是中国共产党。正是在中国共产党的带领下，一百年前，上海的工人阶级有了全新的奋斗目标，有了组织体系；她的诞生给这个城市带来了"新生"。

让我们再近距离观察上海，她变化发展速度最快的阶段是伴随着浦东的开发开放而来。"80年代看深圳，90年代看浦东"，浦东引领了中国改革开放的第二波浪潮，也是中国式现代化最生动的现实写照。

励精图治，经过百年巨变，如今的上海已有了坚定的城市属性——人民城市。我们不会再看到百年前那座在华丽的霓虹下严重两极分化的冷酷都市；我们看到的是一个产业要素齐备，商业贸易发达，市民安居乐业、精神富足，在全球城市中具有资源配置能力的社会主义现代化国际大都市。

一、上海是一座人民的城市

（一）引言

外国朋友来到上海，都喜欢驻足欣赏上海外滩的典雅景象，依傍外滩远眺陆家嘴的现代繁华。从黄浦江两岸迥异的建筑风格中，外宾们体会到中国现代化的巨大成就，同时也会感受到历史与现实的剧烈冲击：为何浦江两岸会如此不同？一百多年来，上海究竟经历了哪些变化？为何会发生如此翻天覆地的变化？为何上海是中国式现代化的亮丽名片？

可以说，中国现代化进程的探索起点在上海。1842 年，中国的大门被迫打开了。1842 年 8 月 29 日，近代中国第一个不平等条约《南京条约》签订。条约规定开放五个通商口岸，上海位列其中。之后的几十年，不断有国外"冒险家"逐鹿上海滩，他们改变了上海的天际线，营造了灯火通明的礼堂，建设了机器轰鸣的现代工厂，使上海获得了"东方巴黎"的赞誉，一位近代日本人甚至称之为"魔都"[①]。当时中国的清朝政府也开始了以"自强""求富"为口号的洋务运动，1873 年，清朝大臣李鸿章在上海成立轮船招商局，从事客运和漕运等运输业务，这是洋务运动最成功的产业之一，也被认为是中国寻求富强的近现代历史开端。

中国式现代化的领导力量诞生在上海。没落的清朝政府最终无法通过自强运动改变中国积贫积弱的旧貌，也无法改变中国当时成为半殖民地半封建社会的事实。民族存亡的危

---

① 1923 年，日本作家村松梢风来到上海，逗留了两个月后回到日本，写出一篇近 5 万字的长文《不可思议的都市"上海"》，次年以《魔都》为书名出版，来描述他在上海的见闻和观感。

机迫切需要一股新的力量来领导中国的现代化。这股力量到了1921年的上海，汇聚成为推动中国式现代化的根本性力量：中国共产党。她的诞生与发展，依托于上海庞大的工人阶层，依托于上海多元并存的城市文化，依托于上海五方杂处的社会特点。她的诞生给这个城市，也给这个国家带来了"新生"，所以毛泽东称上海是"近代中国光明的摇篮"。

上海的发展变化和中国式现代化的筚路蓝缕一样，诠释了"苦难辉煌"的不平凡过程。20世纪二三十年代上海的繁华，是只属于少数人的畸形繁华。在"魔都"的五光十色下，掩映的是衣不蔽体的贫民，摩登礼堂建筑外，也有草皮树枝堆砌的"滚地龙"和"棚户区"①。近代上海极速发展的工业也给城市带来了巨大污染：河流、空气、土壤，均遭到了不同程度的破坏。然而通过几十年来的中国式现代化探索，现在的上海已是共享的、宜居的、亲善的"人民城市"。

我们通过一些比较，可以更好地理解上海在中国现代化进程中取得的翻天覆地的变化及其原因。

（二）从"十里洋场"② 到"人民城市"

1. "十里洋场"的巨大矛盾

一百多年前的上海，城市主体被划分为"租界"。1845年殖民者在上海设立英租界，后来又设立美租界、法租界，再后来英美租界合并为公共租界。由于各种复杂的历史原因，租界成为事实上的"国中之国"，无论是清朝政府、北洋政府，还是南京国民政府，都无法对租界实施直接的管辖权。中国人在租界内被全面"矮化"，在方方面面都低人一等，备受歧视。在政治上，华人没有政治权利。公共租界的工部局长期由外国人组成，没有华人董事，直到1928年才开始有中国人参加董事会。华人在租界的日常生活中也受到很多限制和歧视。例如，著名的跑马场（现在是上海人民广场附近的人民公园）当时禁止华人入内。上海跑马总会可以接受外国人为会员，唯独不接受中国人。1908年，

---

① "滚地龙"和"棚户区"是旧上海许多贫民居住场所，生活条件差，后文会有介绍。
② 旧时对上海"南京路"的简称。南京路全长约5千米，即10华里，密布的都是外国资本、贸易、商行和洋行，故称"十里洋场"。

1920 年上海陆家嘴地区与 2020 年陆家嘴的剧烈反差

上海跑马总会有正式会员 320 名，其他国籍的会员约 500 名，无一为华人。

与中国人备受歧视形成鲜明对比的是，一些殖民者在上海拥有特殊的地位，过着骄纵的生活。著名科学家爱因斯坦曾在 20 世纪 20 年代来过上海，他写道："在上海，欧洲人形成一个统治阶级，而中国人则是他们的奴仆；这个城市表明欧洲人同中国人的社会地位的差别，这种差别使得近年来的革命事件部分地可以理解了。"①上海的工厂大多为殖民者所开设，中国的民族资本正处于起步阶段，还很弱小；上海的服务业虽繁盛，但多服务殖民者，普通上海市民的生活与他们大相径庭。从某种意义上说，当时上海的繁华和摩登，并不属于中国人，也不属于多数人。

2. 从"危棚简屋"到"成套新居"

住房问题是近代上海最为突出的民生问题，被称为"天字第一号"难题。旧上海人口规模巨大，1900 年上海人口超过 100 万人，1915 年超过 200 万人，1930 年突破 300 万人大关，成为中国特大城市，远东第二大城市，也是仅次于伦敦、纽约、东京、柏林的世界第五大城市。到 1947 年，上海的人口数量相当于南京、北平、天津这三个城市人口总和。上海是典型的"移民城市"，来自全国各地的人来到上海打工求生。由于旧上海房价高、房租高，普通打工者无力租房，再加上旧上海殖民者工厂的残酷压迫，导致当时上海工人的生活条件极端恶劣，大量的工人都住在自建的"滚地龙"里。所谓"滚地龙"，就是用竹片做骨架，形成一个半圆形，上面盖上破芦席、破麻包，一头用破物堵住，另一头挂上破草帘或破布做门，就成为"房子"了，里面没有桌椅床铺，是由稻草、芦席和破棉絮组成的地铺。在老上海的一些区域，有成片的"滚地龙"，其中比较典型的就是药水弄。药水弄位于上海西康路以西、苏州河以南的狭小地区，因靠近苏州河区域有两座烧石灰的窑，所以地名就叫"石灰窑"，又因这个地区附近有一家江苏药水厂，所以又称"药水弄"，是沪西著名的"三湾一弄""棚户区"之一。那时流行的歌谣道："宁坐三年牢，不住石灰窑。"在这片居住条件极差的区域内，没有水电等基本的生活设施，到处都是垃圾、臭水坑，病疫时常发生。里面的道路弯弯曲曲、高高低低，没有排水沟渠，一下雨就成了泥浆路，十天半月都不会干，人们称之为"阎王路"。

---

① 《爱因斯坦文集》第三卷，商务印书馆 2009 年版，第 31 页。

旧上海的"滚地龙"

旧上海的"棚户区"

　　新中国成立后，上海大兴土木，开始对"棚户区"进行改造，"滚地龙"逐渐消失，茅草屋换成了土房、瓦房，有的人家还建造了两层楼房。同过去相比，"棚户区"居住状况有所改善，但仍然是各自搭建，没有统一规划和设计，房屋密集，空间非常紧张，也谈不上符合现在所要求的消防、卫生等条件。因为没有独立的厨房和卫生间，大多数情况下，都是几户居民公用，隐患很大。由于住房面积特别狭小，有些底楼的居民只能在自家客厅睡觉，脚伸直甚至都能伸到邻居家中。由于离得太近，家住二楼或三楼对窗的两家人，只需用搓衣板之类的木板搭起一座"天桥"就能很方便地将自家的菜肴与邻居分享，有些关系亲密的邻里甚至采用了"今天你家烧饭，明天我家烧饭"的共享模式，这便是"三湾一弄"特有的"搭天桥"吃饭的场景。这样的弄堂被人们戏称为"一线天"。1982 年关于上海住房的调查显示，上海当时有棚户简屋 216 万平方米，旧式里弄 1428 万平方米，居住在这些危棚简屋和旧式里弄的居民占全市总户数的 65%。上海社科院当时做过一次调查显示，1985 年上海市区缺房户共有 88.09 万户，占市区总户数的 52.28%。[①]

上海住房条件的真正改善是在中国大力实施改革开放政策之后。1987 年 3 月，上海把解决人均居住面积 2 平方米以下特困户工作提上市政府重要议事日程。1992 年，上海市第六次党代会明确提出到 20 世纪末完成上海市区 365 万平方米危棚简屋改造的目标。至 2000 年，经过近 10 年的努力，结合土地批租、房地产开发、市政建设，上海全面实现第六次党代会提出的危棚简屋改造预定目标。

苏州河边的危棚简屋（郑宪章　摄）

近些年，上海以更新改造历史街区的方式，加大力度保护历史建筑和历史风貌，同时又抓紧推进成片二级旧里[②]以下房屋改造。比如 2020 年，上海市中心旧房面积最大的黄浦区，根据上海市委、市政府关于进一步加快推进成片二级旧里改造的总体要求，结合工作实际，研究制定了《2020—2022 三年旧改攻坚计划》，通过市区联合储备、

---

①　《"三湾一弄"变形记》，载赵刚印等《改革开放成就上海》，上海人民出版社 2018 年版，第 194 页。

②　二级旧里的住房条件相对于危棚简屋来说略好一些，属于平房或结构较好的老宅基房屋，居住状况同样不乐观。

苏州河边危棚简屋改造成的居民小区"中远两湾城"（来源：乐浴峰/IP SHANGHAI）

区级单独储备、地产集团政企合作平台等多个渠道，想方设法加快民生改善。2022 年 7月，黄浦区成片二级旧里以下房屋改造全面完成，意味着上海成片二级旧里以下房屋改造收官。在更多人看来，这也标志着以黄浦区为代表的上海中心城区，一边是高楼大厦林立、一边是老旧房屋密集的"二元结构"矛盾得以历史性解决。①

从 1992 年开启大规模旧区改造至今，历届上海市委、市政府都把提高居民居住质量

---

① 曹玲娟：《历史性解决！上海成片二级旧里以下房屋改造完成》，人民日报中央厨房－大江东工作室，2022 年 7 月 27 日。

作为民生保障"头等大事"，一届接着一届干，持之以恒、久久为功。目前，上海终于全面完成成片二级旧里以下房屋改造工作，初步实现旧城区现代化进程，取得了巨大成效：中心城区共计约 165 万户家庭、500 万居民的住房条件明显改善，住房成套率至今已逼近100%，人均住房建筑面积已稳步提高至 2021 年的 37.4 平方米，市民住上整洁的成套住房，过上有尊严的生活，获得感、幸福感、安全感大大增强，真正体现"人民城市"的实际内涵。

3. 从"黑色缎带"到"生活秀带"

上海境内有两条河流穿城而过，也就是我们现在所讲的"一江一河"——黄浦江与苏州河。有人说，相较于黄浦江，苏州河更有资格被称为上海的"母亲河"，因为它通往内陆，在海运不发达的年代，河道贸易有着天然的称霸地位。苏州河也称吴淞江，顺着她朝上游行船可以直达苏州的宝带桥，与大运河连接。1843 年上海开埠后，早期殖民者对贸易、商品、货币的流通方向异常敏感，遂将上海市区范围内长 17 千米的吴淞江称为"苏州河"，寓意联通苏州，财通内陆。当时的苏州河水质非常清澈，是一条风光秀丽的江南水道。

工业文明与环境污染是"双生花"。随着上海开埠，由于苏州河连接着江南地区发达的水路，河两岸便成为各种近代工业的"心头好"。1860 年，英国人在苏州河南岸新闸路桥下办了硫酸厂。15 年后，《申报》的创办人美查兄弟入股，从美国和意大利进口硫黄原料，生产硫酸、硝酸、盐酸。因为硫酸厂排放污染物污染了苏州河环境，租界当局限令其搬迁，美查兄弟把厂子搬到苏州河北岸——那里是华界，租界管不到。[①]

同时，中国早期的民族工业也诞生在苏州河的北岸。1912 年至 1925 年，由于第一次世界大战及战后重建，欧美列强自顾不暇，中国民族工业得到了一个难得的发展机遇。那时的苏州河畔烟囱林立，机器隆隆，两江水道，船行如织。几乎所有学者都认为，苏州河的环境也是在这一时期恶化了。一个有力的证据是上海闸北水厂的搬迁。闸北水厂 1909 年选址在苏州河下游。大约在 1920 年始，苏州河市区段出现局部黑臭，水厂被迫加氯消毒。1928 年，为成本计，水厂迁至杨浦黄浦江边。那时苏州河两岸的

---

① 杨海鹏：《苏州河——中国第一条被污染河流的新生》，《南方周末》2001 年 9 月 27 日。

人口已达 200 万人。岸边林立的工厂吸引了当时江苏、安徽、山东来的一大批难民，他们划着小船来到苏州河两岸，搭起危棚简屋，去工厂打工。生活污水、工业废水乃至乡间农闲时的粪便，几乎直泻河道。

到了 20 世纪 50 年代末，苏州河已像是上海城区胸口的一条黑色的带子。苏州河是潮汐河，河水流动性不强，海潮大时，河水会被潮水顶回去，这条"黑色缎带"便周而复始在城市中游来荡去。曾担任上海市苏州河环境综合整治领导小组办公室副主任的张效国回忆说，90 年代，有人大代表视察苏州河，头上冒汗，心里犯恶心，当场就晕倒在河边。[1] 那时上海刚刚对外开放，欧美人、日本人联袂而至，他们不喝上海的水，而是自备饮用水，这让上海的领导们非常难堪。

虽然从 20 世纪 50 年代开始，上海就启动了苏州河污染治理的规划，然而由于资金、技术等问题，一直力不从心。1986 年，上海有了撬动城市变革的"第一桶金"：获得了外国银行 32 亿美元的贷款。这笔资金中的 16 亿元被用于苏州河的污染治理。1988 年，上海和世界银行共同参与的这个项目被命名为"苏州河合流污水一期工程"。该工程的治理思路不复杂：将苏州河以北 70 平方千米、255 万人口产生的工业、生活污水截流，不再直接排入苏州河及其支流，而是用管道输送到吴淞口，深入长江水底排放。经过 6 年建设，全长 33.39 千米的排污管道于 1994 年竣工贯通。同时，总投资 60 亿元的合流污水治理二期工程——白龙港污水截流工程也开始建设。工程完成后，可每天将经过预处理的 500 万吨污水通过管道输送到白龙港排放。经过几年的努力，苏州河的颜色开始泛出黄色，而不再是从前的柏油色。

经过多年持续不断的整治，苏州河干流在 2000 年基本消除黑臭，2002 年以来市区河段的主要水质指标逐渐好转，稳步改善。2000 年在苏州河污染最严重的断面底泥中发现昆虫幼虫，2001 年市区河段出现成群的小型鱼类。同时，主要支流消除黑臭，水质明显改善。2018 年以来，上海聚焦苏州河两岸贯通和品质提升工程，着眼于满足人民对美好生活的向往，苏州河从单一的水质治理逐步向营造高品质生活岸线转变。河道整洁，市容明显改观，滨河绿地、公园大幅增加，亲水岸线改善了市民的生活环境，苏州河两岸

① 张效国：《曾经黑臭的苏州河是怎样变清的》，上观，http://www.shobserver.com/staticsg/res/html/web/news Detail.html?id=53752&sid=67。

正成为适合居住、休闲、观光的城市生活区，真正实现了"生活秀带"的愿景。如今在苏州河边上，依偎着"苏州河·梦清园环保主题公园"，记录了上海治理苏州河的百年之路，记录了苏州河两岸居民"水清梦圆"的时代惊叹。如果说苏州河曾经是上海的一段黑色记忆，那么改造苏州河则是上海城市发展史上的辉煌一幕，也是中国式现代化过程中人与自然和谐共生理念的体现。

（三）结语

中国式现代化进程中要求"坚持以人民为中心的发展思想"。具体到城市工作，习近平主席曾指出："城市的核心是人，关键是十二个字：衣食住行、生老病死、安居乐

苏州河目前已开通了水上观光项目，真正实现"人民共享"（来源：唐宕/IP SHANGHAI）

业。"① 把城市居民最关切的事务放在城市发展的首位去考虑，这是"人民城市"建设的核心，也是上海，乃至中国几千个城市所共同前进的目标。

上海百年巨大变化有目共睹，上海之所以取得如此成就，成为中国式现代化的亮丽名片，就是因为她实践了"人民城市"的理念，遵循了中国式现代化的内生要求。

中国式现代化致力于全体人民共同富裕而非少数人的美好生活。上海的现代化发展告别了旧时代"十里洋场"的畸形繁荣，告别了服务于少数人群的导向模式，告别了"你住花园洋房，我住棚户简屋"的巨大分化。"人民城市"理念要求"将最好资源留给人民"，而不是留给少数特权者，上海这些年贯通了黄浦江和苏州河的沿河岸线，提供给上海市民大量休憩场所、儿童天地、公共空间，再也不是旧租界时期只有少数人可以进入的"外滩公园"，维护了社会公平正义。

中国式现代化致力于人与自然和谐共生，坚持可持续发展，坚持绿水青山就是金山银山的理念。上海的现代化发展中不可避免地遇到工业化带来的各种"烦恼"，如水的问题、空气的问题，但通过几代人的不懈努力，上海完成了"蝶变"，曾经的"黑色缎带"成为"生活秀带"，苏州河、黄浦江两岸成为上海最聚人气的地标。绿化面积也在不断增加，现在上海每逢周末，天气温和时，大大小小的绿地上到处都是露营的市民，这些都是中国式现代化进程中绿色、开放、共享理念的充分实践。

满足人民对美好生活的向往是我们现代化建设的出发点和落脚点。改革开放后的中国，经济不断发展，人民对于美好生活的向往也不断丰富。在上海，30年前大多数居民的向往可能就是一份稳定的工作，一套中等大小面积的住房。但如今，大多数居民需要更多的休闲空间，需要跑步健身，需要看电影，需要带孩子去更多博物馆、艺术馆，而中国式现代化正是要满足这些期盼，真正实现每个人自由而全面的发展。

① 《习近平著作选读》第一卷，人民出版社2023年版，第412页。

二、上海是一座光荣的城市

（一）引言

中国是一个历史悠久、文化灿烂的文明古国，在历史上曾长期走在世界前列，勤劳、勇敢、智慧的中国人民为人类文明进步作出了卓越贡献。近代以后，由于种种原因，中华民族面临亡国灭种的危机，使中国人民清醒地认识到中国的落后状况，从而开始寻求变革、谋求自强，探索现代化道路。

中国社会向何处去？中国的出路在哪里？中国无数仁人志士进行了艰苦卓绝的探索和可歌可泣的斗争，但一次又一次的失败证明了，不触动社会根基的改良之路行不通，照搬照抄西方的正式制度和发展模式也行不通。中国迫切需要新的思想引领救亡运动，迫切需要新的组织凝聚革命力量，挽救处在水深火热中的人民，挽救处在危亡边缘的国家。

1921 年，中国共产党成立，解决了中国现代化建设的领导力量问题，提供了正确的方向指引和坚强的组织保障。100 多年来，中国共产党团结带领中国人民经过艰辛探索、接续奋斗，推动中国社会主义现代化建设取得了举世瞩目的成就。

上海，是中国共产党的诞生地。中国共产党成立后的 12 年里，除三次短暂迁离外，中共中央领导机关均驻扎上海，在这座城市艰辛探索一条适合中国国情的革命道路，其间发出的一条条指令，照亮了中国革命的前行道路，留下的珍贵的红色印迹，已融入上海城市血脉，铸造了上海城市精神的红色之魂。上海星罗棋布、历史与现代交融的革命历史旧址，生动诠释了中国共产党在内忧外患中诞生、在磨难挫折中成长、在攻坚克难中壮大，与人民同呼吸、共命运、心连心的光荣历史，也是对上海这座光荣之城的伟大注解。那么，这支中国式现代化的领导力量为什么诞生在上海呢？

中共一大会址（何兆赟 摄）

中共一大纪念馆（何兆赟 摄）

（二）现代化国际大都市的红色基因

1. 苦难深重：中华民族百年屈辱在上海的缩影

1840 年，中国处于最后一个封建王朝清朝的统治之中，英国对中国发动了鸦片战争，战争以清朝战败告终，中国开始一步步成为半殖民地半封建社会。战败的清朝政府与外来侵略者签订了不平等条约，上海被迫成为向外商开放的通商口岸，殖民者纷纷踏上黄浦江这片江滩。于是，这条曾经是船夫与苦工踏出来的纤道，成为上海的新地标——"外滩"，林立其上的"万国建筑"恢宏古典，却也投射出中华民族近代的百年苦难和屈辱。正是通过这个长江门户，殖民者逐渐控制和蚕食长江流域这一东西走向的中国经济命脉。殖民者在上海设立租界，在租界中设立独立的行政管理机构、司法机构甚至准军事化武装，形成真正意义上的"国中之国"。于是，上海逐渐形成"一市三治"的行政格局，即当时的上海同时存在"法租界"、"公共租界"（又称"英美租界"）、"华界"（即清朝政府"上海县"）三个政府。上海租界是当时中国其余各个租界面积总和的 1.5 倍，也是当时中国所有租界中历时最久的，从 1845 年产生到 1943 年 8 月结束，长达 98 年。

上海开埠以后，外国近代企业陆续建立，产生了第一批产业工人，他们受到残酷的剥削压迫，是"世界上最苦的"产业工人。中国著名文学家夏衍笔下的"包身工"将当时上海工人的深重苦难展现得淋漓尽致："两粥一饭，十二小时工作，劳动强化，工房和老板家庭的义务服役，猪一般的生活，泥土一般地被践踏，——血肉造成的'机器'，终究和钢铁造成的不同；包身契上写明三年期间，能够做满的大概不到三分之二。工作，工作，衰弱到不能走路还是工作，手脚像芦柴棒一般的瘦，身体像弓一般的弯，面色像死人一般的惨，咳着，喘着，淌着冷汗，还是被压迫着做工。"[1] "美国一位作家索洛曾在一本书上说过，美国铁路的每一根枕木下面，都横卧着一个爱尔兰工人的尸首。那么，我也这样联想，东洋厂的每一个锭子上面都附托着一个中国奴隶的冤魂！"[2]

---

[1] 《夏衍文集：文学》（上），浙江文艺出版社 2005 年版，第 10—20 页。
[2] 《夏衍文集：文学》（上），浙江文艺出版社 2005 年版，第 10—20 页。

事实证明，不触动旧的社会根基的自强运动，各种名目的改良主义，旧式农民战争，资产阶级革命派领导的民主主义革命，照搬西方政治制度模式的各种方案，都不能完成中华民族救亡图存和反帝反封建的历史任务，都不能让中国的政局和社会稳定下来，更谈不上为中国实现国家富强、人民幸福提供制度保障。中国迫切需要新的思想引领救亡运动，迫切需要新的组织凝聚革命力量。

2. 伟大开端：中国共产党在上海的诞生

中国共产党在上海创建的原因择其要者有四：特殊的政治格局、开放的文化氛围、复杂的社会结构和便捷的交通通信条件。[①]

特殊的政治格局提供"政治缝隙"。当时上海法租界、公共租界和华界"各自为政"，使得城市管理极为复杂。这些租界的交界处虽然没有物理屏障的隔绝，但是三个租界当中任何一家的巡捕都不能越界执法。所以，当时的上海因为租界的存在出现了一道特殊的"缝隙"，中共一大、二大、四大的召开都利用了这条"缝隙"。中共一大召开的地方处于法租界的边缘地带，中共二大会址在法租界和公共租界的交界处，中共四大开会的地方在越界筑路[②]区域。

开放的文化氛围塑造思想和干部基础。新文化运动[③]促使中国涌现诸多改造社会的思潮，马克思主义只是其中一种，起初并不占主导地位，无政府主义曾一度占据优势。俄国十月革命的胜利和五四运动[④]的洗礼，使得进步青年在诸多"主义"的反复对比中最终选择了马克思主义。此后，马克思主义在中国迅速传播。思想的觉醒为中国共产党的创建奠定了思想基础。当时的上海已经是中国出版业最发达的城市，繁荣的文化机构肥沃

---

① 上海市委党史研究室、上海市档案局编著《日出东方：中国共产党诞生地的红色记忆》，上海文化出版社、上海故事会文化传媒有限公司 2014 年版，第 14 页。

② 越界筑路是上海公共租界在界外修筑道路，进而事实上取得了一定行政楼管辖权的附属于租界的"准租界"区域。

③ 新文化运动是 20 世纪初中国一些先进知识分子发起的反对封建主义的思想解放运动，其基本口号是提倡民主和科学。

④ 五四运动，是 1919 年 5 月 4 日发生在北京的一场以青年学生为主，通过示威游行、请愿、罢工、暴力对抗政府等多种形式进行的爱国运动。其间，上海工人进行的大罢工，导致上海市内市外及海上陆上交通全部中断，生产停止，给帝国主义和军阀政府造成沉重打击。后来，五四运动的中心由北京转移到上海，运动主体由学生演变为工人。

了进步思想的成长土壤，上海成为当时马克思主义传播的中心。1920年，俄共代表在报告上海之行时说："上海是中国社会主义者的活动中心，那里可以公开从事宣传活动。上海有许多社会主义性质的组织，出版包括报纸、杂志和书籍在内的300多种出版物，都带有社会主义色彩。"① 马克思主义在上海的传播塑造了一批先进知识分子，他们当中很多成为中国的第一个共产党组织——"上海共产党早期组织"的发起人。

复杂的社会结构培育新兴革命力量。开埠后的工业和对外经济的发展使得上海形成了多元的社会结构。最为重要的是，20世纪20年代的上海，工人数量占全国的1/4，有"中国工人阶级大本营"之称。哪里有压迫哪里就有反抗，上海工人悲惨的劳动条件和生活条件使得他们颇具斗争性。1919年五四运动爆发后，陈独秀曾经痛陈"北京只有学界运动，市民不觉醒"，而上海工人举行了大规模的罢工。

便利的交通通信条件为中国共产党在上海更好领导中国革命提供了条件。当时上海的交通比中国其他城市发达，不仅有铁路和内河航线，还有定期通往欧美、日本、东南亚等的轮船航线，有利于人员往来。通信网络上，自1930年起上海陆续与旧金山、柏林、巴黎、日内瓦、西贡、伦敦、莫斯科、东京等地建立了无线电直达电报电路，有利于革命者的信息交流。

1921年7月23日，来自各地共产主义小组的13位代表和2位共产国际代表齐聚在当时上海法租界一大代表李汉俊的住所召开中国共产党第一次全国代表大会，其中5位拥有大学学历，2位大学在读，4位有海外留学经历。召开第六次会议时，法租界的密探闯入，代表们被迫转移到浙江嘉兴南湖上的一条游船上继续举行会议，讨论并通过《中国共产党的第一个纲领》《中国共产党的第一个决议》，决定建立三人组成的中央局，选举陈独秀任书记、张国焘为组织主任、李达为宣传主任，中共一大胜利闭幕。

从图1中国近代历史的V形反转轨迹图可以看到，中国共产党1921年创立后，带领中国人民经过28年浴血奋战，打败日本帝国主义，推翻国民党反动统治，完成新民主主义革命，建立了中华人民共和国。这一伟大历史贡献的意义在于，彻底结束了旧中国半殖民地半封建社会的历史，彻底结束了旧中国一盘散沙的局面，彻底废除了列强强加给中国的不平等条约和帝国主义在中国的一切特权，实现了中国从几千年封建专制政治向

---

① 《联共（布）、共产国际与中国国民革命运动（1920—1925）》，北京图书出版社1997年版，第45页。

人民民主的伟大飞跃；深刻改变了近代以后中华民族发展的方向和进程，深刻改变了中国人民和中华民族的前途和命运，深刻改变了世界发展的趋势和格局。

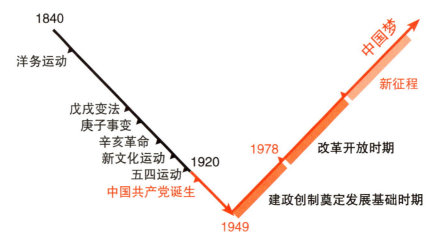

图 1　中国近代历史的 V 形反转轨迹

3. 逆境坚守：中国共产党在上海百折不挠的斗争

中国共产党自 1921 年创立到 1949 年建立新中国，遇到不少困难和挫折，从图 2 中国共产党党员人数变化图我们至少可以看到两次关系生死存亡的危机。其中一次就是 1927 年大革命①失败后的生存危机。1927 年 4 月 12 日，蒋介石在上海发动"四一二"反革命政变②，大肆屠杀共产党员和革命群众，共产党员的人数由 5.7 万人下降到 1 万人。在中国共产党遭受成立以来第一次重大挫折时，中共中央领导机关依然在外部环境最为严峻的上海坚持斗争，使得党在逆境中重生，1928 年 6 月，中国共产党党员人数又迅速增加到 4 万人。从中国共产党诞生到 1933 年初中共中央迁往江西瑞金，除三次短暂迁离外，中共中央领导机关均驻扎上海，因此，上海是当时中国革命运动的指导中心。

---

①　1924 年 1 月至 1927 年 7 月是第一次国内革命战争时期。第一次国内革命战争是中国人民在中国共产党和中国国民党合作领导下进行的反对帝国主义、北洋军阀的战争，亦称"国民革命"或"大革命"。

②　1927 年 4 月 12 日，以蒋介石为首的国民党右派在上海发动反对国民党左派和共产党的武装政变，大肆屠杀共产党员、国民党左派及革命群众。

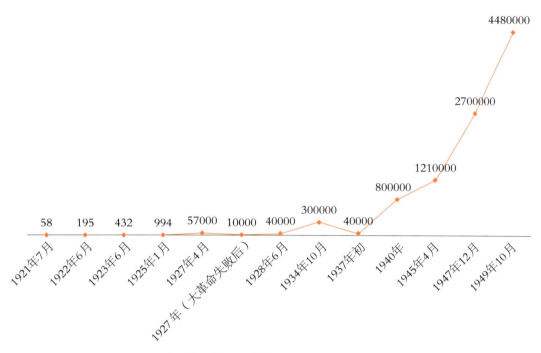

图 2 中国共产党党员人数变化（1921—1949 年）（单位：人）
数据来源：根据中国共产党历次全国代表大会相关文件整理得出

上海现存的 612 处[①]红色文化遗址是幼年时期的中国共产党坚持在最危险的地方开展斗争的光荣历史见证。例如，上海市黄浦区云南中路 171—173 号，人民广场对面一幢不起眼的二层建筑，紧邻当年国民党达官贵人经常出入看戏的"天蟾逸夫舞台"，是当时新修葺的"中共中央政治局机关旧址（1928—1931 年）"所在地，被称为白色恐怖下的红色中枢。1928 年 4 月，在中共湖北省委工作的熊瑾玎受周恩来[②]委派来到上海担任中共中央秘书处会计科科长，负责筹措和管理党的经费，并物色机关办公用房作为中共中央政治局机关。熊瑾玎经过多次考察发现这里紧靠熙熙攘攘的繁华路段，隔壁是热闹的天蟾舞台，又与私人诊所生黎医院为邻，是个险中求安的好地方，适合设立党的秘密机关。于是，熊瑾玎以商人身份租下生黎医院楼上的三间房间，并挂出"福兴商号"的招牌作

---

① 数据来源：《上海市红色资源名录（第一批）》。

② 周恩来 1928 年在中共六届一中全会上当选为中央政治局常务委员，后任中央组织部部长、中央军委书记，为保证中共中央在上海秘密工作的安全，为联系和指导各地区共产党领导的武装斗争，为发展在国民党统治区的秘密工作，起到了重要作用。在这一阶段的大部分时间内，他实际上是中共中央的主要主持者。

为掩护，在此设立了中国共产党中央政治局机关，作为党的秘密办公地点。一般人很难想到，在上海繁华的市中心，敌人眼皮底下，中国共产党中央政治局会在这里办公。从1928年4月至1931年4月，这里见证了中国革命风云变幻的三年，周恩来、邓小平、李维汉、瞿秋白等中央政治局委员在这里工作，领导了最为艰苦的革命斗争——恢复和发展党的组织，加强情报保卫工作，指导根据地建设，确立政治建军的根本原则，领导左翼文化运动，指导全国革命的开展。1931年4月，中央政治局候补委员、中央特科负责人顾顺章被捕叛变。周恩来得知消息后，采取果断措施，将中央和江苏省委机关紧急转移，使党中央机关免遭破坏。从此，"福兴商号"结束了秘密使命，在中共党史上留下了厚重的印记。当熊瑾玎夫妇搬走3天后，即有公共租界巡捕到生黎医院打听楼上住户熊老板的去处。在这座"白色恐怖下的红色中枢"里，中国共产党人用胆识与智慧书写了中国革命重要的一页。

4. 重获新生：中国共产党对上海的尊重与爱护

1949年5月27日，经过整整16天硝烟弥漫的激烈战斗，人民解放军以伤亡3万余人的代价，歼敌15万余人，将上海这座孕育中国共产党和中国革命的远东大都市完整回归人民。[①]

早在党的七届二中全会时，毛泽东就高瞻远瞩地指出进入上海对于中国革命来说是过一大难关。共产党有无能力接管上海，关系到中国共产党在世界上的形象。他说，上海是远东最大的工商业城市，是中国唯一的国际性贸易城市，一定要让这座世界名城完好地回到人民手中。他甚至明确提出：何时进驻上海，须得我们批准。1949年4月27日，第三野战军逼近上海，毛泽东却发来了"不要过于迫近上海"的命令，解放大军紧急刹车，就地开展接管城市的学习。

1949年5月25日，第三野战军夜里攻入上海市区，第二天早上，外面的枪声归于平静后，上海市民打开自家房门，发现穿着破烂军装的解放军官兵全部露宿在梅雨季节湿漉漉的上海街头。美国合众社的报道也记录了当时的场景："中共军队军纪优良，行止有节，礼貌周到……虽然有许多大厦是大开着，可以用来做军营，而中共军队仍睡在人

---

① 刘统：《战上海》，上海人民出版社、学林出版社2018年版，第77页。

行道上……"原来，在渡江战役之前，第三野战军专门制订颁发了《入城三大公约十项守则》，这份守则原件现在被珍藏在中共一大纪念馆中，其中有两条规矩："无故不得打枪""不住民房店铺"。解放军10万大军露宿街头的照片，很快被世界各大媒体刊载。

1949年5月27日，新生的上海，电灯是亮的，自来水未停，电话畅通，工厂学校保护完好，人民解放军创造了战争史上的奇迹。上海解放后，各界群众走上街头欢迎解放军入城，庆祝解放。中国人民解放军迈着整齐的步伐进入市区，接受上海市民的检阅。

（三）结语

习近平在庆祝中国共产党成立100周年大会上的讲话中指出："一百年前，中国共产党的先驱们创建了中国共产党，形成了坚持真理、坚守理想，践行初心、担当使命，不怕牺牲、英勇斗争，对党忠诚、不负人民的伟大建党精神，这是中国共产党的精神之源。"作为中国共产党的诞生地、初心始发地和伟大建党精神的孕育地，上海对中国共产党事业的开创和发展、奋斗历程的艰辛和非凡、始终坚持人民至上的坚守和力行，都有着更深切的认识，上海成为顽强拼搏、接续奋斗，践行人民城市理念、打造人民城市典范，更好地向世界展示中国式现代化光明前景的精神财富。

为人民而生，因人民而兴。中国共产党自成立以来就把为中国人民谋幸福、为中华民族谋复兴确立为自己的初心使命。中共一大召开时，中国共产党只有58名党员，其中22人出自地主官僚家庭、17人出自知识分子家庭，2人出自商人富农家庭，他们绝不是吃不饱饭、穿不暖衣的人，大多数家庭条件还是比较好的，他们之所以参加革命，是为了挽救中华民族于亡国灭种之际，拯救中国人民于水深火热之中。中国共产党之所以能够一次次绝境重生、始终赢得人民的拥护和支持、取得探索现代化建设的成功，根本原因是她始终把人民当家作主和让全体人民过上幸福生活作为自己的目标追求。

始终高扬革命精神。要把理想变为现实，必须发挥革命精神的能动性来战胜困难。在中国共产党的奋斗史上，始终面临着各种各样甚至难以想象的巨大风险挑战。但我们党总是为了人民和民族的利益迎难而上、向险而行，敢于斗争、不怕牺牲，最终取得胜利。据统计，从1921年7月1日中国共产党成立，到1949年10月1日中华人民共和国成立，有姓名可查的牺牲的革命者有370多万人。这就是说，在这1万多个日子里，平均每天就有 370 名共产党员牺牲。任何政党都不可能一贯正确、不犯错误，中国共产党勇于自我革命，敢于承认问题、正确分析原因、坚决纠正错误，所以能够保证在前进的道路上始终具有旺盛活力。

锻造强大的领导力和执政力。中国共产党之所以能够把世界上这个人口最多、历史悠久、文化多样的国度里的亿万人民团结和凝聚起来，创造出以少胜多、以弱胜强的战争奇迹，进而创造出经济快速发展奇迹和社会长期稳定奇迹，原因在于中国共产党拥有强大的领导力和执政力。哈佛大学教授约瑟夫·奈在接受《环球时报》采访时指出："中国的巨大成就正是在中国共产党的领导下才取得的。"[①] 未来，要引领一个世界上人口最多且从积贫积弱困苦中走来的大国建成社会主义现代化强国，中国共产党所面临的国内外难题，都是难以想象的，必须具备强大的领导力和执政力。

---

① 《约瑟夫·奈：中国历史性成就源于中共执政》，环球网，https://m.huanqiu.com/article/9CaKrnK5za0。

三、中国最大经济中心和改革开放前沿

（一）引言

每个国家都有一个或多个"最大"的经济中心，它们是一个国家总体生产力发展的重要驱动力。上海由于独特的近代历史境遇和文化传承，获得了中国最大经济中心城市的地位，如图 3 所示。

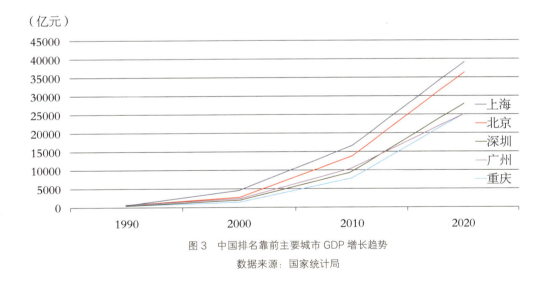

图 3　中国排名靠前主要城市 GDP 增长趋势

数据来源：国家统计局

上海虽不是全球最富的城市，但它作为亚洲的商业和经济中心，也是全球创新和金融中心，国家商业、运输和贸易中心，同时也是世界最繁忙的集装箱港口——上海港的所在地。上海的城市能级和核心竞争力在世界排名中也是十分亮眼的。从总体排名看，根据国际管理咨询公司科尔尼发布的 2021 年《全球城市指数》（GCI），上海全球城市排名较 2018 年提升 10 位，名列世界第十。根据日本森纪念财团发布的 2021 年《全球城市实力指数》（GPCI），上海的全球城市排名较 2018 年提升了 16 位，名列世界第十。

上海的 GDP 从新中国成立之初的 30 多亿元增长到 2022 年的 44600 多亿元，经济总量在全国城市中排名前列。而且它还以不到全国千分之一的土地面积，贡献了全国近十分之一的税收总收入。要探寻上海始终保持全国最大经济中心的秘诀，还需要深入到中国从 1978 年开启的改革开放历史中。

（单位：亿元）

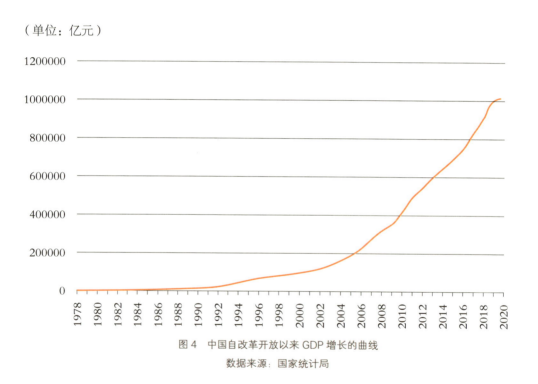

图 4　中国自改革开放以来 GDP 增长的曲线

数据来源：国家统计局

改革开放让中国用近 40 年时间摆脱贫穷，走向富裕，推动了现代化发展。"中国从改革开放之前人均国民收入不到 300 美元发展到今天人均国民收入超过 9000 美元的世界第二大经济体，并且在这期间使得 8 亿人口摆脱贫困。"[1]可以说，没有改革开放就没有今日之中国。没有改革开放也没有今天的上海，正是改革开放使上海再度崛起为亚太区域的中心城市。

---

① 财政部、国务院发展研究中心与世界银行共同发布的报告：《中国减贫四十年：驱动力量、借鉴意义和未来政策方向》，中国国际发展知识中心官网，https://www.cikd.org/ms/file/getimage/1516697201483554817。

那么，中国的改革开放政策为什么能够成功？成功的秘诀就藏在具体的细节里。要破解这个疑问，我们可以再返回到上海这个地方，将它作为中国改革开放的最佳观测点。上海作为改革开放前沿曾发挥了重要作用，并且在当下全面深化改革开放布局中，上海又有了全新定位。从中国改革开放的"排头兵"、"先行者"到"社会主义现代化建设引领区"，上海被赋予改革开放新使命，为中国实现现代化继续作出更大贡献。

（二）浦东开发开放的历程与成就

让我们再把镜头拉近，将上海改革开放的焦点放在浦东。因为浦东的开发开放是中国改革开放的典型中的典型。它代表了中国改革开放在步骤、策略、目标和成效等方面的关键性考虑。

1. 十年之后的重要选择

其实，浦东的开发开放并不是从中国改革开放的第一年开始的，而是在 10 年之后。1980 年 8 月中国批准在深圳、珠海、汕头、厦门设置经济特区，1984 年 5 月决定大连等 14 个沿海港口城市及海南岛对外开放，1988 年 4 月又批准建立海南经济特区，沿海地区经济社会迅猛发展。这一时期的改革开放并没有把上海列入其中，因为改革开放本身就有很强的试验性质，上海在全国经济中的地位太重要了，上海经济的稳定直接关系到全国经济的稳定和发展。在 1989 年这一年，上海工业总产值是 1515 亿元，占全国总产值的 6.9%，财政收入 297 亿元，占全国财政总收入的 10.2%，工业部门几乎覆盖所有行业门类。在整个 20 世纪 80 年代，上海经济增长幅度持续低于全国平均水平，可每年上缴国家财政仍占全国的 1/6，高居榜首。改革开放头 10 年，上海为中国其他地区的改革探索提供财力、人力和物力的支持。所以，在上海推动改革开放一定要慎之又慎。

但是到 20 世纪 90 年代，上海与周边地区相比已经出现明显差距。上海城市基础设施老化、工业技术优势减弱、产业结构不合理等问题已经成为制约上海发展的障碍。经过 10 年的摸索，其他地区已经取得改革开放的试验性成效，在上海这个中国经济中心实行改革开放的时机已经成熟。

1990 年，浦东开发开放被提上了日程。这一年年初，刚从国家领导岗位上退下来的

邓小平来到上海考察，在听取上海领导的汇报后，他把目光投向了与浦西仅一江之隔的浦东。在邓小平的推动下，党中央、国务院经过充分调查研究和论证，于1990年4月正式批准开发开放浦东。浦东开发开放就此拉开了序幕。不甘落后的上海，终于抓住了20世纪最后10年的历史机遇，冲到了改革开放的前沿。

2. 渐进式推进改革开放

表1　浦东开发开放大事记

1990年，成立全国第一个金融贸易区，第一个出口加工区，第一个保税区，第一家证券交易所
1992年，第一家外资保险公司注册开业，第一家合资物流企业成立
1993年，第一个尝试土地实转、资金空转的土地开发模式，第一个设立保税交易市场
1995年，第一家外资银行成立，第一家合资零售企业开业
1996年，成为第一个外资金融机构经营人民币业务试点区域
2001年，第一次赴美国、欧洲招聘国际化高层次人才
2005年，第一个开展综合配套改革试点，转变政府职能和经济运行方式
2007年，第一个金融审判机构上海金融仲裁院成立
2013年，第一个自贸试验区挂牌成立，第一家跨境贸易电商平台建立
2014年，第一个单独设立的知识产权局成立
2015年，第一个综合性国家科学中心成立
2017年，第一个海外人才局成立
2019年，中国（上海）自由贸易试验区临港新片区设立
2020年，确立浦东为高水平改革开放、社会主义现代化建设引领区
……………

如表1所示，30多年来，浦东的开发开放大致经历了三个阶段。[①] 第一个阶段从

①　周振华、洪民荣主编，石良平等著《上海改革开放40年大事研究·卷四·对外开放引领》，上海人民出版社2018年版，第32页。

1990年到2000年，这一时期浦东完成了高起点的总体发展规划和城市基础设施建设。高标准的城市总体规划设计让浦东的开发可以整体地、分步骤地开展，而大规模基础设施建设让浦东的现代化面貌呈现在全世界的面前。凭借改革开放的政策支持，浦东还推出了一些关键性的改革新举措，如土地对外批租、土地二级运转模式、成立国资开发公司与园区等，还有推进"小政府、大社会"的政府经济职能转变，有效吸纳和合理运用外资，引进世界先进技术和管理模式，这使得城市功能格局和产业结构得到全面提升。正是在这个时期，浦东的改革和对外开放让上海拥有了新的发展动能和发展机遇，成为中国改革开放的排头兵。

第二个阶段从2001年到2012年，这一时期以中国加入世界贸易组织（WTO）为标志和上海举办世博会为契机，浦东关注国际通行的经济运行法规的制定和体制环境的培育，将国内市场与国外的不同市场主体和市场体系连接起来。这段时期，浦东大力推动"聚焦张江"战略和金融中心建设，将对外开放的重点从一般生产加工领域扩大到服务贸易领域，像金融保险、信息咨询、会展旅游等，还有国际租赁、国际航运、现代物流、国际商品展示和国家法律服务等，都落实了进一步的开放政策。这使得很多具有国际影响力的跨国公司将地区总部设在浦东，还带动科技研发中心、外资金融机构和专业服务中介都纷纷涌入浦东。这一时期的浦东率先开展了综合配套改革试点，标志着浦东开发开放的内在动力由依靠政策优惠和投资拉动转变为依靠体制创新和扩大开放。

第三阶段从2013年至今，这一时期以中国（上海）自由贸易试验区的成立为标志，浦东继续推进改革开放的先行先试，积极发挥窗口作用和示范意义。自由贸易区在今天的中国开放度是最高的，它推动统筹了国际业务、跨境金融服务、前沿科技研发、跨境服务贸易等功能集聚，强化了开放型经济的集聚功能和区域产业升级。有了这些作为基础，先进制造业和新型产业链才能有长足发展，例如人工智能、集成电路、工业互联网领域，特别是新能源汽车、集成电路两大核心产业，已经成为自贸区临港新片区为中国培育经济发展新动能的鲜明体现。

3. 改革开放成就来之不易

浦东开发开放是中国改革开放的一个缩影，也是先进典型。它在全国创造了多项"第一"，引领国家经济体制转轨和扩大对外开放。通过其他地区还没有的国家优惠政策的倾斜，浦东可以在一些领域先行先试，有了很大的改革自主权，例如，针对当时中国对外资进入的领域限制、产业限制、经营限制和其他限制，浦东做了很多政策性突破，中外合资的外贸企业开始成立，外资银行被允许经营人民币业务等，这些都有利于转变旧的相对封闭的经济发展模式。同时，浦东作为中国改革开放的最前沿，有些领域的改革和开放并没有直接的政策和制度作为依托，而是通过制度创新打破固有桎梏，自主探索、不断试错并总结经验得来的。另一方面，浦东自主探索出的新事物又意味着国家发展和开放的更强有力支持。

从刚开始单向的政策型开放转变为双向的制度型开放格局，浦东的开发开放见证了将制度创新与对外开放结合起来以实现连续突破性发展的可行性。通过推动新的规则、规制、管理和标准的制定与落实，确保了改革开放的可持续性和可复制性。例如，上海自贸试验区建设以来，坚持以制度创新为核心，对标最高标准最好水平，大胆试、大胆闯、自主改，聚焦投资、贸易、金融、事中事后监管等领域，率先构建与国际通行规则接轨的制度体系，形成了外商投资负面清单、国际贸易"单一窗口"、自由贸易账户、证照分离等一批基础性和核心制度创新。在这里形成的 328 项制度创新成果也复制推广到了全国。

浦东开发开放从一开始就是面向世界来谋划改革举措和开放政策的。自从开发开放浦东被提升为国家战略，它引起了全国和世界的瞩目。上海确定了"开发浦东，振兴上海，服务全国，面向世界"的方针，意思是浦东的开发开放的规模是世界级的，它要融入世界经济特别是亚太地区经济的发展进程。30 多年来，浦东累计吸引实到外资超过 1000 亿美元，有 3 万多家外资企业和 370 多家跨国公司的地区总部选择在浦东成立，另外，浦东海港通航全球 600 多个港口，13 个国家和地区在这里设立 100 多家各类外资资管公司。

当然，我们知道改革旧的制度体系需要面对的困难会很多，而对外开放就意味着国际市场环境的风险也会对内部发展和稳定造成冲击。浦东开发开放的成功离不开敢于承担风险、勇于谋划战略布局的政治家以及千千万万高层次人才，是他们为浦东的改革开放出谋划策并付出艰辛努力。所以浦东的开发开放从一开始就非常重视领导者的培养和人才的吸纳。

浦东新区生产总值（亿元）

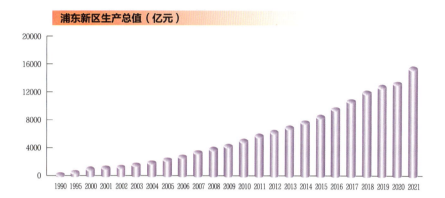

浦东新区财政收入（亿元）

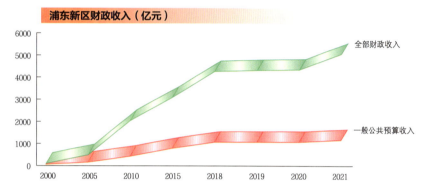

上海证券交易所市价总值（亿元）

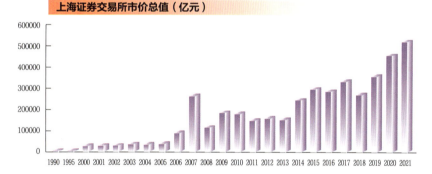

浦东新区集装箱吞吐量（万标箱）

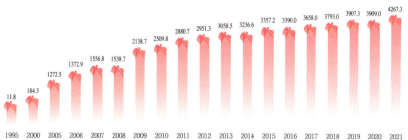

图 5　浦东开发开放成就——1990—2022 年浦东 GDP、财政总收入、上证交易所市价总值、集装箱吞吐量等变化曲线

数据来源：2022 年浦东新区统计年鉴

正如图 5 中所显示的，浦东 30 多年来的改革开放取得的成就是显著的，也证明了这条现代化道路是走得通的。如今，围绕着首创性改革、引领性开放、集成化创新，浦东改革探索全面提速：地区生产总值是 1990 年的 265 倍；450 项引领区建设实施方案完成比例超过 90%；300 多项重要改革成果、51 条"浦东经验"正向全国复制推广。

正是浦东的开发开放，使中国的改革开放推进到更深领域和更高水平，它对全国改革发展的示范作用和辐射带动作用非常鲜明。它的辐射区域包括长江三角洲以及整个长江沿江地区。浦东通过加快推进国际金融、贸易、航运中心的建设，促进了全球资金、技术、信息、人才、货物等的要素配置的全球流动，支撑了整个中国经济贸易快速发展。

如今，中国的现代化进入新的发展阶段，改革的复杂程度、敏感程度和艰巨程度不亚于 40 年前，这就更需要浦东乃至上海为推进全面深化改革开放持续发力。2020 年，在浦东开发开放 30 周年之际，习近平主席宣布浦东作为中国高水平改革开放的最前沿将打造社会主义现代化建设引领区。引领区的定位，将支持浦东在改革系统集成协同高效、高水平制度型开放、增强配置全球资源能力、提升城市现代化治理水平等方面先行先试、积极探索、创造经验。这对上海以及长三角一体化高质量发展乃至我国社会主义现代化建设具有战略意义。

（三）结语

浦东开发开放遵循了世界现代化的一般规律，它在工业化、城市化、市场化、信息化、法治化和国际化等方面都有很多有益拓展。不过，如何运用这些规律带来切实的改变，使本国、本地区不仅积累起现代的物质财富和精神财富，而且能够持续地朝着现代化方向发展，则需要正视现代化的一般规律和本土的特殊情况的有机结合。全盘套用别人的现代化经验和模式，将会付出很大代价。

在这 40 多年中，中国的现代化积累了丰富的经验。

一是试验性改革与渐进式发展。要实现现代化必须改革开放，但要获得成功，中国的经验是改革要选取重要地区先行先试，但是在选取这些试验地区的时候还要综合考虑多重因素，既要有改革开放的示范价值，又要走渐进性的道路，考虑社会承受能力，不可贸然打开国门、放开所有领域，以避免经济崩溃、社会混乱。中国可先在原有体制内一些易操作、震动小、成本低、收益高的地方开始改革，收到相应成效后再扩展到更重要的地区和领域，进行深入探索。还有一些试验性的改革措施和重大项目都需要准备两套方案，以便发生不可预估的情况时有回旋余地，确保改革开放能够延续下去。[①]

二是处理好改革、发展与稳定的关系，用改革推动开放，以开放倒逼改革。发展是目的，改革是手段，稳定是保障。一些国家和地区内部存在的旧体制，模仿西方化的发展模式，这些都制约了经济社会发展，因为现代化之路始终受原来的利益格局和跨国资本利益集团牵制，发展很难让所有人同等获利。在这个时候，以开放倒逼改革，触动旧的利益格局，寻找经济发展动力和利益来源，有助于国家和地区在保持相对稳定的基础上逐步走出一条经济社会发展新路。

三是新举措要可复制可推广。浦东在改革开放时期推出的一系列改革举措虽然绝大部分都是史无前例的，但探索出来的成功措施可以拿到其他地区继续发挥推动发展作用，例如保税区、自贸区、金融区建设目前已经在全国逐步展开，浦东的先行探索发挥了至关重要的作用。

四是充分发掘和利用自身优势，扬长补短。我们并不是想让每个地区都成为上海的浦东，而是提供了一条通过开放发展激活内在优势、形成经济的自我造血功能的道路。国际市场风云变幻，金融、外贸、航运、旅游等产业的开放程度和具体步骤肯定各不相同，这就需要我们有效处理好开放发展与保持自身独立的关系，摆脱过多受因外部环境变化影响而出现内部陷入经济周期性危机的困境，增强现代化发展的持续性。

---

① 中共上海市委党史研究室编，黄金平、龚思文著《潮涌东方：浦东开发开放30年》，上海人民出版社2020年版，第96页。

第二章

创新转型：
走高质量发展之路

　　发展问题一直是世界范围的难题。如何实现生产力的提升？如何解决工业化和城市化过程带来的一系列问题？后起国家和地区在现代化的道路上可以实现赶超吗？如果可以，其动能和路径又是什么呢？长期以来，世界各国都孜孜不卷地在实践中探索上述问题的答案。这个过程是漫长的、曲折的，西方国家花了几百年进行探索，对于前进中遇到的问题和困难又花费了大量时间和金钱去解决。

　　而上海用几十年的时间完成了从工业体系的完整塑造，到现代金融、贸易、航运中心基本建立，再到建设具有全球影响力的科技创新中心，可谓是"浓缩式"发展。截至 2021 年，上海全市工业增加值突破万亿元，位居全国城市首位；人均可支配收入跻身全球发达经济体水平，人民群众获得感不断提升；科技创新引领产业体系升级，不断的制度突破使上海始终站在中国改革开放的最前沿；长三角一体化、进博会①、自贸区、科创板、数字化转型、城市软实力、国际消费中心……这些关键词绘出了上海城市新画像。

　　短短几十年何以取得如此多的成就？每一次战略转型都精准且成功的秘诀是什么？上述问题的答案就藏在上海高质量发展的过程中。

　　高质量发展是全面建设社会主义现代化国家的首要任务，是中国式现代化的本质要求。高质量发展不再简单地以生产总值增长率论英雄，而是要实现创新成为第一动力、协调成为内生特点、绿色成为普遍形态、开放成为必由之路、共享成为根本目的。因此，不断提升产业能级、坚持科技创新和实现绿色生态转型是高质量发展的重要内容。陆家嘴金融城是上海构建现代化产业体系的缩影，也是以产业发展推动城市能级提升的样本。张江科学城是上海经济高质量发展的重要增长极，是上海科技创新的一张亮丽名片。中国宝武集团（上海）的转型过程展现了上海践行推动人与自然和谐共生的发展理念。

　　实现中国式现代化要求高质量发展，如何实现高质量发展，并通过高质量发展提升国家或城市的影响力和竞争力是各国在发展中面临的共同问题。上海聚焦高质量发展动能，在经济创新转型方面成效显著，为高质量发展提供了上海样本。

---

　　① 中国国际进口博览会（CIIE）由中华人民共和国商务部和上海市人民政府主办，中国国际进口博览局、国家会展中心（上海）承办，为世界上第一个以进口为主题的国家级展会。

一、产业转型提升城市能级

（一）引言

当前，世界经济复苏缓慢、增长乏力，有些国家甚至陷入困境，加之全球治理和安全形势面临极大挑战，因此各国都在寻求应对之策。经济要转型，产业要先行，有效推进产业转型升级，有利于培育、壮大新兴产业，拓宽产业结构，增强经济发展的活力与持久力，促进实现经济可持续发展，因此，以产业转型升级推动国家或城市能级提升已成为世界公认的发展模式。但如何选择未来的重点产业呢？培育壮大新兴产业的路径又是什么呢？对于转型中遇到的问题和困难如何破解呢？这就要在高质量发展中找寻答案。

上海在短短几十年的时间里，成功完成了几次产业转型和城市功能的转变提升，每次转型都准确而轻盈，每一次提升都是大的突破。20世纪30年代，在"三二一"的产业结构形态下，上海是集商贸、金融、工业、航运、信息中心为一体的"多功能经济中心"城市。新中国成立到改革开放前，上海城市产业结构由近代后期的商工并重转变为以工为主，且二、三产业在国民经济中的地位发生了根本性倒置。到1977年，三产比重急剧降至19.70%，二产比重陡然升至76.80%，上海由"多功能经济中心"逐步转变为功能较单一的工业城市，进而成为中国规模最庞大的"综合性工业城市"。改革开放后，上海进入产业调整阶段，"服务业发展优先"的思路逐步明确，城市也向着"四个中心"的方向大步迈进。进入新时代，上海加快建设社会主义现代化国际大都市，服务型经济特征日趋显现，突出表现为门类更加齐全、业态更添新颖、层级更趋高端，其中现代服务业发展更是驶入"快车道"，实现"大提速"。与服务业发展并驾齐驱，上海工业进入以发展先进制造业为目标的"发展调整中提升"阶段，产业能级明显"上台阶"，形成一批资本技术密集化特征显著的支柱产业和战略性新兴产业，与服务经济相适应的新型工业体系逐步建立起来，上海处在推进、落实基本建成"五个中心"和社会主义现代化国际大都市目标的深化发展阶段。

　　这背后的高质量发展密码是什么？我们可以从陆家嘴金融城的诞生中找到线索。

（二）陆家嘴金融城的崛起之路

　　"黄浦江边有个烂泥渡，烂泥路边有个烂泥渡镇，行人路过，没有好衣裤。"这首民谣在 20 世纪六七十年代的浦东广为流传，烂泥渡路位于浦东陆家嘴地区，每逢下雨就会水漫金山，遇到暴雨，雨水会积到没过膝盖的深度，雨停后一周水才能慢慢退去，周围百姓苦不堪言。

昔日陆家嘴（郑宪章　摄）

烂泥渡路是当时浦东的一个缩影，陆家嘴与浦西外滩仅一江之隔，但发展差距大，看起来犹如两个世界。当时的浦东以农业为主要产业，工业发展相对滞后，现代服务业几乎没有。

谁能想到，昔日的烂泥渡，几十年后会成长为耀眼的世界级金融城。

如今的陆家嘴经济密度高、体量大。陆家嘴金融贸易区是全国金融机构最集中、金融要素市场最齐备、金融服务体系最完善、金融人才最密集的地区，集聚了 839 家监管类金融机构、13 家国家级金融要素市场和功能性金融基础设施、6000 多家中外金融机构、30 多万名金融从业者，此外，陆家嘴金融贸易区还贡献了浦东 1/2 的商品销售总额、1/3 的实到外资、约 1/4 的社会消费品零售总额，贡献了全市 1/2 的金融业增加值。[①] 以陆家嘴金融城中心区为起点，沿世纪大道一路向东，一条聚集金融和企业总部的黄金走廊正逐步形成，这里区域经济总量突破 6300 亿元，每平千米里超过 200 亿元，培育了 110 余幢税收亿元楼和上海第一幢税收百亿楼。行业内有一种说法："陆家嘴的每栋大厦，都是一条站立的金融街。"

如今的陆家嘴跨国公司集聚度高，产业生态好。陆家嘴集聚了 340 多家世界 500 强企业的分支机构，以及 138 家跨国公司地区总部，有 3/4 总部企业在全球布局发展，管理、贸易、研发、投资、结算等多功能复合型总部 80 多家，为全国之最。完备的金融生态功能体系使陆家嘴成为中外机构"落户"上海的首选之地。

如今的陆家嘴辐射带动能力强，未来不可限量。陆家嘴高楼林立、直耸云霄，其中 632 米高的上海中心大厦是中国最高、世界第二高建筑，总建筑面积近 58 万平方米，相当于外滩第一排所有建筑面积总和，被称为竖起来的"外滩"和垂直的"金融街"。"陆家嘴论坛"吸引各国政府和监管机构的高层领导、全球财经界的领袖人物和国际顶尖专家学者在此对话，人流、物流、资金流、信息流在此汇聚、流动，形成了显著的"财富效应"。夜晚的陆家嘴超高层建筑群灯光华美、流光溢彩，与隔江而望的外滩万国建筑群交相辉映，这里成为上海的经济地标，向人们诉说着上海的过去、现在和未来。

---

① 《全国首个金融贸易区的变迁》，浦东文明网，http://sh.wenming.cn/pudong/pd_yw/201809/t20180918_4833823.htm。

1. 一片滩涂上谋划城市未来

陆家嘴的金融奇迹令世人惊叹。但回到 20 世纪 90 年代，上海面对一片空白的浦东却在苦苦思索，城市未来发展的方向是什么？动能又是什么？

其实早在 20 世纪 30 年代，上海就已经成为中国最大的金融中心。1935 年，中国 164 家银行中，总行设立在上海的就有 58 家，占到总数的 35％，这些总行设立在上海的银行都是全国性的大银行，它们的存款量至少占到全国总存款量的一半。根据相关史料记载，1933 年上海的银行资产总额为 33 亿元，占全国银行资产总值的 89％。与此同时，全国 29 家外商银行中，有 27 家银行在上海设立有分行。曾经的上海是远东第一大都市，这与其发达的金融贸易体系不无关系。这样的繁华在多年后又被提起。1990 年，党中央、国务院作出了浦东开发开放的重大战略决策，与此同时，国务院在这里批准设立了全国第一个也是唯一一个以"金融贸易"命名的国家级开发区——陆家嘴金融贸易区，面积 31.78 平方千米，其中中心区（小陆家嘴）面积 1.7 平方千米。

1991 年 2 月 18 日，农历大年初四上午，邓小平兴致勃勃地来到了那时上海最高的旋转餐厅——新锦江大酒店 41 层的旋转餐厅，窗外晴空万里，阳光明媚。他透过宽敞明亮的玻璃窗眺望上海中心城区的面貌，对身边的人说："我们说上海开发晚了，要努力干啊！"旋转餐厅里挂着两张大幅地图，一张是上海地图，另一张是浦东新区地图，地图旁摆着浦东开发的模型。据在场的同志回忆，当时小平同志就说："金融很重要，是现代经济的核心。金融搞好了，一着棋活，全盘皆活。上海过去是金融中心，是货币自由兑换的地方，今后也要这样。中国在金融方面取得国际地位，首先要靠上海。那要好多年以后，但现在就要做起。"

然而陆家嘴的开发起初并不顺利，很多机构不愿入驻，"宁要浦西一张床，不要浦东一间房"的观念还深植在人们心里。中国人民银行上海分行身先士卒，来到了这片荒凉的土地，这对诸多在浦西隔江而望和在国外隔海相望的外资金融机构起到了示范作用，不少外资银行在拿到人民币的执照后，也都纷纷跨过了黄浦江，搬入了陆家嘴。1995 年，首家外资银行——日本富士银行上海分行在陆家嘴开业，而后三菱银行、渣打银行、汇丰银行、花旗银行等接踵而至。1997 年，上海证券交易所在这里成立，1999 年，上海期货交易所也在这里诞生。随着工商银行、建设银行、农业银行、国家开发银行等众多金融机构的集聚，陆家嘴金融贸易区的金融功能初步集聚，曾经我们做最基本的人民币兑换美元的业务都要花费近一小时，而今交易员轻松点几下手指即可完成。

2. 众多奇迹在此诞生

进入新的千年，陆家嘴金融城加速发展，诸多的"第一"在这里诞生。2000年，首家钻石交易所在陆家嘴成立；2001年，首家合资基金公司在陆家嘴成立；2006年中国金融期货交易所在陆家嘴成立；2007年，首个金融审判机构在陆家嘴成立。陆家嘴金融贸易区初步形成"3+2"现代服务业产业体系，以证券、商品期货、金融期货等为主要内容的现代金融市场体系日渐成熟，基本确立了中国金融中心的地位。

如今的陆家嘴

　　陆家嘴金融贸易区的发展定位不断向前推进。2009 年，国务院通过《国务院关于推进上海加快发展现代服务业和先进制造业、建设国际金融中心和国际航运中心的意见》，陆家嘴金融贸易区围绕金融和航运两大中心展开一系列布局。2015 年 4 月，上海自贸区范围扩展至陆家嘴片区，涉及陆家嘴金融贸易区的 24.33 平方千米，陆家嘴成为中国新一轮金融领域改革和对外开放的试验田和主战场。2016 年 8 月，陆家嘴金融城正式揭牌，陆家嘴金融城理事会、陆家嘴金融城发展局同时挂牌成立，在全国首创"业界共治 + 法定机构"公共治理架构。

　　与此同时，陆家嘴的现代服务业功能不断完善。2015 年，中国首家由中外律师事务所（美国贝克·麦坚时国际律师事务所和北京奋迅律师事务所）联营的办公室在陆家嘴设立；2017 年，中国首家 CEPA，即《关于建立更紧密经贸关系的安排》协议项下的合资全牌照券商——申港证券落户陆家嘴，中国首家经批准的外商独资经营性职业技能培训机构——普华永道商务技能培训（上海）有限公司在陆家嘴注册，这一年的陆家嘴，已经取代香港成为全球人民币资产定价中心，国际话语权和影响力不断提升；2018 年，中国首个国际化期货品种——原油期货在陆家嘴挂牌……2021 年 8 月，《自贸试验区陆家嘴片区发展"十四五"规划》，标志着上海金融中心建设迈向高质量发展新征程，它将继续以高"开放度"和高"含金量"来向世界展示上海，走出一条独具特色的产业引领高质量发展之路。

3. 上海产业引领高质量发展之路

　　陆家嘴金融城的崛起是上海产业引领高质量发展的一个缩影。新中国成立初期，中国迫切需要快速建立独立的工业体系，从一个完全的农业国转变为一个初步的工业国。上海勇挑重任，一马当先，将城市功能从中心城市转变为工业城市，产业结构从以轻纺工业为主转变为完整的现代工业体系，加快工业化进程，增强工业产品生产的能力和水平。凭借优厚的制造业底蕴，上海迅速成长为中国最大的工业城市和最重要的财政收入地区。1980 年中国改革开放之初，上海工业增加值占全国的比重高达 12%，在十几个工业部门具有垄断性的地位，当时中国人结婚都爱买的"四大件"——上海牌手表、永久牌自行车、蝴蝶牌缝纫机和红灯牌收音机都是"上海制造"，当时上海制造的产品就是品质和潮流的象征，被国人追捧。上海制造业的迅速腾飞给上海的城市发展夯实了基础，也给全国的经济发展注入了力量。

20 世纪 90 年代，上海城市发展遇到了瓶颈，唯有突破创新才能谋求更大的发展。在浦东开发开放的同时，上海的产业定位和城市功能也进行了调整，明确产业结构实施大调整，从"二三一"向"三二一"转变，城市空间布局实施中心城区"退二进三"，重建上海多功能中心城市。2001 年，国务院批复《上海市城市总体规划（1999—2020）》，立足于国家赋予上海要崛起成为又一个国际经济中心的战略目标任务，提出要"把上海建设成为经济繁荣、社会文明、环境优美的国际大都市，国际经济、金融、贸易、航运中心之一"。"四个中心"建设的大幕就此拉开，上海的第三产业开始飞速发展，服务业占比不断提升，截至 2022 年，上海第三产业增加值占比已达到 74.1%，曾经制造业一骑绝尘的上海，如今华丽转身为服务业唱主角。

新时代，上海接续奋斗，不断提高城市核心竞争力和国际影响力，加快建设具有世界影响力的社会主义现代化国际大都市，在"四个中心"建设的基础上，提出建设具有全球影响力的科技创新中心。因此，上海的产业发展方向进一步优化调整，不断向科技创新、生态保护等高质量发展方向侧重。上海布局了绿色低碳、元宇宙、数字经济和智能终端四个新赛道产业，以及光子芯片、基因与细胞、类脑智能、新型海洋经济、氢能与储能、第六代移动通信六个未来产业。"大国重器""尖端产品"竞相涌现，关键战略领域创新突破纷至沓来。"蛟龙"入海、"天宫"探月、"北斗"指南、"墨子"升空、大飞机翱翔……这些大国重器背后都有上海印记；创新药、中国芯、最强光、未来车等原创成果也成为上海制造的闪亮名片，上海科技创新综合水平迈入全球主要创新型城市前列。

（三）结语

中国式现代化走高质量发展的道路，如何依靠产业转型升级推动城市的高质量发展，上海的生动实践给予了明确回答。

规划引领，清晰而准确的城市定位是高质量发展的前提。与世界上很多现代化城市的发展过程不同，它们往往是在发展中逐步形成自己的城市特色的，而上海，在每一次城市发展战略的重大转型之前，都有了明确的城市目标定位，而后在中央与地方的众多政策的支持下，轻快而准确地转型。不仅仅是上海，中国很多地区的发展都证明了这个道理，中国的现代化道路之所以走得快速而稳健，锚定目标、找准方向是关键。

锚定产业，产业转型升级是高质量发展的动力。进行产业结构调整和升级是上海走上高质量发展快车道的重要经验，坚实的产业基础是城市功能的载体，也是城市目标的具体体现。因此要依据城市发展目标锚定产业，产业的选择要能服务城市功能。产业转型升级带动了城市功能的提升，城市能级的提升又会带来国家竞争力和影响力的增强，这是中国式现代化发展道路上的一条重要经验。

破除障碍，做好制度安排是高质量发展的保障。中国式现代化的发展过程，是不断理顺政府和市场的关系的过程，不断优化营商环境、建设服务型政府；也是不断为企业提供支持、减轻负担的过程，加强行业共性技术供给、完善知识产权保护制度、减税降费。制度保障为产业转型升级扫清了障碍，实现了高质量发展，也是中国式现代化实现过程中的重要经验。

构建现代化产业体系、实现产业转型升级是建设现代化强国的重要基石，上海每一次城市功能的成功转型都有与之相对应的产业助推，有完善的制度安排作为保障。这些经验对于上海未来的发展也具有重要的启示意义。

二、科技创新赋能高质量发展

（一）引言

第二次世界大战后，在 100 多个中等收入经济体中，只有部分国家（地区）成长为高收入经济体，而大多数发展中国家在经历了一段时期的高速增长后陷入停滞，落入中等收入陷阱。回顾历史，我们发现只有依靠科技创新推动国家产业结构升级，才是经济长期持续增长的核心动力。当前，我国已迈入高质量发展新阶段，要摒弃旧的发展模式，寻找新的发展动能，必须依靠科技创新提供新的发展空间和驱动力，以创新驱动引领高质量发展，从而跨越中等收入陷阱。

2014 年 5 月，习近平主席在上海考察时，要求上海"努力在推进科技创新、实施创新驱动发展战略方面走在全国前头、走到世界前列，加快向具有全球影响力的科技创新中心进军"。到 2020 年，上海具有全球影响力的科技创新中心形成基本框架，建成了一批国家重大科技基础设施和多个研发与转化功能型平台，集成电路、生物医药、人工智能三大产业加快实施，C919 大型客机、量子计算机、北斗导航系统、"天问"、"天和"、"天舟"、"嫦娥四号"、"嫦娥五号"、"奋斗者"号，这些国家战略科技任务背后都有上海科技力量的身影。当前，上海已跻身全球主要创新型城市行列；在世界知识产权组织最新发布的《全球创新指数报告》中，上海－苏州"集群位列"世界科技创新集群第 6 位；在《自然》发布的"2022 年自然指数－科研城市"中，上海从 2020 年的全球第 5 位升至全球第 3 位；在中国科学技术发展战略研究院发布的《中国区域科技创新评价报告 2022》中，上海综合科技创新水平指数继续位列全国第一，科技已逐渐成为上海的一张名片。① 那么，上海是如何提升科技创新水平并为高质量发展提供动能的呢？张江科学城作为上海经济高质量发展的重要增长极，承载着打造具有全球影响力的科技创新中心核心承载区和建设张江综合性国家科学中心的战略任务，它的成长和发展是对上述问题的生动回应。

（二）张江科学城的创新之路

张江科学城位于上海市中心城东南部，浦东新区的中心位置。1992 年 7 月，张江高科技园区开园，成为第一批国家级新区。1999 年，上海启动"聚焦张江"战略，张江高科技园区进入了快速发展阶段。2017 年，张江又被赋予了新的概念——张江科学城，围绕"上海具有全球影响力科技创新中心的核心承载区"和"上海张江综合性国家科学中心"两大目标，转型成为中国乃至全球新知识、新技术的创造之地，以国内外高层次人才和青年创新人才为主的现代新型宜居城区和市级公共中心。从"高科技园"到"科学城"，张江真正实现了由"园区"向"城区"的转变，发展成为"科学特征明显、科技要素集聚、环境人文生态、充满创新活力"的世界一流科学城。在科学园到科学城的转变中，面积从 1992 年 7 月的 17 平方千米到如今规划面积 220 平方千米，不仅实现了空间地理上的扩容，而且用实践走出了一条上海科技创新之路。

1. 自立自强，提升科技创新策源功能

当一个国家进入中等收入阶段后，国内劳动力优势逐渐减弱，经济增长的动力日益依赖技术进步，但技术引进的空间越来越小，尤其是在高技术领域，技术垄断特征明显，因此必须主要依靠自主创新，提升原始创新能力，实现科技自立自强。

基础研究是科技自立自强的根本。近年来，张江科学城加强创新资源整合，全面提升科研基础能力和发展能级。首先，以国家科学中心为引领，张江集聚了一批高水平科技创新机构，比如张江实验室、李政道研究所、上海国际人类表型组研究院等一批顶尖

---

① 《张江综合性国家科学中心建设去年取得了哪些进展？一起来看这份报告怎么说》，上观，http://sghexport.shobserver.com/html/baijiahao/2023/01/12/940853.html。

科研机构，张江药物实验室、上海量子科学研究中心等高水平专业实验室，复旦大学、上海交通大学、同济大学、浙江大学等高校也加速在张江布局科研力量。围绕基础研究领域，张江科学城致力于汇聚各方面精锐力量，提升关键核心技术攻关"大兵团"体系化作战能力，在原创性研究中不断取得突破。其次，作为基础研究的重要支撑，目前张江科学城已初步形成我国乃至世界上规模最大、种类最全、综合能力最强的光子大科学设施集群。大科学设施是提升原始创新能力的重要手段，21世纪以来，物理学界取得的三项重大突破，即中微子振荡、希格斯玻色子、引力波的发现，都是通过大科学设施发现的。2016年以前，上海只有上海光源这一个大科学设施。2016年以后，在政府支持下，上海陆续建设了一批大科学设施，特别是在张江科学城初步建成了一个光子大科学设施集群，如上海光源、硬 X 射线、软 X 射线、超强超短激光、活细胞成像、神光等。① 特别是上海光源，我国第一台第三代同步辐射光源，在全世界范围内已属于先进水平，在国际上首次实现了最高峰值10拍瓦激光放大输出的超强超短激光实验装置，也创造了新的世界纪录。当今世界，同步辐射光源早已是科研创新不可或缺的重要工具，每一条光束都在为全球科学家在结构生物学、物理学等基础前沿研究提供服务。比如，2019年11月15日，百济神州自主研发的 BTK 抑制剂泽布替尼，成为第一款由中国企业自主研发、获准在美上市的抗癌新药。他们正是利用上海光源，获得了泽布替尼与靶点蛋白的高分辨率结构。此外，在生命科学、海洋、能源等领域，还有蛋白质设施、转化医学设施、海底观测网、高效低碳燃气轮机等科技基础设施。对于企业而言，仪器设备属于实打实的"重资产"，在科研经费中占大头，很多中小企业却因价格昂贵买不起、用不上。对此，张江实施共享实验仪器，中小企业不必自建实验平台，无须购买仪器设备，只须登录上海研发公共服务平台网站，即可一键查询近千家科研单位的共享仪器信息，主要技术指标一目了然。

基础研发的产业化是科技创新的主要方向，也是科技创新赋能高质量发展的关键着力点。近年来，上海在张江主动布局一批代表前沿科技的先导产业，提升关键核心技术竞争力，打造产业高质量发展新动能。一方面，集成电路、生物医药以及人工智能三

---

① 李佳佳、郁玫：《"而立"张江踏上"新征程""大咖"引路创新策源续写新辉煌》，中国新闻网，http://www.chinanews.com.cn/cj/2022/11-15/9895147.shtml。

大"硬核"产业，在张江科学城不断取得关键核心技术突破，呈现年均 10% 以上的高增长态势；另一方面，张江科学城正积极跟进新赛道，培育未来产业，引导和集聚优势企业抢先切入数字经济、绿色低碳、元宇宙、智能终端等新赛道，把发展主动权牢牢抓在手里。另外，科学能力建设和产业发展并重始终是张江一大优势。在张江研发产业化过程中的"张江研发 + 上海制造"模式，使张江从研发到制造，形成了支撑全产业链发展的优势。比如，在生物医药领域，上海市发布《关于促进本市生物医药产业高质量发展的若干意见》（2021 年），提出深入实施"张江研发 + 上海制造"行动，重点推进张江研发产业化项目在本市落地，加速创新成果在上海的转化。此外，为了推动研发向制造的转变，张江科学城采取让上市许可与生产许可两分开，利用共享生产车间模式，不自建工厂也能规模量产，不仅企业投资成本节省上亿元，而且产品上市速度提前两年多。

上海光源科学中心俯瞰（来源：胡蔚成 /IP SHANGHAI）

2. 开放包容，打造科技创新梦想之城

"海纳百川、追求卓越"是上海城市精神的重要方面，它与"鼓励成功、宽容失败"的创业精神相融合，形成了张江独特的创新文化和创新生态。张江科学城，无论是地处上海国际化大都市的地理位置，还是法律环境、人们的思维方式和行为方式，都有着明显的国际化特征，使得不同领域的创新主体，可以在张江开放、自由的环境中成长，催生了张江源源不断的创新动力，也成为科技创新企业和人才的梦想之地。有企业家称："小公司刚刚创立不可能一蹴而就，需要很多配套支持，包括一些技术平台，张江都相对完善，所以从大的战略层面，从技术层面，从人才层面，包括从地方政府的扶持上来讲，张江就是我们的首选之地。"①

张江不断深化体制机制改革，加强政策制度创新，形成了一套兼具科学性和创新性的制度体系，营造出"热带雨林式"的创新生态。通过微软人工智能和物联网实验室、IBM人工智能创新中心等大企业开放创新平台的赋能，带动了中小微企业技术水平提升。②

就从一粒新药说起，上海张江科学城创业者陈力团队历时10年研发，向监管部门递交了148盒、1200余册、36万多页药品上市申请材料，装满了一个标准集装箱。但出乎很多人意料，完成如此艰巨的研发工作，就是从张江科学城一间车库起步创办的企业，无须自建任何实验室。陈力团队依托张江科学城开放创新生态中的共享实验仪器、共享样本数据、共享科研人才、共享生产车间，研制出一款全球首创的糖尿病口服新药。2022年9月30日，这款新药被国家药品监督管理局认定为1类创新药并批准上市。而受益于张江科学城良好创新生态环境的，并不止这一个团队。③

人才是创新发展的第一驱动力。张江科学城是产业集聚高地，周边有许多科研院所，除了李政道研究所，现有各类新型研发机构、企业技术中心、公共技术服务平台等近500家，近年来持续建设了张江复旦国际创新中心、浙大上海高等研究院等一批基础研究领域的创新机构，以及上海科技大学等研究型大学，这些都为公司奠定了良好的人才基础。

① 李佳佳、郁玫：《"而立"张江踏上"新征程""大咖"引路创新策源续写新辉煌》，中国新闻网，http://www.chinanews.com.cn/cj/2022/11-15/9895147.shtml。
② 黄海华：《聚焦"大科学"跑出"加速度"》，《解放日报》2022年6月20日。
③ 刘士安等：《构建开放创新生态 上海张江活力四射》，《人民日报》2022年12月9日。

此外，为整合人力资源，张江科学城配套了一系列人才服务措施吸引更多优秀创新人才在这里安家落户。[①]

3. 大胆改革，完善科技创新体制机制

科技创新体制机制是保证科技创新取得成果的重要前提和有效支持。张江发展的每一步，都离不开体制机制的改革创新，是大胆试、大胆闯出来的结果。在上海勇当改革开放排头兵的担当魄力下，张江在政策层面形成了创新优势。例如，颁发首张外国人永久居留身份证，率先试点药品上市许可持有人制度、医疗器械注册人制度，率先探索形成集成电路保税监管模式，率先试点外籍人才口岸签证等。在制度创新的大胆闯和大胆试之下，也带来了举世瞩目的"张江速度"，包括推动国家药品审评长三角分中心、国家医疗器械审评长三角分中心落地张江，新药、器械审评沟通做到零距离；建设全国首家知识产权保护中心，发明专利审查时间从3年缩短到3个月；建设张江跨境科创监管服务中心，物品通关时间从2~3个工作日缩短到6~10小时等。2020年5月，《上海市推进科技创新中心建设条例》正式实施，是全国首例科技创新地方立法，为张江科学城改革创新提供了法律依据。张江的飞速发展，正是因为能大胆跳出体制机制的藩篱，为科技创新和产业发展提供了强大活力和坚实保障。

历经30年发展的张江科学城，坚持自立自强、开放包容和大胆改革的创新之路，依靠科技创新展现出创新发展的韧劲，以科技创新为上海高质量发展提供动力。面向未来，张江科学城正加快向具有全球影响力的科技创新中心进军，努力扩大高水平基础科技供给、打造科技创新高地、优化完善科技创新体系，为国家实现高水平科技自立自强提供有力支撑。

（三）结语

科技创新是中国式现代化的内生动力，也是各国现代化的共同特征。人类历史上历经了三次重大科技革命，每一次科技革命都带来了社会生产力的飞跃，也加速推进了世

[①] 刘士安等：《构建开放创新生态 上海张江活力四射》，《人民日报》2022年12月9日。

界现代化进程。然而，关键核心技术的使用往往壁垒较高，一旦涉及国家竞争也常常面临"卡脖子"问题。面对新一轮科技革命和产业变革带来的机遇和挑战，中国共产党把创新驱动作为高质量发展的抓手以及中国现代化建设全局中的核心。在理念上，坚持把科技自立自强作为国家发展的战略支撑，走自主的创新道路。从"两弹一星"到超级杂交水稻、北斗卫星导航系统、载人航天工程等，历史和实践充分证明，这些关系国民经济命脉和国家安全的关键领域，真正的核心技术、关键技术是要不来、买不来、讨不来的，只能依靠自主创新。

中国始终把科技创新作为现代化发展道路上的重要推动力，并且形成了一些宝贵经验。在战略上，坚持集中力量和科学规划，集中力量是指以国家利益为最高目标，动员和调配全国有关的力量，包括精神意志和物质资源，攻克某一项世界尖端领域或国家级特别重大项目的工作体系和运行机制，这对中国的科技事业发展起到了重要作用；科学规划是指各级政府积极谋划发展科学，为我国科技事业的发展设置战略目标、重点部署和相关配套保障措施。在路径上，将基础研发与产业发展相结合，为高质量发展提供看得见、用得上、摸得着的科技力量，为产业发展新空间的开辟和新动能的打造奠定基础。在方法上，遵循开放包容和大胆改革的精神，打造良好的科技创新生态，营造适于科技创新的环境和氛围，为科技成果的产生和转化提供强有力的制度保障。

以创新驱动发展为关键抓手的高质量发展，是推进中国式现代化的必由之路。当前，世界百年未有之大变局加速演进，我国面临的资源要素约束更紧，受到来自国际的技术、人才等领域竞争压力更大，只有坚定走科技自立自强道路，才能不断开辟发展新领域新赛道，塑造发展新动能新优势，以创新驱动赋能高质量发展推进中国式现代化。

三、以高水平保护推动绿色发展

（一）引言

　　在陆家嘴和张江，当你被熙攘的人流和林立的建筑包围时，一定会感受到资本与产业、科技与创新碰撞中蕴含的发展潜力，但这并非上海高质量发展的全部动能。与世界上很多超大城市一样，上海也面临着人口和产业高度密集、生态环境容量有限、土地资源短缺等问题，破题的关键就在于生态优先、绿色发展，让绿色成为高质量发展的鲜明色彩。那么，上海在高水平保护中实现高质量发展的"绿色密码"到底是什么呢？

2023 年中国龙舟公开赛（上海普陀站）暨第十九届上海苏州河城市龙舟国际邀请赛（来源：王佳斌 / 上海市体育局 × IP SHANGHAI）

横向来看，发源于青藏高原、横贯中国的母亲河长江，在上海注入东海；纵向来看，全球目前共有九条候鸟迁徙路线，上海是其中一条路线上的重要中转点，那些穿梭于南北半球的候鸟将上海视为能量补给站。一横一纵，交汇点上的上海被赋予了更特殊的绿色发展的使命。

100多年前，我国第一场有正式记载的赛艇比赛在黄浦江上进行；100多年后，2022年10月，上海赛艇公开赛在苏州河上开桨。"一江一河"的浪花，见证了上海生态保护的决心和成效。"一江一河"告别了黑臭、逼仄与疏离，一个可赏、可游、可嬉的城市水脉让市民群众得以走进、亲近。

生态环境好不好，要看鸟儿的翅膀往哪飞。上海在快速的城市化过程中，城市鸟类群落受到了很大的冲击。经过几十年的发展，上海人均公共绿地面积从"一双鞋"增加到"一间房"，超过了东京等国际大都市，越来越多的公园和绿地建成，也为鸟儿提供了更多的栖息空间。上海记录到的鸟类有518种，其中水鸟种数约占全国的2/3。

鸟类栖息景观

德国的柏林被称为"野猪之都"，加拿大的多伦多被称为"世界浣熊之都"。现在，野生动物进城的故事也在上海上演：国家二级重点保护野生动物——貉，被发现出现在上海超过 260 个社区和城市绿地中，其实也是"土著"物种的回归。这些生态保护工作被评为"生物多样性 100+ 全球典型案例"。

从"两型社会"到"美丽上海"再到"生态之城"，上海不再满足于"看天""看水""看绿"，而是更加关注生态品质是否有利于提升市民生态福祉，是否有利于满足超大城市人民群众对美好生活的需要，是否有利于增强城市的吸引力、创造力和竞争力，致力于探索协同推进高质量发展和高水平保护的绿色发展新路径、新举措。[①]

（二）高水平保护助推高质量发展的新路径

基于对国际同类城市的调研分析，上海对标最高标准最好水平，直面自身不足：一是上海城市能源基底仍以化石能源为主，阻碍了生态环境质量的进一步提升；二是产业能级不高，高端制造业不能引领国际化、全球化发展新趋势和新方向。

上海把推动经济社会发展绿色化、低碳化作为实现高质量发展的关键环节。一是强治理，上海全面完成 4000 余台分散燃煤设施的整治，2000 余家企业排放设施的改造，33 万余辆黄标车的淘汰；二是提能级，曾立足于钢铁、化工的传统工业大区——宝山区和金山区，落实"南北转型"的战略要求，加快向新型生态文明跨越；三是促创新，钢铁企业突破绿色低碳冶炼技术，发电企业不断刷新火电煤耗世界纪录。同时，提前布局能源创新转型，规划到 2025 年氢能产业规模突破 1000 亿元。

作为钢产量占全球一半的世界最大钢铁集团，中国宝武集团（上海）实现低碳绿色转型是制造业高质量发展的难题，也是上海打造"生态之城"必须突破的瓶颈。我们通过回顾宝武企业绿色转型的案例，来解密一个人口密集、交通便利、产业健全的超大城市是如何"内外发力"，成为高水平保护助推高质量发展的"绿色样本"的。

[①]　本书编写组：《人与自然和谐共生的美丽上海——社会主义现代化国际大都市生态环境治理的探索与实践》，上海社会科学院出版社 2022 年版，第 7 页。

1. 强化顶层设计，形成企业绿色转型的外部压力

2015 年，《巴黎协定》多边谈判正式开启。上海前瞻性地把握到，降低二氧化碳排放将成为人类文明向前推进的一个不可逆进程，并出台了《上海市煤炭减量替代工作方案（2015—2017 年）》，提出要"控制钢铁行业煤炭消费总量，逐步减少其直接燃烧和炼焦用煤"，明确"到 2017 年，宝钢集团[①]用煤量控制在 1300 万吨以内"。事实上，当时宝钢在钢铁行业二氧化碳减排上已经有了一定的思考和技术研发，但资源消耗总量的约束，让其很快意识到二氧化碳末端治理不能治本，要走到传统冶炼工艺的前端去，将低碳冶金技术作为主要研发方向，减少化石能源的一次性输入。2019 年，在国家工业和信息化部和发展改革委的支持和协调下，宝武首个低碳冶金创新试验平台建成投运，成为全球最大规模的低碳冶炼试验装置和开放型创新平台。2020 年 7 月，宝武成立低碳冶金创新中心，从集团层面统一开展低碳冶金创新技术的基础研究和应用研究。

2020 年 9 月 22 日，习近平主席代表中国向世界作出了"2030 年碳达峰、2060 年碳中和"的承诺。时隔仅仅一年，2021 年 9 月 22 日，中国发布了《关于完整准确全面贯彻新发展理念，做好碳达峰碳中和工作的意见》和《2030 年前碳达峰行动方案》，明确了"双碳"时间表和路线图。2022 年 7 月，上海出台了《上海碳达峰行动方案》，重点实施"碳达峰十大行动"，在绿色低碳区域行动中提出，支持推动宝武集团开展碳达峰碳中和试点示范。随着碳排放约束的趋紧，钢铁行业下游制造商纷纷开始加快低碳产品布局和采购战略调整，向上游寻找更加低碳的绿色钢材。这对宝武绿色低碳产品的供应能力提出了更高要求。不绿色转型不仅意味着丧失未来的竞争优势，更会直接损害企业现有的发展成果和效益。宝武绿色发展思路由此发生了重大变化，强调不仅要以低碳冶金和智慧制造实现钢铁生产过程的绿色化，而且要以精品化实现钢铁产品使用过程的绿色化。

（1）绿色制造：探秘"黑灯工厂"里的降碳行动

宝武集团旗下宝钢股份精心打造的智造项目，2020 年入选世界经济论坛评出的全球"灯塔工厂"，成为中国钢铁行业的代表。[②]只有亲眼看见"黑灯工厂"在黑暗中井然

---

① 2016 年 12 月，宝钢集团和武钢集团联合重组，成立了中国宝武钢铁集团有限公司。
② 何欣荣等：《这家亿吨钢厂有"宝"颠覆你的印象》，新华网，http://www.xinhuanet.com/2022-02/16IC_1128381118.htm。

有序、不分昼夜生产的科幻电影般的强大生产能力，才能切身感受到钢铁行业转向智慧化、自动化的魅力。人工行车变成无人行车、机器人替代人工完成 3D（dangerous，dirty，difficult）作业、模型替代人工设定完成集控作业，从而具备了 24 小时黑灯操作的条件。在无人行车库区，抬头可见车间最高处两台上料行车正在用"钢爪"将一卷卷银色的冷轧钢卷精准调运上料。无人化行车自动把钢卷吊到鞍座上，再由自动拆捆带机器人拆捆并自动回收捆带。在车间机组区的炉子段，还有一个能爬高楼、不恐高的机器人——"炉子智能巡检机器人"。虽然工厂里漆黑一片，但在后端的"中枢大脑"——"六合一集控室"的操控台前，三块巨大显示屏实时清晰显示着机器的运转画面。这套智慧工厂管理系统实现了现场管理数字化，通过应用大量数字化、网络化、智能化技术，解决了生产

"黑灯工厂"黑暗中作业井然有序（来源：刘继鸣／宝山区新闻办 ×IP SHANGHAI）

全要素分段式管理的弊端，实现了无缝的全流程一贯制智慧管理，吨钢能耗下降了 15%，吨钢综合污染物下降 30%，可提高 30% 的劳动效率和 20% 的产能，加工成本下降 10%。智能制造已成为宝武提质增效的"利器"，助力企业碳减排。

（2）绿色产品：原来，钢铁是绿色的

过去，我们一提到精品，就是差异化，就是汽车、硅钢、家电等品种。但是在"绿色产品"的理念下，宝武"精品"是能为下游行业减碳和社会用钢升级作贡献的绿色产品。采用宝武的超低损耗取向硅钢制造的变压器替代中国现有配电网高耗能变压器，全国每年将节电 870 亿千瓦时，相当于新建一座三峡发电站。通过钢铁产品使用过程的绿色化，钢铁将成为当今社会最具有循环经济特征的绿色材料，是可以 100% 无限循环利用的永久性资源。正是在这样的思路引导下，宝武围绕建筑、交通、能源等行业材料升级，技术创新的视野和格局被完全打开了。作为全球最大最强的汽车钢板供应商，宝钢股份在 2021 年 4 月 9 日举办了宝钢超轻型、纯电动、高安全白车身 BCB EV（Baosteel Car Body Electric Vehicle）全球首发仪式。BCB EV 可实现钢板制造阶段减少二氧化碳排放约 200 千克，汽车使用阶段减少二氧化碳排放约 950 千克。

2. 有为政府和有效市场形成合力，激发企业绿色转型的内生动力

绿色发展是发展方式的根本性转变，是发展质量和效益的突破性提升。上海把建设国际科创中心和构建现代化产业体系结合起来，让政府和市场"两只手"同时发挥作用。基础性、先导性、战略性的事情由政府来做，比如兴建科研院所、开展基础性研究、搭建公共研发平台，而涉及行业发展的高精尖研究，则交给企业自己来做，政府给政策、给资金、给补贴。

（1）上海以科技创新支撑"双碳"科研布局

上海通过科技创新行动和能力建设，整合上海高校和研究所资源，合理引导、配置、整合，将人才、资本、技术等引入，将丰富的创新要素聚合起来、协同起来、贯通起来，为宝武绿色转型发展打下坚实基础。2021 年度"科技创新行动计划"科技支撑碳达峰碳中和专项项目中，布局了 4 个方向，包括前沿颠覆性技术、二氧化碳捕集利用与封存技术、新型能源技术和工业、产业低碳零碳技术。今年则增加到 7 个方向，包括前沿颠覆性技术、能源系统、建筑交通行业及区域示范、负碳能力提升技术、二氧化碳排放监测技术、资源综合利用技术、碳中和技术集成示范等。中国宝武有望在世界冶金史上留下印记，富氢碳循环氧气高炉技术，将助力宝武实现 2050 年碳中和目标，这比国家碳中和整体目标计划达成时间提前了 10 年。2022 年年末，中国宝武在 2022 年全球低碳冶金创新论坛上正式披露了其低碳冶金的最新成果：富氢碳循环氧气高炉已实现碳减排 20%、固体燃料消耗降低 30% 的效果，且新工艺具有商业化的基础，将于 2023 年大规模推广。

（2）上海将绿色低碳作为高质量发展的"新赛道"

上海一方面从需求端入手，抢抓能源清洁化、原料低碳化、材料功能化、过程高效化、终端电气化和资源循环化的市场需求；另一方面从供给端发力，围绕"新技术、新工艺、新材料、新装备、新能源"五大领域，形成一批关键技术和企业清单。产业新赛道、产品新增长的实质是企业的创新、技术的迭代更新和市场的不断开发。在促进绿色低碳产业发展行动方案中，上海明确提出要综合运用财政、金融、投资、土地等相关政策，充分利用战略性新兴产业等专项资金，支持本市绿色低碳技术突破、产业发展和特色园区建设。

在新兴产业专项资金的引导下，宝武开启绿色低碳的超前布局。宝武设立的低碳冶金创新中心，已吸引了来自 15 个国家的 62 家企业、院校加盟。在上海宝山，宝武（上海）碳中和产业园区也在建设中。据宝地资产副总裁盛郁旻介绍，园区南部区域定位为绿色低碳主导产业核心功能区，发展总部经济、科技服务、创新孵化、人才服务等。北部片区首发项目以绿色低碳冶金技术研发为主，预计 2023 年上半年建成。园区北部另外约 1900 亩将以制造业为主，承接碳中和创新成果转化，打造碳中和相关领域产业化基地。

宝武借助上海国际金融中心建设和金融机构集聚优势，以绿色融资降低成本、以产业基金募集资金，形成"地方引导＋基金投资＋企业发展＋产业回馈"的良性循环，将金融创新与钢铁产业深度结合。中国宝武与国家绿色发展基金股份有限公司于 2021 年发起成立了宝武碳中和股权投资基金，总规模达 500 亿元，首期 100 亿元，是国内市场上规模最大的碳中和主题基金，致力于挖掘风、光等清洁能源潜在发展地区和投资市场上优质的碳中和产业项目；2022 年宝钢股份在上海证券交易所成功发行一期公司债券，这是全国首单低碳转型绿色公司债券，规模 5 亿元，用于钢铁氢基竖炉系统项目。

绿色低碳领域发展速度反映了城市高质量发展的未来潜力。上海在绿色低碳领域的先发布局，能提前吸引企业进驻，汇聚业内人才与资源，较早完善产业链建设，也将具备更多区位优势，成为更多企业落地的主要选择。制造业绿色转型和新兴产业聚集能为城市发展节能减碳，帮助其他传统企业转型，在改善区域生态环境的同时，又进一步拉动区域经济升级发展。

（三）结语

从瑞典斯德哥尔摩首次人类环境会议（1972 年），到气候变化的《巴黎协定》，再到可持续发展理念，以及今天仍有着很深启迪作用的绿色经济、循环经济、低碳经济，中国一直都是全球生态环境治理的重要参与者和坚定实践者。

经过 50 多年的努力，中国在环境污染防治和自然生态保护方面取得了令人瞩目的成就。美国国家航天局研究结果表明，全球从 2000 年到 2017 年新增的绿化面积中，约 1/4 来自中国，中国贡献比例居全球首位。彭博社的报道也正面肯定了中国环境治理的成就，指出中国用 7 年时间实现了美国 30 年大气污染治理的成绩，并因此让中国居民的平均预期寿命增加 2 年。联合国前副秘书长、挪威前环境大臣埃里克（Erik Solheim）评价说，中国能取得这样的成就，是因为中国人民有这样的要求，中国领导层接收到这个信息后决定采取行动，而且采取了非常坚定的行动。"第一也是最重要的经验就是中国高层领导对环境治理的坚定决心和整体规划。"

从规模和速度而言，中国可以称得上是传统工业化模式最大的受益者。但是，为什么中国却将生态优先、绿色发展放在如此重要的地位，坚定不移地走人与自然和谐共生的中国式现代化道路呢？西方的现代化模式存在着"现代化的悖论"，它可以让世界上少数人口过上丰裕的生活，但一旦扩大到全球，就会出现资源环境方面的危机。从数据上看，工业革命近 300 年，全球进入现代化的国家有 20 多个，总人口 10 亿人左右。14 亿多人口的中国实现了现代化，就会把这个人口数量提升一倍以上。艰巨性和复杂性前所未有。需要我们思考的是，中国如果沿着西方式现代化这条路走，还能不能走得通？中国人均资源禀赋严重不足，下一步中国实现现代化强国的目标一定会面临更多的资源环境约束，这决定了中国不可能走西方现代化的老路。

中国离不开世界，世界离不开中国。地球环境及其多样的生态系统，是人类命运共同体的基石，"只有一个地球"的呼唤和初心仍然需要世界各国人民牢牢铭记。中国共产党将人与自然和谐共生作为中国式现代化的本质特征和中国特色，主要表现在三个方面：一是在理念上，我们坚持绿水青山就是金山银山，坚持尊重自然、顺应自然、保护自然，把这三者作为发展的内在要求；二是在道路和路径选择上，我们坚持在发展中保护，在保护中发展，坚持生态优先、绿色发展；三是在方法上，我们强调系统观念，坚持山水林田湖草沙一体化保护和系统治理，统筹产业结构调整、污染治理、生态保护、应对气候变化。这些都是发展中国家迈向现代化可以借鉴的宝贵经验。

以人为本：
打造高品质生活

高品质生活是人民日益增长的美好生活需要得到保障和满足的生活。推动实现高品质生活、增进人民福祉是各国发展的共同愿景。

什么是高品质生活？它的理想类型是什么样的？对于这一问题，早在 1958 年，就有学者提出"生活质量"这一概念，认为"生活质量是指人的生活舒适和便利，精神上有享受和乐趣"。随后《社会指标》一书将生活质量的研究从理论阐述引入到了实证阶段。目前用于评价生活质量的指标十分丰富，如人类发展指数（HDI）、社会进步指数（ISP）、幸福指数（WBI）、社会发展指数（SDI）和美好生活指数等。从理论探讨到指标研究，无一不说明人们对于高品质生活的需求越来越多元化。从国际视野的角度来看，虽然不同指标侧重不同，但对生活质量的评价都离不开三大维度：精神需求、公共生活和品质民生。

中国式现代化的美好未来必将给予高品质生活极大供给。上海始终坚持把最好的资源留给人民，用优质的供给服务人民，把最广阔的舞台给予人民，为高品质生活提供了上海样本。

传承城市文化精神是上海打造高品质生活的卓越追求。上海以城市文脉和城市记忆的传承提升高品质文化生活，不断呼应人民对美好精神文化生活的新期盼。在推动历史街区品质与城市魅力提升过程中，武康路的诞生记生动演绎了建筑可阅读、街区可漫步、城市有温度的城市更新理念。

保障人民生活供给是上海打造高品质生活所不可或缺的。上海以打造 15 分钟社区生活圈提升城市公共生活体验度，更好地回应人民群众对提高生活品质的新需求。在个人与城市的共处融合过程中，梧桐树下的百年新华将带你一览宜居宜业的繁荣社区、多样便捷的幸福社区、活力开放的和谐社区中的美好生活。

营造老龄友好社会是上海打造高品质生活的应有之义。上海以社区"嵌入式"养老模式实现"原居安养"，构建符合老年人期待的高品质社区养老新生活。在上海每三个户籍人口中就有一位老人，老人的生活是否幸福安康牵动着全社会的心，陆家嘴街道的老年居民将与你诉说他们是如何在熟悉的家庭环境、人际关系和社区场域中安度晚年的。

一、传承城市文化精神

（一）引言

对于今天的中国都市人而言，生活有诗意已成为一种自觉追求，甚至成为衡量生活品质的一个重要指标。近些年，"寻找'诗和远方'"成为人们在节假日和闲暇时光里最热爱做的事情之一。这反映出生活在忙碌现代都市里的人们的一种强烈的精神渴望和文化需要——诗意的栖居。去哪里寻找"诗和远方"满足人们对诗意生活的向往呢？唯有"逃离城市"，去遥远的地方吗？何不把人们对诗意栖居的向往转化成城市发展的新动力，让人们在城市里，甚至在家门口就能感受诗意和美好？

近些年来，上海市民欣喜地发现"诗和远方"不再是奢望，而是真的来到了身边。150 个被市民评选出的家门口"小而美""小而精"的好去处，为人们提供了感受诗意与美好的高品质公共空间。它们散落于生活社区、特色街区、工业厂区、生态绿地等不同类型的城市空间中，其中有不少是在对老建筑的保护和活化的基础上发展起来的，并迅速成为远近闻名的上海文化新地标，成为新时代上海城市文化的活力来源。如今，到了周末和假期，上海市民越来越热衷于走出家门，用脚步去丈量这座城市，在漫步中阅读一座又一座老建筑，感受这座城市的昨天与今天，也感受着她独特的诗意与美好，甚而重新发现与认识这座城市。市民们感慨，上海依然日新月异，但却越来越有历史感、有气质、有温度。这座城市不只是容纳最现代设施、最新技术、最活跃资本要素的容器，也是人们安放灵魂、留住记忆和乡愁、感受诗意和美好的精神家园。

那么，这些变化是如何发生的呢？当你漫步于时下上海最热门的打卡地之一的武康路时，是否想过为什么它会成为市民游客寻找"诗和远方"、感受"最上海"魅力的首选之地？它是如何一步步成长为今天这个样子的？下面我们就一起走进武康路。

（二）可阅读、可漫步、有温度——新时代武康路的诞生记

建筑、道路和街区构成城市景观与都市生活的空间，而审美的符号、文化的内涵、

武康路与淮海路交接处的武康大楼

诗意的美感，就藏在这些物质的载体之中。

武康路，位于上海市中心保护规模最大的衡复历史文化风貌保护区的核心。它始建于 1907 年，原名福开森路（Route Ferguson），1943 年改名为武康路。它是一条带文脉的马路，不仅有大师、有历史、有故事，还有可阅读的建筑，以及落叶满地、秋色如画的街巷。这条不足 2 千米的马路，留存着从 20 世纪初筑路开始到 1998 年的各年代建筑，法式、英式、西班牙式，不一而足，堪称"上海近代建筑博物馆"。90 年前，爱尔兰文豪萧伯纳赞扬武康路："走进这里，不会写诗的人想写诗，不会画画的人想画画，不会唱歌的人想唱歌，感觉美妙极了。"武康路的风貌现在依旧，并且被越来越多的人所共享。

这份最优雅醇厚的海派气质之所以被留传下来，则要从上海对历史街区风貌的守护，对老建筑的保护和修缮开始说起。

1. 像对待"老人"一样尊重和善待老建筑

武康路上的老梧桐们见过老房子的多次变身：1986 年底，上海被列为全国历史文化名城。两年多后，市里给全市的老房子造册，逐步确认了 632 处 2000 余栋优秀历史建筑。1999 年，武康路被划进衡复历史文化风貌保护区。2003 年底，衡复保护区启动整治工程。2004 年，《上海市衡山路—复兴路历史文化风貌区保护规划》获正式批准，开启了徐汇衡复历史风貌区保护的序幕。

2007 年，武康路被定为全市首个历史风貌保护的试点马路，保护性整治迈上一个新的台阶。就在这一年，时任上海市委书记习近平在徐汇区调研时指出，"城市中的老建筑，应该像'老人'一样得到善待"。他登上港汇广场 1 号楼的顶楼，从 220 多米高的楼顶俯瞰徐家汇全貌。看到武康大楼等老建筑后，习近平对上海的城市文脉流露出浓厚的感情。他说："上海历史风貌的价值精华就在 4000 多幢老建筑，如果这些老建筑消失了，上海的文脉就切断了，历史风貌就没有了，城市特色也就没有了。对于历史风貌区要防止大拆大建，切实传承好历史文脉。"像对待"老人"一样尊重和善待老建筑，守护上海城市文脉的理念开始深入人心，并在上海后来的城市规划与建设中得到实践、延续和发展。[1]

---

[1] 胡霁荣：《守护城市的文脉》，载赵刚印等《改革开放成就上海》，上海人民出版社 2018 年版，第 252 页。

渐渐地，铁门镂空透了绿，违规商铺被清理，沿街窗户材质、空调外机颜色、遮阳篷规格、店招式样，乃至每棵行道树的树冠直径等，都按历史文脉一一修整妥帖。整治后的武康路，在 2011 年成为上海第一条国家历史文化名街。①

铭牌挂上了，微更新仍在路上。比如，人行道上用来划分自行车停车区域的线条，不再是司空见惯的用白色油漆涂成，而是用青灰色混凝土砖块拼接得来。又比如，环绕武康大楼的架空线被逐步藏进地下，附近天空层层舒朗起来。又好比"落叶不扫"，并非真的完全不扫，而是视落叶堆积程度，带点美术思维、艺术性地扫。点点举措看似不起眼，可连点成线再成面，武康路在不变中变得更美。还有些改变也悄然发生：巴金故居向公众免费开放；沿街每一栋老房子上都有了讲述身世的二维码；文艺青年视此处为圣地，潮人、商户纷纷相中这里，创客们更希冀沾染武康路空气里飘溢的灵气。

2. 守护"原汁原味"的历史风貌，保存诗意的美感

守护老建筑，就是要保留"原汁原味"的历史风貌，守护城市的诗意与美感，保留城市的记忆和人们的乡愁。

守护"原汁原味"的历史风貌离不开对历史建筑的保护与修缮。武康大楼是武康路老建筑保护和修缮的缩影和代表。它位于武康路与淮海中路交接的起点。建于 1924 年的武康大楼，是一座典型的法国文艺复兴风格的建筑，也是上海最早的外廊式公寓建筑。这栋百年建筑出自老上海滩顶顶有名的外籍建筑师邬达克之手，并因 1940 年代以后一些上海文化演艺界名流陆续搬入而变得星光熠熠。但是它真正为今日上海市民和游客所熟知，成为上海最热门的网红打卡地中的爆款，则是从 2018 年对它进行整体性修缮开始的。

2018 年 4 月，94 岁的武康大楼迎来新一轮整体性修缮。主持修缮工程的顾志峰回忆说，这是他参与修缮的难度最大、最复杂的项目。彼时，上海对历史建筑"修旧如故"的高标准、严要求已经有充分认识，"尊重历史"便成为顾志峰为自己和修缮团队树立的一根准绳。

然而，在实际操作中，修缮班组很快发现，仅大楼外立面的清水墙，就面临着风化

---

① 王彦：《武康路：时光纵无痕，旧梧桐年年有新知》，《文汇报》2018 年 4 月 27 日。

程度不一、重点材料泰山砖已停止规模化生产等困难。经历几番试验摸索后，顾志峰与其团队最终创造性地结合砖粉修缮与"由上至下"的墙面修补法，对武康大楼外墙根据不同的风化程度进行了还原和平色修复。如此一来，既保留了不同历史时期清水墙因风雨冲刷留下的独特竖向纹理，也使修缮后的墙面依旧令人感到眼前一新。

老建筑的保护修缮背后是不断精进的工艺和认真负责、实干创新的精神。顾志峰说，修缮老建筑的工艺不光靠前期的积累，更是历任工匠们在修缮现场一点一点"磨"出来的。"在修缮班组，即便是只负责'管'施工的项目经理、安全员，也都对历任建筑修缮的标准和技法烂熟于心。清水墙有4种不同的接缝，这些都要能马上看出来；红砖、黑砖都是清水砖，只是窑变温度不同，也要分辨得出来。"①

2021年开始，上海成立了首家住宅修缮行业技能人才培训基地"徐房集团实训基地·345传习工坊"。这不仅为前来进修的工人完成技术进阶，把普通的"修缮师傅"变为更高阶的"工匠人才"，也为老建筑修缮提供了持续的人才保障。

一座城如何对待自己的过去，就会如何对待自己的未来。像对待"老人"一样尊重和善待老建筑，透露出上海这座城市对历史文化遗产的尊崇与珍视，以及对未来更好的上海的真诚期盼。让城市留住记忆，让人们记住乡愁，已成为上海守护和传承历史文脉的自觉追求。因为，在面对"千城一面"和城市同质化的问题时，上海变得更加自信和从容。

3. 关注民生改善，老建筑里也有美好生活

历史老建筑的保护和修缮，并不只是照着老照片的样子修修补补，粉刷粉刷外墙，力求"原汁原味"。它不只是老房子外在容颜的"修旧如旧"，而是密切关乎房子的"内里"，关系到居住于此的每家每户的老百姓。

武康路上闹中取静、梧桐掩映下的花园洋房，是过去，也是现在许多人心底里的好房子，满足人们对住宅的美好想象。然而过去很长一段时间，老房子里的生活，并非外界所想的日日活在情致里。资料显示，1985年，上海中心区域的平均人口密度高达每平

① 《复活"小辰光"的记忆：他在一砖一瓦里，重现城市的烟火气》，《解放日报》2022年10月22日。《上海保护规模最大历史风貌区已达7.66平方公里，是谁在修这些老房子》，上观，https://www.jfdaily.com.cn/news/detail?id=431991。

方千米 4 万人；石库门里弄里有 70% 的家庭只能在室内或过道中生煤炉，无固定厨房；厨房及煤气的普及率为 38.7%；60% 的居民与他人共用自来水或使用供水站；使用手拎马桶的家庭更高达 80% 以上。老报纸里也记载了当年武康路的实情。约从 1987 年开始，每逢夏季，报纸上都会刊载"停电检修预告"。住户多了，家用电器也逐渐升级，老房子的民用电网不堪重负，一到酷暑就频频告急。这种情形一直持续到 21 世纪初。更难以启齿的还有洋房里的化粪池：洋房弄窄巷子深，抽粪车开不进去，只能靠人力小车运输；每每此时，人人避之唯恐不及。[①]

2007 年，在广泛听取意见、达成共识的基础上，徐汇区启动了置换购房，武康路的部分居民率先签字。按协议，居住在此的居民搬离老房子，用置换款购置自主产权房。这样，老洋房有机会做个全身体检、全身修复，居民有了真正属于自己的宽敞的家。

除了修门面，修房子还是为了让里面的人住得更舒服。2018 年，武康大楼开始新一轮整体性修缮，为了再现这幢百年建筑原汁原味的历史风貌，同时回应居民对美好生活的需要，有关部门着实啃了一次"硬骨头"。

一直以来，由于大楼外面空调机架、晾衣架、花架杂乱，尤其是二层最有特色的水刷石牛腿装饰被空调机架遮挡，严重破坏了大楼的美感。所以，此次修缮的其中一个重点就是规整所有空调机架并将二楼空调机架全部从南侧移到北侧。而就是这个修缮方案，前后改了 12 稿，经过与大楼居民反复协商后才最终敲定下来。一开始，居民们反对，尤其是二楼居民的反对声音最大。为此，上海徐汇区房管局的领导和工作人员多次到每户居民家中进行"面对面"的交流，了解他们的实际需求。当了解到，居民们主要对楼道管线杂乱不满，并且害怕空调管线破坏屋内非常有特色的历史吊顶后，立刻邀请居民共同制定方案，先规整了楼道管线并用吊板进行了遮挡，同时会同专业设计单位多次到各户家中实地踏勘，为每户"量身定制"一套适合自家的中央空调方案。最终，居民们被打动了，修缮方案得以落实。

武康大楼和武康路的火爆，得益于对历史老建筑的保护和对城市文脉的传承，而这

---

① 胡霁荣：《守护城市的文脉》，载赵刚印等《改革开放成就上海》，上海人民出版社 2018 年版，第 253—254 页。

背后既离不开老建筑修缮者和城市管理者深入细致、有"温度"的工作，也离不开人民群众的共同参与、相互的理解与支持。最终受益的是这座城市以及生活、工作和游历在其中的人们。如今，污水、泥泞、一到夏天就跳闸的现象，煤球炉、手拎马桶、粪车统统是前尘往事。武康路不仅门面上满是优秀的历史文化建筑，此间居民也享受到了现代化的设施、合理的空间。他们看得到历史与回忆，也得到物质生活的满足，更加期待美好的生活。

4. 打造共享的公共空间，让老建筑"活起来"

如果说历史建筑的保护修缮是守护城市历史文脉的 1.0 版本，道路保护和整治是 2.0 版本，那么通过将老建筑对外开放，打造成可共享的高品质公共文化空间，让老建筑"活起来"，让历史街区"动起来""靓起来"，从而推动街区整体品质的提升，则是今天上海正在实践和探索的历史文脉保护传承的 3.0 版本。

老建筑和历史街区的风貌保护不是守护城市文脉的最终目的。修旧如旧的老建筑、原汁原味的历史街区也不应是标本，而应该是被注入新的时代活力的城市生命体。秉持这一想法，衡复历史风貌区，通过腾出历史名人故居，更新为市民游客可进入的公共空间，来激活老建筑的活力，并以此带动整个风貌区的活化。

以武康路 393 号为例。这栋建筑几经变身，曾是参与辛亥革命的革命家黄兴的旧居、上海国际图书馆、世界学校、湖南路街道办事处。2010 年起，武康路 393 号功能转变，成了武康路旅游咨询中心、老房子艺术中心，对普通市民游客开放，并为来往于此处的游客提供便捷、周到的公益服务。人们既可以进到建筑内部欣赏老建筑的内部构造与设计，通过建筑内优秀历史建筑模型、美术、摄影等艺术作品，了解和感受整个上海老房子的历史底蕴，翻阅这里的资料或扫一扫二维码阅读老建筑和风貌区的故事，也可以周末来此参加老房子故事会，听听各路专家学者对上海历史的解读，抑或是坐下来歇歇腿，甚至可以和身边的陌生人拉拉家常，看看别人在武康路或是上海的游历里有什么新发现新感悟。

武康路 393 号的变身，可谓旧貌换新颜。它的保护、修缮、活化利用是上海城市更新的一个缩影和代表。近十年来，在上海像这样被"善待"的老建筑越来越多。老房子变身为开放的公共空间，让市民游客可以与老房子产生很多近距离的互动。这些互动以及独特的个人体验是我们被挡在墙外、隔着门、隔着窗所无法产生和获得的。而老房子也在这样的互动过程中获得了新生，焕发出新的活力。

目前，上海已形成由"优秀历史建筑—风貌保护道路—历史文化风貌区"共同构成的"点、线、面"相结合的保护与活化体系，成功塑造历史街区活化实践示范样本，引领城市有机更新的高质量发展。这其中，以武康路为主体的名人故居特色街区、复兴中路—汾阳路为主体的"音乐文化特色街区"和以建国西路—岳阳路为主体的"海派文化慢生活街区"最具特色和代表性。

除此之外，近些年除了把历史建筑原汁原味地传承下去，上海还通过深挖各类文化要素与资源，通过收集整理数百位名人及其旧居的资料，编撰成书，举办展览、宣讲、提供漫步"阅读"老建筑线路导览、添加二维码、建设网上互动平台等形式，努力探索老建筑的创新打开方式，保护传承"最上海"历史文脉，打造城市文化大 IP，不断提升城市软实力。

（三）结语

可阅读、可漫步、有温度的新时代武康路的诞生，是中国式城市现代化的缩影，它折射出今天的中国人对城市高品质生活的理解、认识与期待。

"经济是血肉，文化是灵魂"已成为大家普遍的共识。经历了改革开放几十年的快速发展，人们认识到城市文化对城市发展的重要性，意识到守护城市历史文脉对城市魅力与都市美好生活的重要作用。正如习近平主席所说，"城市历史文化遗存是前人智慧的积淀，是城市内涵、品质、特色的重要标志。要妥善处理好保护和发展的关系，注重延续城市历史文脉，像对待'老人'一样尊重和善待城市中的老建筑，保留城市历史文化记忆，让人们记得住历史、记得住乡愁"①。

如今，通过保护老建筑、守护老街区历史风貌等举措，城市有机更新的发展模式取代了过去推土机式的"大拆大建"模式。我们透过历史遗存看得见自己和这座城市"从哪里来"，也更清楚我们"要到哪里去"。"建筑可阅读""街区可漫步""城市有温度"

---

① 《习近平关于城市工作论述摘编》，中央文献出版社 2023 年版，第 114 页。

的新时代人民城市，让我们在这里开启了诗意的生活，也让城市与我们每一个人在文化和精神上有了更紧密、更有温度的连接，共同构筑起人与城市的生命有机体。

武康路的案例生动演绎了中国在推进城市现代化历程中对城市有机更新的探索与创新。我们吸收借鉴了西方"城市更新"理论，并结合我国国情，提出了"文化是城市的灵魂""像对待'老人'一样尊重和善待老建筑""让人们记得住历史、记得住乡愁""让文化遗存'活起来'"等守护城市历史文脉、指导城市有机更新的新理念。在新时代十年的实践中，我们不止步于对老建筑的保护修缮，而是同时关注与老建筑朝夕相处的居民的生活需求和对美好生活的向往，并通过改善民生，提升街区品质，以实实在在的具体行动惠及更多民众。由此，一条以人民为中心、自觉追求物质文明与精神文明协调发展的"城市更新"的中国道路逐渐形成。而武康路深受市民和中外游客的喜爱，则进一步增强了我们的自信。这让我们更加坚信我们所走的道路，并且会继续坚定地走下去。

二、打造家门口的美好生活

（一）引言

　　长久以来，生活在城市里的现代人，无论是在大城市还是在小城市，都不得不面对拥堵、长时间通勤、高昂的生活成本和钢铁森林里的孤独等一系列生活挑战，严重影响了人们的生活品质。因此，2022 年 6 月 29 日，联合国人居署在最新发布的《2022 世界城市状况报告：畅想城市未来》中指出，城镇化仍然是 21 世纪一个势不可当的大趋势，但是现有的城镇化模式迫切需要改变。报告呼吁，从国家到地方的各级政府作出更大承诺，鼓励创新型技术和城市生活理念需要进一步推行，使人们都能充分享受城市生活的美好。

　　什么是城市生活的美好一刻？也许每个人都有各自的答案：可能是每天去家门口熙熙攘攘的社区菜场逛一逛，感受一下生活的"烟火气"；可能是下楼就可以散步的口袋花园，随时拥抱大自然；可能是不用担心堵车，每天步行就可以到达办公场所；可能是随时可以在街角的咖啡店与朋友见面聊天；也可能是去家附近琳琅满目的社区小店里转转看看……正是这种近在咫尺、又能满足不同人群的多样化需求的便利，才使得城市生活别具魅力。

　　近年来，上海正努力让这种美好一刻变成人人享有的日常生活。在《上海市城市总体规划（2017—2035 年）》（简称"上海 2035"总体规划）的引领下，从 2014 年开始，上海在全国率先提出打造"15 分钟社区生活圈"。"15 分钟社区生活圈"是指人们在慢行一刻钟的可达范围里，可以满足"衣、食、住、行"等日常需求。满足这些需求，需要配置相应的基本服务功能和公共活动空间。生活圈通常采用"1+N"的空间模式布局，完善社区生活圈的功能配置。"1"是指功能整合、空间复合的一站式综合服务中心，"N"是指灵活散点布局的小体量、多功能服务设施或场所。通过构建融合"宜业、宜居、宜游、宜养、宜学"多元功能的城市空间单元，建立以满足社区居民需求为导向的新型社区服务模式，将空间、服务资源与人的活动相对接，从而引领面向未来、健康低碳的美好生活方式，推动实现幼有善育、学有优教、劳有厚得、病有良医、老有颐养、住有宜居、弱有众扶的高品质生活目标。

随着 180 余个项目相继落地，"大城小圈"的建设究竟给我们的生活带来怎样的变化？当你走进长宁区新华路街道，映入眼帘的美丽图景将助你揭晓答案。

（二）"人文新华"的幸福生活

1. 梧桐树下的百年新华

如果你第一次来到新华路，你会发现，路两旁栽满了高大的梧桐树，林荫蔽日芬芳吐翠，树冠在路中间相交，形成了一条美丽的林荫隧道。细细看去，绿树掩映之间，散落着一排排各国式样的老式洋房，让这条长度仅 2434 米的小路有种道不尽的优雅迷人。

美丽的新华路

作为上海第一条花园马路，它的历史可追溯到 1000 多年前的北宋，曾经这里以园林驰名，法华牡丹名冠上海。公元 970 年建成的法华禅寺，比上海县还早 321 年，故有"先有法华，后有上海"之说。近百年来，这里卧虎藏龙、群贤汇集，建筑大师、文人雅士、达官显贵、名流商贾都曾在新华路居住工作。1971 年，上海市政府为了改变外国元首、来宾从虹桥机场到达市中心的交通状况，避免穿越沪杭铁路困难，建造了新华路隧道。1972 年，时任美国总统尼克松访华时，首次通过新华路隧道。从此，新华路又有了"上海国宾道"的美誉。2005 年，新华路被上海市人民政府命名为上海历史风貌保护区，它是中心城区 12 个历史风貌保护区之一。

新华路街道以新华路为中心，位于长宁区东南部，辖区面积 2.2 平方千米，街道内共有各种类型的居住小区 197 个，各类商务楼宇 56 幢 120 多万平方米，实有单位 3800 余家，常住人口 6.9 万人。尽管这里历史底蕴深厚、人文荟萃，但是作为成熟社区，为了更好满足人民的多元需求，也面临着一系列挑战：社区建成度高（96.1%），空间资源有限；居住类型多元，老旧社区占比较大（77%）；人口密度较高，老龄化程度高；基础服务设施保障完善，精准配置欠缺；空间局部亮点突出，整体品质有待提升；人文底蕴深厚，特色彰显略不足；辖区 1/3 的土地是工厂和烟囱，对于另外 2/3 的居民区造成了可想而知的困扰。人民日益增长的美好生活需要和不平衡不充分的发展之间的矛盾，是新华路街道必然要破解的难题。

为此，作为上海市首批"15 分钟社区生活圈"试点，2019 年 1 月，新华路街道正式启动项目建设，聚焦"方案、评估、规划和建设"四个环节，有序推进规划的编制和实施。为推动试点工作，街道成立专项工作组，聚焦居住、就业、出行、服务、休闲、特色等六方面存在的问题、短板、不足进行全面排摸梳理，联合专业设计团队、社区规划师团队共同编制完成了《新华路街道 15 分钟社区生活圈行动规划》。

在规划引领下，新华路街道以"花园社区、人文新华"为愿景，从强化顶层设计到稳步分类实施，发动社会力量共建、共治、共享，打造人人参与构建社区的"新华样本"，通过慢行系统完善行动、睦邻设施落地行动、交往场所营造行动、多元魅力彰显行动、花园社区再造行动及就业空间再生行动大力推进"新华路街道 15 分钟社区生活圈"项目，在打造精品、精致、精细的品质社区道路上，不断收获着、丰富着。

2. 宜业宜居的繁荣社区

就业是民生之本。为了给更多新华居民提供家门口优质就业岗位，在推进"15分钟社区生活圈"建设中，新华路街道的乐业单元，以"营生记"为主题，关注社区中小型商户企业的生活状态，协助他们积极尝试自我展示，并在社区中更好地就业。同时，新华路街道不断提升辖区营商环境，优化企业全生命周期服务，带动就业创业品质的提升。

"到新华去"已经成为企业的明智之选。近年来，为了助力域内企业持续健康成长，新华路街道不断打磨自身的服务技能，在线上依托"新企通"小程序为企业提供全生命周期服务，在线下通过营商服务站，为企业打造综合服务空间。此外，新华路街道还创造性地为企业制定营商服务清单、企业需求清单、街区资源清单3张清单，让企业能够更加契合新华路街道的发展布局。截至2023年，新华路街道共厚植企业3800多家，在时尚创意产业、在线新经济、生命健康赛道、总部经济等领域，吸引和培育了一大批优质企业，呈现出前所未有的勃勃生机。

服务企业归根到底是服务人。为了打造更多年轻一代所向往的富有活力、配套完善的办公环境，新华路街道通过城市更新的方式盘活社区资源，激发经济活力，已完成了多个自主城市更新项目。从工业新华到商务新华，从老旧园区改造到新建经济楼宇，新华路街道实现了社区形态"腾笼换鸟"，不断缔造创新活力的就业空间，投身构建"上海2035"总体规划的中央活动区。在新华，洋溢着一种人人奋斗出彩的精神，展现着天下英才近悦远来干事创业的生动图景。

安居乃民生之要。"我们细细打理着街区，就是希望能用宜居的环境，让住在这里的人拥有一个慢下来的生活。"新华路街道工作人员说。一方面，近年来，新华路街道针对辖区内老旧小区设施老化、功能缺失等难点、堵点、痛点问题，推进改善居住类项目，有效提升居民舒适性。针对售后公房老旧小区环境普遍较差问题，推动新华路、番禺路沿线整街坊"精品小区"建设，完成69个近70.5万平方米小区的改造提升。针对老公房煤卫合用问题，实施番禺路491弄等3个非成套改造项目。实施梅泉别墅、亦村等两个成片历史保护建筑的修缮，完成平武路58弄房屋协议置换工作，平武路98弄房屋动拆迁彻底解决新华路街道最后一片"拎马桶"问题。在建设项目清单的基础上，叠加家门口工程、微更新、微项目、电梯加装、垃圾箱房升级改造，不仅"打补丁"，更要"绣朵花"，为居民打造"适意"的居住环境。

敬老邨 7 号楼的楼道改造前　　　　　　　　　　敬老邨 7 号楼的屋顶改造后

另一方面，新华路街道"扮靓家门口"，打造"美丽街区"。通过疏通慢行"毛细血管"，对外国弄堂等 20 多条街坊道路的功能定位、环境整治、维护管理、自治共治等分类型进行研究。同时，新华路街道围绕"美丽街区"行动，践行"绿化、彩化、珍贵化、效益化"要求，改造新华路沿线绿化面积 4465 平方米、挡土墙 1647 米，借助"品质绿化"，焕新"花园马路"。在新华一号、友谊颂、香花桥路、定西路、光华医院、杨宅路 6 个道路节点打造街区景观，降低高挡墙，提高绿地的通透性。布置景观灯光、休息空间，吸引居民驻足，提高街头绿地的亲和感。改造后的新华路更显低调优雅、沉稳大气。

3. 多样便捷的幸福社区

"15 分钟社区生活圈"建设让居民们家门口的生活也越来越丰富。新华路街道老年人口占街道总人口的 1/3，但街道为老年人所花费的精力却不止 1/3。"让 1/3 的老年人安心了，那另外 2/3 的人就会高兴。"这是新华路街道一以贯之的理念。老年是生命的重要阶段，是仍然可以有作为、有进步、有快乐的重要人生阶段。

新华路街道综合为老服务中心（1）

新华路街道综合为老服务中心（2）

为积极应对人口老龄化趋势，满足老年人"原居安养"期盼，新华街道大力发展"一中心，多网点，全覆盖"的社区嵌入式养老服务体系，为社区老年群体提供"养、医、学、娱、乐"的一站式服务，推动实现街道综合服务圈、社区托养服务圈、居民区活动圈、邻里互助圈、居家生活圈"五圈合一"，打造人民城市幸福养老生活圈。

其中，新华路街道综合为老服务中心作为试点之一，位于街道辖区中部，前身为上海交通大学长宁校区闲置的学生宿舍。2019 年底正式投入运营后，可提供助餐、助浴、长照、日托、医疗、文娱活动等 20 多项服务，以建设"一站式综合服务、一体化资源统筹、一网覆盖信息管理、一门式办事窗口"四大核心功能为目标，围绕"创新、枢纽、配送"工作主线，着力在开放式运营、枢纽式作用、配送式服务等方面下功夫，统筹为老服务资源，完善养老服务网络，促进供需精准对接，逐步形成"满足基本、打造专业、扩大覆盖、强调个性"的运作模式，用"贴心＋有效"的精细化服务织密社区幸福养老网，成为广大社区老年人心中的"幸福港湾"。

老吾老以及人之老，幼吾幼以及人之幼。在打造"15 分钟社区生活圈"的过程中，新华路街道也积极打造儿童友好型社区。儿童友好不仅体现在社区环境布局上，更是一种理念和关怀。具体说来，首先是"Be kid"——是以儿童的心情和视觉想象所有事物，重点在于让儿童从游戏、活动、交流等方面玩得开心，也可以理解为"Be fun"，作为一个儿童的核心需求，也就是玩耍；其次是"Be kind"——是站在儿童的角度，建设童心、健康、教育等儿童友好空间，让孩子感受爱、建立爱、分享爱，也就是"Be gentle"，通过这些友好空间，让他们可以健康、快乐地成长；最后是"N"——字面意义上是 KID 和 KIND 两个概念字母上的差异，从差异中，又延伸出各种儿童友好建设中的可能性，不是简单地叠加，而是通过层层建设实现多维的"N"：Notice（标识）、Nursery（托儿所／幼儿园）、Native（在地）、Named（指定的）、Nature（自然）、Net（社区网络）、Near（附近）、Neighbourhood（邻里）、Need（需求）、Naivete（童心）、Nurture（教育）、Nourishment（健康食物）……使空间与人居的关系更加舒适与友好。

因此，新华路街道全方位、系统化地建设涉及儿童权利、儿童服务、儿童出行等空间，因地制宜，通过顶层设计，持续改善儿童友好城市环境。通过改造华山儿童公园、建设校园周边最美放学路、打造社区文化中心最靓少儿图书馆，提升儿童友好场景，让儿童在新时代快乐成长。2022 年暑假，新华路街道就联系区域内的多所学校，把假期闲置的教室腾挪出来，供附近小区的孩子们参加暑托班，解决双职工家庭的后顾之忧。老人是过去，儿童是未来，人情味的生活，是人和城市互相成就，是人和城市和谐共生。

为了以更优的供给满足居民需求，用最好的资源服务居民，2020 年，新华路街道广泛听取居民意见，按照人口规模适度、服务管理方便、资源配置有效、功能相对齐全的要求，结合"15 分钟社区生活圈"服务体系建设，在街道、居民区、小区层面整体建设布局"市民中心—市民驿站—市民小站"，新华里巷·市民中心便应运而生。

新华里巷·市民中心由位于新华路 359 号的老洋房改造而成，周边有不少居民区。自 2021 年 6 月 30 日开放后，一直人气颇旺。不少附近居民只需步行十几分钟，就可以在这里享受纸质书籍的书香气，体验喜马拉雅电子书的便捷性，欣赏各类文艺视听盛宴，相互切磋书法、绘画等各类技艺，体验数字化带来的生活便利，还能参观位于二楼的百年图片展了解新华路街道百年历史变迁。

4. 活力开放的和谐社区

在长宁区新华路街道，一个小角落发生了令人惊喜的变化。时尚绚丽、亲切真诚、低碳环保、亲子研学、创新设计……看似并不相关的词，竟都发生在这条弄堂的尽头——一栋由闲置建筑改造的新华·社区营造中心里。这是新华路街道构建"人人参与 共创美好街区"的心脏。

为什么说这里是社区的心脏呢？因为作为一种新的社区公共空间类型，新华·社区营造中心定位为社区的"支持中心"，为塑造"人人参与营造美好社区"而提供多种支撑。具体说来，新华·社区营造中心搭建了四大支持系统。

第一，搭建地方生态系统。这里呈现与"15 分钟社区生活圈"的空间网络相叠加的社区社会网络，既有在地资源，也接口外部资源，如专业力量、高校、基金会和支持平台等。来到这里，社区成员不仅可以感受到"新华生活圈"，还可以连接到在地社群，发现社区的积极行动者、创作者、协作者，并基于 Web3 的数字徽章系统小程序 Comupage，搭建数字化社区黄页。

第二，搭建参与式规划阵地。2022 年 9 月，上海市民政局发布《参与式社区规划导则》，将新华·社区营造中心作为参与式规划实践阵地。这里搭建专业的参与式工作坊活动空间，收集与呈现参与式规划与设计、社区行动支持的系列工具包，并结合真实项目持续开展活动。同时，中心不断积累来源于社区各类人群的议题，形成社区提案库，从而形成自上与自下双向互动的接口。

第三，搭建社造共学系统。新华·社区营造中心不仅激发社区成员的主动参与性，也支持社区外部的专业者、关注者能够通过自主学习、项目制学习、驻地实践等，形成以共学为驱动的行动孵化。同时，通过研发系统化的社区营造课程，为社区营造的专业人士赋能。

第四，搭建可持续资金池。新华·社区营造中心以良性运营和多途径筹款模式来支持可持续的、常态化的社区内生行动，并形成支持性的资金池。多途径收益包括空间运营与场所服务收入、政府采购社区服务项目收入、基金会专项合作筹款收入、品牌社区合作收入等。同时，还为社区积极行动者设立支持性项目，以及与基金会进行专项合作。

在这一系统支持下，新华·社区营造中心提出的"一平米行动"就是基于美好的理念：希望在支持社区中，人人都可以为附近带来美好改变。"一平米"，意味着小型化、轻介入，同时强调所有行动的发起须基于在地社区成员对社区议题的主动发现。

2022 年，"一平米行动"以"韧性社区"为主题，票选出 11 组提案。提案行动包括亲子共建自由游戏场、孩子的玩具交换屋、残疾人友好的无障碍地图、为社区商业造点烟火气的商户支持行动、跨代际沟通的长者脱口秀等。

新华路街道整体的社区营造行动是一个开放、动态、持续、系统的过程，也是社区问题再发现、社区议题再定义、连接各方提方案、筹集资源促改变、共享成果共维护的过程，进而形成更好的互信互惠关系，触达更深的议题。在这个过程中，每个社区成员的主体性和能力都在不断成长，最终形成一个共益、共生的社区生态。

（三）结语

长宁区新华路街道通过推进"15 分钟社区生活圈"建设，将最好的资源汇聚在群众身边，践行了"把最好的资源留给人民、用优质的供给服务人民"的承诺，顺应了人民群众对美好生活的向往，是"人民城市人民建、人民城市为人民"的生动实践，对探索一条中国特色的城市建设发展之路具有重要意义。

始终坚持人民至上，最终成为属于人民的城市、服务人民的城市、成就人民的城市。

人民至上，是推进中国式现代化的根本遵循。上海作为人民城市，在城市建设发展中呈现出坚定的人本取向，努力打造人性化城市、人文化气息、人情味生活，不仅要提供高质量的"民生公共品"，亦通过建设全龄友好城市，满足"全人群"深层需求，强化城市的"民心归属感"。中国式现代化的目标，是人的全面发展，让生活在城市中的人，"人人都有人生出彩机会、人人都能有序参与治理、人人都能享有品质生活、人人都能切实感受温度、人人都能拥有归属认同"。

始终坚持让城市的发展成果为所有人共享，提升民生服务的质量和可及性。如果将城市作为一个"有机生命体"，社区则是构成这个"有机生命体"的一个个"城市细胞"，更是服务市民的"最后一公里"。面对社区居民日益增长的多元化服务需求，要实现"以人为本"配备生活所需的基本服务功能与公共活动空间，让人民便捷地享受到与需求匹配的公共服务，关键就在激活社区这个"城市细胞"。因此，上海始终致力于在家门口的"小空间"里做好民生服务的"大文章"，完善"15分钟社区生活圈"，嵌入更多养老、托育、教育、卫生、文化、体育等服务功能，希望通过点点滴滴的改善，让群众家门口有更足的烟火气、更浓的生活味、更强的幸福感。

始终坚持"城市，让生活更美好"，将理想城市的愿景同人民的美好生活紧密相连。自2010年，上海世博会提出"城市，让生活更美好"口号以来，尽管上海城市建设千头万绪，但无论是城市规划还是城市建设，无论是新城区建设还是老城区改造，都聚焦人民对美好生活的向往，合理安排生产、生活、生态空间，走内涵式、集约型、绿色化的高质量发展路子，努力创造宜业、宜居、宜乐、宜游的良好环境，让人民有更多获得感，为人民创造更加幸福的美好生活。

坚持人民至上，让城市发展真正惠及人民，让人民过上美好生活，正是一座城市的活力所在，也是中国共产党的初心使命所在，更是中国式现代化的核心所在。

三、让老人拥有幸福美满的晚年

（一）引言

上海既是一座充满活力的现代化大都市，同时也是中国最佳的养老宜居城市之一。很多人都会认为上海是年轻人的聚集地，但是与大家印象不同的是，这里同样是老年人最向往的长寿地区。家门口的养老服务设施、社区内触手可及的医疗资源、为老人量身定制的助餐计划等，使得上海老年人的生活幸福感与日俱增。

老年人口规模巨大、老龄化水平极高、高龄化趋势明显、老龄化速度超快以及"慢备快老"既是中国也是上海人口老龄化的基本特征。人口老龄化是世界各国在现代化进程中呈现出的共性特征，对人类社会产生的影响是深刻持久的。据联合国预测，2050 年，老龄人口比例欧洲为 28%，北美为 23%，亚洲为 18%，即使是全球年轻人口比例最高的非洲，老龄化率也将从 2017 年的 3% 提升到 6%。[①] 如何应对老龄化的挑战，让老年人拥有乐享生命的高品质生活是全世界共同面临的问题。

"发达国家对老龄化的担忧其实已经持续一个世纪。"[②] 早在 20 世纪 50 年代，西方已将社区居家养老作为社区照顾的重要组成部分，并通过建设养老院等场所集中照料孤寡老人。然而城市中的养老机构往往分布在远郊，距离医疗机构及其他公共设施较远，交通不够便利，像一个"与社会隔绝的地方"。于是，"在合适的环境中养老"的理念逐渐传播开来。

---

① 联合国经济和社会事务部：《世界人口展望报告 2022》，2022 年 7 月。
② 路易斯·阿伦森：《银发世代》，中信出版社 2022 年版，第 525 页。

中国人口老龄化处于世界老龄化演变的承上启下位置，始于老龄化现象从发达国家向发展中国家扩散的历史拐点。根据中国人口普查数据，2000—2020年，中国60岁及以上老年人口占总人口的比例从10.3%上升至18.7%，65岁及以上老年人口占总人口的比例从7.1%上升至13.5%。

中国在老龄化问题伊始就制定了"9073"养老模式，即90%的老年人以居家养老为主，7%的老年人以社区养老为主，3%的老年人以机构养老予以保障。然而随着社会转型，空巢化、少子化等问题相互交织，居家养老面临诸多阻碍。同时，传统的养老机构由于规模较大、灵活性较差、运营成本较高等原因也呈现出结构性的能力不足问题。

上海作为中国最先进入老龄化的城市，对养老服务供给模式的探索也走在全国的前列。根据2022年上海统计数据，上海常住人口中60岁及以上老年人口占比25.0%，户籍人口中60岁及以上老年人口占比36.8%。按照国际标准，上海已进入深度老龄化社会。面对超大型城市寸土寸金、老年人高度集聚的特点，上海选择以"嵌入式养老"作为大城市养老的首选模式。上海为何有这样的选择？社区嵌入式养老是如何为老年人提供公共服务的？上海的老年人又有怎样的感受？下文以上海市浦东新区陆家嘴街道为案例一探究竟。

（二）大城何以安老

1. 原居安养：从"一床难求"到"第二个家"

中国民政部政策研究中心开展的调查显示，超过八成受访老人都倾向于居家和社区养老。[1] 因此，拥有"家门口的养老院"成为老人们的迫切需求。

早在2014年，上海就以社区综合为老服务中心、长者照护之家为主要形式，开展社区嵌入式养老试点工作。同时，中国的其他省市，如北京、重庆、浙江、江苏、安徽、河北、湖北等地也借鉴上海的经验，探索发展嵌入式养老服务。2017年，"嵌入式养老"首次写入国家文件。2019年，上海指出要把社区嵌入式养老服务作为首选模式，"要在

---

① 参见民政部《中国民政统计年鉴（2018）》，中国社会出版社2018年版。

社区内围绕老年人生活照料、康复护理、精神慰藉等基本需求，嵌入相应的功能性设施、适配性服务和情感性支持，让处于深度老龄化的社区具备持续照料能力，让老年人在熟悉的环境中、在亲情的陪伴下原居安养"[①]。

随着上海对城市养老需求的积极回应，养老床位"一床难求"已得到初步缓解。截至 2022 年底，上海新增养老床位 2.65 万张、社区综合为老服务中心 428 家，社区嵌入式养老设施网络基本形成。以小见大，从陆家嘴街道的经验可以窥见整个上海市，乃至全中国对于养老服务的探索。

陆家嘴街道既是上海建设国际金融中心的核心承载区，也是极具人文气息的生活居住区，街道总面积 6.89 平方千米，实有人口约 12.6 万人，其中 60 岁及以上老年人口约 4 万人，独居老人约 1500 人、纯老户家庭的老人约 6000 人、低保老人 100 余人。为满足社区老人原居养老的需求，陆家嘴街道将辖区划分为崂山、梅园、滨江三个区域，并分别设置社区综合为老服务中心。为老服务中心设置有社区托养、医养结合、家庭支持等"一站式"综合为老服务，且不同区域的为老服务中心根据不同片区的特点和老人的需求，提供相应的个性化为老服务。整个陆家嘴街道辖区内的为老服务设施基本形成了密切联动、功能互补、系统衔接的养老服务圈，打造了社区内的高品质养老服务供应链。对于

陆家嘴街道综合为老服务中心分布

街道综合为
老服务枢纽
中心
（崂山区域）

街道综合为
老服务梅园
分中心

街道综合为
老服务滨江
分中心

① 上海市民政局印发《上海市社区嵌入式养老服务工作指引》，2019 年。

居住在寸土寸金的陆家嘴社区的老人而言，镶嵌在社区内的各类为老服务设施，已成为不少老人的"第二个家"。

2. 老有所享：用资源将老人包裹起来

综合为老服务中心能够为老人提供高品质、温馨的照护，用资源将老人包裹起来，让老人需要的精神慰藉、文化娱乐或志愿服务等在社区唾手可得。

位于崂山五村居民区内的街道为老服务中心是一幢4层楼，总建筑面积2420平方米，户外花园450平方米。为老服务中心一楼大厅是养老顾问咨询点，为老年人提供养老政策、养老服务咨询。二楼是日间照护中心，提供对老年人的生活照料、健康服务、文娱活动。三楼和四楼是长者照护之家，共有40张床位，可提供24小时住养服务，且特设失能专区、失智专区。此外，为老服务中心还设有社区助餐点，由社区食堂统一配送午餐，对于住在周边行动不便的老人，还可以提供送餐上门服务。为老服务中心能容纳近百位老人，可以根据老年人需求开展各类主题活动。

老年人的需求结构正在从生存型向发展型转变，因此，养老服务也需要从基础的保

陆家嘴街道综合为老服务中心（崂山区域）

底功能逐渐向多元化的生活方式供给转变。对于相对低龄的老年人而言，养老本身就是一种生活方式，而嵌入式养老的核心就是方便老人。

今年 59 岁的张女士就住在综合为老服务中心（崂山区域）所在的小区内。她在日间照护中心的一天是这样度过的：早上 9：00 在老人专属健身房做操锻炼；10：00 在多功能房间和好朋友聊天；11：30 吃社区食堂统一配送的午餐，12：30 在休息室的电动躺椅上睡午觉；14：00 吃点心，然后根据中心每日活动安排可以选择做手工、看电影、唱歌等。15：00 左右她就会先行离开，去接孙子放学。

张女士所在的这家为老服务中心的前身其实是崂山新村街道办事处，在土地资源如此紧缺的陆家嘴街道，将政府存量资产改造成为老服务空间，充分体现了"把最好的资源留给人民"的重要理念。截至 2022 年，这样的社区综合为老服务中心全上海共有 428 家，实现街镇全覆盖。提供白天照料的社区日间服务中心 825 家。

3. 医养结合：家门口的第一重保障

随着年龄的增长，老人对可及的医疗服务需求日益增高。正所谓低龄老人以养代医，高龄老人以医代养。对于高龄老人，特别是空巢老人，半失能、失能等身体患有疾病的老人来说，需要适时嵌入慢病管理、康复、护理等服务。老年人慢性病大多属于增龄性疾病，通过长期规范的慢病管理，大多可恢复至良好的功能水平，保持健康的生活状态。

陆家嘴街道社区内有许多居民患有多种慢性病，血压、血糖需要监测，慢性病并发症也较为复杂，对康复有很大的需求。现在住在这里的居民已经不需要走出社区，在社区为老服务中心就可以直接对话家庭医生，看病、问诊、开药直至送药到家，一站式服务方便快捷。

医养结合是陆家嘴街道综合为老服务中心的一大亮点，主要包括安心医护、健康管理、康复训练等不同板块。安心医护包括代配药、远程问诊、药物管理、生命体征测量和住院陪护等；健康管理包括日常健康检测、心理慰藉支持、认知症干预训练、认知症预防和慢病管理等；康复训练包括脑卒中／骨折术后康复训练、生活自理能力训练、推拿按摩、家属赋能指导等。

在认知障碍友好社区的建设方面，上海着眼于多普及、早发现、早预防，自 2019 年以来，先后启动老年认知障碍友好社区建设试点，陆家嘴街道也是上海市老年认知障碍友好社区建设的试点之一。

据陆家嘴综合为老服务中心负责人介绍，居民在社区参加活动时，社区工作人员通过观察老人的言谈举止察觉有位老人可能有认知障碍的症状，经为老服务中心增设的认知障碍脑健康机器免费筛查后，发现老人确实已经是早期认知障碍患者。现在这位老人正在一边参加社区服务中心的康复活动，一边前往医院进行药物干预。

积极识别并及时尽早介入干预对于延缓轻度认知障碍向中重度认知障碍转化有着重要作用，可以为"逐渐消逝的记忆"争取宝贵的时间。因此，将老年认知障碍的宣传教育、风险测评、早期干预、家庭支持、资源链接和平台建设嵌入社区为老服务中心，是建立社区专业照护服务体系的重要一环。

中医康复理疗也是陆家嘴街道最有特色、最受欢迎的项目之一。为老服务中心聘请了有资质的护理人员，增加了小型康复器械，每周四都会有三甲医院专业医生前来为老人服务。老人在为老服务中心产生的符合要求的医疗护理费用也可以直接纳入本市医保范围，如果老人需要进一步住院治疗，还可以通过绿色通道快速办理上级转诊。

社区嵌入式养老的老有所医主要是以医疗为保障，以康复为支撑，以实现边医边养、综合治疗为目标，利用"医养一体化"的发展模式，把大病早期识别干预、大病早期康复训练、日常生活、养护疗养、日常学习、护理等综合在一起进行全流程管理，给老年人在家门口建立第一重保障。截至 2022 年，内部设立医疗机构的养老机构在全上海共有366 家，与医疗机构签约的有 729 家。

4. 以食为本：长者膳食改善计划

解决社区养老问题，首要是解决老人吃饭问题。梅园综合为老服务中心食堂占地面积为 200 平方米，打菜的动线长约 10 米。自 2020 年起，这里推出了"长者膳食改善计划"。该计划通过卫生的环境、安全的食品、丰富的菜式、实惠的价格，让老人们在这里实实在在地感受到了社区的温暖。

社区大部分老人几乎每天中午都会来这里吃饭。这里的饭菜很合老年人口味，而且每个菜品都标明了所含有的营养成分，老人可以结合自身状况选择适合自己的饭菜。食堂的开放解决了老年人的一大心病——"年纪大了，做饭太麻烦"。

觉得"做饭太麻烦"的不仅仅是老年人，食堂物美价廉的菜品在深受老年人喜爱的同时，也吸引了周边大批年轻人。政府托底、服务居民的社区食堂让更多的居民实现了在家门口"吃好饭"的愿望。

对老年人而言，食堂通过个性化就餐和智能化助餐两项服务进一步让老人实现了从"有的吃"到"吃得好"的延续。一方面，膳食改善计划给予社区 60 岁以上老人九折、75 岁以上老人八五折的普遍性优惠。对低保、低收入、特困供养、优抚及重残无业等特殊标识老人再实行每天每餐立减 3~5 元，从而实现 10 多元可以吃饱吃好。另一方面，为老服务还让老人享受到了科技红利，在取餐环节实现自动识别价格、自动识别菜品，在支付环节引入支付宝技术团队，实现"刷脸"识别、无感支付，解决了使用实体补贴卡时，老人担心掉卡、食堂担心冒用的两大痛点。

陆家嘴街道推出的"长者膳食改善计划"还实现了三赢局面。一是政府通过搭建平台将政府出资金转为政府提需求，借力陆家嘴社区基金会，采用"线上广泛募集＋线下精准对接"的方式做大资金池，让区域内各类有社会责任感的企业都能够有针对性地参与到助老服务当中。二是企业提供资金，如普惠性折扣由长者食堂的运营方承担，立减部分的补贴由爱心企业承担，并且在收银条上明示餐费总额、折扣项目以及出资企业名称，将原来抽象的慈善变成了实实在在的精准补贴，实现了"长者膳食改善计划"的具体化和透明化。三是由智慧助餐系统精准识别爱心补贴对象，让老人获得实实在在的福利。

为老助餐服务是一项群众关心、社会关注的民生实事，是养老服务体系建设的重要环节，也是实现养老服务向"高质量发展、高品质生活"新时代迈进的重要内容之一。截至 2022 年，这样的老年助餐场所全上海共有 1303 个，月均服务人数为 20.1 万人。

5. 喘息托养："一碗汤"的距离

陆家嘴长者综合照护家园总建筑面积达 1060 平方米，是浦东新区首家集 24 小时中短期住养、日间托养、居家服务、家庭援助等多功能为一体的综合型、嵌入式社区托养机构。这座长者照护之家在陆家嘴街道老年人群体中口碑极高，老人们说："这里硬件装修堪比四星级酒店，软件服务高于五星级标准。"

对于需要全托照护的老人，长者照护之家就在社区里，离家只有"一碗汤"的距离，让老人养老不离家，可以经常见到儿女，也被称为"嵌入式养老院"。

对于需要短期照护的老人，长者照护之家可以为老人提供临时服务，让老人得到悉

陆家嘴街道长者综合照护家园

心的照料，进而让家有老人的年轻居民放心将老人托管在此。

与儿子同住的史女士今年 72 岁，她的儿子因工作有时需要离开上海几个星期，这段时间史女士的儿子不放心母亲独自在家，就会送她住在长者照护之家，等出差回来再接她回家。史女士也很喜欢这样的安排，她说："在这里人多好玩，家里就一个人，从早上起床到晚上一句话都没有人说，心里也不舒服，还是出来散散心，有人讲讲话好。"

长者照护之家与一般的养老院不同，它兼有养老院和日间服务中心的功能，既能够为老年人提供全托照护服务，也能提供短期照护服务。嵌入在社区中的长者照护之家既提升了老年人的安全感、便捷感和幸福感，也提升了亲属关心老年人的及时性、便利性。截至 2022 年，这样的长者照护之家在全上海共有 217 家，床位数共计 6000 余张。

（三）结语

随着全球总和生育率的持续下降、医疗技术水平提升带来的人均寿命延长，全球的养老危机在不断加剧，各国也在为解决养老难题不断努力。作为中国改革开放排头兵、创新发展先行者，上海努力探寻中国特色的老龄化应对之路，积极构建社区全覆盖嵌入式养老服务体系，在解决上海问题的同时，也形成中国方案。

始终坚持以人民为中心，走出一条包括大规模老年人共同富裕的中国式现代化道路。践行全体人民共同富裕的现代化必须兼顾老年人群的生活福祉。嵌入式养老模式将老年人急难愁盼的问题作为首要目标，依托社区"小规模、易布点，小身体、大功能，离家近、更安心"的特点，提供"持续的护理"，将资源和机会提供给期望拥抱新生活的老年人，提升养老服务的质量和可及性。

不断提升老龄社会治理效能，走出一条最大限度惠及全体老年人的养老服务现代化道路。嵌入式养老服务模式通过构建政府、社会、市场、家庭多元主体共建共治共享的社会治理格局，凸出老年人在社会治理和养老服务体系中的主体性，形成老龄社会治理体系和治理能力现代化的上海经验、中国方案。

坚持"人民的美好生活，一个家庭、一个人都不能少"的人民至上立场。中国人口规模巨大的现代化是接近5亿家庭户的家庭总量巨大的现代化。嵌入式养老模式将家庭养老传统文化有机嵌入养老服务体系中，老年人可以"离家不离社区"，可以与子女保持"一碗汤"的距离，实现"有距离的亲密"，继承中国传承数千年的尊老、敬老、养老、孝老的家庭文化传统，在积极应对人口老龄化的同时发挥深厚而独特的文化禀赋优势，让"家门口"养老在养老体系中继续发挥不可替代的作用。

"一个社会幸福不幸福，很重要的是看老年人幸福不幸福。"[①] 中国式现代化是通盘考虑老龄化问题的现代化。让老年人共享改革发展成果、安享幸福晚年，推动老龄事业高质量发展，构建老年友好型社会，是实现中国式现代化的应有之义。未来，走出中国特色积极应对人口老龄化道路的同时，探索实现更高品质的养老服务永远在路上，为老年人打造更高品质的生活，让所有老年人都能有一个幸福美满的晚年是我们永恒的目标。

---

① 2023年1月18日，习近平主席通过视频连线福建省福州市社会福利院时的讲话。

第四章

智慧公平：
实现高效能治理

上海是一座有着 2500 万人左右常住人口的超大城市。每天，有上百万辆汽车穿梭在这个城市的大街小巷，上千万个物流包裹通过快递小哥送到市民们的手中，人们从五湖四海来到这座"魔都"，追寻他们的梦想、创造他们的生活。但另一方面，在光彩照人的霓虹灯下，上海有十几万栋老旧的楼房，有超过 35% 的老龄人口，每天有数不清的问题等待着这座城市的治理者去解决。上海在吸收来自海内外的各方人士等创造经济文化奇迹的同时，保持着全球最佳的安全纪录。这座城市实现了一种热闹而平静的奇妙平衡。隐藏在这一奇妙平衡之下的，可能就是这座城市高效能治理的密码。

现代治理是现代国家的普遍追求。经过改革开放 40 多年的努力，我国形成了具有独特优势、适应基本国情和发展要求的国家治理体系和治理能力，国家治理现代化水平不断提升。

城市治理的现代化是国家治理现代化的重要组成部分，而实现高效能的城市治理始终是上海的不懈追求。当今时代，世界上的许多城市都面临城市更新、社会治安、公众参与等有效治理的难题。上海也不例外，只是上海在应对这些城市治理的共性问题时，有着自己比较有效的治理方式。通过工人新村的旧城改造、城市治理的数字化转型、重大议题的公众参与等若干案例，可以从不同的侧面了解上海城市治理的价值追求、方式方法与技术工具。彭浦新村是上海非常典型的工人新村社区，从彭浦新村一个小区更新的案例中，可以看到中国共产党和中国政府的价值追求，以及中国进行城市更新的主要方式。城市治理的数字化转型是城市治理形态的革命性变化。上海市推行的政务服务"一网通办"是城市治理数字化转型的典型样本，反映了我国在城市治理中不断拥抱创新、不断优化政务服务的不懈追求。关于城市公共空间的建设，则可以通过中远两湾城社区看到在公共利益和私人利益发生冲突的情况下，我国是如何完整有效地吸纳民意、沟通协商，如何创造性地解决问题、平衡利益，如何让各方面都不受损失、感到满意的。

一、城市更新中的旧房改造

（一）引言

城市发展与治理是世界各国探索的普遍性议题，城市更新作为一项全球性发展策略，不仅响应了城市化进程，还有助于解决城市存在的问题。城市更新一词源于西方，"二战"后至今，西方国家城市更新经历了从"清除贫民窟"到"城市复兴"的过程。在中国的城市化进程中，特别是改革开放后，城市发展正面临从粗放到集约、从外延到内涵、从增量到存量的转变。城市安全、治理与发展不仅需要增量建设，还需考虑到存量片区，在已有基础上进行结构调整与功能提升。城市更新是中国建设现代化城市、推进以人为核心的新型城镇化的重要途径，是城市治理体系与治理能力现代化的重要组成部分，是中国式现代化的重要载体。城市更新要回应高质量发展、高效能治理和高品质生活的系统问题，服从于城市治理现代化的目标，服务于城市居民的美好生活愿景。[1] 城市更新工作不仅有助于推动城市转型、提升城市品质，也有助于提高人民生活品质，进一步增强群众的获得感、幸福感、安全感。

当前，中国开始全面推进城市更新行动，从过去以基本生活与经济为中心的改造转变为多元化多目标的系统更新。目前城市更新最重要的几方面就是生产空间的调整、公共空间的优化以及生活空间的完善。这里与所有人的生活息息相关的是完善居住空间，也就是更新城市中广泛存在的老旧小区改造问题。与发达国家的城中贫民窟一样，老旧

---

[1] 朱正威：《科学认识城市更新的内涵、功能与目标》，《国家治理》2021 年第 47 期。

小区也存在着许多治理难题，普遍集中在建筑风貌、社会人口以及经济发展三个方面：建筑布局混乱，卫生条件差；人口混杂，社会问题频发；经济发展缓慢，缺乏活力。为了解决老旧小区改造这一难题，上海是如何积极探索城市更新模式，推进城市高效能治理升级的呢？下面我们来看看上海市静安区彭浦新村旧房改造的实践案例。

（二）彭浦新村旧房改造的探索实践

上海市静安区彭浦新村中的彭三小区建于 1950—1960 年，是当时彭浦新村的第一批住宅小区。当时该小区建好后大多提供给优秀劳动工作者居住，是令人羡慕的住宅区。然而，经过几十年的风吹雨打，房屋逐渐破损老化，出现屋顶漏水、地面积水等问题，同时几户居民共用厨房和卫生间的房屋布局、配套设施不足等，给居民的日常生活带来极大的不便。在此居住的居民改造旧房的意愿非常强烈。为了改善群众的居住环境，2007 年上海市委市政府、静安区委区政府决定将彭三小区列为市区联合试点成套改造项目。彭三小区共有房屋 58 幢，居民 2684 户。其中，成套房屋 15 幢，建筑面积 27000 平方米，居民 696 户；非成套房屋 43 幢，建筑面积 67240 平方米，居民 1988 户，是面积较大的非成套住宅小区。改造项目分五期实施，一至五期的居民已全部回搬，住进了明亮整洁的新房子。

改造以后，小区面貌焕然一新，公共配套设施完善，极大地改善了居民的生活质量。在改造期间，街道干部结合小区实际情况和房屋结构特点，创造和总结出了"改扩建""加层扩建""拆除重建"等改造模式，不仅极大改善了居民的居住环境，也为上海的旧住房成套改造工作提供了宝贵的经验。尤其是彭三小区五期项目创造了上海旧改工作多项纪录：一是该项目是上海市迄今为止最大的非成套改造项目，涉及居民户数最多；二是集中签约首日签约率就达到 96% 以上；三是签约期内签约率达到 100%，创下了旧住房成套改造签约的新纪录；四是在规定时限内完成 100% 搬迁和拆平，再次创造了非成套旧住房改造工作的新奇迹。[①] 上海市委市政府、静安区委区政府在积极推动彭浦新村居民

---

① 《彭浦新村最大改造项目启动》，《劳动报》2021 年 9 月 2 日。

区旧房改造工作中，既回应群众关心的问题、提出科学可行的改造方案和更新机制，也充分获得群众的理解支持、形成了共识，共同把老旧小区改造这件事办好，让老旧小区更加宜居，让人民生活更方便更幸福。

1. 旧房改造起因：回应群众关切

彭浦新村的土地之前是上海北郊的一片田野，1950 年左右随着社会主义建设高潮的兴起，一批机电工业大厂落户原彭浦乡地区，彭浦工业区由此产生。彭浦工业区诞生了新中国第一台大型天线座、第一台推土机、第一台气动电控冷轧机、第一台水管式工业

彭浦新村改造前外观（来源：彭浦新村街道办事处）

改造前彭浦新村居民家里的厨房（来源：彭浦新村街道办事处）

锅炉等，见证了中国工人阶级如火如荼的青春。而当时的上海，大量技术工人和劳动者住在拥挤狭小的旧式弄堂和棚户简屋里，居住环境比较简陋。为了解决彭浦工业区工人和家属的住宿问题，1958 年，上海建设了 4 个住宅小区，形成了最早的彭浦新村。

在当时的条件下，彭浦新村房子的面积结构等可以满足工人们的需求。然而时过境迁，当年人人羡慕的工人新村，开始出现房屋管线老化、墙面渗水、地基不均、沉降严重，小区路面绿化破损，公共基础设施配套匮乏等一系列问题。住在这里的居民大多是退休的产业工人，退休金不高，还有不少需要政府补助的经济困难者。以他们的经济条件，买商品房的可能性不大。况且，很多老工人对彭浦新村有深厚的感情，他们不愿意离开生活了大半辈子的家。面对这一现状，如何改善居民居住环境，让曾经的先进工作者安度晚年，成为彭浦新村在城市更新发展中面临的最突出问题。2005 年，上海市政府下发了《上海市旧住房综合改造管理暂行办法》，彭浦新村旧住房成套改造就在这一背景下应运而生。

2. 旧房改造工作推进：设计科学可行改造方案

旧住房成套改造是指在保留旧住房原有建筑特色和结构前提下，通过调整布局、改善设施、增加设备，使之独立成套的城市房屋修缮行为。拆除重建是成套改造的一种形式，拆除旧房重新建房后就地安置原住户的旧住房改造行为，也称为"拆落地"。旧住房成套改造工程比动拆迁工程还要困难，比如动拆迁工程只要把房子拆掉就算结束了，而旧住房成套改造工程在拆房前要进行详细的调查摸底、方案设计、居民签约、居民搬迁等工作。旧房拆完之后还要为居民租房过渡，新房建成后要组织居民开展选房、回搬等工作。因此，旧住房成套改造工程要比动拆迁工程复杂困难得多，涉及多个环节的工作。

第一，底数排摸。摸底调查工作是旧改工程的第一步。从工作程序上看，底数排摸工作主要是征询居民对改造的意愿。按照政府的相关规定，旧住房改造项目征询需要超过 90% 的居民同意才能启动后续改造工作。因此，旧改办干部在排摸阶段就开始深入了解各个家庭的基本情况，对于可能存有潜在矛盾的家庭进行特别关注，后期签约阶段重点做工作。彭三小区房型较多，尽管居住租赁卡上有房屋居住面积的记录，但是排摸工作人员却不是简单地把数字抄下来。他们拿着测量工具在居民家中实地测量，尽可能给设计单位提供准确可靠的参考数据。旧改办干部不厌其烦地把所有房屋全部测量一遍，做到心中有数。同时，督促北方集团、北安物业派驻专人前往旧改办，对涉及旧改面积结构等问题逐条研究讨论。旧改办还多次主动与北方集团和北安物业进行沟通，逐项分析，反复确认认定标准的合理性、科学性与可操作性，并会同区房管局、北方集团和北安物业召开推进会，逐步完善认定标准。

第二，方案设计。旧改设计方案是否让居民满意，是非常重要的环节，直接关系到后续的签约率。相对于一般的商品房，拆除重建项目的方案设计难度要大得多。比如彭三小区四期项目，最小的房型才 6.5 平方米，最大的房型有 40 多平方米，朝向也各不相同。方案设计既要确保居民原来的房型、面积、房间数量与朝向基本不变，又要在原来房屋面积基础上有一定增加，并配上独立的厨房和卫生间。旧改办干部通过反复核对，最终对彭三小区四期项目梳理出 39 个房型，提供给设计师进行设计，而且从彭三小区四期开始，随着安置标准的提高，新楼内还配备了电梯。设计师像搭积木一样反复组合拼装，多次修改调整，最终确定了设计方案；旧改办再把设计方案反馈给居民，倾听居民的意见和想法后，再让设计师修改设计方案。据统计，400 多户居民的设计方案前后经过 12 轮修改，每次方案修改，设计师都要耐心地为居民解答各种问题。虽然工作辛苦，但旧改办干部非常理解居民的心情，居民居住在旧小区几十年，终于盼来了改造的机会，希望新房可以更宽敞、品质更好。旧改办站在居民立场上考虑问题，尽最大可能让每户家庭都多增加一点面积。①

第三，居民签约。签约环节非常关键，按照规定，三个月时间内签约率要达到 95%以上签约才生效，否则，整个改造工作就要以失败告终。对于拒签者，旧改办干部摆事实、讲道理，耐心和他们沟通交流。旧改办党支部黄书记在做居民工作的时候，提出工作人员要当好"三员"，即"宣传员""会计员""调解员"。"宣传员"要深入学习相关政策，还要善于和居民进行沟通。比如有的居民长期占用了属于公用面积的过道，但这些面积并不在认定范围之内，旧改办干部就要和居民讲清楚有关政策。"会计员"就是要为居民算好经济账。在拆除重建的改造方案中，居民获益是最多的。有些居民不理解设

---

① 《彭浦老旧屋变身高颜值电梯房，比旧改更难的"整容式"操作怎么做到的？》，《解放日报》2019 年 7 月 13 日。

计方案，不肯签约，旧改办干部就帮他们算经济账，原来房子面积有多少，改造后有多少，变成建筑面积有多少，花多少钱可以买为产权房，按照市场价产权值又是多少。通过具体数字，旧改的好处一目了然，居民自然就愿意签约了。"调解员"就是要及时发现各类问题，主动化解各种矛盾。彭三小区五期签约时，旧改办调解了多户家庭矛盾。黄书记说，调解矛盾没有什么诀窍，只有换位思考、真诚以待，才能赢得居民的信任，才能做好旧改工作。①

第四，居民搬迁。在旧房成套改造工作中，一旦项目签约期结束且项目生效后，下一步要做的就是组织居民搬迁。然而搬迁过程并非一帆风顺。因为像彭三小区这样的老旧公房小区，普遍具有老年人多、残疾人多、重病人多的特点，很多房东不愿意把房子租给老年人和病人。面对这种情况，街道干部充分统筹党建资源、行政资源、社会资源，实现诉求精准传递、服务精准投送、问题精准解决。街道组织社区干部收集了周边房产中介提供的租房信息，写在小区内的告示栏内，供居民选择；发动社区干部排摸街道内居民可供出租的房屋，为双方牵线搭桥；协调养老院，接收了部分行动不便的高龄老人暂时安顿。

第五，创新摇号选层。在彭三小区四期的安置方案中，原来的 5 层住宅楼拆除后，新建成 18 层的高层住宅楼，还加装了电梯。原本让居民受益的事情，没想到却产生了新的麻烦，即有些原本住在旧房 5 层住宅中的居民想搬到新房的高楼层居住，这种要求遭到了原低楼层居民的反对。针对原有房屋均为 5 层楼的老式公房，街道旧改办干部拿出了最公平的摇号选楼层方法。摇号在相同房型的居民中进行，只选择楼层。根据规则，原本住 3 层、4 层的居民参加第一轮选层，2 层、5 层居民参加第二轮选层，1 层居民排在第三轮；而摇号的顺序，则按照签约的时间排序，先签约先摇号。为了体现"摇号选层"的公正性，旧改办干部组建了由 8 名居民代表、8 名社区干部组成的监督管理小组，并对摇号全过程进行摄像，以保障居民的合法权益。这一选房方法得到了绝大多数居民的认可。

---

① 《不旧改却让居民住上"新房"，为了一句承诺放弃转干机会》，上观，http://www.jfdaily.com/news/detai?id=113755。

彭浦新村改造后外观（来源：彭浦新村街道办事处）

3. 旧房改造的成效：创造城市高效能治理现代化的生动实践

第一，多元党建力量得到加强。彭浦旧房改造汇聚多元党建力量，培养锻造了一批基层社会治理队伍。一是大量年轻的基层机关干部在基层一线增长见识、提高本领。二是由居委会干部、社区民警、小区居民等组成的志愿者队伍得到壮大。

第二，居民生活质量大大提升。通过旧房改造，居民房屋质量明显改善，小区面貌焕然一新。居民终于住上了梦寐以求的新房，安装了电梯，配备了阳台、独立厨房卫生间等，增加了房屋实际使用面积。小区新建了地下停车库，从根本上解决了停车难的问题。同时，改造后小区的公共配套设施得以完善，设有中心绿地、休闲广场、老年食堂、活动中心等，居民生活的幸福指数大大提升。

第三，改革创新筹措和平衡资金。2020 年 7 月，上海市城市更新中心成立，创设了全市统一的旧改功能平台，通过市场化融资手段，破解旧改资金筹措和平衡难题。城市更新中心联合多家企业和金融机构共同发起总规模 800 亿元的城市更新基金，定向用于投资旧区改造和城市更新项目，将原来的单宗地块旧改转化为捆绑组合的"区域更新"，实现旧改资金的全市平衡、动态平衡、长期平衡，统筹解决了部分地块旧改成本高的难题。①

改造后彭浦新村居民家里的厨房（来源：彭浦新村街道办事处）

在上海市静安区彭浦新村旧房改造的案例中，基层党组织、党员干部等在旧房改造实践中耐心细致做工作，通过排摸情况找问题、走家入户搞调查、设计方案听意见、针对矛盾求排解、出现分歧多沟通，从多方面、多渠道、多部门协调合力解决技术上的难题和群众的困难。该案例也体现了中国在社会高效能治理方面，把群众的向往作为治理的方向，把群众的需求作为治理的追求，把群众的痛点作为治理的重点，把群众的感受作为检验治理成效的标尺，这样才能最大限度调动群众的参与意识和主人翁意识，创造更多生动的城市高效能治理现代化的实践。

（三）结语

城市更新作为一项全球性发展策略，在推进城市化进程、解决城市问题方面发挥着重要作用。中国与西方国家在城市更新的背景、目标、内涵与模式方面具有不同的特征。

---

① 蒋俊杰、刘靖北：《旧改，"上海答卷"是如何写就的》，《文汇报》2023 年 1 月 16 日。

第一，城市更新的背景不同。西方国家城市更新伴随着城市衰败而起，经历了城市快速发展与大规模商业开发阶段，之后进入应对旧城区衰败的过程。中国城市更新是伴随着城市建设与发展而展开，顺应城市发展新理念新形势，是中国式现代化的重要载体。第二，城市更新的目标与内涵不同。西方国家城市更新以问题为导向，致力于解决前期城市更新遗留的社会公平与空间正义等历史性问题。中国城市更新的目的是转变城市发展方式，提升城市品质，推进以人为核心的新型城镇化。相较于西方国家重视社区更新与城市复兴，中国以建设宜居、韧性、创新、智慧、绿色、人文的现代化城市为目标，弥补城市发展中的短板与不足，解决城市经济、生活、生态与安全问题。此外，中国坚持人民城市的核心理念之一便是坚持以人民为中心，以"人民至上"超越"资本至上"，"人民"而非"资本"是决定城市发展的主体标准和价值标准。第三，城市更新的模式不同。西方国家城市更新依托于政府、私有部门、NPO/NGO 和社区的多方参与城市更新运作模式，强调社区与利益主体的作用。我国城市更新大体上形成了"政府引导－市场运作－公众参与"的模式。[①]

在我国，人民城市是中国式现代化在城市领域的重要体现。人民城市的本质就是依靠人民的力量实现发展，发展的目的为了全体人民，发展的成果由全体人民共享。践行人民城市重要理念，就是要把以人民为中心作为改进城市服务和提升治理水平的重要标尺，作为检验城市各项工作成效的根本标准，并贯穿于城市规划、建设、治理、生产和生活的各环节各方面。城市更新中的老旧小区改造坚持居民自愿，健全动员群众参与机制，真正实现改造项目决策共谋、发展共建、建设共管、效果共评、成果共享，用城市老旧小区改造这个"小切口"，推进城市开发建设模式转型、基层社会治理新格局构建的大改革，为城市治理体系和治理能力现代化提供强大动力，让城市老旧小区改造成为基层社会治理的生动实践。上海在旧改过程中，不断探索创新符合实际的城市更新模式和机制，在政策设计上充分调动各方资源和积极性，完善统筹协调、精准高效的工作机制，通过旧区改造走出了一条中国超大城市旧城区现代化治理之路，是中国式现代化的样本典范。

---

① 朱正威：《科学认识城市更新的内涵、功能与目标》，《国家治理》2021 年第 47 期。

二、让城市更聪明更智慧

（一）引言

数字化是人类社会共同面临的发展趋势，加快数字化转型正在成为国际社会的普遍共识。如何运用大数据、云计算、区块链、人工智能等前沿技术推动城市管理手段、管理模式和管理理念创新？如何让城市中数字接入能力强的群体和数字接入能力弱的群体都能相对均等地享受到优质的政务服务？为什么上海政务服务"一网通办"改革能够从全球 100 多座城市的改革做法中脱颖而出，被《2020 联合国电子政务调查报告》列为城市经典案例？回顾上海政务服务"一网通办"的改革举措，就能从中找到答案。

2018 年，上海率先提出政务服务"一网通办"改革，并将其作为优化营商环境的金字招牌。2018 年 4 月，上海市大数据中心成立，聚焦公共数据资源集中统一管理、门户网站维护和信息化基础设施建设等，成为政务服务"一网通办"的主要建设者之一。2018 年 10 月，上海政务服务"一网通办"总门户上线，支持统一身份认证和部分政务服务事项的线上查询、办理。截至 2022 年 10 月，政务服务"一网通办"服务范围涵盖 4500 多个政务服务事项，上海市政府核发的材料中有 97.3% 的材料可以通过电子证照调用、数据共享核验、实施告知承诺、开展行政协助等方式获得，企业和群众在提交审批申请时可以免于提交这些材料。150 项高频事项引入预填表和自动校核机制，企业和群众一次申报通过率不低于 90%。小孩出生、医疗费用报销、公共信用信息修复、社会救助等跨部门事项整合集成办理，实现平均环节减少 70%，平均时间减少 58%，平均材料减少 77%，平均跑动次数减少 72%。截至 2023 年初，上海政务服务"一网通办"总门户累计办件 2.97 亿件，网办率达 84%。"随申办"App 集成了政务服务办事指南查询、政务服务中心办事预约、个人常用电子证照亮证、查询当前办事进度、反馈办事中遇到的问题以及个性化数据查询等功能，成为随时随地联系服务管理对象的载体。区行政服务中心、街镇社区事务受理服务中心"综合窗口"改革成效显著，线下服务精细化水平不断提升。

营商环境就像阳光、水和空气，滋养着企业的成长。经过这些年的努力，上海已经成为全球营商环境改善最大的城市之一。在《2022 联合国电子政务调查报告》中，上海在全球 193 个城市中排名第 10，"地方在线服务指数"进入全球第一梯队，达到非常高的水平。那么，上海是如何从全球数字政府建设的"追赶者"变成"领跑者"的呢？

（二）"一网通办"的丰富场景

1. 准入门槛降低

降低企业准入门槛是优化营商环境的重要途径。2019 年 7 月，上海市浦东新区率先实施"一业一证"改革，首批 3 家企业拿到了全国首张行业综合许可证。首批改革试点的受益者涉及零售、酒店和健身产业。改革前，每开设一家像便利店这样的零售门店，都需要办理食品经营许可证、酒类零售许可证等 5 张许可证，店家不仅需要准备 5 套申请材料，还需要到不同的窗口去办理，在材料齐全的情况下大约需要 38 个工作日，需要提交 40 多份申请材料。改革后，一张行业综合许可证就涵盖了之前 5 张行业专项许可证的功能，店家只需要提交 1 张申请表和 10 份申请材料，4~5 个工作日就可以领取到行业综合许可证。"一业一证"改革有效降低了零售门店的市场准入门槛，零售门店等待开业的时间从 1~2 个月缩短到 1 周，大大节约了零售门店的开业成本。

浦东新区"一业一证"31 个试点行业已经累计发放 3200 余张行业综合许可证，这些行业覆盖便利店、健身场馆、宾馆、饭店、咖啡店、酒吧、药店等。浦东新区"一业一证"改革很快在全市推广，市场主体凭借一张行业综合许可证，就可以在上海全市各区开展经营活动。行业综合许可证通常被店家张贴在店面内部显眼位置，消费者和监管人员可以通过扫描行业综合许可证上的二维码，查看这家店获得的各类行业专项许可证的信息，为社会监督和监管人员的上门监管提供了便利。在"一业一证"改革基础上，浦东新区又推出了市场准入承诺即入制改革举措，符合条件的市场主体只要作出承诺，并提交必要的材料，政府部门就不再进行现场核查，直接发放行业综合许可证，企业等待开业的时间更短了。上海各区都在推行类似的改革。如，星巴克是深受上海市民欢迎的咖啡店，上海也是全球首个星巴克门店数超过 1000 家的城市。上海为星巴克这样的连锁食品经营门店提供了便利化的开业许可服务，现在在上海开一家星巴克新门店，从市场主体发起申请到新店允许开门营业，最快 1 天就可以完成。[①]

浦东新区政务服务中心

浦东新区政务服务中心大厅

---

① 《最快当天能开业，宝山颁发连锁食品经营许可便利化"首证"》，上海市山区人民政府网站，http://www.shbsq.gov.cn/shbs/bsdt/20230308/358855.html。

2. 人才服务上门

人才是企业的核心竞争力，一家 2022 年营收超过 5000 亿元的互联网公司的人事负责人表示，企业每年招聘大量新员工，其中有创业经历的员工的社保纳税情况相对特殊和复杂，企业和员工需要与政府进行大量的咨询和沟通，来回跑动费时费力。徐汇区人才服务中心了解到企业的这类困扰后，率先为区域内的重点企业、对区域税收贡献较大的企业安排专职人员一对一上门服务。企业预约后，政府工作人员会按照约定时间来企业开展政策宣讲、咨询解答、操作培训、材料预审等服务，这些服务深受企业和员工欢迎。有了上门服务后，企业人事负责人会在政府工作人员上门之前征集好企业和员工遇到的各类问题，由提供上门服务的专职人员作出耐心细致的回答，这让企业为员工办理社保和纳税业务更加顺畅。针对在区域内信用程度高、经营状况好的企业，徐汇区人才服务中心还建立了一支由业务骨干组成的 VIP 企业服务队伍，安排专人对接企业，建立一对一在线沟通机制，为企业招聘员工提供"一人一策"的定制化服务，及时解答企业在人才业务办理过程中遇到的问题。政府主动上门服务，为企业吸引人才、留住人才营造了良好的环境，也让企业员工更加认同自己的雇主。

3. 惠企政策普及

近年来，我国下调了增值税税率并出台了一系列面向小微企业的优惠政策，为了让这些惠企政策能够尽快被企业知晓并让企业享受到实惠，闵行区税务局运用大数据技术辅助识别哪些企业还没有享受到这些政策优惠，并安排专门的人员上门为企业提供办事咨询和帮办服务，尽可能让所有符合条件的企业都能够享受到实惠。上海市、区层面还有不同类型的配套补贴服务，如高新技术企业落户临港，可以享受到楼宇补贴政策，但是按照之前的规定，这些企业每个季度都需要提交申请材料，反复申请非常不方便。2022年，临港新片区"一网通办"推出了楼宇补贴"免申即享"服务，通过流程优化，将原来"申请、受理、审核、提交、拨付"5 个环节，简化为"意愿确认、复核拨付"2 个环节，首批 185 家企业享受到"免申即享"服务，大大缩减兑现周期。[①]一些区也在探索通过"数

---

① 《一网通办：坚持人民至上 120 个免申即享事项上线》，看看新闻，2022 年 10 月 20 日，https://www.kankanews.com/detail/6awW5K8x8yX。

据找人、AI 判定"等方式，自动识别补贴对象，以对企业和群众而言最便捷的方式将补贴发放到本人手中。

上海不少区还推出了免登录版企业专属网页，企业专属网页提供政策查询、项目申报、政策解读、政策匹配、结果公示等功能，企业可以通过浏览专属网页查看全部最新的涉企政策，也可以通过政策匹配功能快速匹配适合自身的政策。有的区定期为企业推送相关政策，如当政府得知特定企业咨询过相关政策，或办理过相关事项，或经营管理中可能存在相关需求，当出现新的政策或政策发生变化时，政府会通过企业专属网页向特定类型的企业定向推送相关政策，变"企业找政策"为"政策找企业"，让企业更加准确、及时了解政策动向，鼓励企业把主要精力放在优化经营上。企业专属网页在一定程度上解决了政府诸多惠企政策因为企业不知晓而享受不到的问题，也帮助企业能够方便快捷地了解政策变化，以更好地调整经营布局或优化经营策略。

4. 帮办服务免费

浦东新区企业服务中心的调查数据显示，成立 1 年以内的新企业遇到的问题和困难最多。为了缓解新企业的办事压力，上海推出了免费帮办服务。在浦东新区企业服务中心内部，设有一排帮办服务窗口，办事人员免费为企业提供咨询、填表等一对一服务和指导，手把手教企业完成业务办理。在办事过程中，帮办人员还会主动跟进业务办理进度，帮助企业协调解决业务流转中的问题，让企业尽快完成事项办理。塞夫华兰德是总部位于德国的世界最大的商用车主要零部件制造商，这家企业计划在上海成立一家投资性公司作为地区总部。但是在严控 P2P 类企业的监管环境下，任何新设的投资性企业，在自主核准企业名称时，都需要通过多个监管部门的联审会，消耗的时间相当漫长。于是，这家企业就到浦东企业服务中心帮办窗口寻求帮助。帮办人员在了解企业情况和办理需要后，积极对接相关部门进行沟通协调和业务跟进，最终帮助企业在 3 天时间内完成核名并拿到营业执照，大大降低了企业与政府沟通的成本。[①]

企业和市民到政府办事，不仅可以享受免费的线下帮办服务，还可以享受到免费的线上帮办服务。为了更好地满足企业和群众在办事过程中对政府实时响应的需求，2021

---

① 赵勇、叶岚、李平：《"一网通办"的上海实践》，上海人民出版社 2020 年版，第 136—137 页。

年 9 月，上海政务服务"一网通办"启动了线上帮办系统，致力于打造"网购型"线上
政务客服，高效、专业地满足企业和群众的办事需求。线上帮办系统首批有 35 个高频事
项上线试运行，涵盖了居住证办理、小孩出生、社会保险登记等企业和个人事项，约占
"一网通办"全年总办件量的 1/3，日均帮办次数 400 余次。[①]企业和群众在网上办事过程
中遇到问题，可以点击智能客服进行在线咨询，智能客服依托"一网通办"知识库快速
提供智能问答；当遇到智能客服无法解答的问题时，企业和群众可以根据对话提示申请
"线上人工帮办"，此时，线上帮办平台就自动转接到各业务部门的"线上人工帮办"，
企业和群众可以在网上 PC 端或移动端，通过文字、语音、视频、截图、录音等方式，与
职能部门负责具体办事的专业人员进行在线交互和问答。

5. 延伸服务便利化

在中国，居民到医院看病时，医生会把患者的就诊情况记录在一本小册子上，让患
者自行保管。年轻、身体硬朗的人很少去医院，他们的一本医疗记录册可以用好多年，
但是年纪大、身体弱、患有慢性病的人需要经常跑医院，医疗记录册很快会被写满；有
时候也会出现不小心遗失的情况，这就需要更换或补办医疗记录册。在上海，居民更换、
补办医疗记录册可以到街道或镇社区事务受理服务中心办理。每个街道或镇有一个社区
事务受理服务中心，负责开展社会保险、社会救助、助老助残等相关工作。上海所有的
居民都居住在街道或镇里。但是，上海最大的街道面积为 62.18 平方千米，最大的镇面积
为 96.7 平方千米，老年人、身体弱的人步行无法达到，搭乘公交或搭乘出租车对老人和
患者不太方便。为了解决这个困扰，大宁路街道（面积 6.24 平方千米，7.77 万人）开始
探索在距离居民家门口 5～10 分钟步行距离的位置设置延伸服务点，让出行不便的人能够
很方便地完成医疗记录册的更换或补办，居民还能在延伸服务点办理 130 多个事项，包
括查询医保卡信息和咨询相关业务等。[②]颛桥镇（20.97 平方千米，7.3 万人）社区事务受
理服务中心还设置了手语窗口，为前来办事的聋哑人提供手语服务，并由工作人员全程

---

① 胡蝶飞：《上海上线全国首个"一网通办"线上帮办系统，已帮办 2.4 万次！35 个高频事项可
"网购式"帮办》，《上海法治报》2021 年 11 月 30 日。
② 《把"一网通办"送到居民家门口——静安打造上海首个试点个人政务远程虚拟窗口服务》，
上海市静安区人民政府，https://www.jingan.gov.cn/rmtzx/003008/003008005/20230329/07cc8990-9a74-
430a-81e0-2afb79a897db.html. type=2。

陪伴帮办。对于一些有特殊需要的老人（如卧床或坐轮椅的老人），办事人员还会到老人家中为其提供个性化的精准服务。

6. 政务服务个性化

老年人希望在家门口办事，职场人士希望在单位附近办事，甚至在 PC 端或手机上办事。自 2018 年 3 月 1 日起，上海市在 220 个街道和镇的社区事务受理服务中心、67 个分中心，全面实施"全市通办"，通过数字化交互来替代纸质材料流转，让上班地点和居住地点相距较远的市民可以自由选择去哪个区的政务服务窗口办事，像证件丢失等事项都可以当场办结并领取到补发的新证件，整个过程几分钟就可以完成。同时，为了更好满足职场人士错峰办事的需求，上海市依托智能办事终端实现政务服务"24 小时"不打烊。

7. 移动应用智能化

中国绝大多数网民有使用手机上网的习惯，上海政府服务"一网通办"打造了移动端超级应用，并依托现有移动端社交工具开发了小程序，还将个人服务事项从政府办理事项拓展到公共服务事项，具体涵盖婚育婴幼、文化教育、旅游休闲、社会保障、劳动就业、交通出行、医疗卫生、政府办事、生活服务、法律咨询、养老助老、企业办事、银行保险等多个服务大类，上千种服务内容，满足了不同层次用户的需要。如驾驶员可以查询到附近不同停车场的剩余停车位数量、距离及导航服务，新能源汽车用户可以查询到公用和专用的新能源汽车车充电桩位置分布；年长者可以选择进入"长者专版"页面。"长者专版"字号较大，功能简单，集中提供乘公交、乘地铁、就医和养生科普等长者常用的功能。游客可以查询到热门景点的实时客流量，市民还可以在该应用上阅读上海图书馆的电子书或参观公立博物馆的"云展览"。外籍人士可以进入市民专属网页的外籍人士就医预约专栏，享受英文导医、预约等服务。PC 端总门户还专门提供英文专版，面向在上海的外籍人士提供政策咨询、城市服务和办事指南等。

8. 税务服务精细化

上海有不少外商投资企业，闵行区税务局办税服务厅经常有外籍人士来办理涉税事项，他们中间有些人能够用中文准确地表达自己想要办理的业务，有些人无法用中文清楚表达自己想办的业务。为了更好地满足外籍人士办理涉税事项的需要，办税服务厅专门成立了一支外语服务团队，负责接待和帮助需要提供翻译服务的外籍人士。这支团队能够用外语跟外籍人士沟通办税业务及其具体流程。为了方便外籍人士查询个人所得税纳税记录，税务工作人员和外语服务团队专门制作了一份中英文对照的外籍人士个人所得税 App 操作手册，并为他们送上一份打印好的个人所得税纳税记录，得到了外籍人士的好评。办税大厅经常会遇到到了下班时间，业务还没有办完的情况，闵行区办税大厅推出延时服务制度，只要有人还在大厅等待，税务工作人员就一定会帮他办完业务。偶尔也会发生纳税人因为堵车等原因不得不在办税大厅下班时间之后才能赶到的情况，当接到纳税人的请求电话后，办税服务大厅也会安排工作人员在大厅等候，帮助纳税人在当天办好业务。

（三）结语

中国式现代化是人口规模巨大的现代化。城市是人集中生活的地方，联合国人居署发布的《2022 年全球城市报告》预测，2050 年全球将有 68% 的人居住在城市。2022 年，上海常住人口城镇化率达到 89.3%，上海政务服务"一网通办"的实践案例生动演绎了城市人口规模巨大的发展中国家如何以数字化转型赋能城市政务服务能级提升，对全球各国尤其是发展中国家的数字化转型之路具有较强的参考性和启发性。

坚持"人民城市"重要理念，打造宜居、韧性、智慧城市。人类社会已经进入数字时代，新技术正在深刻影响着城市中的生产和生活活动，让城市更聪明、更智慧，是推动城市治理体系和治理能力现代化的必由之路，前景广阔。在上海，技术赋能和制度创新让企业开办跑出了新速度，一些有个性化咨询和服务需要的企业可以便捷地在办事大厅、线上门户网站或使用智能手机享受到免费的"一对一"帮办服务。办事大厅设置的"综合窗口"，能够为企业和民众提供统一、均质、标准化的政务服务，这既体现了政务服务业务流程的革命性再造，也是整体性政府理念在上海的生动实践。上海"一网通办"正在不断拉近政府和民众的距离，旨在推动实现更加公平、更加普惠、更加高效、更有温度的政务服务。

坚持以用户为导向，打造国际一流营商环境。全球各国的数字政府建设呈现出两种形态：一是注重全程在线发展，忽视了"数字鸿沟"的出现；二是仍然采用传统线下模式，忽视了数字化能力较强的群体的使用便利。相比于这两种形态，上海采用的是线上和线下融合发展的模式，既顾及了线上办事的便捷，又满足了线下办事的需要，是公平、包容、负责的服务理念在上海的生动实践。线上，无论大、中、小、企业都能随时随地接入政务服务，享受办事的高效与快捷；"全程网办"还能为中、小企业节约大量的人事成本和行政成本。线下，持续保留并做优做强实体服务网点，由训练有素的人员队伍提供面对面服务，服务点尽可能向居民区延伸，努力以最便捷的方式满足企业和群众个性化的服务需要，让尽可能多的企业和群众感受到城市发展的速度和政务服务的温度。

坚持统筹效率和公平，推动城市可持续发展。效率和公平是人类社会发展的永恒议题。从全球城市人口规模来看，城市日益成为人类重要的生产和生活空间，如果说城市生产活动追求效率，那么城市生活空间更向往公平。一方面，上海政务服务"一网通办"强调"高效办成一件事"；另一方面，结合《提升全民数字素养与技能行动纲要》，上海持续开展"全民数字素养与技能提升月"活动，努力提升各类群体的数字素养与技能，彰显数字包容。中国式现代化是全体人民共同富裕的现代化，数字时代的红利也应当为全体人民共享，上海实践强调"让线上办事更有速度，让线下办事更有温度"，其背后体现的是"不让一个人掉队"的"共富"理念，是打造"人人都有人生出彩机会、人人都能有序参与治理、人人都能享有品质生活、人人都能切实感受温度、人人都能拥有归属认同的城市"的美好愿景，追求的是城市的永续发展。

三、重大议题中的公众参与

（一）引言

亚当·斯密曾经说，每一个人处在他当时的地位，显然对其经济利益能判断得比政治家或立法者好得多。每一个市场主体也就是经济人的理性行为汇聚起来，就能形成理性的市场经济，它将有助于实现经济利益最大化。这一经济学领域的判断，加以转化就变成了民主政治的基本信念：每个人是其自身利益的最佳判断者，凡是与决策利害相关的个人都有权参与决策的制定，每一个政治主体也就是政治人的理性行为汇聚起来，就能形成理性的民主政治，它将有助于实现政治利益最大化。但是，在公共事务的管理中，每个人都基于个体利益而进行博弈，并不一定能达到最优的结果。中国社会也是一个高度利益分化的社会，但中国社会并不依赖单纯的个体理性而进行博弈。在中国，重大公共事务的治理过程，十分注重公共利益和私人利益的平衡，既要满足公众的参与需求，也要注意不要让私人利益绑架了公共利益。

在任何一个城市，滨水岸线都是稀缺资源。对这一资源的开发、利用和分配，受到城市政治学的深刻影响。黄浦江外滩沿岸伫立的万国建筑群，诉说的是殖民主义时代西方资本逐利上海滩的沉重历史。"一江一河"沿岸突兀的烟囱和锈迹斑斑的工厂，则体现了古老中国希望通过工业化努力追求富强和实现现代化的夙愿。而如今，"一江一河"两岸几乎已经全线贯通，彻底转型为老百姓宜居、宜业、宜乐、宜游的开放式公共空间。江河不改，但空间形态的变化恰恰说明了这座城市主导意志的深刻演变。

"一江一河"岸线贯通，属于滨水空间转型与品质提升的必然要求，对于上海整体城市面貌和沿岸居民居住环境都有很大的助益。经过沿线各级政府和居民区的共同努力，

全线贯通并修缮一新的中远两湾城岸线（郑宪章 摄）

到 2020 年底，苏州河中心城区岸线基本贯通，堵点最后只剩下位于普陀区宜川街道中远两湾城小区内部。这一段约有 1.69 千米岸线，是名副其实的"硬骨头"。中远两湾城是上海市中心城区规模最大的纯居住小区，地块分东西两个区域，总建筑面积 153.4 万平方米，共有 96 个楼栋，住宅总户数 11599 户，常住人口 5 万余人。而这 1.69 千米苏州河沿岸空间，都在中远两湾城小区规划红线范围之内。因此，在一些居民看来，这段风景秀丽的滨水岸线属于两湾城小区业主共有的"私产"。一方面，要实现苏州河沿岸全线贯通，必须从中远两湾城小区红线范围内"挖出"一部分空间来；另一方面，业主的共有物权受到法律的严格保护。公益与私益的矛盾在这里一触即发。

公共事务与个人利益如何平衡？重大公共议题中如何引导公众参与？让我们一起看看两湾城小区的案例。

（二）两湾故事中见民主

1. 公共空间建设与业主权益保护

强制开放没有法律依据，征收回购也无操作可能，中远两湾城小区内的滨水岸线这一段与苏州河沿岸的贯通开放，唯有通过民主程序，在小区业主集体投票同意的情况下才能实现。但是，在一个 5 万多人的超大小区，要达成这样的民主合意何其困难！一是权属难，岸线在小区产权红线范围之内；二是协商难，居民诉求多元，难以形成统一意见；三是对价难，对业主进行补偿的测算对价标准不明确；四是推进难，小区物业选聘争议交织形成连带影响；五是管理难，开放以后担心后续管理不到位造成安全隐患；六是方案难：居民对设计方案众口难调。一开始，居民内部对权属岸线开放共享存在极大争议，最初的意见征询中，有近九成居民反对岸线贯通。一些居民明确提出，小区苏州河沿线土地为小区权属周地，"私域"为何要变为"公域"？"封闭独享"为何要变为"开放共享"？加上不少居民对原先物业公司也有不满情绪，种种因素综合在一起，各方诉求多元难以统一，以至于根本看不到达成一致意见的可能性。

因为反对者甚众，部分赞同开放的业主也因为害怕被孤立，在小区业主群里不敢吱声，反对的声音则越来越响。2020 年初，普陀区政府组织座谈会，业委会成员、居民代表、街道干部坐在一起讨论，有居民代表坚决表示反对。从 2020 年初到当年 10 月，小区所在的普陀区宜川路街道几次征求意见，均因意见不同而无法推进。基层干部认识到，"想为百姓做好事"与"百姓觉得是好事"，并非一回事。

根据业主的意见，反对苏州河贯通的理由主要有以下几点：一是业主对于开放征询的区域享有产权，故有权表达反对；二是小区业主独享的沿河景观步道，既是业主的合法权益和环境利益，也是小区品质的一大卖点；三是一旦开放，曾经稀缺的独享河景房将变为临街房，物业价值将大受影响；四是无偿出让并对社会开放后，地块"权属不明"，容易造成法律关系混乱；五是开放后的管理难以得到保障，很可能出现安全、卫生、噪声扰民等问题；六是改造后道路隔离网严重破坏小区原有设计风格。有业主直言，中远两湾城这条美丽的沿河风景线是广大业主当年付出巨量资金所购，并非他人无偿赐予。小区业主每月支付的物业管理费之中也包括了岸线的相关管理费用。即便全体业主真能一致同意出让，其间也涉及非常复杂的法律关系及资金补偿事宜。而一旦这条岸线出让，今后如果出现问题或者反悔也将再无收回之可能。

但另一方面，小区业主的态度并非铁板一块。有些业主认为，让渡一部分权利开放岸线作为公共空间，小区能够得到相应的补偿收益，只要管理得当并非不可；也有不少业主从公共利益出发，认识到岸线贯通对于整个城市的意义而支持政府的倡议。比如，小区有一位 80 多岁的老党员陈步君就在上级党组织的建议下以个人名义写了一封公开倡议书，力陈苏州河岸线贯通对城市发展和居民生活的意义，号召小区党员和居民全面了解工程，作出客观公正的判断。这封倡议书在社区公众号发表后所引起的反响，远远超出陈步君的预期，当天就有 6000 多名党员和居民作出响应，表达了对于岸线贯通的理解和支持。

可以看到，对于任何一个公共议题，在一定的社群范围内，想要做到众口一声是几乎不可能的。苏州河岸线贯通这一议题，在两湾城业主群内，虽然反对者众多，但支持者也并不少。有意思的是，其中反对者的立场往往非常明确，而且其主张合理合法；而支持者则有可能处于两可之间，从而特别需要加以正向引导。再进一步，按照西方对于民主政治运行的理解，对于公共议题如有争议，要么不同意见的各方分别选派代表进行讨论决定，要么由全体成员根据个人意见举行公投一决高下。问题在于，以投票多少的方式决定公共选择，一来并不一定能够作出真正符合公共利益的决策，二来有可能造成社群内部的分化、对抗甚至撕裂。那么，有没有简单票决以外的更优方式来化解不同利益群体之间的冲突，从而达成一个公共利益最大化且公私利益更加均衡的结果呢？

2. 公私利益之间的冲突与平衡

严复当年用文言语句翻译英国人约翰·穆勒（John·Mill）的《论自由》时，将书名译作《群己权界论》。之所以选用这个译名，严复的用意在于说明个体的自由并非单纯的个人之事，而是应当在与他人的关系中才能得到界定和实现。所谓"群"者，群体、社会公域也；"己"者，自己、个人私域也；也就是说，公共领域和私人领域要区分清楚。穆勒所要表达的规则在于：自由属于个人的领域，国家公共权力对之不能随便干预；而另一类行为属公共领域，则应该从公益出发，实施民主，不能个人专断。公域和私域界限分明，不容混淆，更不能颠倒，以此来确定自主和民主各自的范畴。问题在于，公域和私域是否真的可以一切两半、截然分开？将公域排除在私域之外，有助于公共利益最大化，甚至有助于最大限度保护其中的私人利益吗？

在中远两湾城苏州河岸线贯通过程中，就面临所谓"公域"和"私域"的多重交叉的情况。如果以业主和家户作为私域的主体，那么中远两湾城小区就是一个公域，应当实行民主而非自主原则。如果以中远两湾城小区作为一个独立的物业管理单元，那么它又具有私域的性质，在很多事项的管理上可以实行自主原则。但是，这个小区作为当地街区乃至整个城市的一部分，它又嵌套在更大的公域之中，而需要受到民主原则的约束。可见，所谓公域和私域的划分，以及自主和民主的适用范围，并不能绝对化。

中远两湾城业主据以主张维持现状、拒不开放的最坚实依据，在于物权法所保障的业主共有的宗地使用权。在法律上，两湾岸线归全体业主所共有是特定的历史条件所形成的，这是一个无可辩驳的事实。依法治国是我国的基本国策之一，公民的合法权益受到国家法律的保护是明载于各相关成文法律条款的。政府推动实施水岸开放项目虽合情合理，但前提是不能因此损害业主的合法权益。这一合法主张的逻辑基础在于，中远两湾城小区是一个"私域"，实行自主原则，有权决定是否改变现状，而不容公权力的干预。有的业主就引用英国的著名谚语"风能进，雨能进，国王不能进"，来论证公域私域区分的必要性，以及自身主张的合法性。

但实际上，欧美国家虽然声明私有财产神圣不可侵犯，但在面对重大公共利益需求的时候，他们同样懂得，在对私益进行合法保护的前提下，后者需要给前者让路。即"神圣性"也不是绝对化的，它体现在私益受保护的神圣状态，而不是说私益可以完全凌驾于公益之上。例如，在产权保护最为严格的美国，为了公共利益的需要，私人利益也需要受到一定的限制。几十年前，纽约世贸中心大厦附近是一片低矮的老旧商业区。1962 年，纽约市政府决定对这一地区进行征收，腾出土地建设世界贸易中心大楼。此举遭到商业区业主的强烈反对，代表几百家店家的西下城商人协会对此征地行为提起诉讼。在其被纽约的上诉法院驳回后，官司打到了美国最高法院。美国最高法院于 1963 年 12 月对此上诉予以驳回。后来我们都知道，征地行为得以顺利实施，世贸中心大楼双子塔成为纽约的地标建筑。业主之所以败诉，是因为高等法院大法官们认为，该商业区毗邻华尔街和纽约港，该地段是美国乃至世界经济的象征，世贸大楼的修建将吸引全世界对美国的投资，会给纽约乃至美国带来更大的繁荣，而几百家店铺不能够做到这一点。

苏州河"断点"的贯通是人民城市建设大局，有助于整个上海城市空间品质的提升，具有明显的公共利益属性。而中远两湾城业主要将小区红线范围内的空间"共享"出来，则需要对于私人利益作出一定的让渡。实现公益具有合理性，保护私益也具有合法性。如何在公益与私益之间寻求平衡，考验着政治体制和城市治理的智慧。

不同之处在于，美国社会在面对此类公益与私益的争端时，通常通过司法途径来寻求解决办法；而中国社会则更加相信通过事前的全过程沟通和治理，不必最终诉诸法庭。因此，全过程人民民主提供了一种实现公私利益平衡的可能空间和可行机制。党和政府广开言路、共商共议、利益平衡、沟通解释的过程，实际上就是一个在公益和私益之间寻找最佳结合点的过程，同时也是一个尊重民意、了解民意、实现民意的民主过程。通过践行全过程人民民主，公益和私益之间不仅没有酿成冲突，反而实现了双赢。

利益的冲突是多元社会的基本形态，问题在于，不同的社会以何种方式弥合冲突，以及能否最终在多元利益诉求之间求得共识。在社会冲突之中寻求共识，也是民主政治之所以需要的根本原因。自由主义民主理论主张不同利益团体进行"自由竞争"，最后"票多者胜"，这体现了一种"赢者通吃"的零和博弈思维，不仅难以真正求得共识，反而容易撕裂社会，造成新的不公平和相对剥夺问题。而全过程人民民主强调"有事好商量，众人的事众人商量"，实现了过程民主和成果民主、程序民主和实质民主、直接民主和间接民主、人民民主和国家意志相统一，是全链条、全方位、全覆盖的民主，是最广泛、最真实、最管用的社会主义民主。对于是否开放小区空间，中远两湾城业主存在较为明显的认知偏差和诉求分野，但党和政府没有放任不同利益诉求群体之间陷入相互冲突，也没有诉诸简单的票决机制，而是通过反复征询意见，进行耐心细致的说明解释工作，并且对于业主的利益进行了合理的补偿，最终取得了小区绝大多数业主的认同理解，从而创造出最大共识。

3. 全过程人民民主在多元利益诉求中实现最优解

人们往往没有能力看到超出自身利益之外的公共利益对自身利益最大化的真正价值，

很多时候即使人们看到了这一点，也将由于缺乏实现它的途径和能力而不得不抱憾。所以，在一个缺乏远见的社会，人们总是陷于短期利益的争夺，而很难组织起面向长远的公共行动。要实现多元利益的最优解，既不能迷信所谓个体的理性，也不能迷信所谓自由竞争的民主。"苏州河沿线综合整治，岸线品质提升了，最直接受益的就是小区居民。要想让贯通工程得民心，最重要的是赢得真正的认同，让居民实实在在成为获益者。"宜川路街道党工委书记钱晓莉说："这对我们是个提醒，做好工作必须认真倾听居民的意见和建议，做好民主协商。"

也就是说，相比于因保护私益而使公益得不到满足，在苏州河岸线贯通问题上存在着更优的解决方案。但是，这一更优解，仅仅靠业主自身的理性，以及居民区的民主规则是无法实现的。但如果党和政府作为积极行动者以民主的方式推动实现公共利益的最大化，何尝不是一种更好的民主呢？我们看到，为了推动苏州河贯通，当地政府做了以下几方面工作。

第一，提出了岸线开放的经济补偿方案。开放岸线并不是一个专断意志行为，而是充分尊重业主的理性利益诉求。地方政府意识到，相比于情怀，居民最终要的是实惠。当年小区业主以房价的方式涵盖了土地出让金，这是获得岸线独家使用权的对价行为，也是业主物业权利的真正基础。开放岸线，就意味着受益人必须对业主的这一利益减损或利益让渡作出相应补偿。在这里，受益人是不特定的上海市民或者上海这座城市，支付对价的人只能是上海政府。因此，一方面，政府承诺，岸线开放只涉及空间使用权的部分让渡，不改变小区红线的范围，也就是说不变更法律关系；另一方面，经过专业测算，政府从财政资金中拨付 1.69 亿元注入小区公共账户，作为小区对开放岸线的补偿对价，而且承诺岸线的改造和维护费用由政府承担。

第二，通过各种方式宣传贯通方案，让居民"看到"更优解。比如，发布微信公众号文章。据统计，自 2020 年 12 月 1 日起至今，"丈量宜川"公众号连续推送 104 篇相关文章，总阅读量达 12.2 万，其中原创作品 75 篇，阅读量达 11 万。通过 200 张有代表性的图片海报，设计制作"中远两湾城的昨天、今天和明天"主题微展览，带领居民在历史变迁中讲好"两湾故事"，共同期待崭新的"生活秀带"。开展"社区集中宣传日"，设立 14 个宣传摊位，制作近 300 块宣传版面，张贴千余张海报，发放 15000 余份宣传材料，出动"无人机"拍摄两湾美好景色，在液晶屏上滚动播放宣传短片。针对居民关心的问题，推出"改建后步道还属于我们吗？""1.34亿能做什么？""物业选聘流标了怎么办？"等13个微信小视频，解疑释惑。

第三，听取居民意见建议，了解群众真实想法和需求。街道联合区重大办和设计公司开展设计方案宣讲，组织社区骨干前往已贯通区域实地察看，共计召开宣讲会50余场、实地察看30余次，覆盖各类社区骨干2000余人次。通过意见箱、电子邮件、征询表等渠道广泛收集社区群众意见和建议共计2000余条。街道牵头区重大办、区绿容局、区市政中心、区交管中心、设计单位等部门，邀请业委会及业主能人参加，连续召开关于"沿河楼栋安全""远景路停车""中三区域步道设计""41号楼下设计"等13场业主磋商会。通过磋商会吸纳业主提出合理化的建议和需求，不断完善设计方案。从与设计专家胡老先生、建设监理林老先生等人的交流中，发现和挖掘有专长、有热情、有影响的社区能人、达人和热心人，建立社区"智囊团"。

第四，设立联合接待点，解答群众疑问。在联合接待点，由普陀区重大办、规划和自然资源、绿化市容、房管、司法、设计单位等工作人员联合接待办公，与业主面对面交流，解疑释惑。4个居委会分批召开18场党员和楼组长宣讲会，1000余名党员、楼组长参会。会上，区职能部门、设计公司、专业律师及街道干部、居民区书记通过口述讲解和视频详述，传达最新方案，得到了党员群众的积极支持和响应。有原本反对的业主表示，"听了区重大办的解释，打消了心里的顾虑，最终投了同意票"。

第五，回应群众关切，逐项解决岸线贯通中的具体问题。不少业主对于岸线是否贯通，态度处于两可之间。他们担心的主要是一些实际的问题，比如贯通后安全能否得到保障，日常维护的职责谁来承担，设计施工方案是否符合自身需求，等等。针对这些实际问题，工作组的态度是只要不违反法律法规，尽量满足居民的一切合理关切。比如，将岸线纳入"一网统管"，增加高清摄像头，由街道增派安保人员加强巡逻，即由政府承担贯通后的安全保障工作。岸线设施维护由市政部门承担，减轻居民区物业管理负担。设计施工方案，经过充分讨论后全面听取居民意见。

（三）结语

表面上看起来，苏州河岸线贯通完全是一项由政府推动的工作，似乎同民主不搭界。

但这是一种政府－社会二分法思维方式的结果。如果我们将政府和社会看作是一体的，在公共利益上是具有很多交集的，也就是说在更大的公域范围内来看待这一问题，那么我们完全有理由认为这是一个实现民主意志的过程。首先，上海市贯通"一江一河"是提升城市公共空间品质的公益行为，包括中远两湾城小区在内的诸多经济社会主体都同城市的这一公共利益发生了关联。因此，这并不是一个单纯的小区内部的事务。其次，上海各级政府部门在推动实现公共利益的时候，运用了走访、征询、沟通、解释、补偿等大量尊重民意、发现民意、实现民意的做法，这不是一个政府单方面的意志行为，而是一个追求合意的民主过程。最后，也是最重要的一点是，在运用多种民主方法开展工作之后，上海政府方面最终把决定权交给了两湾城业主。2020 年 12 月 30 日，中远两湾城举行了全体业主表决大会，通过民主投票的方式，最终大多数业主选择了支持岸线贯通的方案。很多时候，民主并不全是社群内部不同利益群体之间的横向博弈，特别是在现代国家，民主政治的实际运转存在着大量纵向上的行动。也就是说，这不完全是社会层面的自主行为，而是国家与社会之间紧密合作，以民主方式实现民意和公共利益最大化的过程。

人民城市人民建，人民城市为人民。城市是由人组成的，城市治理最终落脚在解决人的问题，解决老百姓关心关切的民生问题。人民对美好生活的向往是城市旧改工作的出发点和落脚点，切实改善人居环境，提高人民获得感、幸福感和安全感是检验城市工作成效的重要标准。数字化转型是超大城市治理体系和治理能力现代化的必然要求。习近平主席强调，一流城市要有一流治理，要注重在科学化、精细化、智能化上下功夫。这为加强城市精细化管理和"城市大脑"建设指明了方向。实行人民民主，保证人民当家作主，要求我们在治国理政时在人民内部各方面进行广泛商量。在中国特色社会主义制度下，有事好商量，众人的事情由众人商量，找到全社会意愿和要求的最大公约数，是人民民主的真谛。上海的城市治理始终坚持和落实以人民为中心的理念，积极探索超大规模城市治理现代化的道路，精益求精提升城市治理现代化水平，高效能的治理正在不断助推上海的高质量发展，把城市打造得更精心、更有序、更安全、更温暖。

第五章

共享开放：
为中国和世界贡献上海智慧

　　上海一直将自身发展放在中央对上海发展的战略定位上、放在经济全球化大背景下、放在全国发展大格局中、放在国家对长三角发展的总体部署中思考谋划。从区域发展和中央对上海发展的战略定位看，上海是"全国"的上海。改革开放以来，上海长期致力于帮助中国西部地区消除贫困。消除贫困一直是中国这个拥有 14 亿多人口、世界上最大的发展中国家的发展目标与政治责任。2021 年 3 月初，联合国秘书长古特雷斯给习近平主席发来一封贺信。信中古特雷斯对中国成功消除绝对贫困向中国政府致以最诚挚的祝贺，他指出："这一重大成就为实现 2030 年可持续发展议程所描绘的更加美好和繁荣的世界作出了重要贡献。"自 20 世纪 90 年代以来，以上海为代表的东部地区与西部地区之间形成了长期稳定的对口帮扶关系，塑造了以政府合作为牵引、带动市场与社会力量共同参与的对口帮扶体系，这是中国式现代化推进全体人民共同富裕在空间维度的重要表现。

　　从全球化大背景看，上海是全球的上海。中国系统部署新一轮高水平对外开放，进一步深化进口合作，上海积极参与其中，充分发挥中国改革开放排头兵、创新发展先行者作用。一方面，在中国进一步扩大对外开放进程中，上海打造国际航运中心，港口成为联通区域、联通全球的重要节点、枢纽和平台，洋山深水港作为典型代表，助力上海在中国高水平对外开放进程中发挥先导作用。另一方面，进博会是中国在推进新一轮高水平开放中深化部署进口合作的鲜活案例。五年来，进博会的国际采购、投资促进、人文交流、开放合作的四大平台作用充分发挥，增强了国内国际两个市场、两种资源的联动效应，助益扩大全球总需求，促进了不同国家之间优势互补、互通有无，深度融入了全球经济体系的生动实践，提升了世界经济发展的强劲动能，为中国推动世界经济共同繁荣发展贡献上海智慧。

一、对口帮扶促进共同富裕

（一）引言

曾经的中国，人口的贫困规模之大、贫困分布之广、贫困程度之深世所罕见，贫困治理的周期长，治理的难度巨大。长期以来，中国政府遵循"贫穷不是社会主义，社会主义要消灭贫穷"理念。按照世界银行每人每天 1.9 美元的贫困标准，中国的贫困发生率从 1981 年的 88.1% 下降到 2019 年的 0.6%，贫困人数减少近 8 亿，占同期全球减贫人数的近 75%。

2012 年，当时中国还有 9899 万农村贫困人口，[1] 这个数字比当年世界人口排名第 12 位的国家人口总数还要多。2012 年以来，中国组织实施了人类历史上规模空前、力度最大、惠及人口最多的脱贫攻坚战。[2] 经过 8 年持续奋斗，到 2020 年底，中国如期完成新时代脱贫攻坚的目标任务，按照 2020 年的脱贫标准，即农民人均年收入 4000 元，9899 万农村贫困人口全部脱贫（见图 6），832 个贫困县全部摘帽（见图 7），[3] 12.8 万个贫困村全部出列，[4] 区域性整体贫困得到解决，完成了消除绝对贫困的艰巨任务。脱

---

① 这些贫困人口都是贫困程度较深，自身发展能力较弱，且分散在交通信息闭塞、经济发展落后、自然条件恶劣的地方，与其他地区的人口相比，脱贫成本之高、难度之大超过以往。

② 2012 年，中国政府提出实现全面建成小康社会目标，2012—2020 年的脱贫攻坚战是中央政府自上而下采取的一种国家战略，该战略坚持"绝不能落下一个贫困地区、一个贫困群众"的反贫困理念与原则，实施精准扶贫的行动方略，解决了反贫困"扶持谁、谁来扶、怎么扶"的核心难题。

③ 图6和图7来自中华人民共和国国务院新闻办公室：《人类减贫的中国实践》(2021年4月)，人民出版社 2021 年版，第 14 页。

④ "贫困县、贫困村、贫困户"概念是中国精准扶贫工作中分别从区域与个体层面的一种识别与定义区域贫困和个体贫困的单元化机制，贫困县、贫困村和贫困户都有相应的政策支持。

贫是一个综合性标准，贫困人口的收入大幅度提高，贫困地区农村居民人均可支配收入，从 2013 年的 6079 元增长到 2020 年的 12588 元（见图 8）[①]，贫困人口的福利水平得到保障，"两不愁三保障"[②] 全面实现，教育、医疗、住房、饮水等条件明显改善，既满足了基本生存需要，也为后续发展奠定基础。按照世界银行国际贫困标准，中国减贫人口占同期全球减贫人口近 75%，提前 10 年实现《联合国 2030 年可持续发展议程》减贫目标。

单位：万人

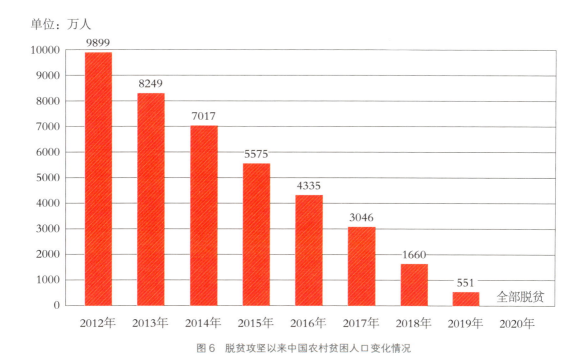

图 6　脱贫攻坚以来中国农村贫困人口变化情况

---

① 图 8 来自中华人民共和国国务院新闻办公室：《人类减贫的中国实践》（2021 年 4 月），人民出版社 2021 年版，第 16 页。

② "两不愁三保障"中"两不愁"是指"稳定实现不愁吃、不愁穿"。"不愁吃"是指根据个人饮食习惯，能够满足主、副食需要（每天 500 克米或面，500 克蔬菜），且能补充每天 100 克左右蛋白质（包括肉、蛋、奶、豆制品等营养食物），有安全饮水；"不愁穿"是指做到四季有换季衣服、日常有换洗衣服。"三保障"是指保障贫困家庭孩子接受九年义务教育，确保有学上、上得起学；保障贫困人口基本医疗需求，确保大病和慢性病得到有效救治和保障；保障贫困人口基本居住条件，确保住上安全住房。

在中国反贫困治理中，作为国际大都市的上海自身并不存在绝对贫困，该项工作中上海如何发挥作用？作为中国式现代化的先行者，改革开放初期上海发展离不开全国各省市大力支持。那么，上海发展起来以后不能独"惠"其身，有责任支持西部地区共同发展。自 20 世纪 90 年代初期以来，以上海为代表的东部沿海地区的 9 个省（市），通过有组织的干部人才交流、资金技术支持等形式对口帮扶西部省份的贫困地区。随着 2012 年以来中国步入脱贫攻坚阶段，以上海为代表的 9 省（市）参与对口帮扶工作的人员、资金、项目等实现了大幅度的上升，[①] 帮助西部贫困地区实现脱贫与共同发展。

单位：个

图 7　脱贫攻坚以来贫困县数量

① 自 2012 年中国提出脱贫攻坚的目标以来的 8 年中，东部 9 省市共向扶贫协作地区投入财政援助和社会帮扶资金 1005 亿多元，东部地区企业赴扶贫协作地区累计投资 1 万多亿元。见习近平《在全国脱贫攻坚总结表彰大会上的讲话》(2021 年 2 月 25 日)。

单位：元

图 8 贫困地区农村居民人均可支配收入

（二）共同富裕实践中的上海力量、上海作为、上海智慧

上海参与对口帮扶有悠久的历史传统，曾以各种方式支内支边①。支援中西部地区，规模最大的要数 20 世纪的"三线建设"②。该项目启动于 1964 年，历时 17 年，是新中国历史上一次规模空前的重大经济建设运动，也是一场以战备为指导思想的大规模国防、科技、工业和交通基本设施建设。当时全国支援各地"三线建设"的有上千万人，作为新中国最大工业基地的上海，就有 150 万人奔赴新疆、贵州、云南等地。改革开放以后，有部分"三线建设者"返回上海，但也有不少人仍生活在当地。应该说，历史上的"三线建设"让上海与西部地区的云南、贵州、新疆兵团等地建立了紧密联系，长期形成了

---

① 支内，即支援内地建设。支边，即支援边疆建设。
② "三线建设"是中国经济史上一次极大规模的工业迁移过程。

良好的合作关系。

1. 多元化的上海专业力量

20 世纪 90 年代开始，在新一轮扶贫大开发战略推进中，根据党中央、政府要求，以上海为代表的东部沿海省市开始了新一轮对口帮扶中西部地区的实践。1992 年，上海对口支援四川省万县地区（现重庆市万州区）和湖北省宜昌市宜昌县（现湖北省宜昌市夷陵区）；1995 年，上海欢送首批 49 名干部启程赴西藏挂职；1997 年，首批 23 名上海干部启程赴新疆阿克苏地区挂职；同年，上海市政府举行仪式欢送首批 12 名干部赴云南挂职；2010 年，第一批共 7 名干部走进青海省果洛州挂职；2013 年，上海第一批 10 名干部启程奔赴贵州省遵义市挂职……自此，每隔三年一个周期，一批批上海的干部人才参与到西部地区的反贫困治理，贡献自己的智慧才干。30 多年的对口帮扶，既是当年支援西部的一种延续，又被赋予了新的时代内涵。

2012 年以来，自从中国开展大规模的脱贫攻坚战后，以上海为代表的东部地区在原来对口帮扶基础上，进一步增加了人员、资金和资源等方面的帮扶力度。到 2020 年 12 月，上海已与中西部 7 省（区、市）20 个市（州）的 101 个县（市、区）形成了对口帮扶关系（见表 2）。大约有 50 多个批次、2000 余名援外干部和人才（例如医生、教师等）到西部地区任实职、担使命。[1] 2020 年底，上海对口帮扶的中西部 7 个省（区、市）、20 个地州市的 98 个国家贫困县（西部地区）[2] 全部如期"摘帽"（摘掉"贫困县"称号），超过 909 万建档立卡贫困户[3] 脱贫出列，其中 200 多万贫困人口是从上海市项目中直接受益脱贫。上海派出的一批批干部人才，是东西部地区对口帮扶工作的"桥梁"与"枢

---

① 上海参与中西部对口帮扶的人员主要分为两类：一是专业的领导干部去对口帮扶地区的政府部门担任领导职务，时间通常为 3 年为一个批次；还有"短期多批"的教育、医疗方面的专业人才，参与时间是 3 个月、半年或 1 年等不同周期，后改为 3 年。

② 上海市对口帮扶的贫困县（区）在 2018—2020 年分批退出贫困县序列。主要包括新疆维吾尔自治区喀什地区下辖的 4 个县（巴楚县、莎车县、泽普县、叶城县），西藏自治区日喀则市下辖的 5 个县（江孜县、拉孜县、亚东县、定日县、萨迦县），贵州省 56 个县（区），云南省 51 个县（区），青海省 6 个县。

③ 中国在脱贫攻坚中探索出一套识别"谁是贫困户"做法，创新了"建档立卡贫困户"机制。针对"建档立卡贫困户"，政府在产业、就业、健康、教育、危房改造、易地搬迁、社会保障、残疾人政策与其他类型等方面有 9 类相应帮扶政策。中央政府为精准掌握建档立卡贫困户实际情况，分别于 2020 年、2021 年分两批对中西部 22 省（区、市）开展国家脱贫攻坚普查。

纽"。他们让上海的帮扶资金在当地使用更精准、更有效，实现了东西部地区之间的资源与优势互补。以上海为代表的东部省市与西部地区一起在反贫、扶贫、减贫和共同发展等方面，展现了地方政府间团结互惠的中国样本。

表 2　上海参与对口帮扶的省（区、市）、市（州）、县（市、区）[①]

省（区、市）	市（州）	县（市、区）
新疆	克拉玛依、喀什、阿克苏（2010 年起调整为喀什）	
西藏	日喀则	
云南	迪庆、丽江、大理、德宏、保山、临沧、普洱、西双版纳、楚雄、昆明、曲靖、文山、红河	
重庆		万州区
湖北	宜昌	夷陵区
贵州	遵义	赤水市、桐梓县、习水县、湄潭县、正安县、道真县、务川县、凤冈县、余庆县
青海	果洛州	

资料来源：上海市人民政府合作交流办公室（2019 年）

2. 精准化的上海作为与上海智慧

上海市政府按照"中央要求、当地所需、上海所能"相结合原则，借助自身拥有的市场、社会和技术等优势，实现东西部地区间的精准化适配。

第一，"中央要求"是对口帮扶工作的政治前提。2016 年，中央政府发布的《关于进一步加强东西部扶贫协作工作的指导意见》明确了东西部地区对口协作工作的目标。该意见指出："东西部扶贫协作和对口支援，是推动区域协调发展、协同发展、共同发展的

---

① 在 2021 年全国东西部协作和中央单位定点帮扶工作推进会后，东部 8 省（市）与西部 10 省（区、市）在会上签订新的东西部协作协议。对口帮扶关系有新调整，上海原对口帮扶的贵州省部分地区调整给广东省，广东原对口帮扶的云南省部分地区调整给上海市（表 2 没有体现这一新变化）。

大战略，是加强区域合作、优化产业布局、拓展对内对外开放新空间的大布局，是打赢脱贫攻坚战、实现先富帮后富、最终实现共同富裕目标的大举措。"中央政府制定长期性、宏观性与原则性的反贫困战略，东部发达地区的地方政府（支援方）和西部地区的地方政府（受援方）根据自身的情况制定具体的对口协作政策。

第二，"当地所需"是对口帮扶工作的精准导向。中国是一个发展中国家，拥有超大规模的人口，地区之间的发展呈现出明显的"不充分、不均衡"的分化。首先，地区间自然禀赋差异巨大。贫困地区往往地处高山地带、缺水地带，产业基础十分薄弱。例如，处于西南边陲的云南省是集边疆、民族、山区、贫困于一体的地区，脱贫攻坚的特殊性、复杂性、艰巨性十分罕见。而且云南省大多数地区处于喀斯特地貌，农业灌溉严重缺水制约当地农业产业发展。针对"用水难"问题，上海干部将上海淼汇科技的"自然能提水"技术引入当地，建成了 32 个自然能提水工程，解决了当地 8.2 万人生活用水，6.4 万亩农田灌溉用水，1.5 万头牲畜和 10 万只羽鸡的饮用水。其次，贫困地区基础设施薄弱。中央政府在西部地区进行大规模基础设施建设，以上海为代表的东部省市的对口帮扶资金主要用于产业、教育、医疗与社会组织等方面建设。例如，针对"配套难"问题，上海的资金既用了修建厂房、冷库、圈舍、管网等配套产业发展必需的基础设施，也用于兴建改造乡村的学校、卫生室、养老院等公共场所。最后，贫困群体间存在发展的时间差。例如，云南是我国直过民族^①主要聚居区，2020 年 11 月 14 日，云南省宣布怒族、傈僳族整族脱贫，至此全省 11 个直过民族全部实现整族脱贫，少数民族群众"住进安居房、过上好日子、养成好习惯、形成好产业"，从刀耕火种的原始社会，实现向全面奔小康的千年跨越。

第三，"上海所能"是对口帮扶工作的落脚点。上海坚持"民生为本、产业为重、规划为先、人才为要"的"十六字方针"，努力为西部贫困地区的发展塑造内生的"造血"机制。首先，构建多元主体参与的帮扶体系。上海参与东西部对口帮扶不仅仅是派出干部人才，还有上海的国有企业、民营企业与社会组织等主体都参与其中。其次，充分发挥上海的多元优势。上海发挥自身所拥有的人才、技术、市场、专业等优势，既让上海的干部、人才、资源、技术等走进当地，大力开展产业、就业、消费、智力等方面的帮扶，帮

---

① 直过民族，特指新中国成立后，未经民主改革，直接由原始社会跨越几种社会形态过渡到社会主义社会的民族。

助当地培训干部、教师、医生、致富带头人等各类人才，也让当地的产品、人才、资源"走出来"，不断增强当地的可持续发展能力。东西部地区之间的对口帮扶重要目标就是要实现地区之间的资源互补。最后，在对口帮扶中，上海主要以干部人才为枢纽，借助帮扶资金，充分利用上海优势，探索全方位、多形式的对口帮扶，主要体现为产业帮扶、就业帮扶、健康帮扶、教育帮扶、贫困村提升、社会公益帮扶、消费帮扶等多种形式。

其中，上海在教育帮扶、产业帮扶、消费帮扶、医疗帮扶等方面具有典型的专业优势，在教育和医疗方面探索了"组团式"的人才对口帮扶模式，为当地打造高质量的教育联盟、医疗共同体。教育方面，坚持因地制宜原则。上海援藏干部、西藏日喀则市教育局副局长、日喀则市上海实验学校校长傅欣，除了与团队成员一起将日喀则市上海实验学校打造成当地的教育标杆，还着眼于当地教育和产业之间发展的联动性，将上海优质的职业教育资源"引进去"。

产业方面，注重当地内生动力与外部帮扶相结合。上海充分挖掘自身的大市场、大平台、大流通的优势，将当地的产品卖到上海。上海市援黔干部、贵州省遵义市道真县副县长周灵，在上海、贵州、重庆之间跑了十几趟，打开了当地蔬菜的销售市场，增加了当地农民的家庭收入，并以重构道真县蔬菜产业组织模式为抓手，塑造有特色的农业品牌。另一方面，将上海的产业园区模式引到当地。上海援黔干部、临港遵义科技城管理有限公司董事长季稼桦，依托遵义市的农产品资源，在当地打造产业园区，并运用科学的管理思路与方法进行招商引资。在云南，上海积极推进"1+16+N"产业园区合作[①]，引导 1300 多家企业在当地投资 600 多亿元，为当地经济赋能。

消费方面，坚持政府主导与市场合作相结合。上海优化当地农特产品产销对接长效机制和工作体系，培育与开发当地更多特色鲜明、品质稳定、竞争力强、辨识度高的区域品牌农产品。上海充分利用市场化力量与平台化机制，打造了"百县百品"项目[②]，它是上海地区特色商品展示、销售的窗口和阵地。上海全市已建立 19 个百县百品直营店、20 个生活馆、169 个专柜，实现线上电商渠道和线下"百县百品"体验厅的结合，实现了"西边产品东边卖"的联动效应。

---

① "1"是指上海，"16"是指上海 16 个区，"N"是指在云南省当地进行产业扩散。
② 2019 年，上海市打造了"百县百品"项目，即从对口帮扶地区分批筛选 100 种左右特色鲜明、品质稳定、竞争力强的区域品牌农产品。

医疗方面，坚持创"三甲"医院和建立医疗联合体相结合。上海医疗人才探索了"组团式"帮扶模式，以当地龙头医院为抓手，通过帮助当地医院"创三甲"，提升当地医院的软硬件，培养当地医疗卫生队伍。同时，借助"互联网＋"打造医疗联合体，提升整个地区医院公共卫生服务能力和水平，实现优质医疗资源的地区间共享。

（三）结语

以上海为代表的东部发达省市参与东西部对口帮扶，推动不同地区之间各层面的结对帮扶，实现人才、市场、技术等方面的资源双向互动，走出了一条地方政府之间共同发展的对口帮扶之路。

坚持以人民为中心的发展思想，坚定不移走共同富裕道路。中国的反贫困治理集中力量解决贫困群众基本民生需求。以上海为代表的东部省市发挥政府的主体和主导作用，发挥市场力量的支持和社会力量的帮扶作用。根据中央、政府的反贫困治理要求，坚持将帮扶资金"80%以上用于基层民生"，将帮扶资金项目沉到贫困县、落到贫困村、绑定贫困户。其中，东西部对口协作[①]方向，90% 帮扶资金用于县以下，对口支援[②]方向，80% 以上的帮扶资金用于县及县以下，80% 以上的帮扶资金用于民生领域，真正将对口帮扶的资金、资源用于支持当地的民生保障和福利提升，不断夯实共同富裕的物质基础、政策基础和制度基础。

坚持经济和社会包容性发展，用发展的办法消除贫困根源。大力推进经济社会包容性发展，将发展作为解决贫困问题的根本性途径。中国实践表明，发展是消除贫困最有效的办法，唯有发展才能更好保障人民的基本权利。改善发展条件，增强发展能力，实现由"输血式"扶贫向"造血式"帮扶转变，让发展成为消除贫困最有效的办法、创造幸福生活最稳定的途径。

坚持发挥集中力量办大事的制度优势，形成共同富裕的共同行动。中国减贫经验表明，推动减贫战略的制定和实施，需要提出可信的政治承诺，增强政府部门内部协调，

---

① "对口协作"主要是由国务院扶贫办牵头的任务，例如援云南、援贵州都属于此类。

② "对口支援"主要由国家发展改革委牵头的任务，例如援新疆、援西藏、援青海属于此类。援助三峡库区属于国家重大工程的特殊对口支援项目，由水利部（三峡办）牵头。

推动多方合作，这都需要一个高效且有能力的政府。中国不仅强化东西部扶贫协作①，推动省、市、县各层面结对帮扶。而且中央政府组织开展定点扶贫，中央和国家机关各部门、民主党派、人民团体、国有企业和人民军队等都积极行动，所有的国家扶贫开发工作重点县都有帮扶单位。各行各业发挥专业优势，开展产业扶贫、科技扶贫、教育扶贫、文化扶贫、健康扶贫、消费扶贫。民营企业、社会组织和公民个人热情参与，"万企帮万村"行动蓬勃开展。中国反贫困工作构建专项扶贫、行业扶贫、社会扶贫互为补充的大扶贫格局，形成跨地区、跨部门、跨单位、全社会共同参与的社会扶贫体系。体现了和衷共济、团结互助的美德，营造了全社会扶危济困的浓厚氛围，传承了中华民族守望相助、和衷共济、扶贫济困的传统美德，形成了人人愿为、人人可为、人人能为的社会帮扶格局。

---

① 2016 年之前对口帮扶名称是"东西部扶贫协作和对口支援"，强调东部地区对西部地区的帮助；2021 年完成脱贫攻坚任务后，"东西部协作和对口支援"，强调东西部地区间的协作。

二、国际航运中心联通世界

（一）引言

中国的现代化建设离不开与世界的互联互通，世界的发展也越发需要中国的参与。全球化时代，中国已经深度融入世界经济发展进程之中，中国在全球贸易体系中发挥着日益重要的作用。尤其是 2001 年中国加入 WTO 以来，深度融入全球化进程，为中国和世界带来了双赢。当前，中国经济总量位居世界第二位，货物贸易总量位居世界第一位，服务贸易位居世界第二位，利用外资稳居发展中国家首位，对外直接投资位居世界第一位，对全球经济增长的年均贡献率连续多年接近 30%。[1] 可见，全球经济的稳定增长离不开中国，中国的发展也需要与世界深化联系。中国进一步深化对外开放，需要打造高水平对外开放门户枢纽，建设现代化联通中外的基础设施平台。港口在互联互通过程中发挥着十分关键的作用，中国约 40% 的能源和 85% 的外贸货物通过港口由海上运输。上海位于长江入海口，是中国经济最发达的城市之一，是中国东部海岸线的中心，开放、创新、包容也已成为上海最鲜明的品格。上海不仅是中国的上海，更是全球的上海，承担着联通世界的重要使命。综观世界，伦敦、纽约、新加坡等世界级城市也都是货物吞吐量排名世界前列的港口城市。上海在加快建设具有世界影响力的社会主义现代化国际大都市进程中，国际航运中心是其中的重要目标。作为中国最大的城市，上海也是世界最大的港口城市之一，上海港集装箱吞吐量连续多年

---

[1] 《入世二十年：中国与世界共赢》，中华人民共和国中央人民政府网，http://www.gov.cn/xinwen/2021-12/10/content_5659688.htm。

位列世界第一、外贸集装箱吞吐量占中国总量的 1/4，国际航运中心成为上海作为全球城市不可或缺的功能之一。作为全球城市，上海除了要打造国际经济中心、国际金融中心，为何还要建设国际航运中心？为什么上海着力推进港口建设，使其成为联通世界的桥梁？

（二）洋山深水港——上海国际航运中心建设的代表性成就

早在 100 多年前，中国近代革命先驱孙中山就提出建设中国三大港的设想，号称东亚第一大都市的上海成为东方大港的候选者。新中国成立后，作为世界观察中国经济的一扇窗口，上海快速发展，对外贸易需求大幅提升，却一直苦于没有能停靠大型集装箱船舶的深水码头，上海建设深水大港的计划呼之欲出，洋山深水港的建成为上海港的发展注入了强劲动力，也是上海打造国际航运中心的重要保障。

1. 上海港的"新成员"

上海洋山深水港是中国首个在微小岛上建设的港口，港区始终保持 24 小时昼夜作业。2021 年，洋山港集装箱吞吐量突破 2280 万标准箱，占上海港全年集装箱吞吐量 4700 万标准箱总量的约 48.5%。尽管近年来国际航运业面临诸多挑战，洋山港迎难而上，吞吐量持续增长，为上海港吞吐量的稳定提升奠定基础。

洋山港的建设与开放浦东有着紧密联系。1995 年底，为支持上海浦东开放，中央政府决定建设上海国际航运中心，这为上海港带来前所未有的发展机遇。面对国际集装箱船舶大型化的发展趋势，建设深水港口成为航运中心建设工作起步之初的重中之重。浙江省舟山市嵊泗县崎岖列岛以北，距上海市芦潮港东南约 30 千米的大、小洋山岛成为新港建设的地点。2002 年 6 月，洋山深水港正式开工建设，工程人员在平均水深 20 多米的岛屿之间，用吹沙填海的方式将岛屿间的海域填平，造出平整陆地，这相当于在有 1000 个足球场面积的土地上，将沙子堆到七层楼的高度，凸显中国雄厚的基础设施建设实力。2005 年 12 月 10 日，洋山深水港区（一期工程）顺利开港，成为中国最大的集装箱深水港。此后，洋山深水港区二期、三期、四期工程顺利竣工并投入使用。

洋山港夜景（来源：黄伟国/IP SHANGHAI）

洋山四期全自助无人码头（来源：黄华英/IP SHANGHAI）

货轮在洋山深水港内

2. 智能港口提升上海港国际影响力

近年来，中国在基础设施关键技术上不断取得突破，洋山深水港四期采用中国自主设计制造的自动化装卸设备。洋山深水港四期码头在全自动系统控制下，无人驾驶的全自动导引车在港区内穿梭往来，搬运集装箱，有效提升了港口作业效率，港口运输业正在迎来一场新的革命性变化。智能革命时代，数字技术在大型基础设施上得到了广泛应用，上海紧抓智能技术革命机遇，加快智能港口建设。2017 年 12 月，洋山深水港第四期自动化码头开港运行，这是全球最大的单体全自动化智能码头，也是全球综合自动化程度最高的码头。在洋山深水港四期码头 2350 米岸线上，风景优美，港区内车流不息。作为全球单体规模最大、综合自动化程度最高的集装箱码头，洋山深水港四期自开港以来，港口吞吐量不断增长，2022 年 5 月 3 日创造了单机每小时装卸 58.95 自然箱的自动化码头作业效率新纪录，让世人见证了"无人码头"的科技魅力，[1] 也向全世界展现了中国经济的韧性。

中国在着力推进科技自主创新的同时，也积极用自身技术推动世界共同发展。洋山深水港四期的技术成果已经在其他地区得到广泛应用，成为中国技术普惠世界的重要代表。2015 年，上港集团从多个国际竞争者中脱颖而出，获得以色列海法新港码头运营权，并于 2018 年正式启动建设。2021 年 9 月 1 日，上港集团以色列海法新港开港，这是以色列 60 年来建设的第一个新码头。该码头应用洋山深水港四期的智能码头技术成果，成为中国向发达国家第一次输出"智慧港口"先进技术和管理经验的典范，也印证了上海正在以科技与基础设施为切口推进更宽领域、更高水平的务实合作，造福世界。

3. 洋山深水港拉动多方资源集聚

洋山深水港的建成推动上海和长三角乃至长江流域各区域资源集聚，使上海港成为中国高水平对外开放的重要窗口，这从上海多港口联动、长三角港口群建设和长江流域协调发展等方面得到突出体现。

第一，洋山深水港作为上海港口群的重要组成部分，助力上海港口群联动，打造

---

① 《"船等货"变"货等船"！上海洋山深水港四期自动化码头满负荷运转》，中央广播电视总台上海总站，https://sh.cctv.com/2022/06/25/ARTIBBVHR7gK4jqg5bWWQmLQ220625.shtml。

"国际中转港"。上海地处长江入海口，江海港口众多，洋山深水港的建成促进上海各港口密切联动，整合资源，共同助力上海的国际航运中心建设。上海积极推动国际集装箱班轮公司开展以上海港洋山深水港区为国际中转港的外贸集装箱沿海捎带①业务试点，上海港积极依托外高桥港和洋山港联合开展货物集拼，开展国际中转，整合了两个港区的货物资源和航线优势，扩充国际中转集拼业务量，这提高了上海港的国际货物运转效率，巩固了上海航运的中心地位。

第二，洋山深水港的建成有利于长三角区域协同发展，助推长三角世界级港口群建设。洋山深水港本身就是上海和浙江两地协调合作的产物，该港在业务上属于上海港港区，但在行政区划上属于浙江省舟山市。上海港与宁波和舟山港两个位居世界十大港口前两名大港达成了合作，签署深化小洋山港区综合开发合作协议，这开创了跨行政区域合作的新模式，有力推动长三角世界级港口群建设和组合港新模式的形成。上海和浙江的外贸联系更为紧密，助推长三角一体化高质量发展。洋山深水港与浙江等其他区域港口形成一体化监管模式，内河港口成为上海港的延伸，实施整体监管，降低水路运输成本，通关流程也得到简化。这些举措推进长三角在物流运输领域协同发展。在区域制度协调上，上海联合江苏、浙江两省积极构建洋山港区域海事联合监管机制，上海海事局制定了长三角一体化研究的实施方案，进而实现口岸监管、交通组织、船舶检验、安全管理等层面一体化建设，满足船舶管理公司对于在洋山深水港及周边水域开展海事联合监管的需求，促进长三角海事一体化融合发展。

第三，洋山深水港的建成推动上海港的腹地从长江三角洲延伸至整个长江流域。上海港积极整合"水路－公路－铁路"物流通道资源，全方位推进长三角区域港口与物流一体化，打造内陆集装箱枢纽。洋山深水港拉动了长江流域江海联运、海海联运的发展。上海港中转功能加强，长江流域更多的货物集聚到洋山深水港运往世界。洋山深水港的建成间接带动长江沿线港口设施建设，推进长江流域尤其是长江上游西部地区扩大对外贸易进出口。作为枢纽港和中转站，洋山深水港优化了长江流域区域港口结构，突出长江黄金水道的优势，促进这一地区的外向型经济发展。可以说聚焦物流链领域，洋山深水港成为中国"构建以国内大循环为主体、国内国际双循环相互促进的新发展格局"的重要平台。

---

① 沿海捎带是指外资或外籍船舶在中国沿海港口之间从事外贸集装箱的国内段运输。

多方资源的集聚不仅推进上海国际航运中心建设，使上海港在全球航运枢纽的竞争中脱颖而出，为上海、浙江和长三角地区乃至整个长江流域的经济发展作出了重要贡献，这有力保障了中国对外开放的顺利实施，为中国参与国际竞争成功构筑了战略支点。

4. 洋山深水港助推自贸区建设

伴随洋山深水港的发展成熟，上海保税区功能也在积极拓展。2019 年 8 月 6 日，中国（上海）自由贸易试验区临港新片区正式设立。随着洋山深水港所在的小洋山岛被纳入临港新片区范围，洋山深水港全球枢纽港功能得到拓展，在沿海捎带、国际船舶登记、国际航权开放等方面加强探索，提高对国际航线、货物资源的集聚和配置能力，洋山深水港迎来又一发展机遇。这带动了像特斯拉在内的诸多国内外企业巨头在临港新片区设址建厂，利用自贸区制度便利，方便产品向海外和中国国内腹地运输。

2020 年 5 月，洋山特殊综合保税区挂牌成立，这是中国目前海关特殊监管区中唯一的特殊综合保税区，是中国国内大循环的中心节点和国际国内双循环的战略链接，凸显中国在制度政策层面凝聚诸多优势要素，为高水平对外开放提质增效。洋山特殊综合保税区在全面实施综合保税区政策的基础上，实施更高水平的贸易自由化、便利化的政策和制度，包括特殊的申报模式、特殊的贸易管制模式、特殊的区内管理模式、特殊的统计制度、特殊的信息化管理模式、特殊的协同管理模式。洋山特殊综合保税区未来将打造新型贸易示范区、全球航运新枢纽、创新业态承载地，至 2025 年，基本形成国际公认、竞争力最强的自由贸易园区框架体系，经济质量和效益显著提高，保税创新业态初步集聚，资源配置能力显著增强，成为服务中国国内和国际双循环发展的重要窗口。作为中国唯一的特殊综合保税区，洋山特殊综合保税区对标国际公认、竞争力最强的自由贸易园区，力争到 2035 年建成国际中转集拼中心、国际分拨及配送中心、国际订单及结算中心、全球销售及服务中心、跨境数字贸易中心等十大中心。依托上海自贸区临港新片区和洋山特殊综合保税区的高水平开放优势，上海市临港产业区国家外贸转型升级基地实现了跨越式高质量发展。基地集聚汽车及零部件生产、国际分拨等功能，各类企业总产值达近 2000 亿元，2022 年出口的新能源汽车占中国新能源汽车出口总数的一半，进出口总额超百亿美元，吸引特斯拉、宝马、奔驰、大众、保时捷、沃尔沃、克莱斯勒等汽车巨头在此落户，并支持上海汽车集团股份有限公司等基地内企业进一步扩展海外营销平台功能，成为"引进来""走出去"的通道和跳板。这都对上海未来比肩全球领先的航运中心提供了有力的制度保证。

从洋山深水港第一至四期的建设，到洋山特殊综合保税区的成立，上海港依托洋山深水港这一大型基础设施，货物吞吐能力大增，标志着上海在国际航运硬件基础设施建设上取得重大突破，助力上海国际航运中心建设。2017 年 5 月 15 日，时任上海市市长应勇会见国际海事组织（IMO）秘书长林基泽（Kitack Lim）一行，林基泽秘书长认为，无论从硬件还是软件看，上海都"已经建成"世界级的航运中心。[①] 未来，上海的国际航运中心建设依然有广阔的发展前景。

一方面，面对互联网、云计算、大数据、区块链等数字技术产业的蓬勃发展，上海将积极把一系列数字技术应用到航运业，促进航运中心建设从传统的实体航运中心发展模式向"实体 + 虚拟"的数字航运中心转型。未来上海的国际航运中心建设将以数字航运为引领，通过数字化实现跨区域的航运服务功能的全球辐射。另一方面，上海的航运中心建设会重点发展航运服务业，做大做强诸如航运金融保险、航运经纪交易、航运仲裁法律、航运咨询信息等高端服务业，大力推进各层级航运功能性机构集聚上海，助推传统航运服务业的数字化转型，使上海真正成为具有全球引领能力的国际航运中心。

（三）结语

面对逆全球化和反全球化思潮抬头，以及某些大国人为设置贸易壁垒，奉行贸易保护政策，中国始终是多边主义和全球化的坚定捍卫者，坚持走高水平对外开放与和平发展道路。随着中国加入《区域全面经济伙伴关系协定》（RCEP）等多边贸易协定，陆海新通道建设不断推进，航运建设有助于带动区域经济一体化，物流需求大幅增加，对中国推动高质量发展、保障全球供应链安全稳定具有重要意义。

一方面，全球化时代，中国式现代化建设助推自身在世界经济中扮演关键角色，中国与世界紧密联系越发离不开发展港口贸易。中国是海洋大国，也是航运大国和造船大

---

① 《应勇会见国际海事组织秘书长林基泽一行》，东方网，http://shzw.eastday.com/G/20170515/u1ai10578612_K27223.html。

国，水上运输、船舶建造、渔业产量、船员数量等指标稳居世界前列，海运航线和服务网络遍布全球。上海港在国际上已成为集装箱航线最多、航班最密、覆盖面最广的港口，上海已经成为中国大陆乃至世界海空枢纽地位双双名列前茅的国际枢纽型城市，上海国际航运中心已经基本建成。上海国际航运中心建设有助于巩固上海在中国对外贸易中的关键地位，有效集聚长三角乃至华东区域优质资源要素，助推中国在全球贸易链、产业链中发挥重要作用，推动高质量的水运基础设施建设，助力中国式现代化建设，为经济全球化注入巨大动能。

另一方面，国际航运中心建设也是践行"一带一路"的重要体现。"一带一路"已成为一项重要的国际公共产品，2023 年是"一带一路"倡议提出 10 周年，共建"一带一路"合作走深走实，为各国开拓出一条通向共同繁荣的发展之路，彰显中国坚定不移走和平发展的现代化道路。上海通过打造国际航运中心，积极在航运领域推进"一带一路"高质量发展，并在顺应绿色、低碳、智能化新趋势的同时，通过加快港口贸易，促进港口、保税区、自贸区的一体化发展，推动长三角一体化协同发展。上海还借助数字时代新兴技术提升航运业效率，通过制度型开放突破航运贸易的制度型约束，协调各部门打造高效的港口贸易体系，通过对接国际制度、国际规则、国际标准，在航运业转型过程中集聚更多高端要素。

上海国际航运中心建设所取得的突出成就，体现出新时代中国式现代化不断取得新进展新突破。中国凭借自身产业优势和资源禀赋，加快航运基础设施建设，提升航运能力，升级航运水平，助推国际贸易的稳步增长和世界经济的繁荣，推动构建人类命运共同体，为增进全球福祉作出了突出贡献。

三、高水平开放推动世界共荣

（一）引言

开放是人类文明进步的重要动力，是世界繁荣发展的必由之路。以开放谋共享之福，以开放汇合作之力为重要抓手，通过持续推动出口合作与进口合作，增强各国发展动能，推动经济全球化不断向前。中国改革开放 40 多年来，成就显著。2012 年至 2021 年，中国对世界经济增长的平均贡献度达 38.6%，是推动世界经济增长的第一动力；中国社会消费品零售总额年均增长 8.8%，成为全球第二大商品消费市场；中国制造业增加值占全球比重从 22.3% 提高到近 29.8%，持续保持世界第一制造大国地位。

传统发展经济学认为，发展中国家在部署发展战略中，更多关注出口，较少关注进口。理由是，更多的出口可以促进就业、拉动经济增长，而更多的进口会减少国内的储蓄率、把市场让出去。近年来，中国系统部署新一轮高水平对外开放，进一步深化进口合作。位列发展中国家的中国，为什么要在对外开放中进一步深化进口合作？其核心举措是什么？成效如何？境外国家要如何参与中国的进口合作、共享市场机遇与发展成果？将这四个问题概括为一个问题，即中国新一轮高水平对外开放中的进口合作方略是怎样的？对此，我们将通过介绍中国在推进新一轮高水平开放中深化部署进口合作的鲜活案例——进博会予以解析。在参与、服务、助推中国新一轮高水平对外开放中的进口合作方略中，上海充分发挥中国改革开放排头兵、创新发展先行者作用，生动回答进博会的举办地和重要主办方"为什么是上海"。

（二）进博会：世界上第一个以进口为主题的国家级展会

　　进博会从 2018 年开始，每年 11 月 5 日至 10 日在上海国家展中心盛大举行。进博会是不一般的展会，区别于以出口或进出口为主题的展会，进博会聚焦进口主题；区别于一般由个别省市或企业组织的展会，中国政府高度重视、积极统筹，由习近平主席亲自谋划、亲自提出、亲自部署、亲自推动，是世界上首个以进口为主题的国家级展会；区别于一般仅以展览为主的展会，进博会重视推动国际共同关注议题的交流、组织国际虹桥经贸论坛；区别于一般以企业产品和理念展示为主的展会，进博会同步推出企业商品展和国家综合展。进博会参展规模较大，从第五届进博会来看，145 个国家、地区和国际组织参展，284 家世界 500 强和行业龙头参加企业商业展。进博会传播层面成效显著，《第五届中国国际进口博览会传播影响力报告》显示，第五届进博会总曝光量逾 56 亿次，五年来关于进博会的总曝光量超百亿次。

第五届进博会南广场（来源：朱伟辉 /IP SHANGHAI）

1. 进博会的举办背景

就举办进博会的国际背景，习近平主席在首届进博会开幕式上深刻揭示，当今世界正在经历新一轮大发展大变革大调整，各国经济社会发展联系日益密切，全球治理体系和国际秩序变革加速推进。同时，世界经济深刻调整，保护主义、单边主义抬头，经济全球化遭遇波折，多边主义和自由贸易体制受到冲击，不稳定不确定因素依然很多，风险挑战加剧。这就需要我们从纷繁复杂的局势中把握规律、认清大势，坚定开放合作信心，共同应对风险挑战。中国通过举办进博会推进全球贸易投资自由化便利化、维护多边贸易体制、推动区域经济一体化、扩大同各国的利益交汇点。

就中国发展而言，通过持续扩大开放、更高水平开放推动中国的高质量发展，是中国办好进博会的强劲动力。一方面，内需和消费是我国经济增长的重要动能，据国家统计局核算，过去 40 年，消费对中国经济增长的平均贡献率高达 58.1%，是毫无疑问的第一动力。关于内需对中国经济增长年均贡献率，10 年来超 100%，达到 105.7%。扩大内需对于发展国内经济意义重大。这种内需具体又表现为人民对高质量消费品和服务的切实需要，在国内商品和服务供给还不能满足消费升级需求的时候，需要畅通进口渠道。另一方面，举办进博会推动产业升级、消费升级、贸易升级，给中国的普通消费者、企业发展、地方发展、经济发展带来了多重机遇。中国希望通过举办进博会，引进先进技术、标准和管理经验，提升国内企业的创新发展水平；通过进口最终产品，倒逼我国企业降低成本、改进工艺、创新技术，从而提升产业竞争优势。通过扩大进口一定程度上解决人民日益增长的美好生活需要和不平衡不充分的发展之间的矛盾，调适供给端与需求端不匹配，低端供给过剩、中高端供给相对不足的结构性矛盾是中国举办进博会的重要考虑。

选择上海作为进博会的举办地和重要主办方的原因，与上海禀赋、上海品格密切相关：第一，地理位置优越。上海港集装箱吞吐量已连续 7 年世界第一，进出口交通方便。上海位于我国沿海居中位置，更容易释放溢出带动效应。第二，会展行业发达。2001 年APEC 会议的成功举办使上海赢得了"世界上最安全的城市"雅号，2010 年世界博览会的举办给上海会展行业带来了契机，会展业国际化、品牌化、专业化、市场化水平进一步提升。第三，营商环境优质。上海拥有公平竞争的市场环境、便捷高效的政务环境、自主便利的投资环境、开放包容的涉外营商环境等，境外企业非常受益。以特斯拉为例，

2019 年，特斯拉在上海以超快速度完成建厂；2021 年，特斯拉上海工厂汽车交付量逾 48 万台，超过北美冠军——特斯拉加州工厂（约 45 万台）。特斯拉创始人兼首席执行官马斯克说，这个惊人的速度是上海市政府和特斯拉团队共同创造的。第四，开放经验丰富。上海是中国改革开放的排头兵、创新发展的先行者。上海在建设自由贸易试验区并向全国推广等开放战略推进方面，积累了较多有益经验。

2. 进博会惠利百姓生活

进口采购是中国举办进博会、推动国际合作的重要内容。五年来，百姓消费升级需求得到较大满足，百姓生活变得更加美好。可以采购多元、高新产品是进博会让百姓生活更加美好的直接表现。经典明星老爷车带来复古体验，元宇宙闪亮登场开启未来，进博会是一场复古与未来的巧妙碰撞；从享誉世界种类繁多的法国奶酪，到香味扑鼻的津巴布韦咖啡豆，再到中外风味融合的"馕披萨"，进博会是一场舌尖上的饕餮盛宴；绿色科技随处可见，时尚定制成为现实，进博会是一次对未来生活的美好畅想。比如，德国卡赫在研发过程中利用先进智能清洁科技，充分挖掘中国消费市场需求，与中国顶尖视觉导航系统团队合作，通过本土研发和生产打造出这款尖端商业 AI 智能清洁产品。它是卡赫扎根中国深度清洁市场、为中国消费者独家研发的智能清洁利器。

进博会惠利百姓生活实实在在体现在了进口交易规模上。五年来，进博会推动成交的累计意向成交规模分别为 578.3 亿美元、711.3 亿美元、726.2 亿美元、707.2 亿美元、735.3 亿美元。《第五届进博会传播影响力报告》显示，"碳中和牛奶"成为高频热词，而纽仕兰也成为第五届进博会重要传播影响力 TOP2 品牌。纽仕兰（上海）乳业有限公司市场总监闫致军介绍："这款新品在进博会首发，进博会后销售同比增长 225%，进博会效应凸显。"除了进博会期间，全年都可以采购进博会相关产品。"6+365 天"常年展示交易平台为交易双方提供了全年可交易的平台。该平台在前四届进博会分别引入境外参展商 502 家、888 家、866 家、920 家，实际进口商品金额分别是 663.5 亿元、801.2 亿元、786.6 亿元、820 亿元。为了在展会后将以展览品方式进口的展品转为保税货物，便利符合条件的商品开展跨境电商网购保税业务，进博会配套推动建设了保税物流中心。这些举措在一定程度上延展了采购周期，助力建设永不落幕的进博会。

采购服务在进博会得到进一步升级，让百姓更便利、更实惠地购买。提供通关、金融等服务是推动采购有序、高效落地的重要内容。比如，对载运进博会展览品的船舶等交通工具，在进出口岸、交通组织、信息服务等方面，提供相应的便捷化、优惠性服务。在媒体采访中，有百姓表示："进博会给我们带来了更新鲜、更便宜的泰国榴莲。"又如，中国建设银行上海分行设立了为进博会提供现场服务的专业支行，针对采购商的大额采购计划及临时的融资需求，建立快速融资的绿色通道，并开发了专属产品，为企业提供高效优质的金融服务，以此推动进口采购，促进"展品"变"商品"。

采购渠道在进博会得到进一步拓宽，满足了更多老百姓的消费需求。引入"直播带货"等本土时髦高效的销售形式是一个典型例子。"直播带货"是近几年在中国快速兴起的一种网络交易，由销售主播在线介绍产品、与意向客户互动交流，意向客户通过点击购买链接、支付价款完成交易。这种交易方式在进博会中被引入，不仅邀请了很多中国客户熟悉的网红主播，还开创了由中国主播带着参展商团队成员一起直播的方式，收效甚好。第五届进博会上，马来西亚咖啡、泰国椰青、日韩美妆等各国好物轮番上架，短短 6 个小时直播的总销售额就达 1.32 亿元；12 万罐来自阿富汗的手剥松子上线 14 秒就售罄。进博会大力推动运用"直播带货"等成效显著的销售形式，有效推进"展品"变"商品"。

3. 进博会促进企业合作

进博会除了推动进口采购，还致力于推动国际投资、促进展客商企业之间的投资合作。五年来，很多企业通过进博会增强了与关联企业的合作，有的找到了新的合作伙伴，有的进一步深化了与既有合作伙伴之间的合作。比如，松下集团连续 5 年参加进博会，与相关企业达成了不少高质量的合作。第四届进博会上，松下与中集安瑞科控股有限公司及其附属公司签订谅解备忘录，围绕松下氢能热电联供模块及技术，携手研发氢电综合应用端集成化产品；此外，继 2020 年与太平洋保险（集团）股份有限公司、三井住友海上火灾保险（中国）有限公司签订战略合作协议以来，松下还与太平洋保险集团旗下养老投资公司签署共同创建《智慧康养实验室》的协议，三方还将合作范围拓展至电动汽车领域，就提供新保险服务及开发新事业签订合作协议。松下集团全球副总裁本间哲朗表示："我们进入中国市场多年，传统产品的销量一直很好，而进博会又为我们提升销量作了助推，进博会期间的订单量大大高于往年同期，全年的订单量也大幅增加。"

进博会期间举办的贸易投资对接会连续四届以来已累计为来自 100 多个国家和地

区的 3800 余家参展商和 7800 余家采购商提供贸易与投资对接撮合服务，达成意向合作 4500 余项。组织投资对接是进博会上规模最大、时间最长的配套活动。除了展间投资对接，还有很多展前对接。举办方组织展商客商到国家会展中心（上海）洽谈、对接投资供需。参展商用"没想到""十分惊喜"描述他们参与投资对接会的心情。比如，德国永恒力叉车中国区总经理白大平表示："之前我们在中国的客户大部分是在中国有工厂的外资企业，这次对接会让我们接触到了很多中国的国有企业，这很让人意外，是个惊喜。"欧姆龙健康医疗（中国）有限公司网络企划部推广经理宋超表示，此前他们仅对中国一、二线城市的医疗市场熟悉，对三、四线城市不熟，投资对接会帮助他们很方便地找到了以往需要花很多成本才能对接上的潜在客户。生物梅里埃公司是法国最大的体外诊断公司、全世界最大的微生物体外诊断公司，它从第二届进博会开始连续参加，在进博会上展示了最新研发的新冠检测诊断产品及微生物实验室整体解决方案、最前沿的抗菌药物科学管理解决方案。"生物梅里埃依托进博会平台，向大众充分展示了公司最新产品及技术，在第四届进博会期间，共举办了 8 场签约仪式，参与了 10 场大型交流论坛及推介会，超 90 个代表团、交易团参观公司展品。进博会创造了很多很好的国际交流合作机会。"

上海优化投资环境、做好国外投资机构入驻保障，以此促进企业合作。虹桥海外贸易中心、进口贸易促进创新示范区、进出口商品集散地等贸易载体在上海建设落地。目前，虹桥海外贸易中心已有丝绸之路国际总商会、上海市对外文化交流协会虹桥海外书院、新加坡企业中心、瑞士中心、中国西班牙商会、中国马来西亚商会、日本商会、法国法语区企业中心、上海台湾同胞投资企业协会、克罗地亚经济商会、巴西圣保罗国家投资局、欧盟商业与创新中心、泰国文化经济协会等 30 多家贸易及服务机构入驻。虹桥海外贸易中心通过已入驻的贸易服务机构，联系全球超过 150 家贸易及投资促进机构。比如，入驻的新加坡企业中心在短短两年时间内就协助 18 家新加坡企业落户长三角。

4. 制度型开放赋能国际合作

制度型开放通过统一规则要素，增强国际交往的透明度和稳定性，生动赋能商品和要素流动性开放。习近平主席在第五届进博会开幕式上指出："中国将推动各国各方共享制度型开放机遇，稳步扩大规则、规制、管理、标准等制度型开放，实施好新版《鼓励外商投资产业目录》，深化国家服务业扩大开放综合示范区建设；实施自由贸易试验区提升战略，加快建设海南自由贸易港，发挥好改革开放综合试验平台作用。"贸易和投资便利化、知识产权保护、营商环境等重要议题被纳入进博会制度型开放实践中。五年来，降低关税、放宽市场准入、深入实施准入前国民待遇加负面清单管理制度、支持自由贸易试验区深化改革创新等开放措施基本落实，有效赋能国际合作。不少国外企业受益于此，比如，马来西亚茂记燕窝的负责人表示："以前很少人知道我们的产品，我们的产品出口非常艰难。我们通过和中国企业合作，让中国代理商在进博会上展示产品，让采购商、消费者更加直观地认识、了解我们的产品。通过在进博会的展示、宣传，我们产品的销量大幅增加。进博会为我们进入中国市场、国际视野提供了很好的机会。"

2022 年 11 月 5 日第五届进博会闵行交易分团集中采购签约在虹桥品汇 A 栋举办（来源：闵行区新闻办 × IP SHANGHAI）

　　上海积极推进制度型开放，在第五届进博会举办前夕出台《上海市服务办好中国国际进口博览会条例》（以下简称《条例》）以优化营商环境是重要实践探索。这是中国首次专门为展会立法，是中国灵动融通世界的实践表达，凸显以秩序、规则为气象格局的"国际范儿"，为中国主动拥抱世界构筑法治环境，充分显现重要法治意义和实践价值。《条例》聚焦"上海市服务办好中国国际进口博览会"主题，将政府部门作为主要的规范主体，以政府行为的法治化、规范化引领其他参与主体行为的法治化、规范化，以法治政府建设引领推动"法治进博"建设，不断体现法治政府效能。一方面，将科学理念能动转化为法规要义，是政府引领其他参与主体高起点、高标准、高质量、高水平办展办会的重要抓手。习近平主席为进博会举办成功，提出开放发展、创新发展、协同发展、绿色可持续发展等发展策略和科学理念。这也充分把握并聚合了国际上关于展会业发展的趋势和共识。《条例》将这些科学理念具体化为绿色办展、科技赋能办展、联动办展等具体规则，由政府引领带动其他参与主体向世界日益展现开放姿态。另一方面，将往届经验主动升华为法规内涵，特别是将政府与市场的互动关系、权责边界方面的经验确立为法规，统筹有为政府与有效市场，确保政府组织办好进博会、体现法治政府效能。进博会是高规格展会，由中国政府而非一般商事主体主办；展会经济展现了社会主义市场经济生机活力，凸显市场在资源配置中发挥决定性作用。科学统筹政府宏观调控与市场调节，实现帕累托最优。为办展单位提供支持、为参展单位提供服务保障、为关联产业和地区带来溢出效应是进博会中政府行为的主要面向，是与进博会相关的服务型政府建设总布局中的子面向。《条例》聚焦这三个维度，分设"支持办展办会""服务和保障""综合效应"等章节，固化行之有效的经验，以此持续释放政府在办好进博会中的引领效能。

　　上海积极探索制度型开放的成效较为显著，在赋能国际合作方面，从多维度释放溢出带动效应：一是时间维度。打造永不落幕的进博会。《条例》明确指引展品在展后如何转为保税货物、如何开展跨境电商网购保税业务；规范虹桥国际开放枢纽搭建常年展示交易服务平台、进口商品展示交易中心、保税物流中心平台。二是空间维度。《条例》明确指引如何在更广空间释放进博会溢出带动效应，联动长三角、服务全国、辐射亚太。三是产业维度。会展业具有高聚集性特点，可有效拉动上下游产业联动发展，并进一步深化社会分工、优化资源配置、节约搜索成本、促进产业升级。对此，《条例》明确指出，政府及有关部门应当制定政策措施，构建展会资源协调共享机制，加强进博会与商贸、旅游、文化、体育等产业联动发展。

（三）结语

开放合作指的是不同国家之间优势互补、互通有无，助益扩大全球总需求、提升世界经济发展的强劲动能。增强国内国际两个市场两种资源联动效应是开放合作的基础逻辑和重要抓手。经过 40 多年改革开放，中国人民基本的生活需求得到了满足，对美好生活的向往也进入了新阶段，消费升级需求越发明显，但国内的商品和服务供给还难以满足消费升级需要。进口高质量产品和服务，引进先进技术、标准和管理经验，推动本国的消费升级、贸易升级、产业升级，是中国扩大进口的重要考虑。此外，中国扩大进口还有助于提升全球总需求，应对世界经济复苏动力不足问题。中国拥有并持续释放超大规模市场优势和内需潜力。中国已成为全球第二大消费市场、第一贸易大国。中国扩大进口可充分发挥其超大消费市场、贸易大国优势，在推动本国经济发展的同时，带动世界经济共同繁荣。在充分认识进口之于本国发展、全球共荣重要性的基础上，中国在进口合作上推动行之有效的中国治理方案：坚持依法治理，推进制度型开放，通过统一规则要素，增强国际交往的透明度和稳定性，生动赋能商品和要素流动性开放；在法治的基础上，推进治理创新，如将国家展和企业展融合、将论坛与展览融合等；凝聚治理合力，如组织投资对接、组织集体采购等；推动治理效应溢出，包括在时间、空间、行业等多维度释放进博会的开放合作效应，其中，以上海为进博会举办地，可以充分运用上海的治理特色、发挥治理优势、释放治理效能。以开放纾发展之困、以开放汇合作之力、以开放聚创新之势、以开放谋共享之福，推动经济全球化不断向前，增强各国发展动能，让发展成果更多更公平惠及各国人民，共同做大"蛋糕"、共赢共享，推进共建人类命运共同体。

后　记

　　上海背靠长江，面向太平洋，长期引领中国开放风气，是一座充满魅力的城市，也是世人眼中的"魔都"。把上海作为中国式现代化的观察样本，不仅因为今天的上海正在加快建设具有世界影响力的社会主义现代化国际大都市，而且在于从其昔日的被动开放饱受屈辱，到如今的主动开放充满自信，故事背后的理念和逻辑可以带给人们诸多启迪。

　　我们组织编写《为什么是上海？——中国式现代化的上海故事》一书，希望读者通过了解上海这座城市的过去、现在和未来，更好地向世界展示中国式现代化的中国特色和光明前景。

　　在中国式现代化的上海生动实践中，方方面面案例俯首可得、举不胜举，本书选取的案例可能不一定能完整、准确、全面展示中国式现代化的最新上海图景。由于本书编写受众特殊性，我们充分考虑世界超大城市发展过程中人们可能普遍关切的现实问题，希望通过这些案例找到超大城市发展中可供对话的空间，为世界超大城市的发展与治理提供中国智慧、上海经验。本书由中共上海市委党校（上海行政学院）的一批青年教师编写，虽然策划这本书，前期做了大量调研咨询工作，但正式启动撰写，到付梓出版只用了半年多时间。这得益于这批青年教师近年来或多或少参与过涉外课程录制或者线上线下涉外交流合作项目等工作，一些案例由录制的课件或现场教学材料转化而来。本书由中共上海市委党校（上海行政学院）教育长罗峰教授策划，罗峰教授多次主持召开专家咨询会、书稿打磨会，确定了本书的写作要求、风格体例、篇章结构，并为本书作序。各章撰写分工如下：第一章由王瑶、甘梅霞、赵恩国撰写，第二章由周静、信瑶瑶、韩旭撰写，第三章由胡霁荣、于健宁、陈煜婷撰写，第四章由孙凌雪、叶岚、汪仲启撰写，第五章由丁长艳、耿召、徐瑜璐撰写。感谢各位作者的倾力付出。

　　中共上海市委党校（上海行政学院）常务副校（院）长徐建刚始终关心、推动着本书的编写、出版。上海市人大常委会原副主任沙海林，上海市社会科学界联合会党组书记、专职副主席王为松，中国浦东干部学院对外交流与培训开发部主任刘根法，上海市委外宣办、市政府新闻办副主任陈怡群，上海市外办新闻文化处处长朱峰，《解放日报》党委原副书记周智强，上海社科院世界中国学研究所所长沈桂龙研究员，上海社会科学院党委宣传部部长吴雪明，华东师范大学社会发展学院院长文军教授，上海大学社会学院院长黄晓春教授，上海外国语大学高级翻译学院党委书记赵美娟教授，中共上海市委党校（上海行政学院）党的建设教研部主任赵刚印教授，《解放日报》理论工作室主编王珍，澎湃新闻第六声总编辑吴挺等专家学者参与了本书写作提纲讨论、书稿审读，对本书的顺利出版提出了许多宝贵的意见和建议。感谢这些领导、专家的大力支持和真知灼见。

中共上海市委党校（上海行政学院）公务员培训处成立编写工作项目组，赵彣、胡静波、欧阳程奕、曹静、徐辉、张元、虞津津、韩圣依等同志承担了大量组织协调工作。国家行政学院出版社做了细致的编辑出版工作，本书以中英文对照方式出版，还得到了上海外国语大学翻译团队的支持，在此一并感谢！

编写供国（境）外学员学习交流的双语读物，是中共上海市委党校（上海行政学院）的首次尝试与探索，由于编者学识、水平有限，再加上时间仓促，疏漏在所难免，敬请各位读者指正。

编者

2023 年 9 月

Preface

The rise and fall of a city are closely related to the development of the country. The political system, historical environment, and development tasks of the country shape and influence the development strategy and path of a city. At the same time, the modernization story of a city is not only its own legend, but also reflects the common process of the country's overall modernization and even modernization in the whole world.

In this sense, Shanghai has a special meaning for China and the world. As a window through which the world sees China and a bridge between China and the outside world, Shanghai is the starting point to examine the modernization process of China and the world.

In the early 20th century, as Mary Ninde Gamewell says in the introduction to her book The Gateway to China: Pictures of Shanghai: To understand China, one must go to Shanghai. Shanghai is a small world, where one can study China up close. In this way, she closely connects Shanghai with China and emphasizes that Shanghai is a window to understand China.

Indeed, Shanghai is a good sample for studying the process and outcome of Chinese modernization. Over the past century, as the birthplace and cradle of the CPC, Shanghai has traveled a rough road of suffering, resistance, and finally prosperity through reform and opening-up, as China has done. It can be said that Shanghai epitomizes China's rise from poverty to prosperity.

In the 1930s, Shanghai became the international financial center of Asia and was known as the "Paris of the East", as the most modern city in China at that time. Its glory, however, only lasted a short period of time. In fact, over the past century, Shanghai has not stayed

firm on the leading position. It has gone through ups and downs. Back in the 1980s, when the tide of reform and opening-up surged in China, Shanghai was left behind. Of course, Shanghai still ranked first in the country in 10 economic indicators, such as total industrial output value, revenues handed over to the central government, and foreign exchange earned through exports, but the city suffered from the largest population density, the smallest road area per capita, the highest proportion of families lacking safe housing, the largest number of traffic accidents, and the highest incidence rate of cancer in Chinese cities.

The revival of Shanghai began after China's reform and opening-up. Deng Xiaoping, chief designer of China's reform and opening-up program, once said, "Shanghai is our 'ace', and reviving Shanghai is a shortcut to realize China's national goals." In the early 1990s, after the start of Pudong's development and opening-up, Shanghai became the Chinese vanguard of reform and opening-up. To date, Shanghai has basically fulfilled its goal of becoming an international economic, financial, trade, and shipping center, and built a basic framework for a science and technology innovation center with global influence. Its core competitiveness has grown remarkably. Within just a few decades, China has completed the industrialization process that has taken developed countries centuries to complete. As a key actor of national strategy and a pioneer of innovation-driven development, Shanghai is embarking on a new journey towards modernization and earning a fame for its good urban governance. Now, Pudong New Area has become a pilot area for socialist modernization, and Shanghai is continuing to play a pioneering and exemplary role.

There are many dimensions for measuring the development of a city, and numbers are more convincing. From 2012 to 2022, the gross domestic product of Shanghai jumped from 2.13 trillion yuan to 4.47 trillion yuan, putting the city ahead of other central cities of China in terms of economic aggregate. Over the past decade, Shanghai has focused on improving people's livelihood. The per capita disposable income of its residents rose from 38,600 yuan to 78,000 yuan, and the average life expectancy extended from 82.41 years to 84.11 years. Now, Shanghai is striving to be a "People's City", giving its people access to the best resources and upgrading its waterfront open spaces to make the city a better and

more enjoyable place for its residents. It has restored the connectivity of embankments of the Huangpu River (45 km) and the Suzhou Creek (42 km). The "rust belt" in the past has transformed into a "life belt" which is clean, beautiful and enjoyable. In 2022, the Port of Shanghai boasted a container throughput of over 47.3 million TEUs, ranking first in the world for 13 consecutive years; the output value of strategic emerging industries as a percentage of the total output value of all industries climbed up to 43%, and the size of three leading industries (IC, biomedicine, and artificial intelligence) reached 1.5 trillion yuan; and the added value of Shanghai's financial industry reached 862.631 billion yuan, up 5.2% over the previous year, equal to 19.3% of gross regional product of Shanghai.

The numbers above fully demonstrate the vitality, charm, and potential of Shanghai. These data are important indicators of the city's modernization, and explain why so many people, including our foreign friends, pay so much attention to China and Shanghai.

In short, Shanghai is growing fast on a solid basis through innovative development. China has goals, plans and strategies for its modernization program. Shanghai's future is not illusory, but tangible. It is undoubtedly the most vivid showcase of the Chinese modernization. As President Xi Jinping said when addressing the celebration of the 30th anniversary of Pudong's development and opening-up, the achievements of Pudong over the past 30 years offer the most convincing evidence of the strength of the system of socialism with Chinese characteristics, and are a vivid demonstration of the country's reform, opening-up and socialist modernization.

As a mega city with a resident population of about 25 million, Shanghai is accelerating its march on the Chinese path to modernization. The modernization efforts of Shanghai have aimed at high-quality development, high-quality living, efficient governance, and high-level openness, covering economic, political, social, cultural and ecological dimensions, which vividly interpret the characteristics and principles of Chinese modernization. Shanghai's modernization does not only produce local impacts, but has also a strong national and international influence. The international influence and attractiveness of Shanghai are increasing day by day. In recent years, Shanghai's utilization of foreign capital has grown

against headwinds. In the first quarter of 2023, the actual utilization of foreign capital reached 7.8 billion US dollars, a year-on-year growth 28.1%; its headquarters economy has developed, with 907 regional headquarters of multinational corporations and 538 foreign-owned R&D centers settled in the city.

When we walk on the streets of Shanghai, we feel that the buildings in Shanghai are telling interesting stories while the parks are relaxing. Also remembering the above development data, many people would consciously or unconsciously ask: Why is it Shanghai that has attained this magic power? Why can Shanghai do all this? These are not only questions scholars and politicians at home and abroad have tried to answer, but also frequent topics we constantly discuss with our foreign guests, including delegations of foreign political parties and many political dignitaries, as well as our compatriots from Hong Kong, Macao, and Taiwan. This book is an attempt to answer these questions. We understand that our foreign friends as well as compatriots from Hong Kong, Macao and Taiwan who come to visit would not stay in Shanghai very long or visit many places, and therefore their understanding of Shanghai would be limited. In order to make up for these limitations, we have organized our faculty to write this Chinese-English bilingual book in order to help them understand Shanghai.

President Xi Jinping once said that Chinese modernization has common characteristics shared by all countries while it shows strong Chinese characteristics. Therefore, when we focus on the history, practices and successes of Shanghai to tell the story of Chinese modernization, we discuss issues which are common concerns of all countries on the road to modernization, such as people's livelihood and well-being, urban governance, poverty governance, openness, and inclusive development. These issues are the basis of dialogue at the global and national levels. At the same time, we're dedicated to summarizing solutions and policy measures at the operational level to address these common concerns, and attempt to present the theoretical basis underlying these concrete practices.

In terms of framework and structure, the book is divided into five chapters. The first chapter, "Great changes over a century: A symbol of Chinese modernization", which is

the general introduction, presents the history of Shanghai as the birthplace of the CPC and Shanghai as the forefront of China's reform and opening-up after briefly describing the history and characteristics of Shanghai's economic and social development. The combination of revolutionary traditions and reform and opening-up has given Shanghai its open, innovative, and inclusive urban character. It is also the key to understanding of Shanghai and explains the source of courage, wisdom, and strength for Shanghai to create miracles of development. The second, third, and fourth chapters focus on the new measures, ideas, and practices of Shanghai in realizing economic and social development over the past decade, focusing on high-quality development, high-quality living, and efficient governance. Chapter 5 "Sharing and opening-up: Contributing Shanghai's wisdom to China and the world" focuses on how Shanghai's development aligns with China's national goals and promotes the country's high-level opening-up, looking beyond Shanghai to the whole country, and even aiming at the world. It showcases Shanghai's vision and commitments as a modern socialist international metropolis with global influence.

Every chapter includes three parts: common problems, case study, and summary of experience and lessons. The rise of Lujiazui Financial City, the strategic development of Zhangjiang Science City, the low-carbon green transformation of Shanghai-based China Baowu Steel Group ("Baowu"), the protective redevelopment of Hengshan Road-Fuxing Road historic area, the creation of 15-minute community-life circles, embedded elderly care services in the central urban districts, the urban renewal projects, the digital transformation of urban governance, public participation in major issues, Shanghai's engagement in East-West cooperation, the construction of Yangshan Deep-water Port as part of its international shipping center, and the China International Import Expo (CIIE)... have painted a picture of Chinese modernization in Shanghai.

This beautiful picture combines vivid description of cases, solid data, moving visuals, and scientific reasoning, revealing the warm emotions and inspirations of the city. It is not only a practical guide on urban development, but also provides insights into the dynamics of its further development. As President Xi Jinping said, "Chinese modernization is a process

led by the CPC", and "the CPC's leadership is a defining feature of Chinese modernization". Shanghai's commitment to being a "People's City" highlights the values Chinese cities adhere to in the course of development. Shanghai has transformed from former foreign concessions and Adventurer's Paradise to today's "People's City", a modern city which is full of vitality and boasts a poetic living environment, and is firmly committed to being a "City of the People and for the People" throughout the entire process of urban development. Everything it does to realize progress is centered around the people, aimed at bringing happiness to people and making their life better. Although the cases in this book present different themes, the values they stand for are homogeneous. It can be said that they are all concrete examples of Shanghai's commitment to people, and its efforts to address their concerns and meet their demands.

This book is a writing project organized and sponsored by Shanghai Party Institute of CPC (Shanghai Administration Institute). For many years, the Institute has adhered to "modern, comprehensive, research-oriented, and open" education, and proactively conducted international exchange programs, which have been widely and highly recognized and appreciated.

I hope that this book, as a book for supplementary reading, can give readers a new perspective to better understand Shanghai and China, and trigger further discussions of China's development and issues in the course of development, thereby helping consolidate friendship, expanding consensus, and strengthening collaboration.

Prof. Luo Feng

Provost of Shanghai Party Institute of CPC

(Shanghai Administration Institute)

September 2023

CONTENTS

Chapter 1

Great changes over a century: A symbol of Chinese modernization

Chapter 2

Innovation and transformation
towards high-quality development

Chapter 3

People-centrism:
Creating a high-quality life

Chapter 4

Smart and equitable:
Achieving efficient governance

Chapter 5

Sharing and opening-up:
Contributing Shanghai's wisdom to China and the world

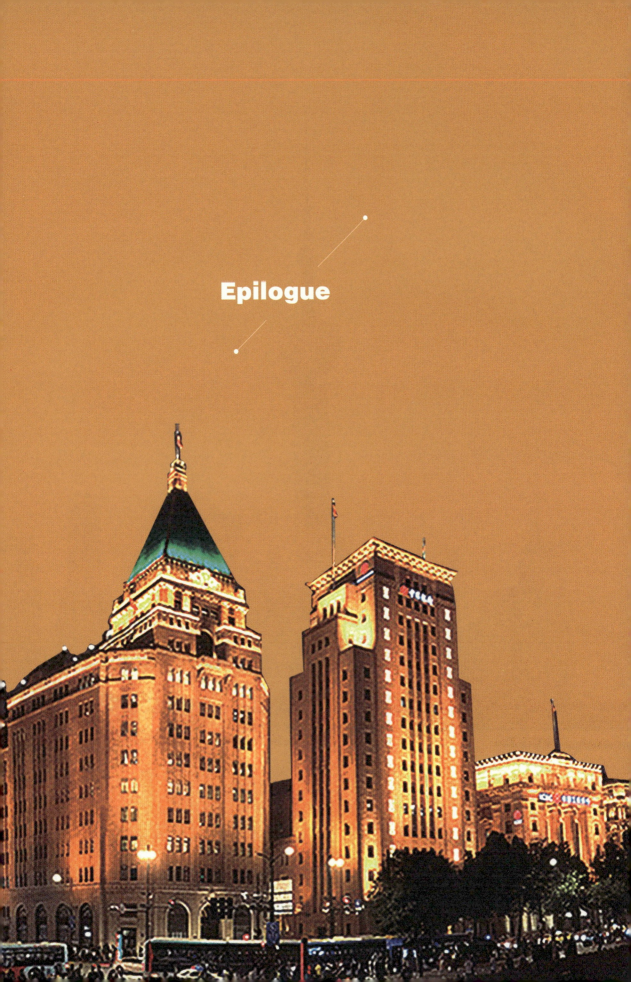

Epilogue

Chapter 1

Great changes over a century: A symbol of Chinese modernization

Foreigners are often advised to come to Shanghai to "read" the story of China over the past century. For example, when visiting Lincoln High School in Tacoma, Washington State, USA on September 23, 2015, Chinese President Xi Jinping told the students in the classroom:

"You can visit Xi'an to understand China's history of the past 1,000 years, visit Beijing for the Chinese history of the past 500 years, and visit Shanghai to witness China's growth over the past 100 years."

How and why can we witness the development of China over the past century in Shanghai? What magical changes had taken place in the city during this period? How did the changes occur? Let's walk with these questions into this magic city: Shanghai.

Shanghai is a young but unique Chinese city. About one hundred and eighty years ago, Shanghai was still a small county on the coast of the East China Sea, standing near the mouth of the Yangtze River. Following the Opium War in 1840, China encountered an upheaval unseen in the past 3,000 years: foreign colonizers "knocked open China's doors" with warships and cannons. Shanghai, however, has since embarked on its own journey to greatness, while witnessing national ups and downs. From the foreign concessions to today's "People's City", Shanghai has risen from the waste land before the founding of the People's Republic of China to become a thriving international metropolis. In this sense,

Shanghai is the epitome of China's modernization process.

The source of power driving the Chinese modernization, namely the Communist Party of China, had also emerged in Shanghai. It was under the leadership of the Communist Party of China 100 years ago, that the working class in Shanghai identified a new goal and organizational system, bringing with it "new life" to the city.

Let's take a closer look at Shanghai. Its fastest growth spurt came along with the development and opening-up of Pudong. It was said that Shenzhen epitomized China's reform and opening-up in the 1980s, and Pudong in the 1990s. In fact, Pudong has played a leading role in China's second wave of reform and opening-up, and provides the most vivid image of Chinese modernization.

Through great changes and development over the past 100 years, Shanghai has established its urban identity as a "People's City". It is no longer a cold and polarized city as it was a century ago, with people starving under the magnificent neon lights. What we see today is a modern socialist international metropolis with a comprehensive industrial chain, a favorable business environment, and citizens living and working in peace and contentment. It is a great city that attracts resources from across the globe.

Shanghai: A People's City

I. Introduction

Foreigners coming to Shanghai would generally visit the Bund for its elegant scenery, and be amazed by the prosperous sight of modern Lujiazui across the Huangpu River. From the vastly different architectural styles on both sides of the waterway, they'd see the tremendous achievements of China's modernization, and wonder about the sharp contrast between the past and the present: Why are the two sides of the Huangpu River so different? What great changes has Shanghai undergone over the past 100 years? Why did such changes occur? Why has Shanghai become a symbol of the Chinese path to modernization?

It can be said that China's path towards modernization began in Shanghai. In 1842, China was forced to "open its door". On August 29, 1842, China signed the first unequal treaty: the Treaty of Nanking. The treaty stipulated that five cities in China should be opened as trading ports to foreign countries, with Shanghai being one of them. In the following decades, foreign "adventurers" competed to establish their presence in Shanghai one after another. They changed the city's skyline, created brightly-lit auditoriums, and built modern roaring factories, earning Shanghai high a fame as the "Paris of the East". One Japanese referred to Shanghai as a "Magic City"[1]. At that time, the Qing government also started

---

[1] In 1923, Tsukaze Muramatsu, a Japanese writer, came to Shanghai and lived in the city for two months. After going back to Japan, he wrote a long essay of nearly 50,000 words, "The Incredible City: Shanghai", which was published as a book *The Magic City* the following year to describe his experiences and feelings in Shanghai.

The sharp contrast between Lujiazui in 1920 and 2020

the Westernization Movement for self-strengthening and growing its wealth. In 1873, Li Hongzhang, prime minister of the Qing Dynasty, set up the China Merchants Steam Navigation Company in Shanghai to engage in transportation business covering water routes for both passenger and commercial use. As a result, the business later expanded into one of the most successful industries, which was considered as the first initiative of China's modernization.

The force that led the Chinese modernization drive emerged in Shanghai. The Qing government was ultimately unable to help its people emerge from poverty through the self- strengthening movement, due to the scarcity of resources, nor could it change China's status as a semi-colonial and semi-feudal society. Facing the national crisis, there was an urgent need of a new force to lead China's modernization. In 1921, this force emerged in Shanghai and afterwards played a fundamental role in promoting Chinese modernization, that being the CPC. Its emergence and development were driven by the vast working class, the inclusive urban culture and the diverse social characteristics of Shanghai. The rise of the CPC had brought new life to this city and even the entire country. Mao Zedong thus referred to Shanghai as the "cradle of modern China".

The development of Shanghai, like the journey of China toward modernization, was an extraordinary process full of glory and hardship. The prosperity of Shanghai in the 1920s and 1930s was only enjoyed by a very limited proportion of the population. In this "splendid" city, there were paupers in rags and modern buildings interspersed with "rundown houses" made of grasses and tree branches in shanty towns. The rapid development of modern industries in Shanghai had also brought serious pollution to the city: the rivers, air and soil had been degraded to varying degrees. However, through explorations on the Chinese path to modernization over the past 100 years, Shanghai has now become a "People's City", which is shared by all, livable and friendly to everyone.

We can better understand these earth-shaking changes in Shanghai during China's modernization process and the reasons behind them through some comparisons.

II. From "Shi-li-yang-chang"① to a "People's City"

1. Miseries in "Shi-li-yang-chang"

More than 100 years ago, Shanghai was occupied by foreign powers and divided into concession areas. In 1845, the British concession was established in Shanghai, followed by the American concession and the French concession, and later the British and American concessions merged and became the International Settlement. Due to various historical reasons, the concession areas in Shanghai became a de facto "state within the country", and neither the Qing government, the Beiyang government, nor the Nanjing National Government could exercise direct jurisdiction over the concession areas. Chinese people were "dwarfed" within the concessions, inferior in all aspects. In particular, they did not have any political rights. The Municipal Council governing the International Settlement was composed of foreigners only and it was not until 1928 that any Chinese joined it. The Chinese people also suffered from many restrictions and discrimination in their daily lives within the concessions. For example, the famous racetrack (now the People's Park near the People's Square in Shanghai) had always been closed to the Chinese. The Shanghai Race Club only accepted foreigners as members, but not the Chinese. In 1908, the Club had 320 formal members and approximately 500 informal members, none of whom were natives.

In stark contrast to the restrictions and discrimination faced by the Chinese people, the foreign colonizers had special privileges in Shanghai and lived a proud and indulgent lifestyle. The famous scientist Albert Einstein visited Shanghai in the 1920s and wrote,

"In Shanghai, Europeans formed the ruling class, while the Chinese people were their slaves. This city shows the difference in social status between Europeans and the Chinese,

---

① A popular name for Nanjing Road in old Shanghai, as the road is about five kilometers or ten li's in total. The road was called "Shi-li-yang-chang" (literally meaning a ten-li street with exotic sights and sounds) also because it was crowded with foreign businesses and merchants.

which partly explained the recent revolutionary events."[1]

Most of the factories in Shanghai were owned by colonizers, and China's national capital then was in its infancy and still very weak. Although the service industry in Shanghai was prosperous, it served mostly colonizers, while the life of ordinary Shanghai citizens was vastly different. In a sense, the prosperity and modernity of Shanghai at that time were not for the Chinese people, nor were they shared by the majority.

2. From dilapidated sheds and shabby houses to completely equipped new homes

Housing has always been one of the most pressing issues in modern Shanghai, known as Shanghai's "No. 1 problem". Old Shanghai had a huge population, over 1 million in 1900, over 2 million in 1915, and over 3 million in 1930, making it a mega city in China, the second largest city in the Far East, and the fifth largest city in the world after London, New York, Tokyo, and Berlin. In 1947, the population was equivalent to the total of Nanjing, Peiping (now Beijing), and Tianjin. Shanghai was a typical "immigrant city" with its residents coming from all over the country. They came to Shanghai as they thought this city was a good place to work and earn a living. Due to the high housing prices and high rents in Shanghai, the vast majority of workers were unable to buy a house there. Furthermore, due to the cruel exploitation of the colonial factories, the living conditions of Shanghai workers were extremely poor at that time. A great many workers lived in self-built run-down houses popularly called "Gun Di Long" (literally meaning huts) by the locals. These huts were semi-circular structures with walls made of bamboo sheets, covered with broken reed mats and hemp bags. One end was blocked with debris, and the other end hung with a broken straw curtain or cloth hanging to make a door. Specifically, there were no tables, chairs, or four-leg beds, but only low beds on the floor, made up of straws, reed mats, and broken-down cotton wool. In some areas of old Shanghai, there were extended patches of run-down

---

[1] The Collected Papers of Albert Einstein (Volume 3) [M]. The Commercial Press, 2009, p.31.

houses, especially along Yaoshui Lane. Yaoshui Lane was located in a small area west of Xikang Road and south of the Suzhou Creek. Because there were two lime kilns nearby, the place was also called "Lime Kiln". It was called "Yaoshui Lane" (literally meaning a lane named after potions) mainly because there was a Jiangsu Potion Factory nearby. It partly constituted the famous shanty areas dubbed "three bays and one lane" (the "lane" being the Yaoshui Lane) in western Shanghai. A popular song at that time went like this, "It's better to be in prison for three years than to live in the lime kiln." In this area with extremely poor living conditions, there were no basic living facilities such as water and electricity supplies, and there were garbage and stinky puddles everywhere, coupled with frequent outbreaks of epidemics. Once it rained, the winding uneven roads in this area, without drainage ditches, became muddy and would not dry until ten days or half a month passed, earning for themselves a nickname the "Yan Wang Roads" (literally meaning the Roads of Hell).

A Gun Di Long hut in old Shanghai

Shanty town in old Shanghai

After the founding of the People's Republic of China in 1949, one after another, the shanty towns in Shanghai were refurbished and the Gun Di Long huts disappeared. The thatched huts had been replaced with earthen or tiled houses, and some families had even built their own two-story buildings. Compared with the past, people's living conditions had improved, but houses were still built at random without unified planning or design. The distance between buildings was not adequate, failing to meet the current requirements for fire protection, hygiene, and other conditions. Because there was no independent kitchen or bathroom, several households had to share the same kitchen or bathroom in most instances, which posed great security risks. Due to the extremely limited housing stock, some residents on the ground floor could only sleep in their own living room, with their feet even "reaching their neighbors' homes". Staying too close, two families living on the second or third floor with their windows facing each other could share their dishes through an "overpass" built with wooden boards such as washboards. Some close neighbors even adopted the sharing mode of "cooking at your home today and my home tomorrow", which may only happen in the "three bays and one lane". In this kind of neighborhood, the residents jokingly remarked that they could only see "a line of sky" between two homes. According to a 1982 survey of housing resources in Shanghai, there were 2.16 million square meters of shanties, and 14.28 million square meters of old-style lanes, which housed 65% of the total population of the city. Another survey conducted by the Shanghai Academy of Social Sciences in roughly the same period showed that in 1985, 880,900 households living in the urban areas of Shanghai needed a home of their own, accounting for 52.28% of the total.[1]

Shanghai's housing problem was finally fixed following China's vigorous implementation of the reform and opening-up policy. In March 1987, Shanghai placed the housing problem of the extremely poor households (with a per capita living area of less than 2 square meters) high on the agenda of Shanghai Municipal People's Government. In 1992, the Sixth Shanghai Municipal Congress of the CPC proposed the goal of completing the

[1] Shanghai's Stories of Reform and Opening-Up [M]. Shanghai People's Publishing House, 2018, p.194.

The dilapidated sheds on the bank of the Suzhou Creek (Photo by Zheng Xianzhang)

renovation of 3.65 million square meters of dilapidated sheds, huts and run-down houses in the urban areas of Shanghai by the end of the 20th century. By 2000, the goal had been achieved after nearly a decade of efforts on many fronts such as land leasing, real estate development, and municipal infrastructure construction.

In recent years, Shanghai has increased efforts to protect heritage buildings and historical sites through old neighborhood renewal and old house refurbishment, accelerating the renovation of buildings more dilapidated than those in level-2 old neighborhoods. [1] For example, in Huangpu District, where the largest concentration of old houses stood, (in accordance with the decision of the CPC Shanghai Municipal Committee and Shanghai Municipal People's Government to accelerate the renovation of level-2 old residential quarters), the "2020-2022 Three-Year Old-House Renovation Plan" was formulated in 2020 based on ground conditions. Through municipal and district-level land reserve, which is the government-enterprise cooperation platform for real estate development, Huangpu District managed to accelerate the improvement of people's living conditions by relocation with compensation. In July 2022, the renovation of buildings more dilapidated than those in

[1] Level-2 old neighborhoods or level-2 old residential quarters are a little better than dilapidated sheds and huts in terms of housing conditions; but mostly they are also bungalows. Although some are buildings or have a well-designed structure, their living conditions are always not favorable.

Once rundown houses were torn down and replaced by a brand-new neighborhood called the "Brilliant City" (Photo by Le Yufeng/ IP SHANGHAI)

level-2 old neighborhoods in Huangpu District was completed, marking the end of old town renewal in Shanghai. In the eyes of locals, this also marked the final and historic resolution of the contradiction between modern high-rise buildings and run-down houses in the city's central urban districts like Huangpu District. [1]

---

[1] Dajiangdong Workshop. Renovation Is Completed for Shanghai's Buildings More Dilapidated Than Those in Level-2 Old Neighborhoods [N]. People's Daily, 2022-07-27.

Since the large-scale renovation of old residential quarters began in 1992, the CPC Shanghai Municipal Committee and Shanghai Municipal People's Government have prioritized improving the residents' living environment. The government has worked tirelessly to achieve its goals. At present, Shanghai has finally completed the renovation of level-2 old neighborhoods and below, and has preliminarily completed the renewal of its old towns. In the central urban areas, the housing conditions of about 1.65 million households, or 5 million residents, have been significantly improved, and 100% of houses are now completely equipped with modern amenities. The average housing floor area per person has risen to 37.4 square meters in 2021. Citizens can live in clean and tidy flats or houses, enjoying a decent and dignified life with a strong sense of gain, happiness and security. This is what a city can offer its people so as to be called a "People's City".

3. From "Rust Belts" to "Life Belts"

There are two rivers that run across the city of Shanghai: the Huangpu River and the Suzhou Creek. According to some, compared with the Huangpu River, the Suzhou Creek is more like the "mother river" of Shanghai because it runs across the central districts and connects to the hinterland, and in the era of underdeveloped sea transportation, river shipments have an undoubtedly dominant position. Going boating upstream in the Suzhou Creek, once known as the Wusong River, one can directly reach the Baodai Bridge in Suzhou, Jiangsu Province, and transfer to the Beijing-Hangzhou Grand Canal. After Shanghai was opened as a treaty port in 1843, early Western colonizers were extremely sensitive to trade and commodity and currency circulation. Therefore, they referred to the 17-kilometer long Wusong River in Shanghai as the "Suzhou Creek", indicating its connection with Suzhou and even the wider hinterland. Bluish-green with crystal clear water, the Suzhou Creek was then a beautiful waterway in the Jiangnan area (the area south of the Yangtze River).

However, industrial civilization came together with environmental pollution, like "twins". As Shanghai was opened as a treaty port for international trade, and there were

well-developed waterways from the Suzhou Creek to the hinterland south of the Yangtze River, both sides of the river became the first-choice sites of modern plants and business operations. In 1860, a British merchant established a sulfuric acid plant under the Xinzha Road Bridge on the south bank of the Suzhou Creek. Fifteen years later, Ernest Major, founder of the newspaper Shun Pao, became a shareholder of the sulfuric acid plant, which imported sulfur raw materials from the United States and Italy to produce sulfuric acid, nitric acid, and hydrochloric acid. As the plant polluted the Suzhou Creek, the authorities of the International Settlement, the Municipal Council, ordered Ernest Major to relocate the plant. Ernest Major thus moved the plant to the north bank of the Suzhou Creek, which was a Chinese sector beyond the Municipal Council's jurisdiction.[1]

China's early national industry also rose in the north bank of the Suzhou Creek. From 1912 to 1925, due to World War I, European and American powers halted their expansion in Shanghai, offering China a golden opportunity to develop its national economy. On the banks of the Suzhou Creek then, chimneys stood tall and machines rumbled. Both rivers were filled with freighters. Almost all scholars believed that the water of the Suzhou Creek had turned foul during this period. A case in point was the relocation of Zhabei Water Plant, which was first located in the lower reaches of the Suzhou Creek in 1909. In early 1920, the water turned black and foul-smelling in the urban part of the Suzhou Creek, forcing Zhabei Water Plant to resort to disinfection through chlorination. In 1928, to save costs, the plant moved to Yangpu District upon the Huangpu River. At that time, the population on both sides of the Suzhou Creek had reached 2 million. Factories alongside the Suzhou Creek attracted a large number of refugees from Jiangsu, Anhui, and Shandong provinces to work. They rowed small boats there and built very poorly equipped sheds and huts nearby. As a result, domestic sewage, industrial wastewater, and even rural fallow manure flowed directly into the Suzhou Creek.

---

[1] Yang Haipeng. Suzhou Creek: The Rebirth of China's First Heavily Polluted River [N]. Southern Weekly, 2001-09-27.

By the late 1950s, the Suzhou Creek had become a "rust belt" in the central area of Shanghai. The Suzhou Creek is a tidal river with low fluidity. When the sea tide is high, water would be pushed back towards the beach, and this "rust belt" snaked back and forth across the city. Zhang Xiaoguo, who once served as Deputy Director of the Office of the Leading Group for the Suzhou Creek Comprehensive Rehabilitation Project, recalled that in the 1990s, a delegate to the National People's Congress inspected the Suzhou Creek, and the trip ended up with sweat on his brow. First feeling nauseous, he finally passed out right on the riverbank.[1] At that time, Shanghai had just opened up to the outside world. European, American, and Japanese people, as well as people from China's Hong Kong and Taiwan came, but they did not drink Shanghai's water. Instead, they brought their own drinking water, which embarrassed Shanghai's leaders.

Although Shanghai began to implement pollution controls for the Suzhou Creek in the 1950s, it failed to meet the planned goals due to financial and technological issues. In 1986, Shanghai earned the first gold opportunity for urban transformation and rehabilitation: it obtained loans from foreign banks, totaling USD 3.2 billion, in which USD 1.6 billion was spent on pollution control of the Suzhou Creek. In 1988, Shanghai and the World Bank cosponsored a project called the Suzhou Creek Mixed-Wastewater Project (Phase I). The framework of this project was not complex: the industrial and domestic sewage generated by 2.55 million people in an area of 70 square kilometers north of the Suzhou Creek would be intercepted, so that sewage would no longer be directly discharged into the Suzhou Creek and its tributaries. Instead, it would be transferred through pipelines to Wusongkou and discharged into the Yangtze River underwater. After 6 years, the 33.39-kilometer sewage pipeline was completed in 1994. At the same time, the Bailonggang sewage interception project began, which was also the Suzhou Creek Mixed-Wastewater Project (Phase II), with a total investment of 6 billion yuan. After the completion of this new project, 5 million tons

[1] Zhang Xiaoguo. How Did the Once Black and Smelly Suzhou Creek Become Clear Again [EB/OL]. Shanghai Observer, http://www.shoberver.com/staticsg/res/html/web/news Detail.html?id=53752&sid=67.

of pre-treated sewage could be discharged through pipelines to Bailonggang daily. After several years, water in the Suzhou Creek turned from pitch black to yellow.

After years of continuous efforts, the Suzhou Creek had basically got rid of black and pungent water by 2000. Since 2002, the key water quality indicators have gradually improved. In 2000, insect larvae were found in the sediment of the once most severely polluted section of the Suzhou Creek, and in 2001, schools of small fish appeared in the river's urban section. At the same time, the water quality of the main tributaries had also significantly improved. Since 2018, Shanghai has prioritized living quality improvement through creating pleasant public spaces on both sides of the Suzhou Creek, with a focus

The Suzhou Creek is now open for sightseeing, proudly displaying its beauty to the local people of Shanghai and visitors (Photo by Tang Dang/IP SHANGHAI)

on meeting people's desire for a better life. Gradually, the efforts on improving the Suzhou Creek shifted from water quality control to bringing quality life to residents in the vicinity. Today, the water is clean, the cityscape has improved, and riverside green spaces have significantly expanded, which gives the residents nearby a better living environment. The banks of the Suzhou Creek are emerging as desired urban spaces for living, leisure, and sightseeing, and forming a "life belt". Now, on the water front, the Suzhou Creek- Mengqing Garden Environmental Theme Park showcases what Shanghai has done to improve the Suzhou Creek over the past 100 years and indicates that residents on both sides of the Suzhou Creek have finally realized their dream of living with clear water. If the Suzhou Creek was once the dark side of Shanghai, its rehabilitation has created the highlight in Shanghai's historical urban development and embodies the concept of harmonious coexistence of man and nature on the Chinese path to modernization.

III. Conclusion

The Chinese path to modernization, in the final analysis, is a people-centered approach to development. President Xi Jinping once pointed out, "The core of a city is its people, and the success of urbanization lies in three elements: easy access to basic necessities; good care during childbirth, old age and illness; and people's living and working in contentment."[1] Addressing the most pressing concerns of urban residents is the core and top priority of building a "People's City", and also the goal of thousands of cities throughout China, including Shanghai.

The great changes in Shanghai over the past century are impressive to all. The reason why the city has made such amazing achievements and become a symbol of the Chinese path to modernization is that it has always been firmly committed to the goal of becoming a "People's City" while taking concrete actions along this path.

---

[1] The Selected Works of Xi Jinping (Volume 1) [M]. People Publishing House, 2023, p.412.

It is a path toward shared prosperity for all rather than just a handful of people. The modernization of Shanghai no longer focuses on the shi-li-yang-chang in the dark history that served only the few, the foreigners, but discards the huge wealth disparity that enabled some to live in houses with gardens, while a great many others had to crowd in shanties. The goal of building a "People's City" requires making the best resources available to the general public, rather than only the privileged. In recent years, Shanghai has created beautiful open spaces alongside the Huangpu River and the Suzhou Creek for Shanghai citizens, unlike the Bund Park which was open only to the few (Westerners). This change ensures social fairness and justice.

Aiming at the harmonious coexistence between man and nature, the Chinese path to modernization also entails sustainable development, based on the philosophy that clean waters and green mountains are as valuable as gold and silver. In its modernization process, Shanghai has encountered various troubles arising from industrialization, such as water and air problems. However, through the unremitting efforts of several generations, the city has completed a dramatic transformation, and the Rust Belts have become Life Belts. The two banks of the Huangpu River and the Suzhou Creek have become the most popular open spaces in Shanghai. The urban green area throughout the city is also being expanded. Now, every weekend in Shanghai, when the weather is fine, there are campers in large and small green spaces. These are all fruits of the city's commitment to green, openness and shared development in the process of modernization.

Meanwhile, at the national level, China has remained committed to people's longing for a better life. After reform and opening-up, China's economy has never stopped developing, and people's living conditions have also continued to improve. In Shanghai thirty years ago, what most residents wanted might have been a good job and a medium-sized house, but today what they expect is more health and recreation activities, such as jogging, watching movies, and visiting museums and art galleries with their children. The Chinese modernization has fulfilled these expectations and realized people's comprehensive development.

Shanghai: A glorious city

I. Introduction

China is an ancient civilization with a long history and splendid culture. It has long been a good example to the world in many ways. The hardworking, brave, and wise Chinese people have made outstanding contributions to the progress of human civilization. In the premodern and modern times, due to various reasons, the Chinese nation had met with a national crisis, through which the Chinese people became aware of our country's weaknesses and began to seek changes and self-improvement, exploring the path of modernization.

Where is Chinese society heading? What is the way out for China? Countless benevolent individuals in China have embarked on arduous explorations and heroic struggles, but time and again, failures have proven that the path of reform without touching the social foundations is not viable, and blindly copying Western formal systems and development models is also futile. China urgently needs new ideological guidance for the salvation movement, a new organization to unite revolutionary forces, to save the people in dire straits, and to rescue the nation teetering on the edge of peril.

In 1921, the CPC was founded in Shanghai, vowing to lead China's revolution and modernization drive and later providing strong organizational support for realizing national goals. For more than 100 years, the CPC has united and led the Chinese people in making remarkable achievements in China's socialist modernization through relentless exploration

Site of the First National Congress of the CPC (Photo by He Zhaoyun)

Memorial Hall of the First National Congress of the CPC (Photo by He Zhaoyun)

and hard work.

Shanghai was the birthplace of the CPC. In the 12 years after its founding, except for three temporary relocations, the leading organs of the Central Committee of the CPC had remained in Shanghai. In this city, the Party had figured out a revolutionary road suitable for China's national conditions. During this period, they had issued orders, which like candles, illuminated the road of the China's revolution. This had left precious legacies to later generations and even fused in the "blood" of Shanghai to form the spirit of this city. Revolutionary historical sites throughout Shanghai, where history and modernity blend, vividly embody the glorious history of the CPC which emerged to save China from internal troubles and foreign invasion, grew up amid China's hardships and setbacks, thrived despite difficulties, and led the Chinese people to create a shared future. This is also part of the glorious history of Shanghai. Then, here is the question: Why was Shanghai a birthplace of the CPC, which leads the Chinese path to modernization?

II. The revolutionary tradition of a modern international metropolis

1. Hardships in Shanghai: A microcosm of the sufferings of the Chinese nation over 100 years

In 1840, during the Qing Dynasty, the last feudal dynasty in Chinese history, the imperial United Kingdom launched the "Opium War" against China, which ended up in the defeat of the Qing Dynasty, gradually reducing it to a semi-colonial and semi-feudal country. The defeated Qing government signed an unequal treaty with the invaders who forced Shanghai to open to foreign merchants as a trading port. Since then, colonists had landed in Shanghai via the Huangpu River. As a result, the narrow muddy path on the west bank of the river, initially paved by Chinese boatmen and laborers, became a new landmark of Shanghai, called the Bund, where magnificent and classical architecture arose. These western buildings were symbols of the suffering and humiliation of the Chinese nation 100

years ago. Beginning from Shanghai as a treaty port, Western colonists gradually invaded and controlled the Yangtze River Basin extending from east to west, which was the lifeline of China's economy. The colonists first established concessions in Shanghai, and built separate administrative and judicial institutions, and even paramilitary armed forces within the concessions, making them "states within a country". As a result, Shanghai gradually formed a unique administrative pattern of "one city, three governments": the French concession, the International Settlement (formerly the British and American concessions), and the Chinese-controlled districts (including the Qing government's Shanghai County). Combined, Shanghai's concessions were 1.5 times the total area of foreign concessions in other Chinese cities at that time, and they were also the most long-standing ones. They were established in 1845 and ended in August 1943, which meant they had existed as long as 98 years.

After Shanghai was opened as a treaty port to foreign merchants, foreign businesses came one after another and hired the first batch of industrial workers in China. Being brutally oppressed, they were largely the most miserable industrial workers in the world. Xia Yan, a famous Chinese writer, vividly described workers' sufferings in Shanghai at that time in a book Bonded Laborers. He said,

"They worked 12 hours a day with two meals of rice soup and one of dry rice, while they had to finish hard labor in workshops as well as family chores of their bosses. They lived in inhumane living conditions. They suffered a great deal. After all, they are all flesh and blood, unlike the machine made of steel. However, their contract period was generally three years, but less than two-thirds of them could fulfill the contract. They worked all day long and had to work even when they were too weak to walk. Their limbs were as thin as reed sticks, their bodies were hunched like bows, and their faces were as pale as those of corpses. They coughed and panted, but still they were forced to continue working." [1]

Robert Merton Solow, an American economist, was quoted as saying that beneath every

① Collected Works of Xia Yan: Literature (Part 1) [M]. Zhejiang Literature and Art Publishing House, 2005, pp.10-20.

sleeper of American railways lay the body of an Irish worker. Similarly, every spindle of Japanese factories in Shanghai carried the flesh and blood of a Chinese "slave worker". [1]

In order to save the nation from crisis and realize national rejuvenation, countless Chinese people with lofty ideals had completed arduous explorations and epic struggles. However, facts had proved that self-strengthening movements could not remove the roots of suffering, including reformism in various names, old-style peasant wars, the Democratic Revolution led by the bourgeois, and various plans to copy the Western political model. They could not save the Chinese nation and perform its anti-imperialism and anti-feudalism tasks, or stabilize China's political and social situation, let alone providing institutional support for the country to achieve national prosperity and create happiness for its people. So, China urgently needed a new force to lead the national salvation movement with new ideas and a new organization to unite revolutionary forces.

2. A great beginning: The birth of the CPC in Shanghai

There are four reasons why the CPC was founded in Shanghai: a special political landscape, an open cultural atmosphere, a complex social structure, and favorable transportation and communication conditions. [2]

A special political landscape means that there was a "political gap" in Shanghai. At that time, the French concession, the International Settlement, and the Chinese-controlled districts were administered separately and independently, making urban management extremely difficult. There was no physical barrier at the borders between these areas, but the police forces of any of the three governments could not cross the borders for law enforcement. Under this circumstance, a special "political gap" existed in Shanghai, and the first, second, and fourth National Congresses of the CPC were convened there using

———————————————

① Collected Works of Xia Yan: Literature (Part 1) [M]. Zhejiang Literature and Art Publishing House, 2005, pp.10-20.

② Sunrise in the East [M]. Party History Research Office of CPC Shanghai Municipal Committee & Shanghai Archives, 2014, p.14.

this political gap. The first CPC National Congress was held on the edge of the French concession, the second at the junction of the French concession and the International Settlement, and the fourth in an area for cross-border road construction. [1]

An open cultural atmosphere shaped the foundation for the spread of advanced ideology and the growth of leadership. The New Culture Movement [2] prompted many thoughts on social transformation to emerge in China. Marxism was just one of them, but at first it was anarchism that played a dominated role before Marxism took root in China. The victory of the Russian Revolution of 1917 and the May Fourth Movement [3] drove the progressive youth to accept Marxism through comparison. Afterwards, Marxism quickly spread nationwide. The national awakening laid the ideological foundation for the establishment of the CPC. At that time, Shanghai was already the most developed city in China in terms of publications, which provided fertile soil for the growth of progressive ideas. As a result, Shanghai became a center of early Chinese Marxism in China. In 1920, representatives of the Communist Party of Russia who visited Shanghai said,

"Shanghai is the center of activities for Chinese socialists, where propaganda can be openly carried out. There are many socialist organizations in Shanghai that published over 300 newspapers, magazines, and books, all for socialist purposes." [4]

As Marxism spread in Shanghai, a group of advanced intellectuals emerged, many of

---

① "Cross-border road construction" refers specifically to the expansion of the International Settlement by building roads beyond its boundary so that the areas the new roads passed became "quasi concessions" over which the Municipal Council of the International Settlement claimed administrative jurisdiction.
② It is an enlightenment movement initiated by a group of Chinese intellectuals to pursue democracy and science and overthrow feudalism in the early 20th century.
③ The May Fourth Movement, taking place in Beijing on May 4, 1919, was a patriotic movement. As the early main participants, young students organized demonstrations, petitions, strikes, and violence against the government. At the same time, a big strike was launched in Shanghai by workers which resulted in a complete disruption of transportation both inside and outside the city, on land and sea, leading further to a halt in production, and finally causing a severe impact on the imperialists and the warlord government. Later and gradually, the center of the May Fourth Movement shifted from Beijing to Shanghai, and the main participants of the movement changed from students to workers.
④ Uniting the Bolsheviks and the Communist International to Advance the Chinese National Revolution (1920-1925) [M]. Beijing Book Publishing Company, 1997, p.45.

whom became co-founders of China's first socialist organization, predecessor of the CPC.

A complex social structure allowed new revolutionary forces to emerge. The development of national industry and international trading after port opening had led to the formation of a diversified social structure in Shanghai. Most importantly, in the 1920s, Shanghai had one fourth of all industrial workers in China, so it was dubbed the "stronghold of the Chinese working class". As a saying goes, wherever there is oppression, there is resistance. The miserable working and living conditions of workers in Shanghai made them combative. After the outbreak of the May Fourth Movement in 1919, Chen Duxiu lamented that there were only academic movements in Beijing and the general public there just had not woken up, while workers in Shanghai had launched large-scale strikes.

Favorable transportation and communication conditions made it possible for the CPC based in Shanghai to lead China's revolution. At that time, the city's transportation network was more developed than that of other cities in China, with not only railways and inland waterways available, but also regular shipping routes to Japan, Europe, America, and Southeast Asia, which facilitated the mobility of personnel. In terms of communication, since 1930, Shanghai had built radio-telegraph circuits for communication with foreign cities such as San Francisco, Berlin, Paris, Geneva, Saigon, London, Moscow, and Tokyo, which boosted information exchange with overseas revolutionaries.

On July 23, 1921, 13 Communist Group delegates from all over China and 2 delegates of the Communist International gathered at the residence of Li Hanjun (one of the Communist Group delegates) in the French concession in Shanghai to hold the first National Congress of the CPC. Among these delegates, 5 had completed university education, 2 were studying in universities, and 4 had studied abroad. When the sixth session of the First National Congress of the CPC was held, special agents of the French concession broke in, and the delegates were forced to transfer to a ship on Lake Nanhu, Jiaxing, Zhejiang Province to continue the meeting. The First Program of the CPC and the First Resolution of the CPC were discussed and passed there, and the Congress decided to establish a three-person Central Bureau, with Chen Duxiu as secretary, Zhang Guotao as organizational

director, and Li Da as director for publicity and communication.

The figure below shows the V-shaped trajectory of modern Chinese history: after it was founded in 1921, the CPC had led the Chinese nation to defeat Japanese imperialism, overthrow the reactionary rule of the KMT (Kuomintang, or the Chinese Nationalist Party), complete the New Democratic Revolution, and establish the People's Republic of China after 28 years of bloody struggle. These moves put an end to the semi-colonial and semi-feudal state of China, the coexistence of diverse governments in China, and the unequal treaties that gave privileges to colonists. They have also realized China's great leap from feudal dictatorship to democracy. Besides, they had profoundly changed the course of development of China since the premodern times and would shape the future destiny of China and the world.

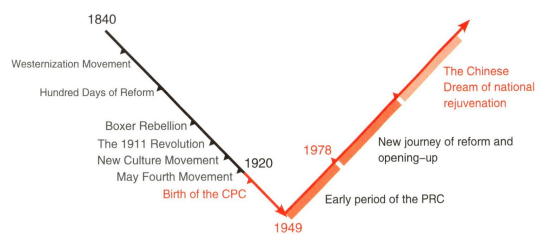

Figure 1　The V-shaped trajectory of modern Chinese history

3. Perseverance against adversity: Endeavors of the Communist Party of China in Shanghai

From the founding of the Party in 1921 to the founding of the People's Republic of China in 1949, the CPC had suffered a great many setbacks. The figure below shows the change in the number of CPC members, and from this figure, we can see the Party had met

with at least two life-or-death crises. One was the defeat of the Great Revolution[1] (co-led by KMT and the CPC) in 1927. On April 12, 1927, Chiang Kai-shek of the KMT launched the Shanghai Massacre[2] on April 12, 1927, killing CPC members and revolutionary masses. The number of CPC members plummeted from 57,000 to 10,000, which meant that 47,000 people had sacrificed their lives for their ideals. After this setback, the CPC's first since its establishment, the leading body of the CPC Central Committee continued their struggle in Shanghai, one of the most dangerous cities for them, and managed to bring back the Party to life in the midst of adversity. In June 1928, the number of CPC members rose to 40,000. From the birth of the CPC to early 1933 when the Central Committee of the CPC moved to Ruijin, Jiangxi Province, the leading body of the Central Committee of the CPC had retained its presence and remained active in Shanghai, except for three temporary relocations. Therefore, Shanghai was the command center of the Chinese revolutionary movement at that time.

The 612 existing historical sites[3] of the Party in Shanghai testify to the glorious history of the CPC, especially its relentless fighting one of the most dangerous cities in its early years. For example, there is an inconspicuous two-story building at No.171-173 Middle Yunnan Road, Huangpu District, opposite the People's Square and adjacent to the Tianchan Yifu Theatre where KMT officials and social dignitaries often watched plays. It once housed the Political Bureau of the Central Committee of the CPC (1928-1931) and was known as the "red center under the white terror". In April 1928, Xiong Jinding, who had been a member of the Hubei Provincial Committee of the CPC, was appointed by Zhou Enlai as an accountant of the Central Committee of the CPC and transferred to Shanghai, where he was first responsible for raising and managing the Party's funds, and completed site selection for

------

[1] The period from January 1924 to July 1927 was the first high tide of the modern Chinese revolutionary move-ment. The war was fought against imperialism and the Northern Warlords under the joint leadership of the CPC and the Kuomintang (KMT). It was also known as the "National Revolution" or "Great Revolution".

[2] On April 12, 1927, the right-wing KMT led by Chiang Kai-shek launched an armed coup in Shanghai against the left-wing KMT and CPC, killing many CPC members, KMT leftists, and other revolutionaries.

[3] Source: Directory of Red Resources in Shanghai (first list).

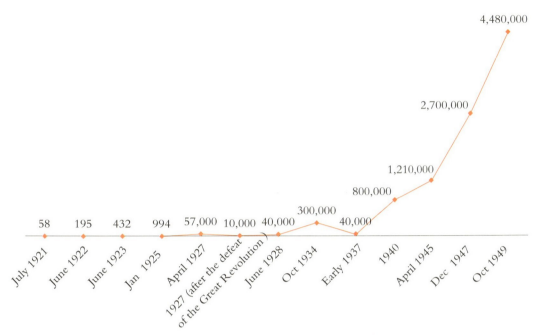

Figure2   Changes in the number of CPC members (1921–1949)（in persons）
Source: Documents of previous National Congresses of the CPC.

the office of the Political Bureau of the Central Committee of the CPC. After inspections, Xiong Jinding found this two-story building which was close to busy roads, and the bustling Tianchan Yifu Theatre and the private Shengli Hospital. It was a safe place in this dangerous city, and thus a good choice for setting up a secret Party organ. Therefore, Xiong Jinding rented three rooms upstairs of Shengli Hospital in the name of a businessman and opened a shop under the signboard of Fuxing Fabric Store. In fact, it was a secret office for the Political Bureau of the Central Committee of the CPC. It's hard to imagine that the Political Bureau would work in the bustling downtown of Shanghai, right under the enemy's nose. From April 1928 to April 1931, this office had witnessed what chaos China had experienced. Among others, Zhou Enlai, Deng Xiaoping, Li Weihan and Qu Qiubai once worked here as members of the Political Bureau, leading China's most arduous revolutionary struggle. They worked hard to enhance and develop the Party, strengthen intelligence and security work, direct the construction of hinterland base areas, establish the fundamental principles for army building, promote the left-wing cultural movement, and guide the course of the

national revolution. In April 1931, Gu Shunzhang, an alternate member of the Political Bureau and head of the Special Actions Section of that Central Committee of the CPC, was arrested and defected. After learning this bad news, Zhou Enlai [1] took prompt measures to transfer the organs of the CPC Central Committee and Jiangsu Provincial Committee to prevent any damage to them. Since then, Fuxing Fabric Store had ended its secret mission but left a mark in the history of the CPC. Three days after Xiong Jinding and his wife moved out, a detective from the International Settlement arrived at Shengli Hospital to inquire about the whereabouts of the upstairs resident. In this "red center under white terror", the Chinese Communists wrote an important page for the Chinese revolution with courage and wisdom.

4. Rebirth: The CPC's respect for and commitment to Shanghai

On May 27, 1949, after 16 days of fierce battle, the CPC-led People's Liberation Army (PLA) wiped out more than 150,000 enemy soldiers at the cost of more than 30,000 casualties, and recaptured the city of Shanghai, this Far East metropolis which was the birthplace and cradle of the CPC and the Chinese revolution. [2]

At the Second Plenary Session of the Seventh Central Committee of CPC, Mao Zedong pointed out with great foresight that taking over Shanghai was a big challenge in the course of China's revolution and tested the ability of the CPC. The success would determine the image of the CPC in the world. He said that Shanghai was the largest industrial and commercial city in the Far East and the only major Chinese city relevant to international trade. There was a need to ensure that this world-renowned city retained its best condition after liberation. Therefore, Mao Zedong explicitly required that the time to take over

[1] In 1928, Zhou Enlai was elected as a standing member of the Political Bureau of the CPC Central Committee at the First Plenary Session of the Sixth Central Committee of the CPC. Later, he became head of the Department of Organization of the CPC Central Committee and Secretary of the Military Commission of the CPC Central Committee. To ensure the safety of the secret network of the Central Committee of the CPC in Shanghai, Zhou Enlai had played an important role in connecting and directing revolutionaries engaged in armed struggles led by the CPC in various districts, and in advancing the CPC's secret work in the Kuomintang ruled areas. Most of the time during this period, he was the main leader of the Central Committee of the CPC.
[2] Liu Tong. Battle of Shanghai [M]. Shanghai People's Publishing House, Xue Lin Publishing House, 2018, p.77.

Shanghai must be approved by himself. On April 27, 1949, the Third Field Army of the PLA approached Shanghai, but Mao Zedong issued an order "not to get too close to Shanghai". The Army immediately slowed down the takeover plan and tried to understand the city and learn how to manage such a large urban area before advancing again.

On May 25, 1949, the Third Field Army occupied the inner city of Shanghai at night. The next morning, after all shooting had ceased, Shanghai citizens opened their doors only to find that all PLA officers and soldiers in ragged uniforms were sleeping on the wet streets. At that time, a report by the United Press International news agency recorded the scene: "The army of the CPC followed strict military disciplines, and behaved in a proper and courteous manners. Although many buildings were open and could be used as military camps, the army still slept on the sidewalk." It turned out that before the battle of crossing the Yangtze River, the Third Field Army had formulated and issued the Ten Rules and Three Great Conventions on Entering the City, which is now shown in the Memorial Hall of the First National Congress of the CPC. There are two rules in it: "No shooting without reason" and "No living in private houses or shops". Photos of 100,000 soldiers of the People's Liberation Army sleeping on the streets were quickly published and forwarded by major media around the world.

On May 27, 1949, a new Shanghai came into being, where lights were bright, running water was available, telephones were in service, and factories and schools were operational after cruel fights, thanks to the precaution taken by the PLA who created a miracle in the history of the war. After the liberation of Shanghai, local people from all walks of life lined the streets to welcome the People's Liberation Army and celebrate the city's liberation. The People's Liberation Army of China marched neatly into the inner city under the watch of Shanghai citizens.

III. Conclusion

At the ceremony celebrating the 100th anniversary of the CPC, Xi Jinping said:

"A hundred years ago, the pioneers of Communism in China established the CPC

and developed the great founding spirit of the party, which is comprised of the following principles: upholding truth and ideals, staying true to our original and founding purpose, fighting bravely without fear of sacrifice, and remaining loyal to the Party and faithful to the people. This spirit is the Party's source of strength."

As the birthplace and cradle of the Party, Shanghai has a deeper connection with the pioneering spirit and the cause of the CPC, having witnessed both its arduous and extraordinary struggles and its commitment to the people. This connection has become the spiritual wealth of Shanghai to continue its great journey, further improve itself as a People's City, set an example in China, and display to the outside world the bright prospect of Chinese modernization. The spiritual wealth is manifest in three facts.

The CPC was born for the people, and is successful because of the people. Since its birth, the CPC has followed its mission of creating happiness for Chinese people and rejuvenating the Chinese nation. At the First National Congress of the CPC, there were only 58 CPC members, of whom 22 were from landlord and bureaucrat families, 17 from intellectual families, one from a merchant family, and one from a rich peasant family. They were by no means people who were hungry for food or clothing. Instead, most of their families were in relatively good condition. The reason why they proactively participated in the revolution was to save the Chinese nation from danger, and to save the Chinese people from painful suffering. The fundamental reason why the CPC has been able to survive, continuously winning the support of the people, and progressing steadily in the course of modernization was that it has always worked towards its original and ultimate goal: letting people become real masters of the country in order to live a happy life.

The CPC has always followed its unbending revolutionary spirit. Now, there is a need to overcome difficulties under the guidance of this revolutionary spirit to turn ideals into reality. Throughout its history, the CPC has faced formidable and unimaginable risks and challenges, but it has risen to all of them to safeguard the interests of the people and the safety and prosperity of the nation, daring to fight and sacrifice. Ultimately, it has achieved a great victory. According to statistics, from the founding of the Party in July 1921 to the

founding of the People's Republic of China on October 1, 1949, more than 3.7 million revolutionaries died whose names could be identified. This meant that during these years, at least an average of 370 CPC members lost their life per day. No political party could always be correct. The CPC is no exception, but it is brave enough to complete self-revolution, admit its problems, analyze the root causes, and resolutely correct mistakes. In this way, the CPC has stayed upon the course of development and progress.

The CPC has acquired a strong leadership and governance capabilities. The secret behind the CPC's success in uniting so many people in such a big country with one of the largest populations, the longest history and the greatest cultural diversity to create military miracles and an economic miracle of rapid development and long-term stability lies in its strong leadership and governance power. As Joseph Nye, a Harvard University professor, said in an interview with the Global Times, the strong leadership of the CPC accounts very much for China's huge achievements so far. In the future, the CPC will continue to lead China, a large country which has shaken off poverty but has limited resources for the largest population in the world, to march towards a great modern socialist country. In the process, the Party must solve difficult and unimaginable problems at home and abroad. However, the Party's exceptional leadership and governance capabilities make it possible for China to cope with any challenges.

China's largest economic center and the forefront of reform and opening-up

I. Introduction

Each country has at least one economic center, which serves as a locomotive for the overall development of the country. Based on its unique modern history and cultural heritage, Shanghai has become such a place for China.

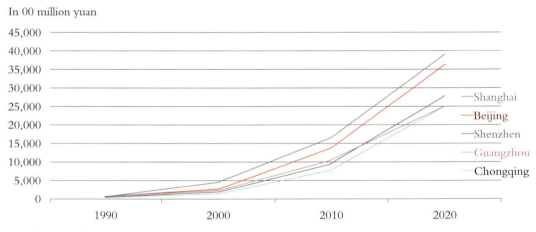

Figure 3   GDP growth trends of top Chinese cities
Source: Chinese National Bureau of Statistics.

Although it is not the richest city in the world, Shanghai is a commercial and economic center of Asia, a global innovation and financial center, a national commerce, transportation, and trade center, and the Port of Shanghai is the world's busiest container

port. Shanghai also ranks high in terms of urban functionality and core competitiveness globally. According to the 2021 Global Power City Index (GPCI) issued by Kearney, Shanghai has raised its overall ranking by 10 places from 2018 to No. 10 in the world. The 2021 GPCI published by the Mori Memorial Foundation of Japan puts Shanghai in the 10th place, up 16 places from 2018.

Shanghai's GDP has increased from over 3 billion yuan in the early years of the People's Republic of China to over 4,460 billion yuan in 2022, the highest among all major Chinese cities. Moreover, it contributes nearly one tenth of China's total tax revenues with less than one thousandth of the country's land. To understand why Shanghai has remained the largest economic center in China, it is necessary to delve deeper into China's history of reform and opening-up since 1978.

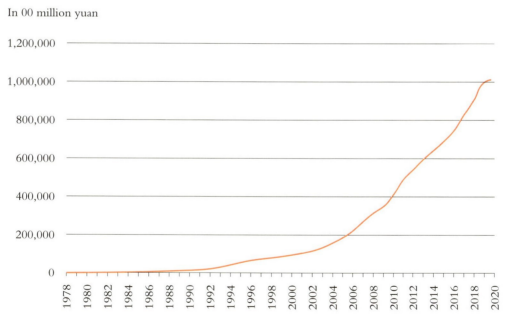

In 00 million yuan

Figure 4　China's GDP growth since reform and opening-up
Source: Chinese National Bureau of Statistics.

Reform and opening-up has enabled China to shake off poverty and move towards prosperity and modernization over the past four decades. China has risen from being a poor

country before reform and opening-up when its per capita national income was less than USD 300 to the world's second largest economy today with a per capita national income exceeding USD 9,000. During these decades, it has lifted over 800 million people out of poverty[①]. Without reform and opening-up, China could not have become so strong as it is today, and there would not have been such a modern city as Shanghai. It is China's process of reform and opening-up that has made Shanghai a central city in the Asia Pacific region once again.

So, how could China's reform and opening-up policy achieve such a huge success? To answer this question, we can take a closer look at Shanghai, a city which has remained at the forefront of China's reform and opening-up. Shanghai has played an important role in China's reform and opening-up, and as China deepens its reform and opening-up policy, Shanghai has found a new role. As the spearhead of China's reform and opening-up, a pioneer of innovative development, and a pilot area for socialist modernization, Shanghai has gained itself a new mission in China's forward-looking drive, and will make greater contributions to China's modernization.

II. History and achievement of Pudong's development and opening-up

Let's zoom in and focus on Pudong on the east bank of the Huangpu River. The development and opening-up of Pudong is a typical case of China's grand reform and opening-up program, so it can be examined to find out China's considerations in terms of steps, strategies, goals, and outcomes.

---

① The Ministry of Finance, the Development Research Center of the State Council, and the World Bank. Forty Years of Poverty Reduction in China: Driving Forces, Reference Significance, and Future Policy Directions [EB/OL]. https://www.cikd.org/ms/file/getimage/1516697201483554817.

1. Pudong: An important choice after ten years

In fact, the development of Pudong did not begin as soon as China started its reform and opening-up program, but ten years later. In August 1980, China approved the establishment of Special Economic Zones in Shenzhen, Zhuhai, Shantou, and Xiamen. In May 1984, the central government decided to open up 14 coastal port cities such as Dalian, as well as Hainan Island, to the outside world. In April 1988, it approved the establishment of the Hainan Special Economic Zone. These moves resulted in rapid economic and social development in the coastal areas. During this period, Shanghai did not appear on the list of reform and opening-up as the policy had a clear experimental character, and Shanghai was extremely important in China's national economy. The stability of Shanghai's economy determined the stability and development of the national economy. In 1989, the total industrial output value of Shanghai was 151.5 billion yuan, 6.9% of China's total, and its fiscal revenues were 29.7 billion yuan, 10.2% of the national total. The city was active in almost all industrial sectors. While its economic growth remained lower than the national average throughout the 1980s, Shanghai still accounted for one sixth of the country's annual fiscal revenues, ranking first in contribution to the national treasury. In the first decade of reform and opening-up, Shanghai provided strong financial, human resources, and material support for other regions of China. So, when it came to Shanghai's participation in reform and opening-up, China had to be cautious.

By the 1990s, there was a significant gap between Shanghai and the advanced surrounding areas. Outdated infrastructure, weakened technological development, and an inappropriate industrial mix had become obstacles to Shanghai's development. After ten years of exploration, other regions of China had achieved exciting development through reform and opening-up, and it was time to implement the same policy in Shanghai, once the largest economic center of China.

In 1990, Pudong's development and opening-up plan was discussed and finally approved. Early that year, Deng Xiaoping, who had just retired as a state leader, took a trip

to Shanghai. After hearing reports from the local leaders, he turned his eyes to Pudong, which was on the other side of the Huangpu River. On his recommendation, the Central Committee of the CPC and the State Council, after thorough investigation and deliberation, officially approved the development and opening-up plan of Pudong in April 1990. Pudong's moment in the sun had finally begun. Shanghai, unwilling to lag behind, finally seized the historic opportunity in the last decade of the 20th century and rushed to the forefront of China's reform and opening-up.

2. Gradually advancing reform and opening-up

Table 1　Milestones of Pudong's development and opening-up

✧ 1990: The first financial and trade zone, export processing area, bonded area, and stock exchange of China were established.
✧ 1992: The first foreign-invested insurance company opened. In the same year, the first joint-venture logistics company was established.
✧ 1993: The innovative development model of investing land use rights in developers was first implemented. In the same year, the first bonded trading market was established.
✧ 1995: The first foreign-funded bank of China was established. In the same year, the first joint-venture retail enterprise opened.
✧ 1996: Pudong became the first pilot area that allowed foreign-owned financial institutions to engage in RMB business.
✧ 2001: Pudong held overseas job fairs in the United States and Europe to attract high-caliber talent with a global outlook.
✧ 2005: Pudong became the first pilot area to transform government functions and shift China's economic mode.
✧ 2007: China's first financial judiciary institution, Shanghai Court of Financial Arbitration, was established.
✧ 2013: China (Shanghai) Pilot Free Trade Zone and the first cross-border trade e-commerce platform were established.
✧ 2014: The first independent Intellectual Property Office was established.
✧ 2015: The first comprehensive national science center was established.

> ✧ 2017: The first Administration of Overseas Talent in China was established.
>
> ✧ 2019: Lingang Special Area of China (Shanghai) Pilot Free Trade Zone (SFTZ) was established.
>
> ✧ 2020: Pudong was chosen to be the vanguard of reform and opening-up at a higher level and China's socialist modernization.
>
> …

Pudong's development and opening-up over the past 30 years can be divided into three stages. [1] In the first stage (1990-2000), Pudong completed a high-standard master plan and urban infrastructure construction. The master plan allowed Pudong to develop in a holistic and scientific way, and a rather complete system of infrastructure ensured the fast modernization of Pudong. To improve the layout of urban functions and industrial sectors, Pudong also launched a series of new reform measures, including land leasing and rental to enterprises, two-stage land development, the establishment of State-owned development companies and industrial parks, and other measures that aimed at promoting the transformation of government roles in economic development, attracting and utilizing foreign capital, introducing advanced technologies and management models from the outside world. It was during this period that Pudong's reform and opening-up created a new development momentum and golden opportunities for Shanghai, and secured a leading position for the city in China's upward trajectory.

In the second stage (2001-2012), utilizing China's accession to the World Trade Organization (WTO) and Expo 2010, Pudong established a set of economic regulations with advanced international standards and created an international institutional environment to attract overseas market entities and align with global market systems. During this period, Pudong worked to implement the strategy of "Focus on Zhangjiang" and build the financial center, shifting the focus of development and opening-up from goods production

---

① Shi Liangping et al. Research on 40 Years of Reform and Opening-Up in Shanghai (Volume 4)[M]. Shanghai People's Publishing House, 2018, p.32.

and processing to services in fields such as finance and insurance, information services, and meetings, incentives, conferences, and exhibitions (MICE). Meanwhile, it promoted further opening up in areas such as international leasing, shipping, international commodity displays, modern logistics, and legal services. This shift resulted in the influx of regional headquarters of world-leading multinational corporations, R&D centers, foreign-owned financial institutions, and professional intermediary agencies. Pudong also took the lead in implementing comprehensive reforms, which shifted the power driving Pudong's development and opening-up from policy incentives and investment to institutional innovation and more advanced opening-up.

In the third stage (from 2013 to present), China (Shanghai) Pilot Free Trade Zone (SFTZ) was established in Pudong, which has remained the first choice for the nation to try innovative policies of reform and opening-up. During this period, as the vanguard of reform and opening-up of China, Pudong has served as a "window" for the world to look into Shanghai and China, as SFTZ represents the country's highest degree of openness. SFTZ not only accommodates international business operations, cross-border financial services, cutting-edge technology research and development, and cross-border trade in services, but also supports the development of an open economy and regional industrial upgrading. More importantly, the establishment of SFTZ has paved the way for the development of advanced manufacturing and new industrial chains, such as artificial intelligence, integrated circuits, industrial Internet, and alternative fuel vehicles. The fast growth of IC and alternative fuel vehicles is a clear manifestation that Lingang Special Area of SFTZ is injecting new momentum into China's economic development.

3. Hard-won achievements of Pudong's reform and opening-up

Pudong is the epitome of China's reform and opening-up. It has created many "firsts" for the country, led the transformation of China's economic system, and stood for a higher-standard opening-up to the outside world. It has always been the first choice to try out innovative policies that have not been institutionalized in other parts of China, and that

has given Pudong a certain level of autonomy. For example, to cope with China's regional, industrial, operational and other restrictions on foreign investment, Pudong was the first area in the country to establish Sino-foreign joint-venture international trade companies and allow foreign-owned banks to operate RMB businesses. These bold moves transformed the original development model of Pudong which was relatively closed. However, as the vanguard of China's reform and opening-up, Pudong has not directly depended on policy and institutional support from the central government, but scored these achievements through its own institutional innovations and explorations. On the other hand, the achievements Pudong scored through its own trials have delivered a strong support for the development and opening-up of Shanghai and China.

Moving from one-way policy-oriented opening-up to two-way institution-oriented opening-up, Pudong's ongoing development and opening-up has proven the feasibility of embedding institutional innovation in opening-up to the outside world, which is indeed a suitable way to achieve sustained development. The formulation and implementation of new rules, regulations and standards have ensured that Pudong's reform and opening-up practices are sustainable and can be emulated and promoted in other regions. Since it was established in Pudong, SFTZ has resorted to institutional innovation, committed itself to the highest standards, and managed to make changes in investment, trade, finance, in-process and ex-post supervision. It has also taken the lead in making major institutional innovations to align with international practices, such as the Negative List for foreign investment, the unified service platform for international trade, free trade accounts, and separation of operating permits and business licensing. Altogether 328 institutional innovations, tried and proved effective in Pudong, have been replicated and promoted nationwide.

Pudong's development and opening-up measures and policies have been designed and implemented from the global perspective. Since it began as a national strategy, Pudong's development and opening-up has attracted extensive attention nationwide and even globally. Shanghai follows the guideline of "developing Pudong, revitalizing Shanghai, serving the whole country, and facing the world", which means that Pudong's

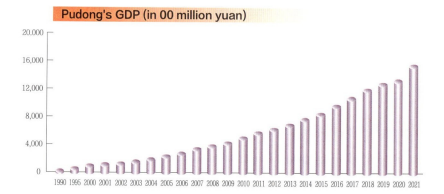

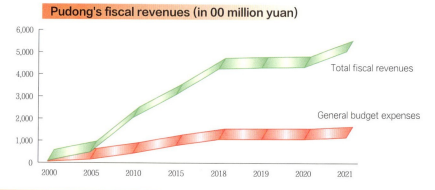

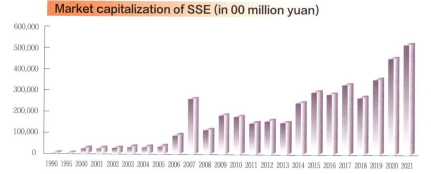

Figure 5   Achievements of Pudong's development and opening-up—Changes in Pudong's GDP, total fiscal revenues, container throughput, and market capitalization of Shanghai Stock Exchange from 1990 to 2022

Source: Pudong New Area Statistical Yearbook 2022.

development and opening-up would be world-class, and Pudong will integrate into the economic development process of the world, especially the Asia Pacific region. Over the past 30 years, Pudong has attracted over USD 100 billion in foreign investment; more than 30,000 foreign enterprises and more than 370 regional headquarters of multinational companies have settled in Pudong; over 600 ports around the world have been connected to Pudong via sea routes; and 13 countries and regions have established over 100 asset management companies here.

It is commonly acknowledged that changing existing mechanisms and systems involves huge challenges, and opening up to the outside world means exposure to risks of the international market which may disrupt the development and stability of the domestic market. In this sense, the success of Pudong's development and opening-up has depended on the determination of politicians who dare to take risks and pursue ambitious goals, as well as millions of people who have contributed their enthusiasm, wisdom, strength and solutions to advance Pudong's reform and opening-up. So, in the course of these policies, Shanghai has always attached importance to the cultivation of leaders and attraction of high-caliber talent.

As the figure above shows, the achievements of Pudong over the past thirty years are phenomenal, which proves that this path to modernization is the correct one. Nowadays, through pioneering efforts, commitment to openness, and integrated innovation, Pudong's development has been accelerated: Pudong's GDP is now 265 times higher than in 1990; over 90% of the 450 pilot plans have been completed; and over 300 outcomes of reform and 51 "Pudong Practices" have been replicated and promoted nationwide.

Through the development and opening-up of Pudong, China's reform and opening-up has risen to a higher level. Pudong has played an exemplary role in China's further reform and opening-up. It has influenced the Yangtze River Delta and even the entire Yangtze River basin. By accelerating the construction of international finance, trade, and shipping centers, Pudong has also helped accelerate the global flow of factors such as capital, technology, information, talent, and goods, making the rapid development of China's

economy possible.

Now, China has entered a new stage of development, and the complexity, sensitivity, and difficulty of reform are no less than 40 years ago. This requires Pudong and even the entire city of Shanghai to continue and even scale up efforts to promote and deepen reform and opening-up in a comprehensive manner. In 2020, on the occasion of celebrating the 30th anniversary of Pudong's development and opening-up, President Xi Jinping announced that Pudong, as a vanguard of China's high-level reform and opening-up, would be a "pioneering area for socialist modernization". This means the central government will support Pudong in exploring new frontiers of reform, such as efficient collaboration, high-level institutional opening-up, expanding access to global resources, and raising the level of urban governance. This has strategic relevance for the high-quality development of Shanghai and the integrated high-quality development of the Yangtze River Delta, and even for China's socialist modernization.

III. Conclusion

Pudong's development and opening-up follows the general rule of modernization, and Pudong has made bold attempts in many areas such as industrialization, urbanization, marketization, informatization, law-based governance, and internationalization. However, in order to realize tangible changes through these moves so that China and Shanghai can not only accumulate material and spiritual wealth, but also get closer to the ultimate goal of modernization, we need to adapt the general rule of modernization to specific local circumstances. Directly copying others' modernization mode or depending too much on others' modernization experience has a high cost.

Over the past 40 years, China has accumulated a wealth of experience in modernization. First, it is necessary to carry out experimental reform and progressive development. Reform and opening-up is a critical step on this path, but the Chinese experience is that some key areas would be selected to try the exploration first. Again, when selecting pilot areas,

multiple factors should be considered. A pilot area must have a high demonstration value, reforms must advance gradually and steadily, and social cohesion must be maintained. The country must not open up too rashly or open too wide, or otherwise economic collapse and social chaos could occur. Reform should start in a few areas under the framework of the original system where targets are more easily attainable, changes cause smaller shocks, and reform has lower costs and high returns, and then any positive outcomes should be scaled up in more regions and fields for further testing and exploration. Major reform measures and projects must have precautionary backups to prepare for any unforeseen situations and ensure the continuity of reform and opening-up. [1]

Second, it is important properly handle the relationship between reform, development, and stability, and to use reform to drive opening-up while using opening-up to fuel reform. Development is the end, reform is the means, and stability provides safeguards for both. The traditional development models of some countries and regions, imitations of the Western model, have posed restrictions on economic and social development. Under the old framework, modernization has always been restricted by the original interest pattern and multinational interest groups, making it difficult for everyone to benefit from development equally. To address this issue, when opening-up fuels reform, the original interest pattern would be changed, and interest groups would seek new sources of interest or motive of economic development, which would drive countries and regions to transform their economic and social development model while maintaining relative stability.

Third, new initiatives should be replicable and expandable. Pudong provides a very good example. Although the reform measures implemented in Pudong are mostly unprecedented, its successful measures and practices can be used to drive development in other regions. For example, Pudong's successful practice of building bonded areas, SFTZ, and the financial center has been replicated and promoted nationwide, and its exploration

---

[1] Huang Jinping & Gong Siwen (compiled by the Research Office of Party History of the CPC Shanghai Municipal Committee). Tide Surging in the East: Pudong's Development and Opening-up over 30 Years [M]. Shanghai People's Publishing House, 2020, p.96.

has played a crucial role in China's overall reform and opening-up program.

Fourth, open development requires exploring and utilizing one's own advantages, enhancing strengths and consolidating weaknesses. China does not expect every region to be like Pudong of Shanghai. Rather, Pudong has provided an example of activating internal advantages through open development and creating internal drivers for economic development. Meanwhile, the international market is changing, and the degrees and specific steps of opening-up key industries such as finance, foreign trade, shipping and tourism are certainly different. This requires us to effectively handle the relationship between open development and maintaining independence to avoid any internal economic cyclical crisis caused by changes in the external environment, and enhance the sustainability of modernization.

Chapter 2

Innovation and transformation towards high-quality development

The world has met challenges on the path of development. How can productivity be increased? How can problems arising from industrialization and urbanization be solved? Can emerging countries and regions catch up with developed countries on the path of modernization? How can it be done? What is the driving force for, and the roadmap to, modernization? For a long time, countries around the world have been trying to find the answers to these questions. This process is long and tortuous, where Western countries have spent hundreds of years, as well as a lot of money.

Over decades, Shanghai has formed a comprehensive industrial system, then worked to build a modern financial, trade, shipping center, and now is committed to becoming a globally influential science and technology innovation center, which could be described as "condensed" development. By 2021, the industrial added value of Shanghai had exceeded one trillion yuan, putting Shanghai in first place among Chinese cities; its per capita disposable income reached the level of developed economies. The people's sense of gain has kept growing, and its industrial system has kept upgrading through scientific and technological innovation. Shanghai remains at the forefront of China's reform and opening-up thanks to continuous institutional breakthroughs. Today, Shanghai is known for its role

in Yangtze River Delta integration, CIIEs [①], SFTZ, the Science and Technology Innovation Board (the STAR Market), its rapid digital transformation, its super strong soft power, and its status as an international consumption center. These keywords indicate the achievements of Shanghai.

How can so many achievements be made within a few decades? What is the secret of Shanghai's success in terms of strategic transformation? The answer to the above questions is Shanghai's high-quality development.

High-quality development is a precondition for building a modern socialist country in an all-round way and a key step on the Chinese path to modernization. It is, however, not simply measured by the growth rate of GDP. Instead, the key metrics for measuring the quality of development are: innovation, balanced development, green development, openness, and shared benefits. Therefore, the essential steps towards high-quality development include: raising the industrial level, advancing scientific and technological innovation, and achieving green transformation. The Lujiazui Financial City is a microcosm of Shanghai's industrial upgrading and modernization, and an indication of the city's efforts to raise its developmental level. Zhangjiang Science City is another important growth pole of Shanghai and a model for Shanghai's scientific and technological innovation. The transformation of Baowu demonstrates Shanghai's commitment to harmonious coexistence between man and nature.

High-quality development is a key condition for China to achieve its modernization goals, but how to achieve it while enhancing the competitiveness of a country or city is a key question faced by all countries. Shanghai has attached importance to high-quality development and has achieved significant results in economic innovation and transformation, providing an example of high-quality development.

---

① CIIE is hosted by the Ministry of Commerce and the Shanghai Municipal People's Government, and organized by the China International Import Expo Bureau and the National Exhibition and Convention Center (Shanghai). It is the first national-level expo on import in the world.

Upgrading the city's growth through industrial transformation

I. Introduction

Currently, the world is suffering from economic slowdown, and many countries are struggling. In addition, there are huge problems threatening global governance and security, which requires all nations to seek countermeasures. To achieve economic transformation, industry upgrading is a top priority as it entails enhancing emerging industries and their competitiveness and expanding into new frontiers, which is a must for the sustainability of economic development. Therefore, promoting the development of a country or a city through industrial transformation and upgrading has become a globally recognized path. But there are still questions: How to identify key industries for the future? What is the roadmap for emerging industries? How to solve the problems and difficulties encountered during industrial transformation? The key lies in high-quality development.

Over the past several decades, Shanghai has completed several rounds of industrial transformation and upgrading of its urban functionality, each of which has led to a breakthrough in city development. In the 1930s, under the sectoral priority framework of tertiary, secondary and then primary industries, Shanghai emerged as multifunctional economic center that integrated commerce, finance, industry, shipping, and information functions. After the founding of the People's Republic of China and before reform and opening-up, Shanghai shifted its focus from commerce and manufacturing to manufacturing

only, reversing the order of the secondary and tertiary industries. By 1977, the proportion of the tertiary industry had dropped sharply to 19.70%, while the proportion of the secondary industry had risen sharply to 76.80%. Shanghai gradually transformed from a multi-functional economic center into a manufacturing city, becoming the largest comprehensive industrial city in China. After reform and opening-up, Shanghai gave priority again to the services sector and strived to become an international economic center, an international shipping center, an international trade center and an international financial center. In the new era, Shanghai is speeding up and scaling up its efforts to build itself into a modern socialist international metropolis, in which the services sector would play a much more important role. It aims to develop an integrated and innovative services sector, and its modern services industries have gained a strong momentum. Meanwhile, Shanghai has also made efforts to upgrade its manufacturing industry, working to promote advanced manufacturing. As a result, Shanghai's industrial output has increased sharply, and a group of pillar industries and strategic emerging industries have emerged that are capital and technology intensive. A new industrial system has gradually been established which prioritizes the service economy. Now, Shanghai is quickening its pace to build itself into an international economic, financial, trading, shipping and sci-tech innovation center and a socialist modern international metropolis.

What is the secret of Shanghai's high-quality development? Lujiazui Financial City provides a clue to explore this secret.

II. Rise of Lujiazui Financial City

There is a popular folk song in Pudong in the 1960s and 1970s: "There is a muddy road, along the Huangpu River, and then a muddy town, along the muddy road. People walk on the muddy road in muddy clothes." This muddy road was in the Lujiazui area of Pudong. Whenever it rained, there would be flooding in this vicinity. After heavy rainfall, floodwaters would rise to the knee, and it would take a week for the water to subside, which was a real

headache for locals.

The muddy road, which was called Lannidu Road, was a microcosm of Pudong at that time. Lujiazui and the Bund on the west bank of the Huangpu River (Puxi) are separated by a river only, but they were worlds apart due to a huge development gap. At that time, agriculture was the main source of income in Pudong, where industrial growth was slow and there were almost no modern services.

This once muddy area has now morphed into a dazzling world-class financial city. It boasts high economic density and a huge economic aggregate with the highest concentration of financial institutions, the most complete financial service, and the highest density of financial talent in China. It is home to 839 regulatory financial institutions, 13 national financial factor markets and financial infrastructure institutions, over 6,000 domestic and

Lujiazui in former days (Photo by Zheng Xianzhang)

foreign financial service institutions, and more than 300,000 financial service practitioners. In addition, Lujiazui Financial City also contributes half of total commodity sales, 1/3 of paid-in foreign investment and about 1/4 of the total retail sales of consumer goods in Pudong, and 50% of the added value of Shanghai's financial industry.[1] From the central area of the Lujiazui Financial City to eastern areas along Century Avenue lies a "golden corridor" that gathers a large number of financial service companies and corporate headquarters. The economic aggregate of the Financial City has reached 630 billion yuan, or over 20 billion yuan per square kilometer. It is home to more than 110 buildings each contributing tax revenues over 100 million yuan, including the first building in Shanghai contributing over 10 billion yuan. There is a saying in the financial industry: "Every building in Lujiazui is a standing financial street."

Nowadays, Lujiazui is home to a large number of multinational companies. Offering a very good business environment, Lujiazui has attracted over 340 Fortune Global 500 companies to set up branches and 138 multinationals to set up regional headquarters. Three quarters of these multinationals have a global presence, and over 80 have set up multifunctional headquarters engaged in management, trade, R&D, investment, and settlement. Shanghai ranks first in China in terms of presence of multinationals. The increasingly complete industrial chain, in turn, has made Lujiazui the first choice for domestic and foreign entities to settle in Shanghai.

Lujiazui now has a strong influence on, and is driving the development of, the surrounding areas, and its future is unlimited. Lujiazui is full of skyscrapers, among which Shanghai Tower, 632 meters high, is the highest in China and the second tallest in the world, with a total floor area of around 580,000 square meters, equivalent to the floor area of all buildings in the first row along the old Bund. It is called the "standing Bund" and a vertical "financial street". Every year, high-ranking officials of governments and regulators, leaders

---

[1] The Changes of the First Financial and Trade Zone in China [EB/OL]. Pudong Civilization Network, http://sh.wenming.cn/pudong/pd_yw/201809/t20180918_4833823.htm.

of the global financial community, and leading international experts and scholars gather at the Lujiazui Forum to share their expertise and insights about financial and economic development. People, logistics, capital, and information congregate in Lujiazui to generate and capture the "wealth effect". At night, the skyscrapers in Lujiazui are brightly lit and glittering, complementing the dazzling Bund on the opposite side of the Huangpu River. This area has become an economic landmark of Shanghai, showing people the city's past, present, and future.

1. Future of Shanghai that has risen out of the mud

The phenomenal development of Lujiazui Financial City has amazed the world. Back in the 1990s, however, Pudong was just a farming area while Shanghai was trying to map out its path to the future. Where should it go? What was the driving force?

In fact, in the 1930s, Shanghai was already the largest financial center in China. In 1935, out of the 164 banks in China, 58 were based in Shanghai, or 35% of the total. These banks were all large national banks, and their aggregate deposits were at least half of the country's total. According to historical records, the total assets of banks based in Shanghai in 1933 amounted to 3.3 billion yuan, 89% of the total in China. Meanwhile, of all the 29 foreign banks in China, 27 had set up branches in Shanghai. In a sense, Shanghai had become the most famous city in the Far East because it had a highly developed financial and trading system. The opportunity to revive the city's prosperity came in 1990 when the Central Committee of the CPC and the State Council made a major strategic decision to develop and open up Pudong. At the same time, the State Council approved the establishment of China's first and only national-level financial and trading zone in China, Lujiazui Finance and Trade Zone, with an area of 31.78 square kilometers, in which the central area called Xiaolujiazui is 1.7 square kilometers.

On the morning of February 18, 1991, then State leader of China Deng Xiaoping enthusiastically went up to the revolving restaurant on the 41st floor of the New Jinjiang Hotel, which was the tallest revolving restaurant in Shanghai at that time. The sky outside

the window was clear and the sun was shining brightly. He looked at the central area of Shanghai through the wide and bright window, and said to people around him, "Shanghai has come late. We must work hard from now on!" On the wall of the revolving restaurant hung two large maps: one was the map of Shanghai, and the other the map of Pudong New Area, beside which was a sand table showing the blueprint of Pudong's future development. As a team follower recalled, Deng Xiaoping said at that time,

"Finance is very important, because it is the core of modern economy. A thriving finance sector is essential to the national economy. Shanghai was once a financial center where currency exchange was convenient, and things will be like that in the future. To become a real member of the global financial community, Shanghai is our first choice. It may take many years, but we must act right now."

The development of Lujiazui, however, didn't get off to a very good start, as many institutions were reluctant to come. So to speak, people still "preferred a bed in Puxi to a room in Pudong." The Shanghai Branch of the People's Bank of China took the bold move to come first and was followed by many foreign financial institutions formerly located in Puxi. After obtaining the RMB license, they crossed the Huangpu River and moved into Lujiazui. In 1995, the first foreign bank, Fuji Bank's Shanghai Branch, opened in Lujiazui, and then Mitsubishi Bank, Standard Chartered Bank, HSBC, and Citibank followed. In 1997, the Shanghai Stock Exchange was established here, and in 1999, the Shanghai Futures Exchange was also born here. After the arrival of a great many commercial financial institutions such as Industrial and Commercial Bank of China, China Construction Bank, Agricultural Bank of China, and China Development Bank, the Lujiazui Finance and Trade Zone took shape with a complete range of financial functions. The most basic service of exchanging RMB for US dollars may have taken an hour previously, but now bank clerks can easily complete it with a few clicks.

2. A place of miracles

In the early 2000s, the development of the Lujiazui Financial City sped up, scoring

many "firsts". In 2000, the first diamond exchange was established in Lujiazui; in 2001, the first joint-venture fund company was established in Lujiazui; in 2006, China Financial Futures Exchange was established in Lujiazui; and in 2007, the first financial judiciary institution was established in Lujiazui. Lujiazui Finance and Trade Zone preliminarily formed a "3+2" modern service industry system, and its modern financial market system embracing securities, commodity futures and financial futures became increasingly mature. At the same time, Shanghai emerged as China's financial market center.

The position of Lujiazui Finance and Trade Zone in China's development continued to rise. In 2009, the State Council issued Opinions on Accelerating the Development of Modern Services and Advanced Manufacturing in Shanghai and Building an International Financial

Today's Lujiazui

Center and an International Shipping Center, beginning the initiative to build finance and shipping centers in Lujiazui Finance and Trade Zone. In April 2015, SFTZ expanded to include an area of 24.33 square kilometers of Lujiazui Finance and Trade Zone. Lujiazui thus became a test ground for the new reform and opening-up of China's financial sector. In August 2016, the Lujiazui Financial City was officially established, along with the opening of the Lujiazui Financial City Council and the Lujiazui Financial City Development Bureau, forming the first co-governance framework in China involving industry and regulators.

At the same time, the modern services sector in Lujiazui continued to improve, becoming more and more complete. In 2015, the first law office jointly operated by a Chinese and a foreign law firm (Baker & McKenzie and FenXun Partners) in China opened in Lujiazui. In 2017, China's first joint-venture fully-licensed securities firm established under Closer Economic Partnership Arrangement (CEPA), Shengang Securities, opened in Lujiazui. In the same year, PwC Business Skills Training (Shanghai) Co., Ltd, the first wholly foreign-owned vocational school in China, was registered in Lujiazui. In 2018, China launched crude oil futures in Lujiazui, the first futures variety on the Chinese mainland open to overseas investment. In 2017, Lujiazui replaced Hong Kong as the global RMB asset pricing center, and its international influence continued to increase. In August 2021, the 14th Five-Year Plan for Economic and Social Development for SFTZ in Lujiazu was released, announcing the new journey towards high- quality development in Shanghai. Shanghai will continue to aim at a high level of openness and create values for the world, pursuing a path towards high-quality development driven by its unique industry mix.

3. Shanghai's path of high-quality development

The rise of Lujiazui Financial City is a microcosm of Shanghai's endeavors to achieve high-quality development through industrial upgrading. In the early years of the People's Republic of China, there was an urgent need to quickly establish an independent industrial system and transform from an agricultural land to an industrialized country. Shanghai bravely shouldered this heavy task and worked to transform itself into an industrial city

by building a modern industrial system. To this end, Shanghai reduced the proportion of the textile industry in its sector mix and improved the capacity and quality of industrial production. Through relentless innovation and at the same time building on its industrial strength, Shanghai rapidly regained its position as China's largest industrial city and became China's biggest contributor of fiscal revenues. In 1980 at the beginning of China's reform and opening-up, Shanghai accounted for as much as 12% of China's total industrial added value and had a monopolistic position in more than a dozen industrial sectors. At that time, the "four big things" that Chinese people would buy when getting married were all "Made in Shanghai", including: a "Shanghai watch", a "Forever bicycle", a "Butterfly sewing machine" and a "Red Lantern radio". At that time, goods made in Shanghai stood for quality and fashion, and were sought after by people nationwide. The rapid growth of its manufacturing sector laid a solid foundation for its urban development and injected impetus into the economic development of China.

In the 1990s, Shanghai met with bottlenecks in its urban development, and could only go further through continued innovation. As Pudong opened up and sped up its development, Shanghai adjusted sectoral priorities in economic development and urban governance. The "2+3+1" sectoral pattern (first secondary, then tertiary and last primary) was changed to a "3+2+1" pattern (first tertiary, then secondary and last primary), while the urban spatial layout was also adjusted to give more space to the tertiary sector instead of the secondary sector. In this way, Shanghai had intended to rebuild itself as a multifunctional city. In 2001, the State Council approved the Shanghai Urban Master Plan (1999-2020), which specified the strategic goals and tasks assigned by the central government to Shanghai. According to this document, Shanghai would become an international economic center, an international metropolis boasting economic prosperity, a diverse and prosperous culture, a clean and beautiful environment, and one of the foremost international economic, financial, trade, and shipping centers in the world. After this grand program began to be implemented, Shanghai's tertiary industry began to develop rapidly, with the proportion of the services sector continuously increasing. In 2022, the added value of the tertiary industry reached

74.1% in Shanghai. The services sector became predominant in this city, which was once the manufacturing hub of China.

In the new era, Shanghai continues to improve its core competitiveness and international influence, accelerating the construction of a modern socialist international metropolis. On the basis of the construction of the "Four Centers (international economic, financial, trading, and shipping center)", it has proposed to build a sci-tech innovation center with global influence. It continues to update its industrial development plan, putting increasing value on high-quality development, sci-tech innovation, and environmental protection. Shanghai has identified four major areas of development: green and low-carbon, Metaverse, digital economy, and smart terminals, and picked six future directions: photonic chips, gene and cell technology, brain-inspired intelligence, new marine economy, hydrogen energy generation and energy storage, and 6G mobile telecommunication. In recent years, China has launched a series of "pillar products" and "cutting-edge products", which are important innovations in key strategic areas. The best-known examples are: Jiaolong, China's first manned deep-sea submersible, Tiangong space station, the BeiDou Navigation Satellite System, the quantum science satellite Mozi, and the soaring large airliner. Shanghai is behind all these important technological breakthroughs. Shanghai is also known for many other original innovations such as new medicine, computer chips, ultra-intense and ultra-short lasers, and intelligent connected vehicles. All this proves that Shanghai is one of the major innovative cities in the world.

III. Conclusion

The Chinese path to modernization requires high-quality development and industrial transformation. The experience of Shanghai provides a clear answer to how to promote the high-quality development of a city.

A clear development plan and accurate urban positioning are prerequisites of high-quality development. Unlike many other modern cities in the world which have often

shaped their own urban characteristics gradually during development, Shanghai, before each major transformation, has developed clear development goals, and then, with the support of the national and local policies, worked to achieve these goals and complete its desired transformation. Not only Shanghai, but also many other parts of China have also proven the effectiveness of advanced development planning. The secret of China's rapid and steady modernization is that it has set clear goals which stand for the right direction of progress.

Industrial restructuring, or prioritizing some industries, is a key step for achieving high-quality development. The need to adjust and upgrade the industrial structure is an important lesson from Shanghai's success in high-quality development. Robust industrial growth is critical to enhance urban governance and achieve development goals. Therefore, industries must be chosen wisely based on the city's development goals. Industrial restructuring will lead to improvement in urban functions, and the improvement of a city's development level will also lead to the enhancement of national competitiveness and influence, which is an important lesson from Chinese modernization.

Proper institutional arrangements would safeguard high-quality development. The Chinese path to modernization is a continual process of changing the relationship between the government and the market, and enhancing the service function of the government to optimize the business environment. It is also a continual process of providing support for and reducing burdens on enterprises, increasing the supply of shared technologies, improving intellectual property rights protection, and reducing taxes and fees. With strong institutional support, obstacles to industrial upgrading and restructuring would be cleared away, and high-quality development could be realized. Providing proper institutional support is another important lesson from Chinese modernization.

Building a modernized industrial system and achieving industrial upgrading are key cornerstones for building a strong modern country. In every round of transformation, Shanghai has been supported by corresponding industry restructuring and sound institutional arrangements. This experience has important implications for the future development of Shanghai.

High-quality development empowered by scientific and technological innovation

I. Introduction

After World War II, out of over 100 middle-income economies, only some have grown into high-income economies, while most developing economies have stopped moving ahead after experiencing a period of rapid growth and then fallen into the "middle-income trap". Looking back at this history, it can be found that the key driving force for long-term economic growth has been industrial upgrading driven by scientific and technological innovation. Now, China has entered a new stage of high-quality development. It is necessary to abandon the old development model and seek new development momentum through scientific and technological innovation to escape the middle-income trap.

In May 2014, during a visit to the city, President Xi Jinping requested that Shanghai should strive to stand at the forefront of the world in technological innovation and lead China in implementing the innovation driven development strategy, and thus accelerate its efforts to build a globally influential technological innovation center. By 2020, Shanghai had completed the basic framework of such a science and technology innovation center, under which a number of national major science and technology infrastructures and multiple platforms for R&D and commercialization had been set up. Three emerging industries (integrated circuits, biomedicine, and artificial intelligence) have developed rapidly. Shanghai has also played a key role in a series of strategic achievements for China including

the C919 large passenger aircraft, quantum computing, the BeiDou Navigation Satellite System, the Tianwen mars mission, the Tianhe space station, the Tianzhou cargo ship, the Chang'e-4 and Chang'e-5 moon landers, and the Endeavor submarine. Now, Shanghai has established itself as one of the major innovation-driven cities in the world. In the latest Global Innovation Index published by the World Intellectual Property Organization, the Shanghai-Suzhou cluster ranks 6th in the world. In the Science Cities 2022 list published by Nature, Shanghai has risen from the 5th place in 2020 to the 3rd spot. In the China Regional Science and Technology Innovation Evaluation Report 2022 by the Chinese Academy of Science and Technology for Development (CASTD), Shanghai continues to rank first in China in comprehensive scientific and technological innovation, and is highly reputed for its technological strength.[1] So, how has Shanghai improved its scientific and technological innovation abilities and thus driven its high-quality development? As a key driver of Shanghai's high-quality development, Zhangjiang Science City shoulders the strategic mission as a core area of the sci-tech innovation center with global influence and a comprehensive national science center. The development of Zhangjiang is in itself a good answer to the above question.

II. Innovations in Zhangjiang Science City

Zhangjiang Science City is in the southeast of Shanghai, at the center of Pudong New Area. In July 1992, Zhangjiang High-tech Park opened and became one of the first national high-tech parks of China. In 1999, Shanghai launched the "Focus on Zhangjiang" strategy (the Zhangjiang strategy), after which Zhangjiang High-tech Park entered a stage of rapid development. In 2017, Zhangjiang was given a new name (Zhangjiang Science City) and two major tasks (becoming the core area of Shanghai as a science and technology innovation

---

① What Progress Was Made in the Construction of the Zhangjiang Comprehensive National Science Center Last Year?[EB/OL]. Shanghai Observer, https://sghexport.shobserver.com/html/baijiahao/2023/01/12/940853.html.

center with global influence and becoming a comprehensive national science center). Through working to realize these goals, Zhangjiang has transformed into a national and even global center for creating new knowledge and technologies. It is now a modern livable urban district and a municipal-level public center for high-level talent and young innovative talent from home and abroad. While growing from a "high-tech park" into a "science city", Zhangjiang has transformed from a "park" into an "urban area". Its aim is to become a world-class science city with strong scientific and technological capabilities, a concentration of sci-tech resources, a sound natural and cultural environment, and a strong momentum of innovation. Over the past years, Zhangjiang has expanded its planned area from 17 square kilometers in July 1992 to 220 square kilometers today, and more importantly it has trail-blazed a path for Shanghai to enhance scientific and technological innovation.

1. Stronger innovation capabilities attained through self-reliance and strength

When a country enters the middle-income stage, it may lose some advantages as labor is no longer cheap in the country, and economic growth relies more and more on technological progress. However, the space for importing external technologies is becoming smaller and smaller, especially in high-tech fields where technological monopoly is common. Therefore, it is necessary to enhance independent innovation capabilities and achieve technological progress through self-improvement.

Basic research is the foundation for sci-tech self-reliance and strength. In recent years, Zhangjiang Science City has strengthened the integration of resources for innovation and thus comprehensively improved its scientific research capabilities. First, as a Comprehensive National Science Center, Zhangjiang has gathered a large group of high- level science and technology innovation institutions, such as Zhangjiang Laboratory, the Tsung-Dao Lee Institute, and the International Human Phenome Institutes (Shanghai), and high-level professional laboratories including Zhangjiang Laboratory of Pharmaceutical Science, and Shanghai Research Center for Quantum Science. Prestigious universities like Fudan

University, Shanghai Jiao Tong University, Tongji University, Zhejiang University, etc. have also accelerated the establishment of their own scientific research facilities in Zhangjiang. Focusing on basic research, Zhangjiang Science City is committed to gathering elites to enhance its capabilities for making breakthroughs in key technologies, or in original research. Second, as an important center for basic research, Zhangjiang Science City is now home to the largest, most diverse, and most comprehensive cluster of photon source and other scientific facilities in China and even in the world. It is well known that scientific apparatuses are critical for growing capabilities for original innovation. Since the dawn of the 21st century, three major breakthroughs in physics, namely the discovery of neutrino oscillation, the Higgs boson and gravitational waves, have been made in large-scale scientific facilities. Before 2016, the Shanghai Synchrotron Radiation Facility was the only scientific apparatus in Shanghai. Since that year, with the support of the central government, Shanghai has built a number of scientific apparatuses, especially a cluster of photon facilities in Zhangjiang Science City, including the Shanghai Synchrotron Radiation Facility (SSRF), hard X-ray, soft X-ray, super-intense ultra-fast lasers, living cell imaging, and the Shenguang laser facility. [1] Shanghai Synchrotron Radiation Facility, the first world-class third-generation synchrotron radiation light source in China, deserves special attention. It is the first ultra intense and super-intense ultra-fast experimental laser facility in the world with a maximum output of 10 petawatts, which was then a new world record. In today's world, synchrotron radiation light sources have become an indispensable tool for scientific research and innovation. They are used by scientists around the world for research into structural biology, physics, and other fields. For example, on November 15, 2019, the BTK inhibitor Zanubrutinib, independently developed by a Chinese company BeiGene, became the first new cancer drug ever developed by a Chinese company and approved for marketing in the United States. They achieved this by using Shanghai Synchrotron Radiation Facility to

---

[1] Li Jiajia & Yu Mei. Zhangjiang Embarks on a "New Journey" with Cutting-edge Facility and Innovation Strategy [EB/OL]. China News Network, http://www.chinanews.com.cn/cj/2022/11- 15/9895147.shtml.

obtain a high-resolution structure of Zanubrutinib and its targeted protein. In addition, there are also protein facilities, translational medicine facilities, seafloor observatory networks, efficient and low-carbon gas turbines, and other scientific and technological infrastructure for research in life sciences, oceans and seas, and energy. For enterprises, instruments and equipment are "heavy assets" that may consume most of the research investment and funding so many small and medium-sized enterprises cannot afford such a heavy investment. To resolve this problem, Zhangjiang implements the sharing of experimental instruments. Small and medium-sized enterprises do not need to build their own experimental facilities or purchase their own instruments and equipment. They only need to visit the website of Shanghai R&D Service Platform, where they can find the information of shared instruments from nearly a thousand scientific facilities, and the main specifications of such instruments are clear at a glance.

The commercialization of outcomes of basic research and development is essential for scientific and technological innovation, and the key step in empowering high-quality development through scientific and technological innovation. In recent years, Shanghai has managed to bring to Zhangjiang a host of emerging industries using cutting-edge technologies, which is a major move to produce breakthroughs in key and core technologies and create new momentum for high-quality development. As a result, companies in three key industries (biomedicine, integrated circuits and artificial intelligence) have made breakthroughs in key technologies in Zhangjiang Science City, registering an annual growth of over 10%. In addition, Zhangjiang Science City has followed new trends closely, proactively cultivating future industries, encouraging competitive enterprises to brave new frontiers such as the digital economy, green and low-carbon industries, Metaverse, and smart terminals. Besides, equal emphasis is put on building scientific capabilities and fostering industrial development, which has long been a key strength of Zhangjiang. The model of "Zhangjiang R&D + Shanghai Manufacturing" has placed Zhangjiang in a better position to support the development of complete industrial chains from R&D to manufacturing. For example, in the field of biomedicine, Shanghai has issued Opinions on

Promoting the High-quality Development of the Biomedical Industry in Shanghai (2021), proposing the implementation of this innovative model and the commercialization of R&D outcomes in Shanghai. Meanwhile, to promote the commercialization of R&D outcomes through manufacturing, Zhangjiang Science City has separated marketing authorization from production authorization, and promoted the model of shared workshops, which enables large-scale production without building new factories. This innovative model has not only saved on investment costs by billions of yuan, but also accelerated the launch of products by more than two years.

2. An open and inclusive city for realizing science and technology dreams

Shanghai is an open and inclusive city that embraces changes and pursues excellence,

Bird's-eye view of Shanghai Synchrotron Radiation Facility Science Center (Photo by Hu Weicheng/ IP SHANGHAI)

and encourages entrepreneurship, rewarding success and tolerating failure. It has formed, in Zhangjiang, a unique culture and ecosystem of innovation. Zhangjiang Science City is very international, whether in terms of its geographical location, legal environment, and people's way of thinking and behavior, allowing innovative entities in different fields to grow in an open and free environment. It has also provided a strong innovative momentum and has become a dreamland for innovative and ambitious enterprises and talent. As entrepreneurs agree,

"Small companies cannot be successful overnight. They need a lot of support, including some technology platforms. Therefore, Zhangjiang is our first choice to settle down because of its abundant talent pool, government support and innovation resources."

Zhangjiang has continued to deepen institutional reforms, strengthened institutional innovation, and formed a reasonable and innovative system, creating an innovation ecosystem like a "tropical rainforest". Having access to the artificial intelligence platforms such as IoT & AI Insider Lab (Microsoft) and Watson Build Artificial Intelligence (AI) Innovation Center (IBM), small and micro enterprises can further improve their technological capabilities.[1]

Let us learn the story of Chen Li, an entrepreneur in Zhangjiang Science City, who spent 10 years developing a new drug. Over the past 10 years, he submitted 148 boxes, over 1,200 volumes, and over 360,000 pages of documentation to regulatory authorities in order to obtain authorization for marketing this new drug. The documentation could fill a standard shipping container. To the surprise of many people, however, his team had completed arduous research and development from a garage in Zhangjiang Science City and had never built any laboratory. Thanks to the open innovation ecosystem of Zhangjiang Science City, Chen Li has developed a new oral drug for diabetes, the world's first, by sharing experimental instruments, sample data, scientific research fellows and production workshops. On September 30, 2022, this new drug was recognized as a Class-I new drug

---

① Huang Haihua. Focusing on "Big Science" and Running at Full Speed[N]. Jiefang Daily, 2022-06-20.

by National Medical Products Administration and approved for marketing. This is not the only team in Zhangjiang that has grown up in the favorable innovation environment of Zhangjiang Science City.[1]

It is widely acknowledged that talent is the first driving force for innovation-driven development. Zhangjiang Science City is an industrial park surrounded by research institutes. In addition to the Tsung-Dao Lee Institute, there are nearly 500 research and development institutions, enterprise technology centers, and public technology service platforms. In recent years, research institutions dedicated to basic research such as Zhangjiang Fudan International Innovation Center, Zhejiang University Shanghai Higher Research Institute, and research universities including Shanghai University of Science and Technology have emerged here. This has laid a solid talent foundation for businesses. In addition, to attract and retain human resources, Zhangjiang Science City has launched a series of talent service measures aimed at outstanding innovative talent.[2]

3. Reforms to improve the institutions and mechanisms for scientific and technological innovation

Institutional arrangements and mechanisms for scientific and technological innovation are prerequisites for achieving scientific and technological innovation results, underlying every step in Zhangjiang's development. Bold reforms have produced remarkable results. While Shanghai is the spearhead of reform and opening-up in China, Zhangjiang has continued to make institutional innovations. For example, Zhangjiang has issued the first permanent residence permit to foreigners, created a licensing mechanism for pharmaceuticals sales and medical device registration, implemented an innovative integrated circuit supervision model, and started a pilot project of issuing visas for foreign talent at the port of entry. Such bold institutional innovations have brought about an amazing "Zhangjiang

---

[1] Liu Shian. Building an Open Innovation Ecosystem in Zhangjiang [N]. People's Daily, 2022-12-09.
[2] Ibid.

speed": Zhangjiang took quick action to land the Yangtze River Delta Center for Drug Evaluation and Inspection of NMPA and the Yangtze River Delta Center for Medical Device Evaluation and Inspection of NMPA in Zhangjiang to facilitate communication in new drug and device evaluation, while building the first intellectual property rights protection center in China, where the time for reviewing and approving invention patents is drastically shortened from 3 years to 3 months. It also established the Zhangjiang Cross-border Science and Technology Innovation Supervision and Service Center where customs clearance for goods is reduced from 2-3 working days to 6-10 hours. In May 2020, the Regulations on Promoting the Construction of Science and Technology Innovation Centers in Shanghai was put into effect. It is the first local legislation safeguarding scientific and technological innovation in China and provides a legal basis for further reforms and innovations in Zhangjiang Science City. In short, the key to the rapid development of Zhangjiang is that it has boldly torn down institutional barriers, which has boosted scientific and technological innovation and industrial development.

Over the past three decades of development, Zhangjiang Science City has followed a path of self-reliance, self-strengthening, openness, inclusiveness, and bold reform. Driven by innovation, it has achieved phenomenal development and injected impetus into Shanghai's high-quality development. Facing the future, Zhangjiang Science City is accelerating its march towards a globally influential sci-tech innovation center, striving to expand the high-standard supply of basic technologies and improving institutional arrangements for scientific and technological innovation to provide strong support for China to achieve greater self-reliance and strength in science and technology.

III. Conclusion

Scientific and technological innovation is the key driving force of Chinese modernization and a common feature of modernized countries. Across human history, there have been three major technological revolutions, each of which has led to a leap

in social productivity and accelerated the process of civilization and modernization. However, the application of key technologies is often restricted, especially in the context of international competition. Facing the opportunities and challenges brought by the current round of scientific and technological revolution and industrial transformation, the CPC regards innovation as the key to high-quality development and the core factor in China's modernization drive. It is believed that self-reliance and self-improvement in science and technology can provide strategic support for national development and China will stay committed to independent innovation. From the "two bombs and one satellite" project, super hybrid rice, BeiDou's Navigation Satellite System, to manned space flight, the history and practices of China in achieving technological progress have fully proven that in key areas of national economy and security, core technologies can only be attained by independent innovation, rather than buying or begging.

China has consistently regarded sci-tech innovation as a crucial driving force in its path towards modernization, and it has accumulated valuable experiences in this regard. Strategically, China adheres to a policy of concentrating its efforts and implementing scientific planning. "Concentrating efforts" refers to the approach of prioritizing national interests as the ultimate goal, mobilizing and allocating all relevant resources across the country, including spiritual willpower and material resources, to tackle cutting-edge areas or nationally significant projects. This approach has played a crucial role in the development of China's scientific and technological endeavors. "Scientific planning" refers to the proactive planning by various levels of government to develop science and technology and set strategic goals, priorities, and related support measures for the advancement of China's scientific and technological pursuits.

In terms of a roadmap, we will provide visible, practical, and tangible technological support for high-quality development by carrying out basic research, to lay a solid foundation for exploring new frontiers and creating new driving forces for industrial development. In terms of methods, we will embrace openness, inclusiveness, and bold reforms, create a sound ecosystem and build an enabling environment for innovation,

and provide institutional support for the generation and industrialization of technological achievements.

Innovation-driven high-quality development is the only way to promote Chinese modernization. At present, great changes unseen in a century are occurring across the world. China is facing tighter constraints on resource availability and greater competition from other countries in technology, talent, and other fields. Only by staying on the path of self-reliance and strength in science and technology can we continue to push back frontiers of development, create new driving forces and advantages, and further promote Chinese modernization.

Green development through high-level protection

I. Introduction

In Lujiazui and Zhangjiang, facing bustling crowds and towering buildings, you will feel the development potential of Shanghai, and be amazed by the agglomeration of capital, the prosperity of industry, the advancement of technology and the power of innovation.

The 2023 China Dragon Boat Open (Shanghai Putuo) and the 19th Shanghai Suzhou Creek City Dragon Boat Invitational (Photo by Wang Jiabin/ IP SHANGHAI)

These, however, are not the sole driving forces for high-quality development in Shanghai. Like many megacities in the world, Shanghai also faces problems such as high population and industry density, limited environmental capacity, and land resource shortage. The key to solving these problems lies in protecting the environment and prioritizing green development. So, how can Shanghai achieve high-quality development and high-level protection simultaneously?

Shanghai is at the estuary of the Yangtze River that, originating from the Qinghai-Tibet Plateau and horizontally crossing the territory of China, flows into the East China Sea. Vertically, there are nine migration routes for migratory birds worldwide, and Shanghai is an important transit point on one of them and a food supply station for those migratory birds that shuttle between the northern and southern hemispheres. Shanghai, at the intersection of a horizontal river and a vertical migration route, has been given the special mission of green development.

More than 100 years ago, China's first officially recorded rowing competition was held on the Huangpu River, and more than 100 years later, in October 2022, the Head of the Shanghai River Regatta took place on the Suzhou Creek. The waves of the Huangpu River and the Suzhou Creek have witnessed the determination and effectiveness of Shanghai's environmental protection. The Huangpu River and the Suzhou Creek are no longer black, foul smelling, or loathsome. Instead, they have become part of a city-wide water network that can be enjoyed by all citizens.

Birds serve as a reliable indicator of a healthy ecological environment. During the rapid urbanization of Shanghai, the local bird community has been greatly impacted. After decades of development, the per capita open space in Shanghai has increased from "one pair of shoes" to "one room", surpassing the level of many international metropolises such as Tokyo. More and more parks and green spaces have been built, providing increased habitats for birds. There are 518 bird species observed that have been recorded in Shanghai, in which water birds account for about two-thirds of the country's total.

Berlin is well known as the capital of wild boars, while Toronto in Canada is called

A bird habitat

the world's raccoon capital. Now, the story of wildlife entering the city is being told in Shanghai: raccoon dogs, which are under second-class protection, have been found in over 260 neighborhoods and open spaces in Shanghai. It is the return of an indigenous species. This story is selected as one of the "100+ Biodiversity Positive Practices and Actions Around the World".

Moving from a resource-saving and environment-friendly society to a "beautiful Shanghai" and then to an eco-city, Shanghai is no longer only satisfied with a blue sky, clear water and green spaces, but pays more attention to whether the environmental quality can positively impact the well-being of citizens, meet the needs of its residents for a better life, and enhance the attractiveness, creativity, and competitiveness of the city. Shanghai is, as always, committed to exploring new paths and measures for green development to achieve

both high-quality development and high-level protection. [①]

II. Combination of high-quality development and high-level protection

Based on research and analysis of similar cities around the world, Shanghai benchmarks itself against the highest standards after identifying its own shortcomings. First, Shanghai still depends on fossil fuels as its major primary energy source, which impedes the improvement of its environment. Second, the industrial grade is not high, and advanced manufacturing is not strong enough to lead the city in the direction of internationalization and globalization.

Shanghai prioritizes accelerating its transition to green development, which is considered as a crucial element for high-quality development. The first step is to enhance governance. Shanghai has completed the renovation of over 4,000 coal-burning facilities, the renewal of pollutant-emitting facilities of over 2,000 enterprises, and the phasing out of over 330,000 "yellow-labeled" high-emission vehicles. The second is to upgrade its industrial system. Baoshan and Jinshan districts, which were once dominated by steel and chemical production, have implemented a strategic transformation and accelerated their march towards ecological civilization. The third is to promote innovation. Steel companies have achieved breakthroughs in green and low-carbon smelting technologies, while power generation companies have continuously set world records for reducing coal consumption in thermal power generation. The fourth is to proactively develop and implement strategies for energy innovation and transformation, with an overall goal to create a hydrogen energy industry with a market size exceeding 100 billion yuan by 2025.

As the world's largest steel conglomerate accounting for half of the world's steel

① A Beautiful Shanghai Characterized by the Harmonious Coexistence of Humans and Nature: Innovative Practices of Ecological Governance in Socialist Modernized International Metropolis[M].Shanghai Academy of Social Sciences Press, 2022, p.7.

production, Baowu faces the challenge of achieving a low-carbon green transformation, which is crucial for the high-quality development in the manufacturing industry. The transformation underlies Shanghai's endeavor to build an eco-friendly city. By reviewing the green transformation of Baowu, we can unravel how a densely populated megacity, with its excellent transportation infrastructure and well-developed industrial sectors, pools both internal and external efforts to become a "green model" that balances high-level protection with high-quality development.

1. Strengthened top-bottom strategic planning to guide the green transformation of enterprises

In 2015, the multilateral negotiations on the Paris Agreement officially began. Shanghai quickly recognized that reducing carbon dioxide emissions would become an irreversible process for human civilizational advancement. Therefore, it issued the Shanghai Work Plan for Coal Reduction and Replacement (2015-2017) and proposed to "control the total coal consumption in the steel industry and gradually reduce its direct combustion and coking coal usage". The Work Plan included a target to "limit Baowu's coal consumption to 13 million tons by 2017". At that time, Baowu had already considered a reduction in carbon dioxide emissions across the steel industry and conducted necessary technological research and development. Due to the constraints of total resource consumption, Baowu also realized that end-of-pipe carbon dioxide treatment was not a fundamental solution. Instead, it needed to address the frontend of traditional smelting processes, prioritizing low-carbon metallurgical technologies to reduce the input of fossil fuels. In 2019, with the support and coordination of the Ministry of Industry and Information Technology and the National Development and Reform Commission, Baowu's first low-carbon metallurgical innovation platform was completed and put into operation, becoming the world's largest experimental facility and open innovation platform for low-carbon smelting. In July 2020, Baowu established the Low-Carbon Metallurgical Innovation Center to carry out basic and applied research on low-carbon metallurgical technologies at the group level.

On September 22, 2020, President Xi Jinping pledged on behalf of China to achieve carbon peaking by 2030 and carbon neutrality by 2060. One year later, on September 22, 2021, China issued Opinions on Completely, Accurately and Comprehensively Implementing the New Development Concept and Doing a Good Job in Carbon Peak and Carbon Neutralization and the Action Plan for Carbon Dioxide Peaking Before 2030, which defined the timetable and road map for carbon peaking and carbon neutrality goals. In July 2022, Shanghai issued the Implementation Plan for Carbon Peaking in Shanghai, highlighting the "Top Ten Actions for Carbon Peaking". As a key initiative of the Implementation Plan, Shanghai then issued its Green and Low-Carbon Regional Action which emphasized the need to support Baowu in carrying out pilot demonstration projects for peaking carbon emissions and achieving carbon neutrality. Subject to stricter carbon emission regulations, downstream manufacturers have accelerated their efforts to mainstream low-carbon products and adjust their procurement strategies, seeking greener steel materials from suppliers in the steel industry. This requires Baowu to provide green and low-carbon products. Failing to undergo a green transformation not only means losing competitive advantages but would also directly undermine the existing development achievements and benefits of the company. As a result, Baowu's approach to green development has undergone a significant change. It now emphasizes the need for low-carbon metallurgy and intelligent manufacturing to achieve green steel production processes, but also a commitment to quality goods to achieve the green utilization of steel products.

1) Green manufacturing: Exploring carbon reduction measures in the Dark Factory

Baosteel, a subsidiary of Baowu, has developed an intelligent manufacturing project that was recognized as a global "lighthouse factory" by the World Economic Forum in 2020, making it a champion of China's steel industry.[1] Only by witnessing the powerful production capabilities of its "Dark Factory", which operates efficiently day and night in

---

① He Xinrong et al. Baosteel's Plant, with a Capacity of Billions of Tons of Steel Production, Stands out for Its Innovative Practices that Can Shatter People's Preconceived Notions about Steel [EB/OL]. News.cn,http://xin-huanet.com/2022-02/16IC_1128381118.htm.

darkness, reminiscent of a sci-fi movie, can one truly feel the charm of the steel industry's shift towards intelligence and automation. This Dark Factory is made possible by several factors, including the transition from manual to unmanned crane operations, the replacement of human labor by robots for 3D (Dangerous, Dirty, and Difficult) jobs, and the utilization of models replacing manual configuration for centrally controlled operations. Within the factory, in autonomous crane areas, two feeding cranes at the top of the workshop can be seen accurately transferring and loading rolls of silver cold rolled steels. The cranes automatically lift the steel rolls onto the saddle, and then automatic strapping robots unpack them and recycle the packaging materials. In the furnace section, there is also a robot that

Baowu's "Dark Factory" running well in darkness (Photo by Liu Jiming/ Baoshan District Information Office × IP SHANGHAI)

can climb tall buildings without fear, which are intelligent inspection robots for monitoring furnaces. Although the factory is pitch dark, at the backend in the Integrated Control Room, three large screens clearly display the operation of machines real time. This smart factory management system, utilizing digitalization, networking, and smart technologies, addresses the drawbacks of previous segmented management, and has achieved seamless management throughout the entire process. Digital transformation has resulted in a 15% decrease in energy consumption per ton of steel produced, a 30% reduction in comprehensive pollutants per ton of steel produced, a 30% and 20% increase respectively in labor efficiency and production capacity, and a 10% reduction in processing costs. Intelligence has become a powerful tool for Baowu to improve quality and efficiency, supporting the company's efforts in carbon emissions reduction.

2) Green products: Rediscovering steel's eco-friendly potential

Traditionally, the term "quality goods" refers to differentiated items like automobiles, silicon steel, and household appliances. However, Baowu now defines them as green products that contribute to carbon reduction in downstream industries and the upgrading of steel application in various sectors of society. For instance, transformers in which Baowu's ultra-low-loss silicon steel replaces energy-consuming ones in China's power supply and distribution system can save 87 billion kilowatt hours of electricity annually, equivalent to the generation capacity of the Three Gorges power station. Owing to the widening utilization of green steel products, steel is becoming an environment-friendly material sought after by the circular economy in the world today and a perpetual resource that can be 100% recycled. Understanding this value of steel, Baowu has opened its arms for technological innovation to support the upgrading of industries such as construction, transportation, and energy. As the world's largest and most influential supplier of automotive steel plates, Baosteel launched the Baosteel Car Body Electric Vehicle (BCB EV), an ultra-lightweight, pure electric and highly secure white vehicle body, on April 9, 2021. BCB EV can reduce carbon dioxide emissions by approximately 200 kilograms during steel plate manufacturing and 950 kilograms during automotive usage.

2. Fostering government-market collaboration to activate the intrinsic drive for green transformation of enterprises

Green development stands for a fundamental shift in the development mode, and a breakthrough in the quality and efficiency of development. Shanghai has successfully embedded industrial system modernization into the construction of an international science and technology innovation center, allowing both the government and the market to play their own roles simultaneously. Basic, pioneering, and strategic tasks are handled by the government, such as establishing research institutes, conducting basic research, and building public research and development platforms. Meanwhile, enterprises are dedicated to applied research to support and advance industry development, and in this process, they receive governmental support in forms of preferential policies, funding, and subsidies.

1) Supporting scientific research to fulfill the carbon-peaking and carbon-neutrality goals

Shanghai pools and directs the resources and efforts of local universities and research institutes by encouraging sci-tech innovation actions and capacity building. It has worked to attract talent, capital and technologies and gather multiple elements of innovation to lay a solid foundation for the green development of Baowu. In 2021, the Sci-Tech Innovation Action Plan to support the carbon peaking and carbon neutrality goals pointed out four directions of technology development: cutting-edge disruptive technologies; technologies of carbon dioxide capture, utilization, and storage (CCUS); alternative-fuel technologies and industries; and low-carbon and zero carbon industrial technologies. This year's Action Plan has seven directions: cutting-edge disruptive technologies; energy systems; construction and transportation industries and regional demonstrative projects; negative emissions technologies; carbon dioxide emissions monitoring technologies; recycling of resources; and demonstrative carbon neutrality technologies. Baowu is expected to leave a mark in the metallurgical history of the world. Its hydrogen-rich carbon cycle blast furnaces will help Baowu achieve the carbon neutrality goal by 2050, which is 10 years ahead of China's deadline for achieving this target. At the end of 2022, Baowu disclosed its latest achievement

in low-carbon metallurgy at the 2022 Global Low Carbon Metallurgy Innovation Forum: the hydrogen-rich carbon cycle oxygen blast furnace, which cuts carbon emissions by 20% and solid fuel consumption by 30%. The new process will reach a commercial scale in 2023.

2) Regarding green development as a new track for high-quality development

Shanghai starts from the demand side, keenly spotting the surging demand for clean energy, low-carbon raw materials, functional materials, efficient processes, terminal electrification, and resource recycling. On the other hand, efforts are made from the supply side, encouraging the development of key technologies and enterprises in five major areas: new technologies, new processes, new materials, new equipment, and new energy. This new track of industrial and product growth depends on the innovation of enterprises, the iterative updating of technologies, and the steady development of the market. In its action plan to support green and low-carbon industrial development, Shanghai has explicitly announced that it would implement mutually enhancing fiscal, financial, investment, land-use and other policies, and provide special funds, such as the special fund for strategic emerging industries, to support breakthroughs in green and low-carbon technologies, industrial development, and the construction of characteristic industry parks.

Using the special fund for emerging industries, Baowu has launched an advanced green and low-carbon development plan. Its Low-carbon Metallurgical Innovation Center, as an open platform, has attracted 62 enterprises and universities from 15 countries. In Baoshan District of Shanghai, Baowu Carbon Neutrality Industrial Park is also under construction. According to Sheng Yumin, vice president of Shanghai Baodi Real Estate, the southern part of the Industrial Park will be a core functional area of green and low-carbon industries, and will be a center of regional headquarters of multinationals, a center for scientific and technological services, a center for innovation incubation, and a center for scientific services. The northern part, which is expected to be completed in the first half of 2023, will focus on the research and development of green and low-carbon metallurgical technologies. An area of 1900 mu (approximately 127 hectares) in the northern part will be given to the manufacturing industry which will commercialize research outcomes in carbon neutrality,

and thus become an industrial base for carbon neutrality.

Seizing the opportunity of international financial center construction and utilizing the agglomeration of financial institutions in Shanghai, Baowu has managed to reduce financial costs and raise industrial funds through green financing, forming a virtuous cycle from local government guidance, fund investment, enterprise development to industry output, which deeply embeds financial innovation into the steel industry. Baowu and the National Green Development Fund Co., Ltd. jointly launched the Baowu Carbon Neutrality Equity Investment Fund in 2021, with a total scale of 50 billion yuan, with the first phase reaching 10 billion yuan. It is the largest carbon-neutrality fund in China and is committed to exploring opportunities to invest in clean energy sources like wind power and photovoltaic power and high-quality carbon-neutrality projects. In 2022, Baosteel issued a corporate bond (Phase I) for its hydrogen-based shaft furnace project on the Shanghai Stock Exchange. With a scale of 500 million yuan, it is the first green low-carbon corporate bond in China.

The speed of the shift to green low-carbon development reflects a city's prospect of high-quality development. Shanghai's early action to push green low-carbon industrial transformation helps it attract enterprises and gather talent and other resources to land complete industrial chains, which together with its geographical advantages, make it a first choice for enterprises. The green transformation of the manufacturing industry and the clustering of emerging industries can save energy, reduce carbon emissions, and drive the transformation of traditional enterprises. Therefore, while improving the local environment, green transformation also drives the upgrading of the regional economy.

III. Conclusion

China attended the first United Nations Conference on the Human Environment in Stockholm in 1972 and has tried proactively to address the climate change crisis immediately after the Paris Agreement was adopted. It is firmly committed to sustainable development, embracing the green, circular and low-carbon economies respectively. China

has always been an important participant and resolute practitioner of global environment governance.

After 50 years of hard work, China has made remarkable achievements in pollution prevention and control to address environment issues. NASA's research indicates that China has led the world in greening the planet, accounting for around one fourth of the newly added green area in the world from 2000 to 2017. A report by Bloomberg News also affirms China's achievements in environment governance, stating that the country has scored the achievements of air pollution control within 7 years that had taken the United States 30 years, and has thereby increased the average life expectancy of Chinese residents by 2 years. Erik Solheim, former Deputy Secretary General of the UN, and former Norwegian Minister of Environment, commented that China has achieved such a success because Chinese people demanded it and after receiving this message, the Chinese leadership has taken very firm actions. "The first and most important thing is the firm determination of China's top leaders to improve environmental governance and their overall planning."

In both scale and speed, China has been the biggest beneficiary of the traditional model of industrialization. However, why does China prioritize environmental protection and green development, and remain so firmly committed to harmonious coexistence between man and nature? It is because the Western model is cursed by the "paradox of modernization". Under the Western model, only a small proportion of the world's population can live a prosperous life, but which may cause a crisis of resources and environment as the scale of modernization expands. Statistics show that in the 300 years since the Industrial Revolution, over 20 countries have completed modernization worldwide, with a total population of about 1 billion. As China has a current population of over 1.4 billion, it is more difficult and complex for the country to modernize. One needs to think twice about whether China can follow the Western path to modernization. With seriously insufficient resources per capita, China will inevitably face more resource and environmental constraints when achieving its goal of becoming a great modern country. Therefore, China cannot follow the old path of Western modernization.

China cannot develop alone, and the world cannot grow healthily without China. Nature and its diverse ecosystems are the cornerstone of a community with a shared future for humankind. People from all over the world should bear the welfare of the Earth in mind. The CPC regards the harmonious coexistence of man and nature as the essential feature of the Chinese modernization. It is mainly reflected in three aspects: first, adhering to the principle that clear waters and green mountains are invaluable assets, and that respecting, adapting to, and protecting nature are the internal requirements of development; second, adhering to environmental protection throughout the course of development and prioritizing ecological protection and green development; and third, adopting a systematic and holistic approach to conserving and improving mountains, waters, forests, farmland, grassland, and desert, encompassing industrial restructuring, pollution control, environmental protection, and response to climate change. These are the lessons that developing countries can learn when they're moving towards modernization.

Chapter 3

People-centrism: Creating a high-quality life

A high-quality life means people's growing expectations for improving their well-being are consistently met, and it is a shared goal of all countries to improve their people's well-being.

What is high-quality life? What is an ideal one? The concept of "quality of life" can be traced back to 1958 when John Kenneth Galbraith referred to it as a totality of "life comfort, convenience, spiritual enjoyment and pleasure." Then there was the book called Social Indicators advancing study on the quality of life from theoretical elaboration to empirical research. At present, many scientific indicators are used to evaluate the quality of life, such as the following: Human Development Index (HDI), Index of Social Progress (ISP), Well-being Index (WBI), Social Development Index (SDI), and OECD Better Life Index. Basic theories and specific indicators proposed show people's increasingly diversified demands for a high-quality life. These international studies have put forward indicators focusing on different aspects. Among them, three are indispensable: spiritual needs, public life, and high-quality livelihood.

Modernization will make high-quality life possible for Chinese people. Shanghai, the largest city in China, stands out as a prime example. It always offers the best resources to its residents, serves people with top-quality supplies and presents the most extensive opportunities for individuals to thrive.

Inheriting the spirit of urban culture, Shanghai is unwaveringly making efforts to create a high-quality life. The city is also intensifying efforts to enrich the cultural life of its citizens based on urban cultural heritage and city memory, answering the call of meeting people's growing needs for a better spiritual and cultural life. With such efforts, the rebirth of Wukang Road can be seen among those revitalized historical blocks and unique urban charm. It vividly demonstrates urban renewal through readable buildings, blocks for leisurely walks, and people-centered city development.

Ensuring sufficient supplies for citizens' well-being is indispensable for Shanghai to create a high-quality life. Shanghai aims to build 15-minute community-life circles and provide better experience of urban public life. These efforts are made to meet people's increasing needs for a life of higher quality and deepen connections between residents and the city. The century-old Xinhua Road, lined with wutong trees (Chinese parasol trees), offers a glimpse into what can be called thriving communities which are perfect for living and working - communities of diversity, convenience and happiness, and a vibrant, open and harmonious society for better lives.

Creating age-friendly communities is a key step toward high-quality life. Shanghai adopts community-based elderly care to support aging-in-place, offering high-quality services living up to expectations of seniors. According to statistics, there is one person aged 60 or above in every three permanent residents in Shanghai. Whether all elderly citizens live a happy and healthy life is important to the whole society. The elderly residents in Lujiazui Subdistrict will tell you how they spend their old age with home-based care services, and their interpersonal relationships in communities.

Continuing the urban culture

I. Introduction

For today's Chinese urban residents, a lifestyle of poetic beauty has become what they keenly pursue, and sometimes it is even an important indicator to measure their quality of life. In recent years, "pursuing poetic beauty and dreams" has become one of the most popular things for people to do during their holidays and other leisure time. This reflects the strong spiritual desire and cultural need of people living in busy modern cities, or "poetic dwelling" in other words. Where can they find the "poetic beauty" they are longing for? Is "escaping the city" and going somewhere far away the only choice? Why not take people's longing for poetic dwelling as a new driving force for urban development? In this sense, they can enjoy poetic beauty in the city they live in, even in their neighborhoods.

In recent years, Shanghai citizens are happy to find that poetic beauty and dreams are no longer some wishful thinking, but something tangible within their reach. 150 top spots are recommended as great places at doorway. These small but beautiful locations provide high-quality public spaces for locals to immerse themselves in an air of poetic elegance. These lovely spots are located in residential quarters, characteristic blocks, factories, and green spaces. Many of them were developed by local governments following policies of protecting and revitalizing old buildings, and have quickly become well-known new cultural landmarks, serving as a source of vitality for Shanghai urban culture in the new era. Nowadays, on weekends and during holidays, Shanghai citizens are increasingly eager to

step out of their homes, explore the city and soak up the historical vibes of old buildings, understand the city's past and present development, and see its unique poetic beauty. That's their way of rediscovering Shanghai. Citizens are amazed that Shanghai is moving forward quickly, but it is becoming more historical, elegant, and people-centric. The metropolis is home to the most advanced facilities and technologies across China, and is known as the country's economic powerhouse. It also serves as a spiritual home for people to relax themselves, keep memories of the old days alive, and experience poetic beauty.

So, how did these changes occur? When you take a walk along Wukang Road, one of the most popular attractions in Shanghai, would you wonder why it has become the first choice for citizens and tourists to experience poetic beauty and is regarded as a place with the most distinctive Shanghai characteristics? How did it gradually grow into what it is today? Let's take a walk on Wukang Road together.

II. An approachable landmark suitable for leisurely walks and featured by people-centered development: Rebirth of Wukang Road in the new era

Buildings, roads, and blocks make up urban landscapes, forming spaces where city life takes place. Within these physical architectural entities are aesthetic symbols, cultural essence, and poetic beauty.

Wukang Road is located at the core of the Hengshan Road-Fuxing Road historic area, the largest protected historic area in downtown Shanghai. Built in 1907, it was originally named Route Ferguson and renamed Wukang Road in 1943. It is a road of culture closely related to brilliant architects, history, and stories, sending vibes of approachable old buildings, and offering glimpses into picturesque historic streets and alleys covered in autumn leaves. This road, less than 2 kilometers long, is lined with buildings from the early 20th century to 1998 featuring diverse styles ranging from French, British, to Spanish and more. That is why it is called the "gallery of pre-modern buildings" of Shanghai. 90 years

ago, the Irish writer George Bernard Shaw praised Wukang Road: "Walking here, people who can't write poems want to write poems, people who don't know how to paint want to paint, people who can't sing want to sing. It's wonderful." It is still true and the beauty of Wukang Road is shared by ever more people.

Wukang Building (once called I.S.S Normandy Apartments) located at the junction of Wukang Road and Huaihai Middle Road

This most elegant and mature Shanghai style has been passed down thanks to the city's efforts to protect historic legacies, especially the protection and repair of old buildings.

1. Respect and treat old buildings as if they were the venerable elderly

The tall wutong trees on Wukang Road have witnessed several rounds of transformation of old houses: At the end of 1986, Shanghai was listed as a National Famous Historical and Cultural City. More than two years later, the municipal government started to compile a list of old houses across the city and finally determined over 2,000 architectural heritage buildings on 632 sites. In 1999, Wukang Road was included in the Hengshan Road-Fuxing Road historic area. At the end of 2003, a renovation project was launched there. And in 2004, the "Plan for the Conservation of the Hengshan Road-Fuxing Road Historic Area" was officially approved, marking the beginning of protecting this historic area in Xuhui District.

In 2007, Wukang Road was selected as the first street for the city's pilot project of heritage preservation which marks a higher level of protective renovation. In the same year, Xi Jinping, then Secretary of the CPC Shanghai Municipal Committee mentioned "old buildings in Shanghai should be treated as if they were the elderly" during his inspection tour in Xuhui District. He ascended to the top floor of Building 1, Ganghui Square. From the top, which was over 220 meters high, he had a panoramic view of Xujiahui, a cultural center in the district. After seeing historic buildings such as the Wukang Building, he showed strong determination to preserve the urban cultural heritage of Shanghai. He said,

"The essential parts of Shanghai's historic legacies are preserved in more than 4,000 old buildings. If they disappear, urban cultural heritage of Shanghai will no longer exist, and the historic legacies and unique charm of Shanghai will be lost. In historic areas, it is crucial to prevent large-scale demolition and construction, and ensure effective preservation of historic legacies."

The concept of valuing and preserving old buildings like caring for the elderly has been deeply ingrained in people's minds, leading to increased efforts to protect Shanghai's urban cultural heritage. This philosophy has been implemented and further developed in

subsequent urban planning and construction. [1]

Thanks to these efforts, hollowed iron doors were removed to display the greeneries behind, and shops failing to meet regulations were cleared away. To match the style of historic legacies, more efforts were made to adjust the materials of windows along the street, the colors of outdoor air conditioning units, specifications of sunshades, store signage styles, and even the crown diameter of each street tree. After renovation, Wukang Road was listed as a national historical and cultural street in 2011, the first street in Shanghai to be given such an honor. [2]

The nameplates have been put on, and mini renovations are still on the way. For example, bicycle parking area lines on the sidewalks are no longer painted in common white color but constructed with interlocking blue and grey concrete bricks. The cobweb of overhead electricity lines surrounding the Wukang Building will be removed and put underground, leaving open space for a clear sky above. "Not sweeping the fallen leaves" does not mean literally, but rather it indicates sweeping in an artful way with fallen leaves displaying an aesthetic beauty. These actions may seem trivial, but the dots can be connected into a line and extended to a surface, adding beauty to Wukang Road while retaining its essence. Other changes have also quietly occurred: Ba Jin's House is open to the public free of charge; every old house along the street has a QR code for visitors to scan and learn the background; Wukang Road attracts literary youth to this venerated spot, offers opportunities to trendsetters and merchants, and provides makers with inspirations everywhere.

2. Safeguard the authentic historic legacies and preserve poetic beauty

To safeguard Shanghai's old buildings, we must preserve the original historic legacies, protect the poetic beauty of Shanghai, and preserve people's memory of the city and love for

---

[1] Hu Jirong. "Preserving historical legacies of Shanghai", Reform and Opening-up Makes Shanghai Renowned [M]. Shanghai People's Publishing House, 2018, p.252.
[2] Wang Yan. Wukang Road Witnessing the Passage of Time, and Old Wutong Trees Showing New Vitality [N]. Wenhui Daily, 2018-04-27.

homeland.

To achieve this goal, a key step is to protect and repair historical buildings. The Wukang Building is an example of efforts to revitalize old buildings on Wukang Road. It stands at the beginning of the intersection of Wukang Road and Huaihai Middle Road. Built in 1924, it embodies the typical French Renaissance style and represents the oldest veranda-style apartment building in Shanghai. This century-old apartment block was designed by Ladislav Hudec, a Hungarian-Slovak architect impressing old Shanghai with his outstanding creativity. The building has attracted many Shanghai celebrities and artists to live there since the 1940s. That is why it has paramount historic value. But what truly makes it well-known to Shanghai citizens and tourists, as well as a popular hit among Shanghai's mostly visited destinations for internet celebrities? The answer lies in its overall renovation project started in 2018.

In April 2018, the 94-year-old Wukang Building was ready for a new round of overall renovation. Gu Zhifeng, the leader of the historic building repair team, recalled this was the most challenging and complex project he had ever participated in. At that time, the Shanghai government made great efforts to revitalize old buildings in response to the call of "restoring authentic style of old buildings". Following these high standards and strict requirements, Gu made "preserving historic value" of these legacies a guiding principle for his repair team.

However, during the operations, the team quickly found that the mere repairing of the fair-faced brick wall of the building's facade would be a demanding task. Their challenges include varying degrees of weathering and a lack of the key material, Mount Taishan brick. After several rounds of experiments, Gu's team finally came up with a new method: combining brick powder repair with a "top-down" approach to restore different degrees of weathering on the exterior walls of Wukang Building and reduce color differences. In this way, it preserved the unique vertical texture on fair-faced brick walls left by the wind and rain erosion over time, imparting refreshing charms to the repaired walls.

The renovation project was supported by the continuous improvement of manufacturing process, as well as worker's conscientiousness, strong sense of responsibility, and

their practical innovation. Gu said techniques used to repair old buildings were based on accumulated experience in the earlier stage, and gradually developed by craftsmen on restoration sites. In his team, project managers and safety officers responsible for "coordinating" the construction were familiar with standards and techniques of building repair. For example, a fair-faced brick wall may have four types of seams, which should be immediately spotted. Red bricks and black bricks are both fair-faced bricks, but they are produced in kilns under different temperatures. This difference should be kept in mind.

In 2021, Shanghai launched the first training base on renovation skills for residential buildings: Xufang Group Training Base (345 Workshop). The workshop enables trainees to refine their skills, transforming "repair workers" into "craftsmen". In this sense, the base ensures stable supply of professionals specialized in preserving historic properties.

How a city treats the past determines its future development. Respecting and treating old buildings as if they were "the elderly" indicates the city's reverence for historic and cultural heritage, and it has a sincere plan for a better future. To revive historical splendor and keep memories of the city, Shanghai fuels efforts to protect and inherit its historical legacies. Now the city has become more confident in its uniqueness as comparatively speaking, the cityscape of some other cities becomes more and more homogenized.

3. Enjoyable life in old buildings

Protecting and repairing old buildings is more than fixing and whitewashing exterior walls based on how they originally appeared in old photos. It is not merely about external appearance of old houses being "restored like the old ones", but closely related to the refurbished interior for people living there.

Garden houses on the busy Wukang Road are covered by dense green foliage of wutong trees. They are ideal to live amongst for many people in the past and now, providing examples of the best imaginable residence. However, for a long time in the past, life in old houses was not as enjoyable as people outside had imagined. Data show that in 1985,

the average population density in downtown Shanghai reached 40,000 people/km^2; 70% households in Shikumen Lane could only use coal stoves indoors or in hallways, and did not have a dedicated kitchen; only 38.7% households had kitchens and gas supply; 60% residents shared tap water or collected water from the public supply stations; more than 80% households used closestools. The actual situation of Wukang Road back then was also reported in old newspapers. Since around 1987, newspapers had reported "power outage notices" every summer. The growing number of residents and power supply needed to drive upgraded household appliances put a heavy burden on the power lines connected to old houses, leading to power failures during the scorching summer. This situation was not improved until the beginning of the 21st century. Besides, these western-style houses had septic tanks. For narrow and deep alleys, fecal suction trucks failed to get in. Rickshaws were used to transport feces. At that time, everyone would frown upon and hurry to keep away from these rickshaws. [1]

In 2007, after collecting opinions of residents and obtaining their permit, Xuhui District government launched the policy of house replacement. Some residents at Wukang Road responded quickly by signing their names on the replacement agreement. According to these agreements, residents shall move out of the old houses. Then they could use the compensation money to purchase a self-owned property. In this way, the original Western-style houses could get thorough examinations and repair, while residents would have a spacious home which truly belongs to them.

In addition to improving the facade, repairing a house means to allow people living there a more comfortable life. In 2018, the new round of overall renovation of the Wukang Building was carried out. In order to restore the original historical style of the century-old building and meet the needs of residents for better living conditions, the relevant departments made great efforts to resolve knotty problems.

---

[1] Hu Jirong. "Preserving historical legacies of Shanghai", Reform and Opening-up Makes Shanghai Renowned [M]. Shanghai People's Publishing House, 2018, pp.253-254.

For a long time, the beauty of those old buildings was seriously impaired by messy clothes racks, and flower racks on the exterior walls, and air conditioning racks which even obstructed distinctive terrazzo bracket decorations on the second floor. In this renovation plan, all the air conditioning racks would be cleared away, except those on the second floor, which would be moved from the south to the northside. This plan had been revised 12 times based on rounds of negotiations with involved residents before it was finally decided upon. At the beginning, the residents opposed the plan, especially those living on the second floor. To address their concerns, officials of Shanghai Xuhui Housing Management Bureau visited each household many times for face-to-face communication to gain a full understanding of their actual needs. Officials learned that the residents were worried about corridor pipelines in disorder and afraid that air conditioning pipelines would damage the unique suspended ceiling. They immediately invited residents to jointly develop a renovation plan. First, they tidied up the corridor pipelines and covered them with hanging boards. Then, they worked with professional design teams and conducted multiple on-site visits to each household before offering an individualized central air conditioning plan. In the end, the residents agreed and the repair plan was implemented.

The growing popularity of Wukang Building and Wukang Road is attributed to the protection of old buildings and the preservation of urban cultural heritage. These achievements are inseparable from the meticulous and "people-centric" work of historical building repairers and urban managers, as well as the common participation, understanding and support of the residents. The ultimate beneficiaries are the entire city and the people who live, work, and travel here. Nowadays, sewage, mud, power failures during summer, briquette stoves, closestools, and fecal suction trucks are all things of the past. Wukang Road, lined as it now is with excellently restored historic buildings also enables residents to enjoy modern facilities and sufficient space. It is in this place full of history and memories that they live a comfortable life today and look forward to a better future.

4. Shared public space breathing life into old buildings

If the protection and repair of historical buildings is version 1.0 for safeguarding urban historical and cultural heritage, the road protection and renovation would be version 2.0. Version 3.0, which Shanghai is practicing and exploring focuses on opening up old buildings to the public, creating high-quality public cultural spaces, revitalizing historic heritage and making old blocks dynamic and beautiful, thereby promoting the overall quality of the neighborhoods.

Preserving old buildings and historical neighborhoods is not the ultimate goal of safeguarding urban cultural heritage. Renovated old buildings and authentic historical blocks should not be outdated "specimens", but urban beings in and of themselves bringing vitality in the new era. Following this principle, Hengshan Road-Fuxing Road historic area vacated former residences of historical celebrities and updated houses into public spaces accessible to citizens and tourists. These efforts renew old buildings and drive forward the revitalization of the entire historic area.

Take the building at 393 Wukang Road as an example. The role of this building has undergone several rounds of transformation: from the former residence of the Chinese revolutionary Huang Xing (military leader of the April 1911 Uprising in Guangzhou), Shanghai International Library, World School, to Hunan Road Subdistrict Office. Since 2010, efforts have been made to change its functions. Now it serves as the Wukang Road Tourism Information Center and Xuhui Historical Building Art Center, providing convenient and thoughtful free services for citizens and tourists. You can enter the building, appreciate the internal structure and design, and also learn the history of the old house through the heritage architecture models, fine arts, photographs and other works of art. You can read the written documents here or scan the QR codes to learn stories of the old buildings and the historic area, or come here on weekends, join the story-telling session of the old house, and listen to Shanghai history told by experts and scholars. You can also sit down, take a rest, or even chat with nearby strangers to see what new discoveries and insights others have during

their travels on Wukang Road, or across the city.

The transformation of the building at 393 Wukang Road can be described as a rebirth. Its protection, repair and revitalization are a showcase of Shanghai's urban renewal efforts. In the past decade, more old buildings in Shanghai have been treated with such care. They serve as open public spaces, allowing citizens and tourists to have close interactions with the architecture. These interactions and unique personal experiences would not be possible if people were blocked by walls, doors, and windows. The old houses, therefore have also gained new vitality through this interactive process.

At present, Shanghai has a protection and revitalization system focused on "heritage architectures, protected roads, historic areas", corresponding to "dots, lines, and surfaces". The city is a symbol of successful practices to activate historic districts, leading to high-quality urban renewal. The most outstanding examples are as follows: the celebrities' former residence block on Wukang Road, the "street block with intensive music culture" on Fuxing Middle Road-Fenyang Road, and the "slow living block of the Shanghai style" on Jianguo West Road-Yueyang Road.

In recent years, in addition to keeping the original essence of historical buildings, Shanghai has tried to make the best use of various cultural elements and resources, collected information about hundreds of celebrities and their former houses, compiled books, held exhibitions, given lectures, provided guided tours of old building routes, developed QR codes, and built online interactive platforms. In this way, it explores innovative ways to introduce old buildings, protects and inherits the historic legacies with the most distinctive Shanghai characteristics, creates big brands of the urban culture, and continuously enhances the soft power of the city.

III. Conclusion

Wukang Road in the new era features approachable architecture, streets suitable for leisurely city walks, and people-centric development. It serves as an epitome of Chinese

modernization, reflecting high-quality life, which is understood and expected by Chinese people today.

It is widely agreed that "economy is the flesh and blood, while culture is the soul". After decades of rapid development since reform and opening-up began, people have realized urban culture is an integral part of urban development. Thus, safeguarding urban historical and cultural heritage is significant to maintaining an urban life full of charm and beauty. President Xi Jinping said:

"The historical and cultural heritage of a city shows wisdom of great people in the past, and is an important symbol of the city's essence, quality and characteristics. We are required to properly handle the relationship between preserving the past and urban development, pay close attention to passing down urban historical and cultural heritage, respect and treat old buildings as if they were the venerable 'elderly', and preserve the historical and cultural memory of the city, in the urban space and in the mind of people." [1]

Nowadays, efforts to protect old buildings and safeguard historic legacies in old neighborhoods contribute to proper urban renewal and development approaches which replace large-scale demolition and construction methods. We can see through historical relics where this city came from and have a clearer understanding of where we are heading. Shanghai as a People's City in the new era is characterized by approachable buildings, streets for leisurely walks, and people-centered development. It enables residents to enjoy their poetic life, strengthens the bonds of culture and spirit with individuals, and makes concerted efforts with locals to improve the life ecosystem of citizens and their environs.

The case of Wukang Road demonstrates China's exploration and innovation of urban renewal in the process of promoting urban modernization. Instead of copying western theories of urban renewal, it has been applied according to Chinese national conditions, with the proposal of new ideas such as "culture as the soul of a city", "respecting and

---

[1] Central Committee of the CPC Party History and Literature Research Institute. Excerpts from Xi Jinping's Remarks on Urban Development [M]. Central Party Literature Press, 2023, p.114.

treating old buildings as if they were the elderly", "keeping history and people's memories of the city", "bringing vitality to cultural relics", to protect urban historic legacies and guide urban renewal. Over the past ten years, efforts have been made to protect and repair old buildings. Closer attention has been paid to living standards and life quality of nearby residents. Actions to improve people's livelihoods and the neighborhood environments have brought benefits to more people. As a result, the Chinese-style urban renewal, which focuses on people's needs and coordinated development of material and spiritual civilization, has gradually taken shape. Wukang Road renovation is a case of successful application of these aforementioned actions. The popular tourist spot is deeply loved by citizens in Shanghai, and visitors from across the country and the world, which further enhances our confidence in people-centered urban development. Firmly convinced that the city is headed in the right direction, it should continue to follow this path with unwavering determination.

Creating a better life for citizens

I. Introduction

For a long time, modern urban dwellers, whether in large cities or small towns, have had to face a series of life challenges, including traffic congestion, long commutes, high living costs, and loneliness in the concrete jungles. These issues have significantly impacted people's quality of life. Therefore, on June 29, 2022, the UN Habitat Programme highlighted in its latest World Cities Report 2022: Envisaging the Future of Cities that urbanization remains an unstoppable trend in the 21st century, but the existing urbanization model urgently needs to change. The report calls for greater commitment from governments at all levels, from national to local, to encourage the implementation of innovative technologies and urban living concepts. By doing so, people can fully enjoy the beauty of urban life.

What can be called a wonderful moment of urban life? Perhaps everyone has a different answer. It could be going to the bustling community vegetable market nearby every day, visiting a "pocket park" for strolling downstairs and embracing nature as you like, walking to where you work without worrying about traffic jams, sitting in a coffee shop at the street corner where you can meet and chat with friends at any time, or browsing community shops with a superb collection of products near your home. These accessible conveniences show a city's ability to meet diverse needs of different groups of people, and they are what make urban life unique and full of charm.

In recent years, Shanghai has been striving to make these wonderful moments an integral part of daily life for all. Guided by the Shanghai Master Plan 2017-2035, the

megacity has rolled out detailed plans to build 15-minute community-life circles since 2014, making it the first city in China to put forward such proposals. A "15-minute community-life circle" refers to a residential zone where people can meet their daily needs, such as clothing, food, housing, and transportation, within a 15-minute walkable radius. To fulfill these requirements, appropriate basic service facilities and public activity spaces are necessary. The layout of a 15-minute community-life circle typically follows a "1+N" spatial model, which involves the integration of various services and amenities in a one-stop comprehensive service center ("1") and the flexible scattered placement of small-scale, multifunctional service facilities or venues ("N") to enhance the functionality of the community. The city has built urban spatial units "suitable for work, living, travel, elderly care, and education", established new community service models focused on the needs of residents, provided spaces, service resources for people, and led the way toward future-oriented, healthy, and low-carbon lifestyles. In this sense, people's access to childcare, education, employment, and medical services, which are essential to a high-quality life, can be assured.

With more than 180 projects implemented, how has urban planning and life circle development changed the lives of citizens? When you visit Xinhua Road Subdistrict in Changning District, the beautiful scenes would catch your eyes and help you find the answer.

II. Happy life in the Xinhua Road Subdistrict

1. Centennial Xinhua Road lined with wutong trees

If you come to Xinhua Road for the first time, you will find that tall wutong trees are planted on both sides of the road. The green foliage of trees provide shade, and their crowns intersect over the middle of the road, forming a lovely tree tunnel. Take a closer look, and you may find lanes along the tree-lined road are filled with historical Western-style villas, adding elegance and charm to the 2,434-meter-long street.

Xinhua Road, a beautiful street

As the earliest garden road in Shanghai, the history of Xinhua Road can be traced back to the Northern Song Dynasty (more than 1,000 years ago). It was famous for its landscape gardens and the Fahua Peonies. The Fahua Temple was built in 970 AD, 321 years earlier than the establishment of Shanghai County, hence the idiomatic saying "there was Fahua Temple before Shanghai County came into being". Over the past century, this area has been home to a galaxy of extraordinary people: brilliant architects, literati, dignitaries, the famous and the rich. In 1971, Municipal People's Government built Xinhua Road Tunnel for diplomatic purposes, aiming to provide leaders and guests from other countries with a smoother journey from Shanghai Hongqiao International Airport to the downtown area by saving them the trouble of crossing Shanghai-Hangzhou Railway. In 1972, Richard Nixon was the first sitting US president to pass through this tunnel during his visit to China. Since then, Xinhua Road has become well-known as Shanghai State Guest Road. In 2005, Xinhua Road was listed as a historic area by Shanghai Municipal People's Government. It is one of the 12 historic areas in the city's downtown area.

Xinhua Road Subdistrict with Xinhua Road at the heart is located in the southeast of Changning District, covering an area of 2.2 square kilometers. It is home to a total of 197 residential communities of various types, 56 commercial buildings covering a floor area of over 1,200,000 square meters, accommodating over 3,800 business entities and 69,000 residents. Despite a rich historical and cultural heritage, well-developed functional communities also face challenges to meet diverse needs of residents: limited space resources caused by high community completion rate (96.1%); multiple types of housing, with old communities taking a large proportion (77%); high population density and high degree of aging; lack of accurate configuration despite complete basic infrastructure; overall quality to be improved despite prominent local highlights; impressive cultural heritage with its unique charm unexplored; factories and chimneys occupying one third of the land in the district jurisdiction, which causes distress to people in the residential area. People's need for a better life and their development are unbalanced and insufficient. It is a problem to be solved by Xinhua Road Subdistrict on its way toward further development.

Therefore, as one of the first pilot projects to build 15-minute community-life circles, Xinhua Road Subdistrict officially started construction in January 2019, focusing on "proposal, evaluation, planning and construction", developing and implementing construction plans in a well-organized way. The local government also set up a special working group to identify and sort out problems and shortcomings in six aspects: housing, employment, travel, services, leisure lifestyle, and special charm. Together with a professional design team and a community planner team, they have developed the "Xinhua Road Subdistrict 15-Minute Community-Life Circle Action Plan".

Guided by the plan, the local government strives to build garden communities of happiness, with efforts ranging from strengthening central planning to steadily implementing classification, mobilizing social resources for co-development, co-governance, and sharing, while involving everyone in community development. By improving the slow traffic system, providing facilities in the neighborhood, creating communication venues, showcasing diverse charm, and reconstructing Garden Community and Employment Spaces, the

Xinhua Road Subdistrict steps up efforts to implement 15-minute community-life circle project, continuously creating a high quality, exquisite, and refined community life for local residents.

2. Prosperous communities suitable for business and daily life

A good employment rate is essential to the wellbeing of the public. To provide high-quality jobs for more local residents in their neighborhoods, and further promote the construction of a 15-minute community-life circle, the Employment-friendly Unit of Xinhua Road Subdistrict launched the campaign of "living for life". It pays close attention to the living conditions of small business owners in local communities, and helps job-seekers to demonstrate their competence and gain extensive career development opportunities on their doorstep. At the same time, Xinhua Road Subdistrict continuously improves the business environment within its jurisdiction, optimizes lifecycle services for enterprises, and improves the quality of employment and entrepreneurship.

Setting up offices at Xinhua Road has become a wise choice for enterprises. In recent years, in order to boost sustained and healthy growth of enterprises in the region, Xinhua Road Subdistrict has stepped up efforts to improve service skills. The local government uses "Xin-Qi Connecting" App to provide online full lifecycle services for companies, and provides comprehensive offline services through business service stations. In addition, Xinhua Road Subdistrict has creatively developed three lists for companies focusing on business services, enterprise needs, and block resources, allowing companies to better align their goals with community development. By 2023, there are over 3,800 key companies in the Xinhua Road Subdistrict. From fashion and creative industries, the online new economy, healthcare to headquarters economy, a large number of high-quality enterprises have been attracted to this area and developed in full swing, showing great vitality to boost local economic growth.

To serve companies means to serve people. To create a vibrant and well-equipped office environment popular with younger generations, Xinhua Road Subdistrict has mobilized

community resources, unleashed economic vitality, and completed multiple independent urban renewal projects. It has developed from an old industrial district into a local economic center featuring new office buildings for business activities. It has also created an innovative and dynamic employment space, and is committed to building itself into a central activity district according to the Shanghai Master Plan 2017-2035. People here show a spirit of being exceptional and enterprising, attracting the like-minded to gather in Xinhua Road Subdistrict for career success.

Comfortable housing is fundamental to people's happiness. "We manage our neighborhoods with great care, hoping to create a livable environment which allows residents to enjoy lifestyles at a slower pace", said an official from the local government. In recent years, Xinhua Road Subdistrict has intensified efforts to implement projects improving residential conditions and ensure local residents a more comfortable life by solving issues caused by aging facilities and incomplete functionality in old residential areas.

Corridor and roof of Building 7 in Jinglao Estate before and after renovation

To improve quality of after-sales public housing in old residential areas, efforts have been made to build communities along Xinhua Road and Panyu Road into "quality residential areas". Renovation and upgrading of 69 residential areas have also been completed, covering a floor area of nearly 705,000 square meters. To address issues caused by shared use of coal and sanitation in public housing, three non-apartment renewal projects were launched on Lane 491, Panyu Road. Efforts have also been made to renovate two protected historical areas, that is, Meiquan Villa and Yicun, and complete the agreed replacement of houses on Lane 58 of Pingwu Road. In this way, people in Xinhua Road Subdistrict would never need to use closestools. In addition to basic programs on the construction project list, efforts have been made to provide services available at doorstep, carry out micro updates, micro projects, elevator installation, and garbage bin room upgrading and renovation. In this way, the local government works to improve living standards and create a comfortable living environment for residents.

Xinhua Road Subdistrict works to revamp neighborhoods into comfortable blocks. When implementing the slow traffic system, research was conducted on the functions, environmental improvement, maintenance and management, autonomy or co-governance of more than 20 neighborhood roads, including Lane 211 and Lane 329. Besides, the local government has taken the initiative to develop beautiful street blocks following the principle of "greening, vibrancy, value, and efficiency". This project includes the renovation of a 4,465-square-meter green space and a 1,647-meter long retaining wall along Xinhua Road, revitalizing the "Garden Road" through high-quality greening efforts. Block landscapes have been created at six road nodes: Xinhua No.1, Youyisong, Xianghuaqiao Road, Dingxi Road, Guanghua Hospital, and Yangzhai Road. High retaining walls were reduced to offer open space for views of green spaces. Landscape lighting and rest spaces are in place. Residents can enjoy their leisure time here, forming a closer relationship with the green street spaces. The renovated Xinhua Road is thus more elegant and beautiful.

3. Happy communities of diversity and accessibility

Constructing 15-minute community-life circles has enriched the cultural lives of residents, especially elders at their doorways. The elderly people account for one-third of the population in Xinhua Road Subdistrict, but the government spends more than one-third of its efforts on the elder people. "If our senior citizens live a comfortable life, their family members would be happy." This is the principle followed by the local government. Old age is an important stage of life and can be full of achievement, progress and happiness.

To respond proactively to population aging and meet the expectations of the elderly for home care, Xinhua Road Subdistrict vigorously develops a community-based elderly care service system with the characteristics of "one center, multiple outlets, and full coverage". Such a system will provide one-stop services for the elderly in the local community, including elderly care, medicine, education, and entertainment, and will promote the establishment of the "subdistrict comprehensive service circle, community care service circle, residential district activity circle, neighborhood mutual assistance circle, and home life circle". These five circles are meant to constitute a happy elderly care life circle in People's City.

The Comprehensive Senior Service Center of Xinhua Road Subdistrict is one of the pilot projects for elderly care. Located in the central part of the subdistrict, it was formerly a vacant student dormitory belonging to Changning Campus, Shanghai Jiao Tong University. Since it was officially put into operation at the end of 2019, it has provided more than twenty services such as meal assistance, bathing assistance, long-term care, daycare, medical care, and cultural and entertainment activities. There are four core roles the center plays: one-stop comprehensive services, integrated coordination of resources, information management through a single web portal, and a comprehensive service hall. The center has functioned as a distribution hub that offers and delivers innovative services. By coordinating resources for elderly care services, improving the network of elderly care services, and promoting precise coordination of supply and demand, the center has gradually developed an operational model

Comprehensive Senior Service Center of Xinhua Road Subdistrict, Changning District (1)

Comprehensive Senior Service Center of Xinhua Road Subdistrict, Changning District (2)

that meets basic needs, showcases professionalism, expands coverage, and emphasizes individuality. The community's network of happy elderly care has been tightly woven with thoughtful and effective refined services and becomes a happy harbor in the hearts of the elderly within the large community.

As Mencius urged, "Treat with the reverence due to age the elders in your own family, so that the elders in the families of others shall be similarly treated; treat with the kindness due to youth the young in your own family, so that the young in the families of others shall be similarly treated." In the process of building a 15-minute community-life circle, Xinhua Road Subdistrict is also actively building a child-friendly community. Being child-friendly is not only reflected in the environment of the community but also means more attention and care for kids. It is a project named "Be Kid". It means reimagining everything with a childlike mood and mind and focusing on how to make children happy with games and other activities. The second project is "Be Fun". After all, a core requirement of a child is to play. The third is "Be Kind". It requires us to build child-friendly spaces from their perspective, promoting health and education and allowing children to feel, believe, and share love. Be gentle. Through these friendly spaces, they can grow up healthy and happy. "N", literally, refers to the differences in letters between the two concepts. Based on these differences, we find out the possibilities of building various child-friendly scenarios. It is not simply overlapping, but adding multidimensional concepts to "N" step by step. "N" may refer to Notice, Nursery, Native, Named, Nature, Net, Near, Neighborhood, Need, Naivete, Nurture, and Nourishment. All these concepts make the relationship between space and human habitation more comfortable and people friendly.

Therefore, Xinhua Road Subdistrict works on children's rights and welfare in a comprehensive and systematic way. It builds on local facilities and continuously promote a child-friendly urban environment through central planning. By renovating Huashan Children's Park, constructing the most beautiful school path around the campus, and establishing the most beautiful children's library in the community cultural center, the children-friendly environment has been enhanced to enable children to grow happily in the

new era. In the summer of 2022, Xinhua Road Subdistrict contacted multiple local schools to vacate classrooms for children in nearby neighborhoods to attend summer care classes. This helps address the concerns of two-income families. Elderly people represent the past, and children the future. A humane life is a mutual achievement between the people and their city as well as a harmonious coexistence between both.

To meet the needs of residents through better supplies and serve them with the best resources, Xinhua Road Subdistrict extensively listened to the opinions of the residents in 2020. In accordance with the requirements of moderate population size, convenient service management, effective resource allocation, and relatively complete functions, "Xinhua Lane· Citizen Center" emerged as the residents' requirement. It combined with the construction of the "15-minute community-life circle" service system and developed an overall layout of "Center-Station-Stop" at district, subdistrict, and residential district levels.

"Xinhua Lane · Citizen Center" is a re-development of an old Western-style house located at 359 Xinhua Road, with many residential areas surrounding it. Since opening on June 30, 2021, it has been very popular. Many nearby residents only need to walk for more than ten minutes to enjoy the familiar fragrance of paper books, experience the convenience of Himalayan e-books, and enjoy various literary and artistic audio-visual feasts. They can come here and share skills in calligraphy, paintings, and other forms of art, and benefit from the convenience brought by digitalization. They can also visit the century-old picture exhibition on the second floor to learn about the historical changes in the Xinhua Road Subdistrict over the past century.

4. A harmonious community with vibrancy and openness

Amazing changes have taken place in a small corner of Xinhua Road Subdistrict in Changning District. Fashion and gorgeousness, friendliness, and sincerity, low carbon and environmental friendliness, parent-child inquiry learning, innovation, and design... These words are seemingly unrelated but they are what has happened in the Xinhua Road Community Center, which was transformed from a vacant building at the end of the alley.

This building is known as the heart of Xinhua Road Subdistrict construction which aims to build a community where everyone can participate in creating a beautiful neighborhood.

Why is it called the heart of the community? As a new type of community public space, Xinhua Road Community Center is positioned as the local hub "support center", providing various types of assistance for shaping a beautiful community where everyone participates. Specifically, Xinhua Road Community Center has established four major support systems:

First, the Center has established a "local ecosystem". This presents a community-based social network that overlaps with the spatial network of the 15-minute community-life circle, including internal and external resources such as professional forces, universities, foundations, and support platforms. Here, community members can feel the "Xinhua life circle" connect themselves to the local community and discover the community's active actors, creators, and collaborators. Based on "Comupage", an App built on Web 3 digital badge system, a digital community yellow page is taking shape.

Second, it has established a "participatory planning platform". In September 2022, the Shanghai Civil Affairs Bureau issued Guidelines for Participatory Community Planning, which designated Xinhua Road Community Center as a practical platform for participatory planning. This place is to build professional participatory workshops which collect and present a series of toolkits for participatory planning and design, community action support, and continue to carry out activities in conjunction with real projects. At the same time, this platform will continuously accumulate issues from various groups in the community, and form a community proposal library, thus forming a two-way interaction interface between top and bottom.

Third, it has established a "community-based building and learning system". The Xinhua Road Community Center not only stimulates the active participation of community members, but also provides support for professionals and followers outside the community to form action incubation driven by collaborative learning through self-directed learning, project-based learning, and on-site practice. At the same time, developing systematic community-based courses will empower professionals in community building.

Fourth, it has established a "sustainable funding pool". The Xinhua Road Community Center supports sustainable and normalized community endogenous actions by forming a supportive fund pool through healthy operations and a multi-channel fundraising model.

The fundraising sources included the operation revenue of the community facilities and services, government procurement of community service projects, fundraising from the foundation's special cooperation projects, and revenues derived from community cooperative projects. At the same time, supportive projects were established for community active involvers, and special collaborations with foundation organizations were launched as well.

With these four supportive systems, the Community Building Center introduced an initiative named "One Square Meter Action", which was based on the idea of pursuing a better life. The Center hoped that in the community supported by the systems, everyone could bring positive changes to the neighborhood. "One Square Meter" means miniaturization and light intervention. And the Action emphasizes that all actions must be initiated based on the active discovery of community issues by community members.

In 2022, One Square Meter Action held a vote under the theme of "Resilient Community", and eleven proposals were selected by the organizer. The proposals included a free parent-child playground, children's toy exchange house, disabled-friendly accessible map, merchant support actions enlivening the community market, and elderly talk show facilitating cross-generational communication.

The overall community building of Xinhua Road Subdistrict is an open, dynamic, continuous, and systematic process. It is also a process of rediscovering community problems, redefining community issues, engaging all parties for solutions, leveraging resources to promote changes, and sharing and maintaining the achievements, thereby forming a better mutual trust and reciprocal relationship so as to tackle more profound issues. In this process, the willingness and abilities of each community member would be constantly growing, which would ultimately lead to the formation of a mutually beneficial and symbiotic community eco-system.

III. Conclusion

By promoting the construction of "15-minute community-life circles", Xinhua Road Subdistrict of Changning District has fulfilled the promise of leaving the best resources to its residents and delivering the best services to them. The construction of such circles meets the people's yearning for a better life and was a vivid illustration of a "city built by the people and for the people", which is of great significance to explorations for a path of urban construction and development with Chinese characteristics.

All in all, Shanghai has always been adhering to the principle of "people first" and has ultimately become a city that belongs to the people, serves the people, and helps the people to succeed. "People first" is the fundamental principle to promote the Chinese modernization. As a people's city, Shanghai has shown a firm humanistic orientation in urban construction and development, striving to become a modern city with a humanistic atmosphere and more human touch. It not only provides high-quality "public supply for people's livelihood", but also meets the deep needs of everyone and strengthens the "sense of belonging" of the citizens by building a friendly city for all ages. Shanghai has been committed to advancing the Chinese path to modernization, whose goal is to realize the all-round development of people, so that everyone living in the city can have the opportunity to shine in life, orderly participate in city governance, enjoy a quality life, feel the warmth and care from the city, and have a sense of belonging to the city.

Shanghai has been always sharing the achievements of urban development with everyone, and improving the quality and accessibility of livelihood services. If you regard a city as a biological organism, then the communities would be its cells. If you regard the undertaking of serving everyone in the city as a journey, then community service would be the last mile. In the face of the growing diversified needs of community residents, the key to achieving the "people-centered" provision of basic service functions and public activity spaces required for daily life, is to activate the "urban cells", the communities, so that people

can enjoy convenient public services that match their needs. Therefore, Shanghai has always been committed to making as much progress as possible in daily life services in the small space of communities, such as improving 15-minute community-life circles, and increasing facilities in elderly care, child care, education, health, culture, sports, and so on. Shanghai hopes that through these gradual improvements, citizens can enjoy a warmer and happier life.

Shanghai has always been adhering to the principle of "Better City, Better Life", and committed to aligning the vision of an ideal city with the better life of the people. Since the above slogan was put forward during Expo 2010, Shanghai's focus has rested on fulfilling the people's longing for a better life. In the face of myriad tasks of urban construction, no matter whether it is concerning urban planning or urban construction, construction of new urban areas or the renovation of old urban areas, Shanghai has rolled out a series of effective measures. For example, reasonable arrangements have been made for production, living, and ecological spaces, high-quality development paths that are intrinsic-oriented, intensive, and ecologically friendly have been pursued, and efforts have been made to create an environment that is conducive to employment, living, entertainment and tourism, so as to provide people with a greater sense of gain and create a happier and better life for them.

Adhering to the principle of people first, or making urban development truly benefits the people, and allowing them to live a better life, is the source of a city's vitality, the original mission of the CPC, and the core of Chinese modernization.

Efforts to help the elderly enjoy a happy and fulfilled life

I. Introduction

Shanghai is not only a vibrant modern metropolis, but also one of the best livable cities for the elderly in China. Many people might think that Shanghai is a magnet for young people, but what sets it apart from everyone's impression is that it is also the most desirable city for the elderly in terms of longevity. The care services and facilities near home, accessible medical resources within the community, and customized meal assistance plans have contributed to the increasing sense of happiness in the lives of the elderly in Shanghai.

The accelerating population aging in Shanghai and in other parts of China as well, is characterized by the large scale and extremely high and fast-growing proportion of the aged population, increasing human longevity, and the lag in preparation to cater adequately for this population. Population aging is a common feature presented by countries around the world in the process of modernization, and its impact on human society is profound and lasting. According to the United Nations' estimates, the proportion of the total population aged over 65 in 2050 will be 28% in Europe, 23% in North America, 18% in Asia, and even in Africa, which has the highest proportion of young people in the world, the proportion will increase from 3% in 2017 to 6%.[1] How to deal withthe challenges of aging and let the

---

[1] Population Division of the Department of Economic and Social Affairs of the United Nations Secretariat. World Population Prospects 2022 [R]. 2022.

elderly population enjoy a high-quality life is a question to be answered by all countries around the world.

"Developed countries have been concerned about the issue of population aging for a century."[1] Since the 1950s, Western countries have regarded home-based elderly care as an important component of community care, and focused on the construction of elderly homes and similar facilities to hold old people who need care. However, elderly care homes in cities were often located in remote suburbs, far from medical institutions and other public facilities. Due to poor availability of transportation facilities, they were "isolated from society". In this context, the concept of "elderly care in a friendly environment" has gradually spread.

The aging of China's population is a historical turning point of the process of world aging where this phenomenon has spread from developed countries to developing ones. According to China's census data, from the year 2000 to 2020, the proportion of the elderly aged 60 and above in the total population increased from 10.3% to 18.7%, and the proportion of the elderly aged 65 and above increased from 7.1% to 13.5%.

When the aging problem first arose, China formulated a "9073" model, which means that 90% of the elderly would mainly rely on home-based care, 7% on community-based care, and 3% on institutional care. However, as society has transformed, issues such as "empty nests" and declining birthrates are intertwined, adding many obstacles to home-based elderly care. At the same time, traditional elderly care institutions experienced deficiencies in structural capacity, poor flexibility, and high operating costs due to their large scale.

As the first in China to become an aging city, Shanghai is at the forefront of exploring how to provide elderly care services. According to the statistics of Shanghai in year 2022, 25.0% of the permanent population in Shanghai were aged 60 and above, and 36.8% of the registered population were in the same category. According to international standards, Shanghai gives host to a severely aging population. Faced with the characteristics of megacities with limited land and high concentrations of elderly people, Shanghai has chosen

---

① Louise Aronson. Elderhood[M]. CITIC Press Group, 2022, p.525.

"community-based elderly care" as the preferred mode of supplying elderly care services. Why did Shanghai make such a choice? How does the community-based elderly care serve the elderly? How do senior people in Shanghai feel about it? This article takes Lujiazui subdistrict, Pudong New Area as a test case to study.

II. Elderly care in Lujiazui Subdistrict

1. Aging-in-place: From "hard to get enrolled" to "living in a new home"

According to a survey conducted by the Policy Research Center of the Ministry of Civil Affairs of the People's Republic of China, over 80% of the surveyed elderly tended to receive care at home and in the community.[1] Therefore, a "nursing home at the doorstep" has become an urgent need for the elderly.

As early as 2014, Shanghai launched a pilot project on community-based elderly care mainly in the form of senior service centers and elderly homes. At the same time, other provinces and cities in China, such as Beijing, Chongqing, Zhejiang, Jiangsu, Anhui, Hebei, and Hubei, have also learned from the experience of Shanghai and explored the development of community-based elderly care services. In 2017, "community-based elderly care" was first included in national documents. In 2019, Shanghai pointed out that community-based elderly care services should be the preferred mode.

"Corresponding functional facilities, adaptive services, and emotional support should be embedded in the community to meet the basic needs of the elderly, such as daily care, rehabilitation care, and spiritual comfort. This will enable communities in a severely aging society to have continuous elderly care capabilities and allow the elderly to age in place in familiar environments and geographically close to their family."[2]

---

[1] Ministry of Civil Affairs of the People's Republic of China. China Civil Affairs' Statistical Yearbook (2018)[J]. China Social Sciences Press.2018.

[2] Shanghai Civil Affairs Bureau. Guidelines on Community-based Senior Services in Shanghai[D]. 2019.

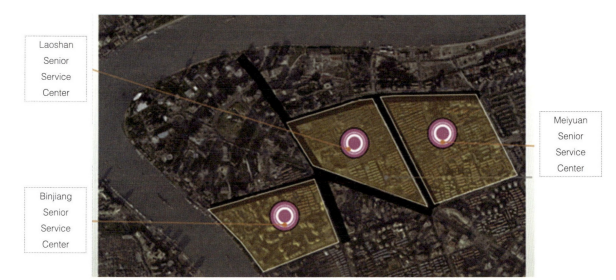

Laoshan
Senior
Service
Center

Meiyuan
Senior
Service
Center

Binjiang
Senior
Service
Center

Distribution of senior service centers in the Lujiazui Subdistrict

Thanks to the proactive response from the government of Shanghai to the demand for urban elderly care, the difficulty of getting enrolled in a care center for the elderly has been alleviated. In the past five years, Shanghai has added 26,500 elderly care beds, 428 senior service centers. The network of community-based elderly care facilities has basically formed. From the experience of Lujiazui Subdistrict, we can picture the exploration of elderly care services in Shanghai and even across China.

Lujiazui Subdistrict is not only a core functional area in the international financial center, but also a residential district with abundant history and culture. The total area covers 6.89 square kilometers, with a population of about 126,000, including about 40,000 elderly people over the age of 60, about 1,500 seniors living alone, about 6,000 old people in all-senior households, and more than 100 seniors living on subsistence allowance. To meet the needs of the elderly for aging-in-place, Lujiazui Subdistrict has divided its jurisdiction into three areas: Laoshan, Meiyuan, and Binjiang, and has set up comprehensive senior service centers in these areas. These centers provide access to one-stop services for the elderly, including community care, medical care, and family support. In addition, they offer customized services according to the characteristics of the locality and the needs of their

elderly. The elderly care facilities in the entire jurisdiction of Lujiazui Subdistrict have basically formed a closely linked, functionally complementary, and systematically connected network and a high-quality elderly care service supply chain has been shaped within the community. For the elderly living in the downtown Lujiazui community, the elderly care facilities integrated into the community have become their "second homes".

2. High-quality life for the elderly: Making full use of resources to serve them

The senior service centers can provide high-quality and warm care for the elderly by making full use of all resources, and make the spiritual support, cultural entertainment, and volunteer services that the elderly need accessible within the community.

The senior service center located in the residential area of Laoshan Village 5 is a 4-story building with a total floor area of 2,420 square meters and an outdoor garden of 450 square meters. The lobby on the first floor is an elderly care information center, providing information on elderly care policies and services. The second floor is a day care center that provides daily care, health services, and recreational facilities for the elderly. The third and fourth floors are a 24-hour elderly home, with a total of 40 beds. It contains a disability care zone and dementia care zone. In addition, the senior service center has a community canteen, and the lunch there is supplied by the community kitchen. For elderly people who are unable to move around, door-to-door delivery service are also available. The Laoshan Senior Service Center can accommodate nearly a hundred elderly people and can carry out various themed activities tailored to their needs.

The core of the community-based elderly care is to facilitate the living of the elderly with adequate living conditions. The overall demand of the elderly is shifting from meeting their basic needs to developing diversified lifestyles. Therefore, elderly care services also need to gradually evolve in this direction. For elderly people at a relatively young age, elderly care is a way of life in itself.

59-year-old Ms. Zhang lives in the community where Laoshan Senior Service Center is

Laoshan Senior Service Center in Lujiazui Subdistrict

located. She spends her day at day care center in this way: she does some exercise at 9:00 am in a dedicated gym for the elderly. At 10:00, she chats with her friends in a multi-functional room. At 11:30, she has lunch which is delivered to the center from a central kitchen. At 12:30, she takes a nap in the electric massage chair. At 14:00, she has dim sum and then does handwork, watches movies, and sings songs, etc. Her activities are arranged according to the timetable of the center. At around 15:00, she leaves the center to pick up her grandson from school.

The predecessor of the elderly service center where Ms. Zhang spends time in is actually the former office site of Laoshan New Village Subdistrict. Because of the fact that land resources are extremely limited in Lujiazui subdistrict, the government decided to transform an old building into a space for the elderly, fully reflecting the commitment to "leaving the best resources to the people". By 2022, there were 428 comprehensive senior service centers and 825 day care centers covering almost every part of Shanghai.

3. Combination of medical and nursing care: Care at the doorstep

Elders demand increasingly accessible medical services as they grow older and older. Younger elderly people need more daily care, while for older elderly people, healthcare plays a more important role. For elderly people, especially those living alone and those with semi-disabilities or disabilities, and others with physical illnesses, it is necessary to provide services such as prevention and treatment for chronic disease and elderly care. Chronic diseases in the elderly are mostly age-related, many can recover through long-term standardized chronic disease management. Most of the elderly people are able to return to good functional levels and continue a healthy lifestyle.

Quite a few residents in the community suffer from various chronic diseases. Their blood pressure and blood sugar need to be closely tracked and monitored. The complications of chronic diseases are complex, which is the reason for great rehabilitation demand. The residents living here now no longer have to go to the hospital. They can go directly to family doctors and receive the prescription at the community service center. Later the prescribed medicine will be delivered to their homes. That is how fast one-step service takes care of everything.

The integration of medical care and elderly care is the highlight of senior service in Lujiazui Subdistrict, involving different sectors such as reassuring medical care, health care, and rehabilitation training. Medical care includes drug prescriptions, remote consultations, drug management, vital sign measurements, and inpatient care; health management includes daily health testing, psychological support, dementia intervention training, cognitive disorder prevention, and chronic disease prevention; rehabilitation training includes rehabilitation training after stroke/fracture surgery, self-maintenance ability training, massage, and family empowerment guidance.

In terms of building dementia-friendly communities, Shanghai focuses on knowledge promotion, early detection, and early prevention. Since 2019, pilot projects have been launched for the construction of a friendly community for seniors with cognitive impairment. Lujiazui Subdistrict is also one of the pilot projects for building a friendly community for seniors with cognitive impairment in Shanghai.

According to the elderly service center, during the community activities, staff found that an elderly lady may suffer from cognitive impairment judging from the way she spoke. After the free checkup carried out by the cognitive disorder brain health machine in the elderly service center, she was indeed diagnosed with an early-stage cognitive disorder. Now residents can participate in rehabilitation activities at the community service center while going to the hospital for medication intervention at the same time.

Actively identifying and intervening in a timely way plays an important role in delaying mild cognitive impairment transition. It helps moderate and delay severe cognitive impairment. Therefore, it is essential to establish a professional community care service system. Some of the important elements of the system are the combination of promotion and education, risk assessment, early intervention, family support, resource links, and the construction of community service platforms for the elderly suffering from cognitive impairment.

Traditional Chinese Medicine physical therapy and rehabilitation is also one of the most distinctive and popular projects in Lujiazui Subdistrict. Qualified nursing staff are hired for the elderly service center, and the number of small rehabilitation equipment has been increased. Professional doctors from tertiary hospitals come to serve the elderly every Thursday. The eligible medical and nursing expenses incurred by the elderly in the elderly service center can also be directly included in the scope of medical insurance. If elderly people need further hospitalization and treatment, they can also quickly go to higher-level referrals through the green channel.

The community-based elderly care medical services are mainly based on medical care and rehabilitation. The goal is to combine health care and medical care for comprehensive treatment. With the "integration of medical and elderly care" development model, the first protection shield for the elderly shall be established through the integration of early identification and intervention of serious diseases, early rehabilitation training of serious diseases together with self-care capability, nursing care, daily learning, etc. As of 2022, 366 elderly care institutions in Shanghai have established internal medical elderly care institutions, and 729 have signed contracts with dedicated medical institutions.

4. Action plan for elderly nutrition improvement

The first priority in solving the problem of community elderly care is to tackle the food and nutrition problem of elderly people. The Meiyuan comprehensive senior service center cafeteria covers an area of 200 square meters, with a serving line of about 10 meters. Since 2020, the "Action Plan for Elderly Nutrition Improvement" has been implemented here. The plan allows elderly people to truly feel the warmth of the community through a hygienic environment, safe food, colorful dishes, and affordable prices.

Most elderly people in the community come here for lunch every day and they enjoy the food a lot. Each dish has its nutritional content attached to it. Elderly people can choose the food according to their own needs. The cafeteria has solved a big problem for the elderly. "As I am getting older, cooking becomes a daily burden", and old man said.

It is not only the elderly who find "cooking too troublesome". The high-quality and affordable dishes in the cafeteria are not only enjoyed by the elderly, but also a large number of young people in the neighborhood. The community cafeteria, which is supported by the government and serves residents, has enabled more residents to "eat quality food" within reach.

For the elderly, those cafeterias further promote their dining experience through smart dining and intelligent meal assistance services. On the one hand, the dietary improvement plan provides a universal discount of 10% for elderly people over 60 years old and 15% for elderly people over 75 years old in the community. For elderly individuals with special indicators such as low social security benefits, low income, extreme poverty, special care, and severe disability without employment, their daily meal expenses at the center are reduced by 3-5 yuan, ensuring that they can afford to eat well. On the other hand, the development of technology has also allowed the elderly to enjoy the convenience of services. Automatic price recognition and dish identification are implemented during meal collection, while the payment process incorporates the expertise of Alipay's technical team, enabling facial recognition and contactless payment. This addresses the concerns of elderly individuals regarding the loss or misuse of physical subsidized payment cards, which were

previously major issues for both the elderly and the canteen staff.

The action plan for elderly nutrition improvement launched by the Lujiazui Subdistrict has achieved positive results stemming from the following three aspects. First, the local government has converted its role from funding into collecting demands on a specific platform, cooperated with the Lujiazui Community Foundation and expanded the funding pool through online fundraising and offline precise alignment of demands, allowing socially responsible enterprises in this area to participate in targeted elderly care services. Second, these enterprises, serving as fundraisers, have covered costs such as inclusive discounts and subsidies for discounts respectively borne by the operators of the elderly cafeterias and these enterprises. In addition, the total amount of meal expenses, discounted items, and names of fundraisers are clearly shown on cash registers, making the action plan more concrete and transparent, rather than an empty promise. Third, the intelligent meal assistance system will accurately identify the recipient of subsidies, providing the elderly with substantial benefits.

In brief, the meal assistance service for the elderly is a practical matter that concerns everyone and the wider society. It is an important part in building the elderly care service system and achieving high-quality elderly care services in the new era. As of 2022, there were a total of 1,303 elderly meal assistance facilities across Shanghai, serving an average of 201,000 elders per month.

5. Respite care within the "warm-soup proximity"

An elderly home in Lujiazui Subdistrict, which covers a total floor area of 1,060 square meters, is the first comprehensive and embedded community care institution in Pudong New Area that integrates 24-hour short- and medium-term care, day care, home services, family assistance, and other functions. It has a high reputation among the local elderly who remarked, "the equipment and decoration here is comparable to a four-star hotel, and its service is better than that of five-star hotels."

This elderly home is a good choice for those elderly people who require full care.

Conveniently located in their neighborhood, it is within a "warm-soup proximity" (an optimal distance between family members, defined by the possibility to deliver a bowl of soup before it gets cold). It allows the elderly to enjoy elderly care without leaving home or separating from their children. Such a kind of elderly home is thus known as the integrated elderly care institution.

It is also suitable for elderly people who only need short-term care, as it provides meticulous temporary services for them, making their children feel assured and satisfied.

Ms. Shi, 72 years old this year, has been living with her son who sometimes needs to leave Shanghai on business for a few weeks. During that time, what worries Ms. Shi's son most is leaving his mother alone at home, so he will take her to the elderly home and pick her up after the trip. Ms. Shi was very happy with this arrangement and commented. "It's fun herewith so many people my age. When living alone at home, I have no one to talk to the whole day and I feel quite uneased. It's better to come out and relax and talk with someone."

A senior service center in Lujiazui Subdistrict

The elderly home, different from those common elderly care institutions, serves simultaneously as an elderly care home and a day care center with both full care and short-term care services for the elderly. Located in the neighborhood, the elderly home not only enhances the sense of security and happiness of the elderly, but also helps their children and relatives to attend to them in a timely and convenient manner. As of 2022, there were 217 elderly homes in Shanghai, with a total of over 6,000 beds.

III. Conclusion

As the global fertility rate continues to decline and the average life expectancy rises thanks to the advancement of medical technologies, the crisis in global elderly care is intensifying, pushing governments to solve this problem. By actively building a community-wide elderly care service system and transforming the Shanghai-specific solution into a uniquely Chinese solution, Shanghai, the vanguard of China's reform and opening-up and the pioneer in innovation-driven development, is also striving to put forward solutions with Chinese characteristics to address this problem.

Shanghai always takes the people as the center and embarks on a Chinese journey to modernization that features a large-scale common prosperity for all the elderly. One of its moves is the integrated elderly care model that takes the urgent problems of the elderly as the top priority. It is built into the neighborhood and of small scale, multi-functional and closer to home, ensuring provision of "continuous and satisfying care services", while offering resources and opportunities to the elderly who hope to enjoy quality old age, improving the quality and accessibility of elderly care services, and achieving the modernization of common prosperity for all in tandem with the well-being of the elderly.

This model exemplifies Shanghai's effort to continuously improve its governance efficiency of the aging society and blaze a modernized path of elderly care services that maximizes benefits for all elderly people. It is designed to build a social governance pattern that is jointly built, governed and shared by multiple parties, such as government, society,

the market, and family. It gives primacy to the elderly in social governance and elderly care service systems, and forms a Shanghai experience and Chinese plan for modernization of the governance system and capacity.

Shanghai adheres to the principle of the CPC that puts people first and "in the course of pursuing a happy life, not a single family or person should be left behind", as China's modernization is a huge task that involves nearly 500 million households. Shanghai has built an integrated elderly care model that organically integrates the traditional culture of family elderly care into the elderly care service system. It allows the elderly people to leave their home but not leave the neighborhood, maintain a "warm-soup proximity" with their children, and achieve "a sense of intimacy at a distance" It inherits the traditional family culture of filial piety, respecting and caring for the elderly, that has been passed down in China for thousands of years. In short, this model responds proactively to the issue of population aging and in the meantime leverages China's profound and unique cultural endowment advantages to continue to play an irreplaceable role in the elderly service system.

"The happiness of a society mostly depends on the happiness of the elderly population."[1] Chinese modernization is an overarching task that comprehensively considers the population aging issues and has fundamental requirements of enabling the elderly population to enjoy the achievements of reform and development and to live a happy life, promoting the high-quality development of the elderly, and building a friendly society for them. In the future, while proactively exploring solutions with Chinese characteristics to population aging, providing higher quality elderly care services is always high on the agenda. It is China's eternal goal to create a higher quality life for the elderly and enable them to have a happy and fulfilling life in old age.

---

[1] Speech by President Xi Jinping via video link to the Fuzhou Social Welfare Institute in Fujian Province on January 18, 2023.

Chapter 4

Smart and equitable: Achieving efficient governance

Shanghai is a huge city with a permanent resident population of around 25 million. Every day, millions of cars shuttle through the streets and alleys, and tens of millions of packages are sent to citizens through express delivery. People from all over the world come to this city to pursue their dreams and to improve their lives. On the other hand, Shanghai has over 100,000 old buildings and more than 35% of the population consists of elderly people, and therefore, countless problems await the city's administrators each day. Unlike many megacities throughout the world, Shanghai maintains the world's best safety record while absorbing people globally to create economic and cultural wonders. This city has achieved a balance between liveliness and tranquility. What underlies this wonderful balance may be the key to efficient governance in this city.

Modern governance is a common pursuit of most countries. After over 40 years of efforts in terms of reform and opening-up, China has formed an efficient governance system and capacity with unique advantages to meet basic national conditions and developmental requirements, and the modernization level of national governance has constantly improved.

The modernization of urban governance is a vital part of State governance modernization, and efficient urban governance has always been Shanghai's goal. In today's era, many cities around the world are facing challenges to effective governance such as urban renewal, social security, and public participation. Shanghai is no exception,

but it has its own effective urban governance approaches when dealing with the common issues of urban governance. In this chapter, we will present several cases, such as the digital transformation of workers' new villages through old town renewal, effective urban governance and public participation in major public governance affairs, to show the approach, methods and technology tools of urban governance in Shanghai. The Pengpu New Village described in this chapter is a very typical workers' new villages community in Shanghai. Through the case of community renewal in Pengpu New Village, we can see the pursuit of the CPC and the Chinese government, as well as the primary approaches of urban renewal in China. The digital transformation of urban governance is a revolutionary change. The Government Online-Offline Shanghai portal is a typical example of digital transformation to improve urban governance, which reflects the city's unremitting pursuit of innovation and optimization of government services. The third case in this chapter relates to the construction of urban public spaces. The case of the Brilliant City, a neighborhood where there is a conflict between public and private interests, provides some inspiration on what is the most effective way for the government to garner public opinion and work with the public to solve problems, guarantee interests, and ensure that all parties are satisfied.

Renovation of old houses in urban renewal

I. Introduction

Urban development and governance are universal issues explored by countries around the world. As a global development strategy, old town renewal, or urban renewal, is not only part of the process of urbanization, but also helps to solve the problems that exist in cities. The term "Urban Renewal" originates from the West. Since World War II, urban renewal in Western countries has gone through a process from "poverty elimination" to "urban revitalization". In the process of urbanization in China, especially after the reform and opening-up, urban development is facing a transformation from extensive to intensive, from expansion to enhancement, and from increment to stock. Urban safety, governance, and development not only require construction, but also need to take existing districts into account and make structural adjustments and functional improvements based on existing foundations. Urban renewal is an important way for China to build a modern city and promote a new type of urbanization centering around people, which is an important part of the modernization urban governance system and capacity. In addition, it serves as an important carrier of the unique Chinese path to modernization. Urban renewal should resolve issues of high-quality development and life and efficient governance, comply with the goal of modernization of urban governance, and serve the vision of a better life for urban

residents[1]. Urban renewal not only helps to promote urban transformation and improve urbanization quality, but also helps to improve people's quality of life, further enhancing their sense of gain, happiness, and security.

Currently, China has been promoting urban renewal across the country, and its priority has shifted from addressing basic living necessities to a diversified and multi-goal systematic renewal. At present, the most important aspects of urban renewal are the adjustment of production space, the optimization of public space, and the improvement of the living environment. What is closely related to everyone's life here is the improvement of living space, which refers to the renovation of old residential areas that are common in cities. Like urban slums in developed countries, there are also many governance challenges in old residential areas, which are generally concentrated on three aspects (architecture, population, and economic development): first, chaotic architectural layout, poor sanitation conditions; second, mixed population and frequent social problems; third, slow economic development, and lack of vitality. In terms of solving the problem of renovating old residential areas, how has Shanghai actively explored urban renewal models and upgrade efficient urban governance? Let's look at the practical case of the renovation of old apartment blocks in Pengpu New Village, Jing'an District, Shanghai.

II. Old apartment renovation in Pengpu New Village

Peng San community in Pengpu New Village, Jing'an District, Shanghai was built in the 1950s, and was one of the first residential communities in Pengpu New Village at that time. That community was provided for excellent labor workers to live in, making this area an enviable residential district. However, after decades of natural erosion, the houses became dilapidated, resulting in problems such as roof leakage and ground waterlogging. At the

---

① Zhu Zhengwei. Scientific Understanding of the Meaning, Function and Goal of Urban Renewal[J]. National Governance, 2021(47).

same time, the facts that several households shared kitchens and bathrooms, and that there were insufficient supporting facilities also brought great inconvenience to residents' daily lives, thus spurring them on to renovate their old houses. In order to improve the living conditions of the residents, in 2007, the CPC Shanghai Municipal Committee and Shanghai Municipal People's Government, as well as the CPC Jing'an District Committee and Jing'an District People's Government, decided to list Peng San community as a joint apartment renewal project. Peng San community is a large residential quarter with a total of 58 apartment buildings accommodating 2,684 households, including 15 buildings with complete apartments with an area of 27,000 square meters accommodating 696 households. There are also 43 buildings with non-complete apartments with an area of 67,240 square meters and 1,988 households. The renovation project was implemented in five phases, and residents from phases one to five have all moved back and now live in bright and tidy new houses.

After the renovation, the community has taken on a new look, with complete public supporting facilities, greatly improving the quality of life for residents. During the renovation period, subdistrict officials combined the actual situation of the community and the structural characteristics of the houses to create renovation models such as renovation, expansion, adding stories, demolition, and reconstruction. This not only improved the living environment of residents, but also provided valuable experience for the renewal of old residential quarters of old houses across Shanghai. The fifth phase of the project of Peng San community has set multiple records for Shanghai's old apartment renovation: first, this project is the largest non-complete apartment renewal project in Shanghai, involving the largest number of households; second, the signing rate on the first day of centralized contract signing reached over 96%; third, the signing rate eventually reached 100% during the signing period, setting a new record for signing contracts for the complete renovation of old houses; and the fourth is to complete 100% relocation and demolition within the specified time limit, once again creating a new miracle in the renovation of non-complete apartments.[1] In

---

① Pengpu New Village's Largest Renovation Project Launched[N]. Labor News, 2021-09-02.

actively promoting the renovation of old houses in Pengpu New Village, the CPC Jing'an District Committee and Jing'an District People's Government, as well as the CPC Shanghai Municipal Committee and Shanghai Municipal People's Government, have responded to the concerns of the residents, proposed scientific and feasible renovation plans and renewal mechanisms, and fully gained the understanding and support of the residents, forming a consensus. Together, they have successfully completed the renovation of old residential areas, making the community more livable and making people's lives better and more convenient.

1. Reason for the renovation: A response to public concerns

The land of Pengpu New Village used to be a farm field in the northern suburbs of Shanghai. Around 1950, with the rise of socialist construction, a group of large electrical machinery plants settled in the former Pengpu town, resulting in the creation of the Pengpu Industrial Zone. This zone has witnessed the flourishing youth of the Chinese working class, with the birth of the first large antenna base, the first bulldozer, the first pneumatic-driven and electronically-controlled cold rolling mill, and the first water tube industrial boiler. At that time, a large number of technical workers and laborers lived in cramped old alleys, lanes and shanties, amidst poor living conditions. In order to solve the accommodation problem for workers and their families in Pengpu Industrial Zone, four residential communities were built in 1958, forming the earliest Pengpu New Village.

Under the conditions at that time, the area and structure of houses in Pengpu New Village could meet the needs of workers. However, times have changed, and workers' new villages have begun to face a series of problems such as aging housing pipelines, water seepage on walls, uneven foundations, serious settlement, damaged road greening infrastructure in residential areas, and a lack of public infrastructure support. Most of the residents living here are retired industrial workers with low retirement wages, and there are also many disadvantaged individuals who need government subsidies. It is infeasible that they buy commercial housing. Moreover, many veteran workers have a deep affection for

Pengpu New Village before renovation (Photo by Pengpu New Village Subdistrict Office)

Kitchen in Pengpu New Village before renovation (Photo by Pengpu New Village Subdistrict Office)

Pengpu New Village, and they are unwilling to leave their homes where they have lived for most of their lives. Improving the living environment of residents and enabling former exemplary individuals to spend their days in peace has thus become the most prominent problem Pengpu New Village faces when it comes to urban renewal and development. In 2005, the Shanghai Municipal People's Government issued the Interim Measures for the Management of Comprehensive Renovation of Old Houses in Shanghai, and the complete renovation of old housing in Pengpu New Village emerged in this context.

2. Promotion of renovation: Designing scientific and feasible renovation plans

The complete renovation of old houses refers to the act of refurbishing urban houses by adjusting the layout, improving facilities, and adding equipment, while retaining the original architectural characteristics and structure of the old housing stock. Complete renovation involves the demolition and reconstruction of old houses and the on-site resettlement of original residents, a process known as "demolition and reconstruction". The complete renovation of old houses is even more difficult than housing demolition and relocation, since the latter only requires demolishing the house. The renovation project of old houses requires detailed surveys, project design, resident signing relocation agreements, and resident relocation. After the demolition of old houses, it is necessary for residents to rent a temporary accommodation. After the completion of new houses, residents would be invited to select their units and then move back. Therefore, old house renovation projects are much more complex and difficult than demolition-relocation project, as it involves multiple steps.

First, a baseline survey. It's the first step of the renovation project. From the perspective of work procedures, a baseline survey mainly involves asking about residents' willingness for renovation. According to relevant government regulations, more than 90% of residents' consent for old house renovation is required to initiate subsequent renovation work. Therefore, the staff of urban renewal affairs office (the UR Office) need to have a deep understanding of the situation of each family during the screening stage, paying special attention to families that may have potential conflicts, and focusing on the work in the later contract signing stage. There were many types of houses in the Peng San community. Although there was a record of the residential area on the residential rental certificate, the survey staff did not simply copy the numbers. They must use accurate tools to conduct on-site measurements in residents' homes, providing accurate and reliable reference data to design units as far as possible. Staff of the UR Office would tirelessly measure all houses,

ensuring that they had a clear and precise understanding. At the same time, they urged North Group and Bei'an Property to send dedicated personnel to the UR Office to discuss issues related to the area structure of the old renovation one by one. This office also actively communicated with North Group and Bei'an Property several times, analyzed each item, confirmed the feasibility, scientific nature, and operability of the recognition standards, and held promotion meetings with the District Housing Administration Bureau, North Group, and Bei'an Property to improve the identification standards.

Second, project design. Whether the renovation design scheme satisfies residents is very important, since it directly affects the subsequent signing rate. Compared to ordinary commercial housing, the design of demolition and reconstruction projects is much more challenging. For example, the size of houses in Peng San Community Renewal Phase IV Project ranged from 6.5 to 40 square meters, with different orientations. Project design should not only ensure that the original type, area, number of rooms, and orientation of the residents remain unchanged, but also increase the original housing area to a certain extent with independent kitchens and bathrooms. After cross-checking, staff of the UR Office finally sorted out 39 housing types for this project and provided them to the designers. Starting from Phase IV of Peng San community, with the improvement of resettlement standards, the new houses would be also equipped with elevators. After multiple modifications, the design plan was finally determined. The UR Office would provide feedback on the design plan to the residents, listen to their opinions, and then ask the designer to make any necessary modifications. According to statistics, the design plans of over 400 households had undergone 12 rounds of revisions before and after, and every time the plans were modified, designers patiently answered various questions from the residents. Although the work was hard, the officials of urban renewal affairs office understood the feelings of the residents very well. After living in the old houses for decades, the residents finally got the opportunity for renovation, and therefore they hoped the new houses could be more spacious and of better quality. The UR Office considered issues from the perspective

of residents and strives to increase the living area of each household as much as possible. [1]

Third, residents signing relocation contracts. The contract signing process is crucial. According to regulations, the signing rate must reach over 95% within three months before the signing takes effect. Otherwise, the entire renovation work will end in failure. For those who refused to sign, staff of the UR Office would present the facts, be reasonable, and patiently communicate and exchange ideas with them. Secretary Huang of the Party branch of the UR Office proposed that staff should be good at communication, accounting and mediation. Staff responsible for communication should study in depth relevant policies and be adept at communicating with residents. For example, some residents had long occupied corridors that were shared areas, but which were not within the designated living space. The UR Office must clarify the relevant policies with the residents, as an accountant calculates economic accounts for them. In the renovation plan of demolition and reconstruction, residents benefited the most. Some, however, did not understand the design plan and refused to sign a contract, thus spurring the UR Office to help them calculate the economic benefits. The original size of the house, the size of the house after transformation, floor area, how much money should be spent on purchasing a property rights house, and what the value according to the market price value would then be. Through specific figures, the benefits of the old reform were clear at a glance, and residents were then naturally willing to sign contracts. A mediator would promptly identify various issues and concerns, and address them proactively. When the fifth phase community was signed, the UR Office mediated conflicts among multiple households. Secretary Huang said that there was no magic one-size-fits-all solution to eliminate conflicts, but only by thinking from a different perspective and being sincere could the trust of residents be won, thus allowing a good job to be done in the renewal project. [2]

---

[1] Pengpu Old Houses Are Transformed into High-value Elevator Houses. How Did the "Cosmetic Surgery" Operation Complete, since It Is more Difficult than the Old Reform? [N]. Jiefang Daily. 2019-07-13.
[2] Enable Residents to Live in "New Houses" without Reforming Old Ones, for a Promise to Give up the Opportunity to Transfer [EB/OL]. Shanghai Observer, http://www.jfdaily.com/news/detai?id=113755.

Fourth, resident relocation. In the renovation of old houses, once the project signing period ends and the project takes effect, the next step is to organize resident relocation. However, the relocation process was not smooth sailing. Because old public housing communities like Peng San Community generally have a large number of elderly, disabled, and seriously ill people, many landlords are unwilling to rent their houses to them. Faced with this situation, subdistrict leaders fully coordinated party-building resources, administrative resources, and social resources to achieve precise transmission of demands, delivery of services, and resolution of problems. Community officials collected rental information provided by surrounding real estate agencies and wrote it on the notice board in the community for residents to choose from. Community officials were also mobilized to search for rental housing available to residents in the community and bridge the gap between the two sides. Elderly service centers were also contacted to temporarily accommodate some elderly people with mobility difficulties.

Fifth, new unit selection by drawing lots. In the resettlement plan for Peng San Community Phase IV, the original 5-story residential building was demolished and 18-story apartment buildings were built in that place, with elevators installed. However, this change, which was intended to benefit the residents, unexpectedly created new problems. Some residents who originally lived on the top floors of the 5-story old houses wanted to move to the top floors of the new 18-story apartment buildings, which was opposed by the original low-floor residents. For the old apartment buildings with five floors, the subdistrict officials came up with the fairest method of floor selection by drawing lots. The lots would be drawn by residents of the same room type, the result was only used for selecting floors. According to the rules, residents who originally lived on the 3rd and 4th floors would participate in the first round of floor selection, residents on the 2nd and 5th floors would participate in the second round, residents on the first floor would come in the third round, and the order of lot drawing is determined according to the contract signing time, or by the first-come, first-served principle. In order to demonstrate the fairness of floor and unit selection lottery, leaders of the UR Office formed a supervision and management team consisting of 8

Pengpu New Village after renovation (Photo by Pengpu New Village Subdistrict Office)

resident representatives and 8 community officials, and filmed the entire lot-drawing process to ensure the legitimate rights and interests of residents were upheld. This housing selection method was approved by the majority of residents.

3. The effect of renovating old residential areas: Creating a vivid example of efficient urban governance

First, the robustness of Party building has been strengthened. The renovation of old communities in Pengpu New Village has strengthened Party building and cultivated a group of the primary level social governance officials, as reflected in the following aspects: on

one hand, a large number of young government officials at the primary level have gained insights and improved their skills for serving the local residents; on the other hand, collaboration among volunteers composed of neighborhood committee officials, community police officers, and community residents has been strengthened.

Kitchen of residents in Pengpu New Village after renovation (Photo by Pengpu New Village Subdistrict Office)

Second, the quality of life of residents has been greatly improved. Through the renovation of old houses, the housing quality of residents has significantly improved, and the community has taken on a new look. Residents have finally moved into their dream homes equipped with elevators, balconies, independent kitchens and bathrooms, and a noticeable increase in the actual usable floorspace. The community has built an underground parking garage, solving the parking problem. At the same time, the public supporting facilities in the renovated community have been improved, with central green spaces, public squares, elderly cafeterias, recreation centers, etc., greatly improving the happiness index of residents.

Third, raising and balancing funds through reform and innovation. In July 2020, the Shanghai Urban Renewal Center was established, creating an integrated old renovation functional platform throughout the city. Through market-oriented financing methods, the problem of raising and balancing old renovation funds was solved. The Urban Renewal Center, together with a number of enterprises and financial institutions, has jointly launched

an urban renewal fund with a total scale of 80 billion yuan, which is targeted to invest in the reconstruction of old areas and urban renewal projects, transforming the original single plot old renovation into a bundled combination of regional renewal. This has resulted in the following: a city-wide equilibrium balancing, respectively, of old renovation funds, while comprehensively solving the high-cost problem of old-stock renovation of some land parcels.[1]

The case of old house renovation in Pengpu New Village offers a perspective into the meticulous work of the primary-level Party organizations, as well as Party members and leaders in the process of old house renovation. To identify issues through investigation, conducting surveys from door to door, collecting opinions on designs, seeking solutions to conflicts, communicating when disagreements arise, and coordinating and working together with multiple parties and government departments to solve technical and public difficulties are part and parcel of this tried and tested process. This case also reflects China's emphasis on efficient social governance, where the aspirations of the people serve as the direction for governance, meeting their needs is the goal of governance, their satisfaction is the focus of governance, and finally, their feelings are the benchmark for testing the effectiveness of governance. Only in this way can the mobilization of the masses' awareness of participation and ownership be maximized, allowing for the creation of more vivid and streamlined modern practices of urban governance.

III. Conclusion

Urban renewal, as a global development strategy, plays an important role in promoting urbanization and solving urban problems. China and Western countries have different characteristics in terms of the background, goals, and models of urban renewal. First, different backgrounds of urban renewal. Urban renewal in Western countries has emerged

---

① Jiang Junjie & Liu Jingbei. Old House Renovation: How Is It Done in Shanghai? [N]. Wenhui Daily, 2023-01-16.

with the decline of cities, experiencing rapid urban development and large-scale commercial development, and then entering the process of responding to the decline of old urban areas. Urban renewal in China is carried out with urban construction and development, conforming to the new concept and new situation of urban development, and is an important carrier of the Chinese path to modernization. Second, different goals and understanding of urban renewals. Urban renewal in Western countries is problem oriented and committed to addressing historical issues such as social equity and justice left over from early urban renewal periods. The purpose of urban renewal in China is to transform the model of urban development, improve urban quality, and promote a new type of urbanization centered around people. Compared to Western countries that attach great importance to community renewal and urban revitalization, China aims to build modern cities that are livable, resilient, innovative, intelligent, green, and humane, to make up for the shortcomings and deficiencies in urban development, and to resolve urban economic, living, ecological, and safety issues. In addition, as one of the core commitments of China, "People's City" means putting people at the center and prioritizing people over capital. People, rather than capital, are considered the primary determinant and criterion of urban development. Third, different models of urban renewal. Urban renewal in Western countries relies on a multi-party participation model of government, private sector, NPO/NGO, and community in urban renewal operations, emphasizing the role of communities and stakeholders. China's urban renewal has generally formed a model consisting of "government guidance, market operation, and public participation".[①]

The commitment to building the "People's City" is an important embodiment of the Chinese path to modernization in the urban context. The essence of the "People's City" is relying on the power of the people to achieve development. Development is intended to benefit all people, and the fruits of development are shared by all. Building the "People's City" means taking the people-centered approach for improving urban services and raising

---

① Zhu Zhengwei. Scientific Understanding of the Meaning, Function and Goal of Urban Renewal[J]. National Governance, 2021(47).

governance levels, as a fundamental standard for testing the effectiveness of various urban work, and to run through all aspects of urban planning, construction, governance, production, and life. Urban renewal of old residential areas adheres to the voluntary participation of residents, improves the mechanism of public participation, and truly realizes the decision-making, development, construction, management, effectiveness evaluation, and achievement sharing of renovation projects. Through renovation of old house residential quarters, Shanghai aims to transform its urban development mode and build a new pattern for primary level social governance, thereby providing strong impetus for urban governance systems and modernization of governance capacity, and transforming old urban communities into a primary level practice of grassroots social governance. In the process of old houes renovation, Shanghai explores and innovates practical urban renewal models and mechanisms, mobilizes resources and enthusiasm from all parties in policy design, and improves upon a coordinated, precise and efficient working mechanism. Through the reconstruction of old areas, Shanghai has paved the way for modernizing governance in the old towns of mega-cities nationwide, serving as a model and example of Chinese path to modernization.

Making the city smarter

I. Introduction

Digitalization is a common trend in human society, and accelerating digital transformation is becoming a universal consensus in the international community. How to utilize cutting-edge technologies such as big data, cloud computing, blockchain, artificial intelligence, etc., to promote innovation in urban management methods, models, and concepts? How to ensure that both digitally capable and digitally disadvantaged groups in cities can equally enjoy high-quality government services? Why was the integrated service portal Government Online-Offline Shanghai recognized as a classic case by the United Nations E-Government Survey 2020? By reviewing the innovative measures of Government Online-Offline Shanghai, we can find the answers.

In 2018, Shanghai became the first to propose an integrated online-offline government service mechanism and took it as a key initiative to optimize the business environment. In April 2018, the Shanghai Municipal Big Data Center was established, focusing on centralized and unified management of public data resources, maintaining the portal website, and constructing information infrastructure. It became a primary driving force behind the establishment and operation of Government Online-Offline Shanghai. In October 2018, Government Online-Offline Shanghai was launched, enabling unified identity authentication and online inquiry and processing of certain government services. As of October 2022, the service scope of Government Online-Offline Shanghai covers over 4,500 administration

matters. About 97.3% of the materials issued by the Shanghai municipal government can be obtained through electronic certificates, data sharing verification, implementation of commitment notices, and administrative assistance, eliminating the need for enterprises and citizens to submit these materials during application. For 150 high-frequency matters, pre-filled forms and automatic verification mechanisms were introduced, with a first-time approval rate of no less than 90% for enterprises and citizens. Cross-departmental matters, such as birth registration, medical expense reimbursement, public credit information restoration, and social assistance, were integrated and streamlined, reducing the average number of steps by 70%, the average processing time by 58%, the average materials required by 77%, and the average number of visits by 72%. As of early 2023, the total number of cases handled through Government Online-Offline Shanghai has reached 297 million, with an online processing rate of 84%. Suishenban, a smart phone App for Government Online-Offline Shanghai, integrates various features like government service guidance, appointment scheduling at government service centers, access to personal electronic certificates, tracking current processing status, providing feedback on encountered issues, and personalized data inquiry. It has become a convenient means for citizens to access services and manage their needs anytime, anywhere. The opening of Comprehensive Service Windows at district-level administrative service centers and subdistrict-level community affairs service centers has yielded significant results, while the offline services have continuously improved their precision and efficiency in providing services.

A good business environment is like sunlight, water, and air, in that it nourishes the growth of enterprises. After years of efforts, Shanghai has become one of the cities with the most significant improvement in the global business environment. In the United Nations E-Government Survey 2022, Shanghai ranks 10th among 193 cities worldwide, and enters the top tier on the Local Online Service Index, reaching a "very high" level. So, how has Shanghai transitioned from a "follower" to a "leader" in the global tide of government digitalization?

II. Applications and benefits of "Government Online-Offline Shanghai"

Convenient access. Lowering the entry threshold for enterprises is an important approach to optimizing the business environment. In July 2019, Pudong New Area took the lead in implementing the "one integrated license" initiative, and three enterprises obtained the first industrial license in China. The beneficiaries of the first batch of reform pilot projects included retail, hotel, and fitness industries. Before this reform, for every retail store like convenience store, it was necessary to apply for five separate licenses, including a food business license and a liquor retail license. The store needed not only to prepare five sets of application materials, but also to go to different windows to apply. With complete materials, it would take approximately 38 working days and over 40 application materials would be required. After the reform, one integrated license covers the functions of the previous five. Stores now only need submit one application form and 10 application materials to receive the industrial license within 4-5 working days. The one integrated license initiative has effectively lowered the market entry threshold for retail stores, reducing the waiting time for retail stores to open from 1-2 months to 1 week, greatly saving their start-up costs.

More than 3,200 comprehensive licenses have been issued in 31 pilot industries of Pudong, covering convenience stores, fitness venues, hotels, restaurants, coffee shops, bars, pharmacies, etc. The one integrated license initiative in Pudong New Area was quickly promoted throughout the city, and market entities can carry out business activities in various districts of Shanghai with a comprehensive industrial license. Such a license is usually posted in a prominent position inside the store by the store owner. Consumers and regulatory personnel can scan its attached QR code to view the information of various industry specific licenses obtained by the store, providing convenience for social supervision and on-site supervision by regulatory personnel. On the basis of this initiative, Pudong New Area has also launched the "market access commitment is instant entry" reform measure.

As long as eligible market entities make commitments and submit necessary documents and materials, government departments will no longer conduct on-site inspections, directly issuing an industrial license instead, thereby reducing the waiting time for enterprises. Similar reforms are being implemented in various districts across Shanghai. Starbucks is a popular coffee shop for local citizens, and Shanghai is also the first city in the world with over 1,000 Starbucks stores and has provided streamlined opening license services for chain food stores such as this beverage outlet. Today, if you want to open a new Starbucks store in Shanghai, the process can be completed as quickly as 1 day from the date of the application being initiated by the market entity to the granting of permission to open the new store for business. [1]

Talent services. Talent is the core competitiveness of a company. The HR manager of an internet company with a revenue of over 500 billion yuan in 2022 stated that the company recruits a large number of new employees every year. Those with entrepreneurial experience have special and complex social security tax situations, and the company and employees need to conduct a lot of consultation with the government, which is time-consuming and laborious to run back and forth. After learning about the difficulties faced by enterprises, the Xuhui District Talent Service Center took the lead in assigning dedicated personnel to provide one-on-one door-to-door services for key enterprises in business zones and enterprises that have made significant contributions to taxation revenues of the district. After the enterprise makes an appointment, government staff will come to their premises according to the agreed time to provide policy lectures, consultation and answers, operation training, material pre-examination and other services, all of which are highly welcomed by the enterprise and employees. After providing on-site services, the HR of the enterprise will survey and collect various problems encountered by the enterprise and employees before government staff attend to them in person. The dedicated personnel who provide on-site

---

[1] Baoshan Offers Food Business Permit Facilitation: A Shop Can Open within One Day [EB/OL]. Shanghai Baoshan District People's Government official website. http://www.shbsq.gov.cn/shbs/bsbt/20230308/358855.html.

Pudong New Area Administrative Service Center

Hall of Pudong New Area Administrative Service Center

services will provide patient and detailed answers, making it smoother for the enterprise to handle social security and tax affairs for employees. For enterprises with high credit levels and good business conditions in the district, the Xuhui District Talent Service Center has also established a VIP enterprise service team composed of "business backbone", arranged for dedicated personnel to connect with the enterprise, established a one-on-one online communication mechanism, and provided customized services of "one person, one policy" for enterprise recruitment, while answering the problems encountered by the enterprise in the talent service processing process in a timely manner. The government's proactive door-

to-door service has created a favorable environment for enterprises to attract and retain talent and has also enhanced employees' satisfaction with their employers.

Preferential policies for enterprises. In recent years, China has lowered the value- added tax rate and introduced a series of preferential policies for small and micro enterprises. In order to make these preferential policies for enterprises known to enterprises as soon as possible so that they can enjoy the benefits, the Minhang District Taxation Bureau utilizes data technology to assist in identifying enterprises which have not yet gained access to or benefited from these policies. They arrange for dedicated personnel to visit the company to provide consultation and assistance services, so as to ensure that all eligible enterprises can enjoy practical benefits. There are also different types of supporting subsidy services at the city and district levels in Shanghai. For example, high-tech enterprises that settle in Lingang Special Area of SFTZ can enjoy the subsidy for settlement. According to previous regulations, these enterprises were required to submit application materials every quarter, which caused a lot of inconvenience. In 2022, the Lingang Special Area implemented a new policy giving enterprises access to government services without prior application for building subsidies. Through process optimization, the original five stages of "application, acceptance, review, submission, and disbursement" were simplified into two stages of "willingness confirmation, review and disbursement". The first batch of 185 enterprises enjoyed the access to government services without a prior application service, greatly reducing the redemption cycle.[1] Some districts are also exploring ways to automatically identify subsidy recipients through methods such as "data matching and AI determination", in order to distribute subsidies to individuals in the most convenient manner for enterprises and the general public.

Many districts in Shanghai have also launched a "no-login" version of the "enterprise exclusive webpage", which provides functions such as policy inquiry, project declaration,

---

[1] Government Online-Offline Shanghai Portal: 120 "No need for Application" Matters Handled Online [EB/OL]. Knews, http://www.kankanews.com/detail/6awW5K8x8yX.

policy interpretation, policy matching, and results disclosure. Enterprises can view all the latest enterprise related policies by browsing the exclusive webpage, and can quickly match their own policies through the policy matching function. Some districts regularly push relevant policies to enterprises. For example, when the government becomes aware that a specific enterprise has inquired about or dealt with related policies, or when there may be relevant needs in their business operations, the government will target specific types of enterprises and push relevant policies through the "enterprise webpage" when new policies are issued or policy changes occur. This transforms the process from "enterprises seeking policies" to "policies seeking enterprises", enabling enterprises to more accurately and timely understand policy trends and encouraging them to focus on optimizing their operations. These webpages to some extent solve the problem of enterprises not being able to benefit from beneficial policies due to lack of awareness, and aid them conveniently and quickly understand policy changes, thereby adjusting their business layout or optimizing their business strategies.

Assistant services. According to the survey data from the Pudong New Area Enterprise Service Center, new enterprises established within one year have encountered the most difficulties. In order to alleviate the pressure for these enterprises, Shanghai has launched free assistance services in the service center, where a row of "ASSISANT" service windows have been set, and the assistant staff provide free one-on-one services and guidance for enterprises to consult and fill out forms. As part of the process, the staff will follow up in a timely manner and help enterprises coordinate with different departments, aiming to solve problems in business flow. Such step-by-step assistance has helped enterprises to complete business transactions as soon as possible. For example, SAF Holland GmbH, the world's largest manufacturer of major components of commercial vehicles, headquartered in Germany, planned to establish an investment company as its regional headquarters in Shanghai. However, due to the strict regulation of controlling P2P enterprises, it would take a considerable amount of time for it to go through joint review meetings held by multiple regulatory departments to verify its name. So, this company went to the "ASSISANT"

window for help. Understanding the situation and needs of the company firstly, the assistant staff actively communicated and coordinated with relevant departments and stayed current with the progress. Ultimately, the company completed the name verification and obtained the business license within 3 days. In this way, the cost of communication between the enterprises and the government was greatly reduced. [1]

Now, free assistance services both offline and online have been provided to enterprises and citizens who have to deal with government-related businesses. In September 2021, an online assistance system was added to Government Online-Offline Shanghai, aiming to create an "online shopping-like" government customer service that efficiently and professionally meets the needs of enterprises and the public. It has included the first batch of 35 high-frequency tasks in a trial operation, such as residence permit application, child birth registration, social insurance registration, etc. The tasks completed through the online system accounted for about one-third of the total tasks on the platform of "Government Online-Offline Shanghai" throughout the year, with an average daily assistance frequency of over 400 contact events. [2] In the system, the staff of enterprises and citizens can also click on smart chatbots for online consultation when encountering problems. Utilizing the knowledge base of Government Online-Offline Shanghai, the chatbot can quickly provide answers. If there is any question that the chatbot can't answer, enterprises and citizens can apply for human customer support from dialogue prompts, then they would be automatically transferred to the page of human support from various business departments, where they can interact with and raise questions to professional personnel responsible for specific tasks in pertinent offices by sending texts, voices, videos, screenshots and recordings via PC or mobile platforms.

① Zhao Yong, Ye Lan, Li Ping. Internet Plus Government Services [M]. Shanghai People's Publishing House, 2020, pp.136-137.

② Hu Diefei. The First Online Assistance System in China has Been Launched in Shanghai, Which has since Assisted Residents to Complete more than 240,000 Tasks. 35 High-frequency Tasks Can Be Finished via the Government Online-Offline Shanghai[N]. Shanghai Law Journal, 2021-11-30.

Extended services. In China, when citizens visit hospitals for medical treatment, doctors always record their medical condition in the Medical Recording Booklet that should be kept by the citizens themselves. Young and physically strong people rarely go to hospitals, and their booklets can be used for many years. However, some elderly, weak, and chronically ill individuals frequently attend hospital, and their booklets can get rapidly filled. Sometimes, they may even fail to find them, then they can go to the subdistrict-level or town-level Community Service Center for a replacement. To serve the citizens of Shanghai living in various areas, each subdistrict or town has a Community Service Center responsible for social insurance, social assistance, elderly and disabled assistance, and other related work. However, some subdistricts and towns are so large that the elderly and the physically weak people cannot reach their service centers on foot. For example, the largest subdistrict in Shanghai covers an area of 62.18 square kilometers, and the largest town 96.7 square kilometers. Moreover, taking public transportation or taxis is not very convenient for the elderly patients. Therefore, some subdistricts and towns have started to provide extended services. For instance, Daning Road Subdistrict (covering an area of 6.24 square kilometers with a population of 77,700) has begun to establish extended service stations at a distance of 5-10 minutes' walk from citizens' doorsteps, which allows people living with the challenges of immobility to easily get a new medical record booklet. What's more, the extended service stations have provided over 130 types of services, including checking medical insurance card information and consulting-related business. [1] The Community Service Center in Zhuanqiao Town (covering $20.97km^2$ and having 73,000 citizens) has also set up sign language windows, where the staff will accompany and assist the deaf and disabled people throughout the entire process. For some elderly people with special needs (such as the bedridden or those confined to wheelchairs), the assistance staff can provide personalized and precise services to their homes.

---

[1] Extended Government Services Delivered at People's Doorsteps in Jing'an District, Shanghai [EB/OL]. Jing'an District People's Government offcial website, https://www.jingan.gov.cn/rmtzx/003008/003008005/20230329/07cc8990-9a74-430a-81e0-2afb79a897db.html?type=2.

Personalized government services. In general, elderly people hope to find government services at their doorstep, while professionals hope to solve government-related affairs near their workplace, even on a PC or mobile phone. Against this backdrop, Shanghai released the "City-wide Service" in 220 subdistrict/town-level community service centers and 67 subcenters on March 1, 2018. The aim of the program is to replace the circulation of paper materials with digital interaction, which allows citizens to freely choose which district's government service window to go to, if their workplace is far away from where they live. On each service window, it will only take a few minutes to get things done, such as the reissuing of lost documents. At the same time, in order to better meet the demand of professionals for staggered working hours, Shanghai has achieved the goal of providing 24-hour government services through intelligent service terminals.

"Super App" for mobile devices. The vast majority of Chinese netizens are used to using mobile phones to surf the internet. Therefore, the government of Shanghai has created a mobile app called "Super App" as the mobile version of "Government Online-Offline Shanghai" and developed Apps utilizing the existing mobile social network Apps. It has also expanded the range of personal services from government-related affairs to public services, covering marriage and childbirth, cultural education, tourism and leisure, social security, labor employment, transportation, medical and health, government affairs, life services, legal consultation, elderly care, enterprise affairs, bank insurance and various other service categories. More than a thousand services have met the needs of citizens at different levels. With the App, drivers can check the remaining number of parking spots in different parking lots, the distance between them and the parking lot, and how to navigate to them, and new energy vehicle users can make clear the distribution of public and exclusive EV charging stations. In particular, the elderly can choose the "For Seniors" page, which has a large font size and simple functions that are frequently used by them, including taking public transportation, taking the subway, seeking medical treatment, and promoting health education. Moreover, tourists can check the real-time passenger flow of popular attractions, and citizens can read e-books from the Shanghai Library or visit the online exhibition of

public museums on this App. Foreigners are also catered for, as they are provided with the medical appointment column on the citizens' exclusive website, where they can read medical guidance and make appointments in English. The PC-based portal of "Government Online-Offline Shanghai" also provides an English version specifically for foreign residents in Shanghai, offering policy consultation, city services, and guidance for various administrative procedures.

Tailored tax services. There are many foreign-invested enterprises in Shanghai, and it is common to find foreigners handling tax related matters at the Minhang District Taxation Bureau's Tax Service Hall. Some of them can express exactly what they want in Chinese, while others cannot. To better serve foreign nationals in handling tax related matters, the Tax Service Hall has established a foreign language service team to assist foreign residents who require translation services when handling tax-related matters. This team is able to communicate with foreigners about tax affairs and their specific procedures in the target languages. In order to facilitate foreigners to access personal income tax records, tax officers and the foreign language service team have specially created a bilingual user guide of the tax App and provided them with a printed copy of the personal income tax records, which has been praised by foreigners. The Tax Service Hall often encounters situations where officers cannot complete their work within working hours. Therefore, it has introduced a flexible service-hour extension system, which means as long as there are persons still waiting, tax officers will definitely meet their demands. In rare cases where a taxpayer arrives at the tax service hall after working hours due to circumstances such as traffic jams, the tax service hall will arrange for staff to wait and assist the taxpayer in handling their tax affairs on the same day upon receiving a request call.

III. Conclusion

Chinese modernization is a modernization with a vast population, and cities are where people gather to live. According to the World Cities Report 2022 released by the UN

Habitat, it is predicted that 68% of the global population will be living in cities by 2050. In 2022, Shanghai's urbanization rate among its permanent residents reached 89.3%. The case of Government Online-Offline Shanghai vividly demonstrates how a developing country with a massive urban population can empower city government services through digital transformation, providing strong reference and inspiration for the digital transformation of countries around the world, especially developing nations.

Adhering to the important concept of people's city, Shanghai is building a livable, resilient, and smart city. The world has entered the digital age, and new technologies are profoundly impacting production and daily activities in cities, making them smarter and more intelligent. This is the essential path to modernize urban governance systems and capabilities, with promising prospects. In Shanghai, technology empowerment and institutional innovation have accelerated business establishment, and enterprises with personalized consultation and service needs can easily access free "one-on-one" assistance at service halls, on online portals, or smartphones. The "Comprehensive Service Windows" set up in service halls provide unified, standardized government services to both enterprises and the public. This not only reflects a revolutionary transformation of government service processes, but also represents the practical application of holistic governance philosophy in Shanghai. Government Online-Offline Shanghai is continually bringing the government closer to the people, aiming to achieve more equitable, inclusive, efficient, and warm government services.

Adhering to a user-oriented principle, Shanghai is creating an internationally leading business environment. The digital government construction in countries worldwide generally presents two trends: one focuses on full online development, overlooking the emergence of the "digital divide"; the other still relies on traditional offline methods, neglecting the convenience for those with strong digital capabilities. In contrast, Shanghai adopts a model of integrating online and offline services, and strives to create a better business environment where: online, all large, small, and medium-sized enterprises can access government services anytime and anywhere, enjoying the convenient and speedy online service; and "Fully

Online Service" can significantly reduce personnel and administrative costs for small and medium-sized enterprises. Offline, Shanghai continues to optimize and strengthen physical service centers, where well-trained personnel provide face-to-face assistance, extending service points as much as possible into residential areas, striving to meet the personalized service needs of enterprises and the public in the most convenient way, allowing as many businesses and people as possible to experience the city's speed of development and warmth of government services.

Balancing efficiency and fairness, Shanghai promotes sustainable urban development. Efficiency and fairness have always been enduring issues in human society's development. With the increasing urban population worldwide, cities have become vital spaces for human production and living. While urban production activities pursue efficiency, urban living spaces lean toward fairness. On the one hand, the Government Online-Offline Shanghai in Shanghai emphasizes "efficiency in accomplishing tasks." On the other hand, in conjunction with the "Action Plan for Enhancing Digital Literacy and Skills for All", Shanghai continues to hold the "Month for Enhancing Digital Literacy and Skills for All", striving to improve the digital literacy and skills of all groups, highlighting digital inclusivity. Chinese-style modernization is about the shared prosperity of all people, and the dividends of the digital age should be accessible to everyone. Shanghai's practice emphasizes "making online transactions faster and offline services more considerate", which embodies the "common prosperity" concept of "leaving no one behind". Shanghai spares no efforts to build a city where "everyone has opportunities to excel in life, everyone can participate in governance in an orderly manner, everyone can enjoy a high-quality life, everyone can truly feel the humanistic care, and everyone has a sense of belonging", and achieve the ultimate goal of "Better City, Better Life".

Public participation in governance affairs

I. Introduction

Adam Smith once said that every individual, it was evident, could, in his local situation, judge much better than any statesman or lawgiver could do for him. The rational behavior of each market entity, also known as an economic individual, can converge to form a rational market economy, which will help to maximize economic benefits. Similarly, this economic judgement can be transformed into a basic belief of democracy: every single person is the best judge of their own interests, and all individuals who have a stake in the decision have the right to participate in its making. The rational actions of each political subject, that is, the political person, can converge to form a rational democracy, which will help to maximize political interests. However, in the management of public affairs, everyone "plays games" based on individual interests and may not necessarily achieve the optimal results. Chinese society features high differentiation by interests, but it does not rely solely on individual rationality for "gaming". In governance of major public affairs, China attaches great importance to the balance between public interests and individual interests. It seeks to satisfy the demands for public participation while ensuring that private interests do not overshadow the public interest.

In any city, waterfront areas are scarce resources. The development, utilization, and distribution of these resources have been deeply influenced by urban politics. The historical buildings along the Bund of the Huangpu River tell the story of the heavy historical impact

of Western capital seeking profit during the era of colonialism. The abrupt chimneys and rusty factories along the banks of the Huangpu River and the Suzhou Creek reflect ancient China's aspiration to pursue prosperity and modernization through industrialization. Nowadays, the Huangpu River and the Suzhou Creek riverbanks on both sides have become fully continuous, completely transforming into an open public space that caters to the living, working, leisure and transportation needs of the people. The rivers remain unchanged, but the changes in spatial form precisely demonstrate the profound evolution of the dominant will of this city.

The connectivity of the Huangpu River and the Suzhou Creek embankment is essential

The connected and renovated riverside of the Brilliant City (Photo by Zheng Xianzhang)

为什么是上海？
Why Shanghai?

for the transformation and quality improvement of waterfront space, and it is of great help to the overall urban appearance of Shanghai and the living environment of riverside residents. Through the joint efforts of governments at all levels governing residential areas along the rivers, by the end of 2020, the connectivity of Suzhou Creek and roads in central urban area had been achieved, except for the "bottleneck" part inside a residential area named the "Brilliant City" in Yichuan Subdistrict, Putuo District. This stretch of riverbank, approximately 1.69 kilometers long, was truly a hard nut to crack. It was within the plot plan of the Brilliant City, the largest residence-only area in the central urban area of Shanghai that the community would be divided by the river into two areas, an east area and a west area, with a total floor area of 1.534 million square meters and 96 buildings with the total number of residential households standing at 11,599, and a resident population of over 50,000 people. Therefore, some residents there regarded this beautiful riverbank as their private property. On the one hand, to achieve full connectivity of the Suzhou Creek waterfront, it was necessary to reserve some space within the red line of the Brilliant City. On the other hand, the joint ownership of residents was strictly protected by law. The contradiction between public interest and private interest was imminent here.

How to balance public affairs with personal interests? How to guide public participation in significant public issues? Let's take a look at the case of the Brilliant City.

II. Democracy in the case of the Brilliant City

1. Public space development and protection of property owners' rights

To the property owners of the Brilliant City, there was no legal basis for mandatory opening of the community area and no possibility of expropriation and repurchase. The opening up of this area could only be achieved with the collective vote and consent of the property owners. But how difficult it was to reach a consensus in such a super large

160

community with over 50,000 residents! Difficulties arose from six aspects. First, ownership: the riverbank property belonged to the community. Second, negotiation: a consensus was hard to reach under residents' diverse demands. Third, consideration: the calculation criteria for the compensation to property owners were not clear. Fourth, progress promotion: disputes over the selection and employment of residential properties were intertwined and formed a joint impact. Fifth, management: concerns about potential safety hazards were caused by inadequate follow- up management after opening-up. Sixth, renewal: residents had difficulty adjusting their opinions on the design plan. In the beginning, there was a great controversy among residents regarding the riverbank opening. In the initial consultation, nearly 90% of residents opposed the riverbank connectivity. Some residents had explicitly proposed that the land along the Suzhou Creek in the community belonged to the surrounding areas of the community. Why should private space become public space? Why should closed and exclusive spaces become open and shared? In addition, many residents felt dissatisfied with the former property management company. With various factors combined, it was difficult to unify the diverse demands of all parties, and the chance of reaching a consensus was slim.

As many opponents were there, some homeowners who agreed with the opening-up were also afraid of being isolated and kept silent in the property owner group, while the voices of opposition were becoming increasingly louder. At the beginning of 2020, the Putuo District Government organized a symposium, where members of homeowners' associations, resident representatives and subdistrict officials gathered together to discuss matters. Some residents expressed strong opposition. From the beginning of 2020 to October of that year, the office of Yichuan Road Subdistrict in Putuo District where the district is located solicited opinions several times, ending up with no progress due to divergent views. The primary level officials realized that "things regarded as good for the people" was not the same as "things regarded as good by the people".

According to the property owners, the main reasons for opposing the riverbank connectivity along the Suzhou Creek and the Huangpu River were as follows: first, property owners have the right to express opposition due to their ownership of the open consultation

area; second, the riverside landscape exclusively enjoyed by community owners is not only the legitimate rights and environmental interests of property owners, but also a selling point of overall community quality; third, once opened, the scarce river view houses would become street facing houses, greatly affecting their property value; fourth, the gratuitous transfer and public opening may result in unclear property ownership and potential legal complications; fifth, it is difficult to ensure the management after the opening-up, which may lead to problems related to safety, hygiene, and noise disturbance; and sixth, the road isolation network after renovation may severely damage the original design style of the community. Some property owners explained that they invested a considerable amount of money to acquire the beautiful riverside view of the Brilliant City, which was not provided to them for free. The monthly property management fees paid by these owners also covered the associated management expenses for the waterfront area. Even if all property owners genuinely agreed to the transfer, it would entail intricate legal relationships and financial compensation issues. Once the waterfront was handed over effortlessly, there would be no chance of reclaiming it in the future, even in the event of problems or regrets.

On the other hand, the attitudes of community property owners were not unanimous. Some thought that by relinquishing some of their rights to make the waterfront a public space, the community could receive compensatory benefits, provided there was proper management. In addition, numerous property owners, with public interests in mind, acknowledged the importance of waterfront connectivity for the entire city and supported government initiatives. For instance, Chen Bujun, an 80-year-old veteran CPC member in the community, penned a public proposal at the suggestion of the CPC. He highlighted the importance of Suzhou Creek waterfront connectivity for urban development and residents' lives, urging community residents, particularly CPC members, to fully understand the project and make unbiased, just assessments. The response to this proposal after its publication on the community's official media account far exceeded his expectations. On the same day, more than 6,000 CPC members and residents responded, expressing their understanding and support for the riverbank connectivity.

It can be seen that for any public issue, it is almost impossible to achieve consensus within a certain community. There are both supporters and opponents among the property owners of Brilliant City on the Suzhou Creek embankment issue. Interestingly, the opponents' positions are often very clear and their claims are reasonable and legitimate while supporters may be in a middle ground, requiring some positive guidance. Furthermore, according to the Western understanding of democratic governance, if there is a dispute over public issues, either representatives from different parties with different opinions will be selected for discussion and decision, or all members could hold a referendum based on their personal opinions. However, the problem is that determining public choices based on the number of votes may not necessarily lead to decisions that meet with public interests, and may also lead to internal division, confrontation, and even tearing-apart the community from within. Then, to maximize public interests and balance public and private interests, is there a better way to resolve conflicts among different interest groups beyond simple voting?

2. Conflicts and balance between public and private interests

When Yan Fu, a thinker in the late Qing Dynasty, used classical Chinese sentences to translate the book On Liberty by the British intellectual John Stuart Mill, he translated its title as On the Boundaries of Rights of Groups and Individuals. He chose this title to illustrate that individual freedom is not simply a personal matter, but should be defined and realized in relationships with others. "Groups" refer to different groups and the public space while "Individuals" refer to literally individuals and the private space. That is to say, the public space and the private space should be clearly distinguished. The rule that John Mill intended to express is that freedom belongs to the private space, therefore the public power cannot interfere with it arbitrarily. And another type of behavior belongs to the public space, which should be based on public welfare and democracy, and cannot be decided merely by individuals. The boundaries between public and private space should be clear and cannot be blurred, let alone be reversed, in order to determine categories of autonomy and democracy. The question is, can public and private space be separated completely? Does the exclusion

of public space from the private sphere help to maximize public interests and even protect private interests to the greatest extent?

In the process of providing connectivity along the Suzhou Creek embankment, there were multiple intersections between the public and private spaces. If property owners and households were the main entities of the private space, then "Brilliant City" was a public space and the principle of democracy rather than autonomy should thus be implemented. If, on the other hand, "Brilliant City" was used as an independent property management unit, it then acted as a private space and the principle of autonomy could be followed in dealing with many matters. However, as a part of the local district and even the entire city, this community is nestled within a larger public space and needs to be constrained by democratic principles. Therefore, it can be seen that the division of public and private space, as well as the scope of applying autonomy and democracy, cannot be divided absolutely.

The solid basis for property owners' will to maintain the current situation and their refusal to join the project lies in the common land use rights guaranteed by the Real Right Law of the People's Republic of China. In legal terms, it is an undeniable fact that the embankment is jointly owned by all owners under specific historical conditions. Law-based governance is one of the basic national policies in China. The legitimate rights and interests of citizens are protected by national laws, which are clearly stated in relevant written legal provisions. Although it is reasonable for the government to promote practical projects, the premise is that it cannot harm the legitimate rights and interests of property owners. Since Brilliant City is a private space, which means the principle of autonomy should be followed, property owners are within their rights to decide whether to change the current situation without intervening public power. Some property owners employed the famous British proverb "the wind, rain and storm may enter, but the King may not" to argue for the necessity of distinguishing between public and private space, as well as the legitimacy of their own claims.

In reality, although European and American countries declare that private property is sacred and inviolable, they also understand that under the premise of legal protection of

private interests, in the face of major public interest needs, private interest should make way for the public interest. That is, the "sanctity" of private property is not absolute. It is reflected in the sacred state of protecting private interests, rather than saying that private interests can completely override public welfare. For example, in the United States where property rights protection is the strictest, private interests also need to be restrained to meet public interests. Decades ago, near the current site of the World Trade Center, there were old low-rise commercial districts. In 1962, the New York City Government decided to expropriate the district and free up land for the construction of the World Trade Center. This move was strongly opposed by the property owners of the commercial district, and the West Side Association of Lower Manhattan representing hundreds of stores filed a lawsuit against this land acquisition. After being rejected by the New York Court of Appeals, the case went to the Supreme Court of the United States, which rejected the appeal in December of 1963. Later on, the land acquisition succeeded, and the World Trade Center became a landmark in New York. The property owners lost the lawsuit because the High Court justices believed that the commercial district, being adjacent to the Wall Street and the Port of New York, were prime symbols of the United States, and even the world economy. The construction of the World Trade Center would attract global investment to the US and bring greater prosperity to New York and the nation as a whole, something hundreds of stores could not achieve.

The Suzhou Creek waterfront connectivity is a big urban construction project, which helps to improve the overall spatial quality of Shanghai and has obvious positive attributes for the public interest. And if the property owners of Brilliant City were required to "share" the space within the "red line" of the community, they would need to transfer some private interests. It is reasonable to realize "public interest" while also legitimate to protect "private interest". The question of how to strike a balance between the welfare of the public and its private counterpart provides a stern test for political system and urban governance.

The difference between the American and Chinese society, when they face such interest disputes, is that the former usually seeks solutions through judicial means while the

latter believes more in a holistic process of communication and negotiation before things deteriorate to the point of resorting to the courts. The holistic "whole process" Chinese approach of "people's democracy" provides possibilities and a feasible mechanism for achieving the balance between public and private interests. The party and the government, open to good advice as they are, engage in consultation and discussion while making trade-offs through communication and explanation, which is in fact the best process of finding the right balance point between public and private interests. It is also a democratic process that respects, understands and realizes the peoples' aspirations. By practicing this whole-process people's democracy, public and private interests will not come into conflict, but can engage in a mutual win-win relationship.

The conflict of interests is a fundamental manifestation of a pluralistic society. The questions are how different societies can resolve such disputes and whether consensus can ultimately be reached between different interests. This is why democracy is needed. Liberal democracy theory promotes the idea that different interest groups engage in free competition and the party with more votes wins. This theory reflects zero-sum thinking, which believes in the winner takes all. This kind of thinking not only makes it difficult to achieve true consensus, but also easily tears apart society and causes new inequities and relative deprivation. On the contrary, the "whole-process people's democracy" emphasizes that "everything can be discussed, and everyone can discuss what they want". It has thus achieved the unity of the following manifestations of democracy: procedural, outcome-oriented, substantive, direct and indirect democracy as well as the will of the state. It is a full-chain, all-round and comprehensive form of democracy, which is the most extensive, authentic and effective socialist democracy that exists. In the case of the Brilliant City, obviously, there were different considerations and demands among property owners regarding whether to open up the community space. The party and the government had not allowed different interest groups to fall into conflict. Instead of simply resorting to a voting mechanism, they patiently and meticulously explained the development vision and compensated for the interests of property owners by repeatedly seeking their opinions.

Finally, the majority of residents in the community got to understand the practice and different interest groups reached a consensus that benefited all to the greatest extent.

3. Whole-process democracy as an optimal solution for diverse interest demands

People often lack the ability to see the true value of public interests beyond their own narrow view of maximizing their own interests. Many times, even if people see this value, they still lack the means and capabilities to fully realize it. Therefore, in a society lacking foresight, people are always caught up in the fight for short-term benefits, and have found it difficult to take long-term actions in the public interest. Adam Smith's judgment is reasonable most of the time, but in many cases, it is also unreasonable. If he is always reasonable, then it is difficult to explain why humans engage so often in foolish short-sighted behavior. So, blind trust cannot be placed in the rationality of individuals, nor in free-market democracy.

"The comprehensive renovation of the Suzhou Creek embankment has brought quality improvement and the most direct beneficiaries are the residents of the community. The most important thing to win public support for the embankment project is to win genuine recognition from people and make residents the true beneficiaries."

Qian Xiaoli, Secretary of Party Working Committee of Yichuan Road Subdistrict stated, "This is a reminder to us that if we want to do our work well, we must carefully listen to the opinions and suggestions of the residents and carry out democratic consultation."

That is to say, in terms of conflicts between public and private interest, there is a better solution to the problem of the Suzhou Creek embankment. However, this better solution cannot be reached solely with the rationality of property owners themselves or the democratic rules of the residential district itself. What if the party and the government, as active participants, promote the maximization of public interests in a democratic way? Is that not a better form of democracy? In order to promote the embankment project along the Suzhou Creek and the Huangpu River, the local government has completed the following work:

First, they proposed an economic compensation plan for opening up public access to the embankment. This was not an arbitrary act but a practice that fully respected the interests and rational demands of property owners. Local governments recognized that homeowners ultimately value tangible benefits over sentiment. The housing prices of this community covered the land transaction fees, which was a consideration in obtaining the exclusive right of embankment and the true foundation of the owner's property rights. Opening the embankment means that beneficiaries must make corresponding compensation to property owners who have subsequently suffered an impairment of benefits or transfer of interests. Here, the beneficiaries are unspecified Shanghai citizens or the city of Shanghai itself, so the one paying consideration can only be the Shanghai government. Therefore, the government, on the one hand, promised that opening embankment only involved the partial transfer of rights to use of space, without changing the scope of the "red line", that is, the legal relationship set up within the community. On the other hand, with professional calculations, the government allocated 169 million yuan from financial funds to the public account of the community as compensation of consideration for opening of the embankment. Additionally, the government has promised to bear the costs of the renovation and ongoing maintenance.

Second, the connectivity plan was promoted through various channels to make residents "see" the optimal solution. For example, articles were published on the WeChat public account. According to statistics, since December 1, 2020, "Measuring Yichuan", the Wechat Official Account of Yichuan Road Subdistrict Office, has continuously posted 104 relevant articles, with a total-read count of 122,000, including 75 original articles with 110,000 views. A micro exhibition themed "Yesterday, Today, and Tomorrow of the Brilliant City" was designed and organized with 200 representative image posters, leading residents to relay stories of the Brilliant City in the midst of historical changes and jointly look forward to a new beautiful life. The "Community Focused Communication Day" was also established. On this day, 14 promotional booths were set up, nearly 300 promotional pages were produced, over a thousand publicity posters were posted, and over 15,000 promotional materials were distributed. In the meantime, drones recorded beautiful scenery of the two

bays and LCD screens repeatedly aired the promotional videos. To address the concerns and clarify doubts of residents, 13 WeChat videos were launched to provide explanations and solutions, with video titles such as: "Will the renovated walkway still belong to us?" "What can we do with 134 million yuan?" and "What should we do if the property selection bids fail?"

Third, residents' opinions and suggestions were sought to find out what was on their minds and what they needed. For example, the subdistrict office of Yichuan Road joined hands with Putuo District Major Construction Projects Office and design companies to hold sessions to clarify their design plan, and organized community resident representatives to visit the already connected areas for on-site inspections. In total, more than 50 lecture sessions were held and over 30 on-site inspections were arranged and more than 2,000 community resident representatives participated in these events. A comprehensive poll was conducted via suggestion boxes, emails, and consultation forms and over 2,000 opinions and suggestions were gathered from the community. The subdistrict office connected Putuo District's Major Construction Projects Office, Landscaping Administrative Bureau, Public Utilities Center, Transportation Center, and design companies to jointly launch 13 consultation sessions, and invited the board of the homeowners' association and the property owner representatives to attend. During these sessions, pertinent issues were discussed, including the safety of buildings along the river, parking on Yuanjing Road, design of trails in the middle three areas, and the design of building No. 41 ground area. Through direct consultation, the government took reasonable suggestions and demands from residents into consideration to continuously improve the design plan; through communication with people like design expert Mr. Hu and construction supervisor Mr. Lin, talented people who have expertise, enthusiasm, and influence in the neighborhood were identified and a community think tank was created.

Fourth, a joint reception desk was established to address residents' enquiries. At the desk, staff from Putuo District Major Construction Projects Office, the offices for planning and natural resources, urban landscaping, housing management, the judiciary, and design

companies worked together and communicated with property owners face-to-face to answer their questions. Apart from that, four neighborhood committees hosted a series of 18 sessions for CPC members and building resident representatives, with over 1,000 of them attending. During these sessions, people from functional departments of the subdistrict office of Yichuan Road and design companies, lawyers, street-level workers, and the residential area CPC Secretary explained and demonstrated the latest plan via videos and gained support from CPC members and residents. A resident who used to oppose the idea eventually changed his stance and said, "The explanation from District Major Construction Projects Office dispelled my doubts, and ultimately I voted in favor of the motion."

Fifth, people's concerns were responded to and specific issues brought by riverbank connectivity were resolved one by one. Many property owners were ambivalent in terms of their stance on riverbank connectivity. Their main concerns were about practical issues, such as whether safety could be guaranteed after the connection; who would bear the responsibility of daily maintenance, and whether the design and construction plan would meet their individual needs. Faced with such a situation, the riverbank connectivity working group strived to meet every resident's demand, as long as they were reasonable and did not run against laws and regulations. For example, the working group would incorporate riverbank management into the one-stop city regulation system and install more high-definition cameras; the subdistrict office would assign more security personnel to strengthen patrolling, which means that the government would be responsible for securing safety after the connection; the maintenance of riverbank facilities would be undertaken by the municipal authorities, thereby lessening the burden on residential district property management companies; and when the construction plan was being hammered out, residents' opinions would be fully considered after thorough discussion.

III. Conclusion

At first glance, waterfront connectivity appeared to be a government driven initiative

that seemingly had no connection to democracy. But this notion emanates from a binary mindset that separates the government from society. Rather, the government and the people should be viewed as a collective whole, which then shows that the two sides have many areas of shared public interest. In other words, from a broader public perspective, it is clear that this is a road towards democracy. First, the waterfront connectivity along the Huangpu River and the Suzhou Creek was an activity that promotes Shanghai's public welfare and enhances the quality of urban public space. It was something that concerns the public interest and is therefore closely associated with many economic and social entities, including the Brilliant City community. Therefore, this is not a purely internal matter confined to the residential community alone. Second, when promoting for the realization of the public good, various levels of government departments in Shanghai have adopted democratic methods like visitations, consultations, communications, explanations and compensation to poll public opinion and deliver what people want. Instead of acting unilaterally, the government adhered to the principle of democracy throughout the process by consulting the public in order to reach a consensus. Third, and most importantly, after utilizing various democratic methods, the Shanghai government ultimately left the issue to the property owners of the Brilliant City to decide. On December 30, 2020, the Brilliant City community held a property owner referendum conference, in which over 80% of homeowners ultimately voted "yes" to the riverbank connectivity plan. In a nutshell, democracy is often a lot more than horizontal competition between different interest groups within a community, especially in modern countries, where there are a large number of vertical interactions in the actual operation of democracy. In other words, it is not solely an autonomous action at the societal level but rather a close collaboration between the State and society, aiming to maximize democratic representation and public interest.

Built by the people and for the people, cities are all about people, and urban governance ultimately is about solving people's problems and addressing the livelihood issues that concern them. Fulfilling people's dream for a better life is the starting point and goal of old town renewal work, since effective improvement in living environments, enhancement

in people's sense of gain, happiness, and security are important standards to measure the effectiveness of urban management work. For megacities, digital transformation is an intrinsic requirement in modernizing governance system and governing capacity. As President Xi Jinping once emphasized, a first-class city should have first-class governance, with a focus to make governance more scientific, refined and smarter. This provides guidance for strengthening fine-grained urban management and the development of "smart cities". Moreover, the public must be engaged through extensive discussions in various aspects of governance, as this is essential to democracy and key to ensuring that the people run the country. Under the Chinese socialist system, it is easy to discuss things and people's decisions are in their own hands, since it is the essence of democracy to find the greatest common denominator of social will and demand. Shanghai's urban governance has always adhered to and implemented a people-centered approach. The city has been actively exploring the path of modernization of urban governance in megacities, and striving to achieve excellence in this regard. With the help of efficient and effective governance, Shanghai has been continuously promoting its quality-oriented development, while making the city a more refined, orderly, safer, and more humanistic place for its residents.

Chapter 5

Sharing and opening-up: Contributing Shanghai's wisdom to China and the world

Shanghai has always planned its own development in full alignment with the central government's strategic arrangements, the megatrend of economic globalization, the national development model, and the master plan for development in the Yangtze River Delta. In this sense, Shanghai can be called a "city of the country". Since the launch of the grand program of reform and opening-up, Shanghai, which has no absolute poverty problem has been committed to helping the western regions of China eliminate poverty. What's more, eradicating poverty has been a long-term development goal and political responsibility of China, the world's largest developing country with 1.4 billion people. In early March 2021, António Guterres, Secretary-General of the United Nations, sent a congratulatory letter to Chinese President Xi Jinping in which he praised the Chinese government for its successful elimination of absolute poverty. He said that by this significant achievement, China had made an important contribution to the goal of building a better world as laid out in the "2030 Agenda for Sustainable Development". Since the 1990s, China's eastern regions, as represented by Shanghai, have built long-term relationships with their paired regions in the west, shaping a paired-up assistance system in which inter-governmental cooperation serves as the major force to mobilize market and social entities. This is a symbol of the Chinese path to modernization and China's commitment to common prosperity for all in the spatial dimension.

In the background of globalization, Shanghai is also a city of the world. As China implements a new round of high-level opening-up, including deepening cooperation on imports, Shanghai proactively participates in this process and plays its role as a vanguard in China's reform and innovation-driven development. On one hand, as China opens its door wider, Shanghai has aspired to become an international shipping center. Ports in Shanghai, such as the Yangshan Deep-water Port, have become important nodes, hubs, and platforms for connecting with regions in the rest of the world, aids in the city's aim of playing a leading role in China's high-level opening-up. On the other hand, CIIE is a vivid case of China's commitment to deepening and deploying import cooperation and promoting a new round of high-level opening-up. Over the past five years, CIIE has played a significant role in promoting international procurement, investment, cultural exchange, and open cooperation. CIIE has also enhanced the links between domestic and overseas markets to pool resources, contributing to the growth of global demand for international cooperation, and highlighting complementary advantages and connectivity between countries. Through hosting CIIE, Shanghai has been fully integrated into the global economic system and become a strong force in the global economy, contributing Shanghai wisdom to China's efforts to promote the shared development around the world.

East-west pairing up to promote common prosperity

I. Introduction

China was once plagued by poverty at a scale and a level of severity that has rarely been seen elsewhere in the world. As a result, the cycle and difficulty of poverty alleviation for China are beyond imagination. Fully aware that socialism does not necessarily mean poverty, the central government of China has worked hard to eliminate poverty. Measured by the international poverty standard as defined by the World Bank, which is 1.9 US dollars per person per day, China's poverty rate decreased from 88.1% in 1981 to 0.6% in 2019, and the number of people living in absolute poverty dropped by nearly 800 million, which was approximately 75% of global poverty reduction during the same period.

In 2012, China still had 98.99 million impoverished people in rural areas [1], a number that exceeded the total population of the 12th most populous country in the world in the same year. Since 2012, however, China has fought a tough and resolute battle against

---

[1] This impoverished population in the rural areas had long been plagued by poverty and lived in under-developed regions with poor living conditions and insufficient infrastructure. The scale and difficulty of poverty alleviation in these regions have rarely been seen elsewhere in China.

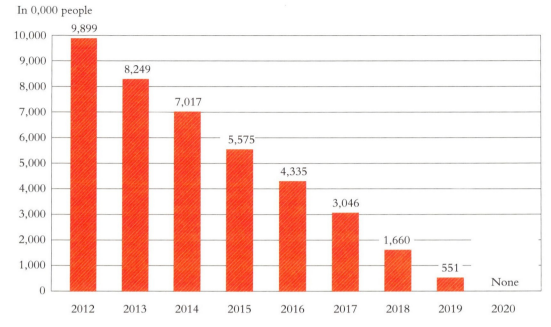

Figure 6　Changes in the number of poor rural residents in China after poverty alleviation

Source: The State Council Information Office of the People's Republic of China. China's Practice in Poverty Reduction (April 2021), People's Publishing House, 2021, p.14.

poverty[1], which is unprecedented in human history in scale, intensity, and the size of population it benefits. After 8 years of sustained hard work, by the end of 2020, China had basically fulfilled its poverty alleviation goals. By the 2020 national poverty standard (the annual income of people in rural areas per capita lower than 4,000 yuan), China had lifted 98.99 million people in rural areas out of poverty (see Figure 6), while at the same time 832 poverty-stricken counties (see Figure 7 below) and 128,000 poverty-stricken villages[2] were removed from China's poverty list. By then, China had eliminated region-wide poverty

---

[1] In 2012, the Chinese government set the goal of building a moderately prosperous society in all respects. From 2012 to 2020, the Chinese government continued to fight the "tough battle against poverty", which is a master plan dedicated to targeted policy implementation on poverty alleviation to ensure that no one will be left behind. This master plan helped identify the targets of poverty alleviation and determine who will carry out the work and how they should do it.

[2] The concept of poverty-stricken counties, villages and households is created by the Chinese government to identify and define impoverished populations at different levels. The government has applied targeted poverty alleviation policies to support these counties, villages and households.

178

and completed the arduous task of absolute poverty eradication. As part of the significant progress in poverty alleviation, China has employed a holistic approach to improving the living conditions of the impoverished population. The nation has witnessed a significant increase in the income of the impoverished population, with the per capita disposable income of rural residents in poverty-stricken areas increasing from 6,079 yuan in 2013 to 12,588 yuan in 2020 (see Figure 8 below). In this course, the well-being of the impoverished population and their access to food, clothing, compulsory education, basic medical service, and safe housing ("two assurances and three guarantees")[①] have all been realized. Access to drinking water in rural areas has also been significantly improved. Through these

Figure 7　Number of poverty–stricken counties after poverty alleviation

Source: The State Council Information Office of the People's Republic of China. China's Practice in Poverty Reduction (April 2021), People's Publishing House, 2021, p.14.

---

① Two Assurances and Three Guarantees refers to assurances of adequate food and clothing, and guarantees of access to compulsory education, basic medical services and safe housing for impoverished rural residents. The "two assurances" will resolve the problems of food and clothing for impoverished rural people. The "three guarantees" will help enhance the rural population's ability to offset risks and develop, and will create conditions for steadily resolving their problems of food and clothing.

improvements, China has not only met the basic needs of its population in poverty-stricken rural areas but also laid a solid foundation for future development. Judging by the World Bank's international poverty line, the number of people lifted out of poverty in China was approximately 75% of the world's total during the same period, and China had fulfilled the poverty reduction goal under the 2030 Agenda for Sustainable Development 10 years ahead of schedule.

As an international metropolis, Shanghai did not suffer from the problem of absolute poverty. How has Shanghai played its unique role in China's battle against poverty? As a case in point, Shanghai, a pioneer of Chinese modernization, could not have achieved its development in the early days of reform and opening-up without the strong support of all other Chinese provinces and cities. Naturally, after it became wealthy, Shanghai was bound

In yuan

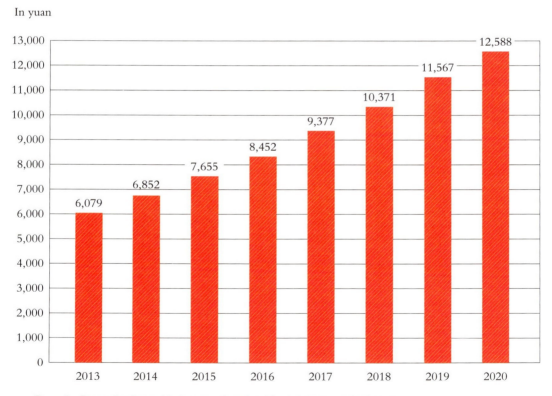

Figure 8   Per capita disposable income of rural residents in impoverished areas

Source: The State Council Information Office of the People's Republic of China. China's Practice in Poverty Reduction (April 2021), People's Publishing House, 2021, p.16.

to offer support to the rest of China in return. Since the early 1990s, nine richer provinces and provincial-level cities in the eastern coastal region, including Shanghai, have offered paired-up assistance to the impoverished areas in China's western provinces by sending officials and professionals to offer hands-on help and providing funds and technological support, among others. As China entered the critical stage of poverty alleviation, paired-up assistance projects including the number of personnel and funds provided by the eastern coastal provinces and cities, significantly increased[1], helping the impoverished areas in China's western regions achieve poverty elimination and reach economic development goals.

II. Shanghai's contributions and practices to achieve common prosperity

Shanghai has a long tradition of participating in China's paired-up poverty relief projects supporting the central and western regions of China through multiple programs, with the "Third Front" construction program[2] being the largest in the 20th century. Launched in 1964 and lasting 17 years, this particular program was a super large-scale construction and economic movement since 1949. This program, originally launched for defense purposes, had focused on national defense, science and technology, industrial engineering, and transportation infrastructure, and involved tens of millions of people who participated in projects across various hinterland regions. 1.5 million participants from Shanghai, the largest industrial center of China at that time, went to Xinjiang Uyghur Autonomous Region, Guizhou, Sichuan and Yunnan Provinces respectively. After the

---

[1] Since China set out to fight the "tough battle against poverty" in 2012, nine prosperous provinces and provincial-level cities in eastern regions had channeled over 100.5 billion yuan in total to support their paired regions. Enterprises in the eastern regions had also invested more than 1 trillion yuan in their target impoverished areas. These figures are abstracted from President Xi Jinping's speech at the National Poverty Alleviation Summary and Commendation Conference (February 25, 2021).

[2] The "Third Front" construction program is a super large-scale construction and economic movement in China's economic history. It was a response to the complicated international situation during the Cold War in the early 1960s.

initiation of reform and opening-up, some participants in the "Third Front" program returned to Shanghai while many others remained. Through this program, Shanghai fostered long-term cooperation with Yunnan, Guizhou, and Xinjiang Production and Construction Corps in western China.

1. Diversified professional support from Shanghai

Since the 1990s, the Chinese central government has issued new rounds of development-oriented poverty alleviation measures. In this context, rich provinces and provincial-level municipalities like Shanghai took the initiative to implement a new round of paired-up assistance projects for the central and western regions. In 1992, Shanghai paired up with counties of Wanxian, Sichuan Province (now Wanzhou District, Chongqing Muricipality) and Yichang, Hubei Province (now Yiling District, Yichang City, Hubei Province). In 1995, Shanghai sent the first batch of 49 officials to Tibet to serve in temporary positions. In 1997, 23 Shanghai officials went to serve in temporary positions in the Aksu Prefecture, Xinjiang. In the same year, the Shanghai Municipal People's Government held a farewell ceremony for 12 officials who went to Yunnan Province to serve in temporary positions. In 2010, 7 officials from Shanghai went to Golog Prefecture, Qinghai Province to serve in temporary positions. In 2013, 10 officials from Shanghai went to serve in temporary positions in Zunyi City, Guizhou Province. This history goes on and on. Today, batches of officials from Shanghai are sent to the western regions to participate in anti-poverty reduction schemes every three years and make remarkable contributions to the great cause of seeking common prosperity. After 30 years, Shanghai has not only preserved the tradition of helping China's western regions, but also endowed this program with a new meaning.

Since the start of the tough large-scale battle against poverty in 2012, rich provinces and provincial-level municipalities like Shanghai have continued to offer help, including personnel, funds, and other resources, to under-developed regions of China. By December 2020, Shanghai had paired up with 101 counties (including county-level cities or districts) in 20 prefectures and autonomous regions of 7 provinces (including provincial-level

regions or municipalities) (see Table 2 below). In about 50 batches, around 2,000 officials and professionals (such as doctors and teachers)[1] have been sent to the western regions to fulfill special missions or serve in temporary positions. By the end of 2020, 98 national-level poverty-stricken counties[2] in 20 prefectures and autonomous regions of 7 provinces in the western regions which paired up with Shanghai had been removed from China's list of poverty-stricken counties as scheduled; over 9.09 million registered poor households[3] were lifted out of poverty; and more than 2 million poor people had directly benefited from Shanghai's assistance. Officials and professionals from Shanghai have participated in poverty relief projects and helped bridge the development gap between the eastern and western regions of China. Through their work, funds donated by Shanghai have been used more effectively and have been more aligned with local conditions, so complementary advantages of the eastern and western regions have been realized. Shanghai has provided a great example of solidarity between China's eastern and western regions and win-win outcomes achieved by regional governments in their joint efforts to eliminate poverty and promote mutual development.

---

[1] The personnel dispatched by Shanghai to support impoverished western regions is divided into two categories: officials and professionals. Officials are sent to serve in positions in local governments every three years while professionals in education and medical care industries are sent to impoverished western regions on a short-term basis, ranging from three or six months or a year. Later on, these professionals are sent to Shanghai's target regions every three years.

[2] From 2018 to 2020, impoverished counties and prefectures paired up with Shanghai had been successively removed from China's poverty list. This included 4 counties in Kashgar Prefecture, Xinjiang Uyghur Autonomous Region, 5 counties in Shigatse city, Tibet Autonomous Region, and 56 counties and prefectures in Guizhou Province, 51 counties and prefectures in Yunnan Province, and 6 counties in Qinghai Province.

[3] The Chinese government created an innovative practice of poor household registration in its efforts to fight the tough battle against poverty. Besides, for registered poor households, the government set out targeted policies covering industrial development, employment, health care, education, inhospitable house renovation, relocation of impoverished residents, social safety net, disabled population, and more. To deliver targeted poor household registration, the government decided to perform a national census on impoverished population in 22 provinces, autonomous regions and provincial-level cities in the central and western regions from 2020 to 2021.

Table 2 Provinces, cities and counties pairing up with Shanghai[①]

Provinces/Municipality	Cities/Prefectures	Counties/Districts
Xinjiang	Karamay, Kashgar and Aksu (adjusted to Kashgar since 2010)	
Tibet	Shigatse	
Yunnan	Diqing, Lijiang, Dali, Dehong, Baoshan, Lincang, Pu'er, Xishuangbanna, Chuxiong, Kunming, Qujing, Wenshan and Honghe	
Chongqing		Wanzhou District
Hubei	Yichang	Yiling District
Guizhou	Zunyi	Chishui City, Tongzi County, Xishui County, Meitan County, Zheng'an County, Daozhen County, Wuchuan County, Fenggang County and Yuqing County
Qinghai	Golog	

Source: Cooperation and Exchange Office of Shanghai Municipal People's Government (2019)

2. Targeted actions and Shanghai's wisdom

The Shanghai Municipal Government, in accordance with the principle of combining "central government's requirements, local needs, and Shanghai's capabilities", utilizes its own market, social, and technological advantages to achieve precise adaptation between the eastern and western regions.

[①] In 2021, a meeting was held to advance the east-west pairing-off cooperation on poverty alleviation and strengthen efforts made by the central government-affiliated institutions in targeted poverty alleviation. During the meeting, new pairing-off cooperation contracts were signed. Shanghai's paired regions have changed from impoverished regions in Guizhou Province to those in Yunnan Province. This change, however, isn't reflected in Table 2.

First, it is a political mandate from the central government for Shanghai to implement paired-up assistance projects. In 2016, the Guiding Opinions on Further Strengthening Poverty Alleviation Cooperation between the Eastern and Western Regions issued by the central government set down the goals of targeted cooperation between China's eastern and western regions. The Opinions pointed out that cooperation on poverty alleviation between the eastern and western regions would be a big move to promote coordinated, synergetic and common development. Those opinions stand for visions of the central government to strengthen inter-regional cooperation, optimize the industrial layout, and expand new space for opening-up. They were significant measures to fulfill the goal of eliminating poverty by fostering win-win cooperation, in which regions that got rich first are supposed to help the less-developed regions until common prosperity is achieved. Besides, the central government has formulated long-term anti-poverty strategies and guiding principles, allowing the local governments in the prosperous eastern regions (supporters) and the local governments in the less-developed western regions (recipients) to develop specific poverty relief policies based on their own conditions.

Second, paired-up assistance focuses on meeting the real needs of economic development and local conditions of China's under-developed regions. China is a developing country with a super large population and suffers from inadequate and uneven regional development. There are significant differences in natural endowments between regions. Poor regions are often located in high mountains and water-scarce areas where industrial infrastructure is insufficient. For example, Yunnan Province is a mountainous region on the southwestern frontier of China, and its economy is under-developed, so the majority of ethnic minority populations in Yunnan are plagued by poverty. It can be said that the complexity and difficulty of poverty alleviation in Yunnan are beyond imagination. Moreover, Yunnan has wide karst areas. This unique geographic feature poses a severe challenge for local agricultural development due to water scarcity in karst regions. To address water scarcity in karst areas, officials from Shanghai proposed a water supply solution using micro-hydro-power technology, which suits local conditions. This

underlying technology was developed by Shanghai Miaohui Energy and Technology Co., Ltd. Afterwards, 32 micro-hydro-power projects were built throughout Yunnan, ensuring the supply of domestic water for 82,000 residents, irrigation water for around 10,543 acres of farmland, and drinking water for 15,000 heads of livestock and 100,000 feather broilers. At the same time, infrastructure remains inadequate in impoverished areas. To address this problem, the central government conducted large-scale infrastructure construction projects in the western regions and channeled assistance funds coming from the eastern provinces to industrial development, education, healthcare, and the development of social organizations. Funds to tackle the infrastructure inadequacy have covered key infrastructure projects such as factory buildings, cold storage facilities, animal pens, and pipelines. Funds have also been used to build and renew public spaces such as schools, clinics, and elderly care institutions in rural areas. Last but not least, there is a development gap between poverty-stricken groups. For example, Yunnan is home to major communities of ethnic groups that directly transitioned from the primitive society to socialist society without undergoing democratic reforms after the founding of the People's Republic of China. On November 14, 2020, the Yunnan Poverty Alleviation Office announced that the Nu and Lisu ethnic groups had been lifted out of poverty. By then, 11 ethnic groups with cross-stage development in Yunnan Province had all shaken off poverty. Today, the living standards of all ethnic groups in Yunnan have improved significantly, with ethnic minorities moving from inhospitable areas into government- subsidized housing. With improvements in living conditions and the economic environment, ethnic minorities have cultivated healthier habits and enjoyed better employment opportunities. In this sense, ethnic minorities in Yunnan have accomplished a millennial jump from communities depending on slash-and-burn farming to modern communities.

Third, giving access to Shanghai's resources and expertise is the starting point of targeted poverty relief assistance. As mentioned above, Shanghai has mobilized a great many professionals and officials to implement paired-up poverty relief projects in line with the goals of the central government. Shanghai has also implemented targeted measures to improve the wellbeing of people in poor areas and promoted industrial development

according to the local conditions. These steps, which have enhanced the sustainable growth of local economies in the western regions, form a multi-participant system. In addition to sending officials and professionals to target western regions, Shanghai has encouraged state-owned enterprises, private enterprises, and social organizations in Shanghai to participate in this program. To aid paired up western regions, Shanghai has contributed its intellectual, technological, and material strengths and helped the western regions train local officials and professionals such as teachers, doctors, and entrepreneurs. In addition, Shanghai has also helped them to sell their products in Shanghai and elsewhere and facilitated talent exchange to enhance the sustainable development of the targeted under-developed regions. One of the important goals of paired-up poverty relief assistance is to achieve resource complementarity between China's eastern and western regions. Once again, Shanghai fully leverages its intellectual and financial strengths to help the western regions in many ways. For example, Shanghai has helped to promote industrial development, employment, healthcare, education, reconstruction of impoverished villages, social welfare, and consumption.

In all these areas, Shanghai boasts an exceptional availability of resources in education, industrial development, consumption, and health. To help the target regions, Shanghai has developed a grouped model of intellectual support in education and health, contributing to the establishment of high-quality communities of educational and medical professionals in under-developed areas. In education, efforts have been made to integrate Shanghai's own resources with the locals'. Fu Xin, a Shanghai official, was sent to Tibet and served as deputy director of the Education Bureau of Shigatse City and president of the Shanghai Experimental School there. He had worked with his team to build Shanghai Experimental School in Shigatse City into an exemplary middle school. Besides, he had paid special attention to the correlation between education and industrial development in Shigatse, striving to channel high-quality vocational education resources from Shanghai to the poverty-stricken areas.

In terms of industrial development, efforts have been made to foster one-on-one cooperation to unleash the potential of the local economy in the western regions of China.

To aid the target regions, Shanghai fully leverages its market, platform, and circulation advantages. For one thing, such cooperation has made it possible for local products to be sold in the Shanghai market. Zhou Ling, an official from Shanghai, served as the sub-prefect of Daozhen Gelao and Miao Autonomous County, Zunyi City, Guizhou Province. To find markets for locally grown vegetables, he repeatedly traveled between Shanghai, Guizhou, and Chongqing, contributing to the increase of the income of local farmer households. He also worked to build an agricultural brand through restructuring the vegetable industry in the county. For another, Shanghai's industrial park models are replicated in the target regions it has paired up with. Ji Jiahua, chairman of Zunyi Lingang Technology City Management Co., Ltd., was another Shanghainese official sent to Guizhou to facilitate the development and sales of locally produced agricultural products. While there, he built industrial parks suited to local conditions and implemented favorable administration rules to attract businesses and investment. In addition, Shanghai also works with Yunnan Province to promote the "1+16+N" cooperation model for industrial parks: designating officials to oversee paired-up cooperation between 16 districts of Shanghai and 16 prefecture-level municipalities and autonomous prefectures of Yunnan, and help enterprises headquartered in Shanghai set up production bases in Yunnan. This cooperation model has drawn more than 1,300 enterprises to invest a total of over 60 billion yuan in Yunnan, thus revitalizing the regional economy.

On the consumption side, the government-led intervention work with market-based approaches proceeded on a mutually enhancing basis. To promote the sales of local agricultural products produced in the under-developed areas, Shanghai optimizes the cooperative production-marketing mechanism with targeted western regions, giving more visibility to their high-quality, competitive, and specialty agricultural products. Making full use of its market and business platforms, Shanghai has launched the "100 Products from 100 Counties" program[1], which created a perfect platform to promote featured products from

---

[1] In 2019, Shanghai started the "100 Products from 100 Counties" program, under which the city selected about 100 quality and competitive specialty products from its paired regions, and helped promote the sales of these products in Shanghai.

various counties and facilitate their sales. Shanghai has established 19 direct-sale stores, 20 lifestyle halls, and 169 specialty counters under this program in total. These stores integrate e-commerce platforms with offline experience halls, building a link between China's western and eastern regions.

In the area of health, efforts have been made to build Grade-A tertiary hospitals and form medical consortia. To improve medical conditions in target regions, Shanghai has developed a grouped model of paired-up assistance in the medical field, under which batches of medical professionals and funds are deployed to upgrade the hospital infrastructure and develop professionals in leading hospitals in the under-developed regions, helping more local hospitals to blossom into Grade-A tertiary hospitals. In the meantime, Shanghai has built Internet-based medical consortia, extending high-quality medical resources to target regions, and improving the healthcare service efficiency in the hospitals there.

III. Conclusion

Rich provinces and provincial-level cities in the eastern regions like Shanghai have offered targeted assistance to the western regions of China and promoted paired cooperation at all levels between east and west, advancing two-way flows of resources including talent, market, and technology. This practice of paired-up assistance for poverty relief has paved the way for regions of China to achieve win-win outcomes.

China has remained loyal to the people-centered development philosophy and unswervingly followed the path of common prosperity. China's anti-poverty governance focuses on the basic needs of the impoverished population, while local governments at all levels in eastern provinces and provincial-level cities like Shanghai have taken the initiative to mobilize market and social entities to support the national anti-poverty movement. As per the requirements of the central government, local governments in eastern provinces have consistently allocated over 80% of poverty relief funds to meet the basic living needs of the impoverished population, and tried to make sure all funds are well spent in every

impoverished county and village to benefit every poor household. Around 90% of the total poverty relief funds are directly channeled to areas below the county level under "paired-up cooperation" projects [①], while over 80% of the east-west paired-up support funds [②] are directed to impoverished areas at or below the county level. It can be said that more than 80% of poverty relief funds are used to improve people's livelihoods in the poverty-stricken areas, in part by supporting farming, and consolidate the material, policy and institutional foundation of common prosperity.

China is committed to eliminating the root causes of poverty by promoting inclusive economic and social development, or by the development-oriented approach. China's practices and achievements in poverty alleviation indicate that development is the most effective way to eliminate poverty and only development can really guarantee people's basic rights and meet their basic needs. Following this development-oriented principle, China continues to improve the economic conditions of people in the less-developed western regions. Shifting from an assistance-oriented approach to a development-oriented approach, the Chinese mode of poverty alleviation focuses on empowering the poor, testifying to the fact that development is the most reliable path towards prosperity.

China has leveraged one of the strengths of its socialist system: the ability to pool resources to support major development programs and mobilize national solidarity to achieve common prosperity. China's practices and achievements indicate that the formulation and implementation of poverty reduction strategy require credible political commitment, inter-government coordination at all levels, and multi-party participation, all of which cannot proceed without an efficient and effective government. China has strengthened paired-

---

① "Paired-up cooperation" is an initiative championed by the State Council Leading Group Office of Poverty Alleviation and Development that encourages the rich eastern regions to help less developed regions like Yunnan Province and Guizhou Province through cooperative projects.

② "Paired-up support" is an overall arrangement made by the National Development and Reform Commission. Shanghai's assistance to impoverished regions in Xinjiang, Tibet, and Qinghai Province follows such an arrangement. An exception is the program of assisting the Three Gorges Reservoir region, which is led by the Ministry of Water Resources.

up east-west cooperation on poverty alleviation[①], at the levels of provinces, cities, and counties. Besides, the central government has organized a point-to-point poverty alleviation movement, with all government organs, political parties, social organizations, state-owned enterprises, and the people's army proactively engaging in this movement, and all national-level impoverished counties have access to support from a counterpart in the prosperous regions in east China. At the same time, China's poverty alleviation has been multi-pronged, focusing specifically on industry, science and technology, education, culture, healthcare, and consumption. Private enterprises have also participated in the national poverty alleviation movement through the "10,000 Enterprises Revitalizing 10,000 Villages" project. In short, China has built an inclusive poverty alleviation system consisting of special projects, industrial development, and social relief, encouraging the participation of all entities, regions, and sectors of society. China's poverty alleviation also has boosted social values, as it emphasizes the spirit of solidarity and mutual assistance, preserves the traditional Chinese virtue of reciprocity, and helps bring people together in times of difficulty.

---

① Before 2016, the government used "paired-up assistance" to refer to the assistance offered by prosperous east- ern regions to targeted impoverished western regions. After China eradicated extreme poverty in 2021, the name changed to "paired-up east-west cooperation", with a focus on synergic cooperation between the east and west parts of the country.

An international shipping center that connects Shanghai with the outside world

I. Introduction

China could not have developed alone without connection with the rest of the world, and the world could not have prospered without China. In its march towards modernization, China has become deeply integrated into the world economy and plays an increasingly important role in the global trading system. Since China joined the WTO in 2001, it has forged closer and deeper connections with different parts of the world and created win-win outcomes. At present, China ranks second in the world in economic aggregate, ranks first in trade of goods, and ranks second in trade in services. It ranks first among developing countries in terms of foreign capital inflow and ranks first in foreign direct investment. Its annual average contribution to global economic growth stands close to 30%.[1] It can be concluded that the stable growth of the global economy is not possible without China,while on the other hand, China's prosperity depends on deepening ties with different parts of the world. Therefore, China needs to create a high-quality gateway for high-level opening-up and build a modern infrastructure network to connect China with the world. Ports are important transportation hubs in achieving this, as about 40% of China's energy supplies

---

[1] 20 Years in WTO: China Contributes to a Win-win World [EB/OL]. State Council of the People's Republic of China, http://www.gov.cn/xinwen/2021-12/10/content_5659688.htm.

and 85% of its goods for sale in overseas markets are transported by sea. Besides, Shanghai, being one of the most economically developed cities in China, is located at the Yangtze River Estuary and enjoys multiple advantages to become an international shipping center. For example, it is at the center point of China's eastern coastline and is known for its openness, innovation, and inclusiveness. What's more, as a Chinese city with global influence, Shanghai undertakes the important mission of connecting China with the world. Naturally, turning itself into an international shipping center is a very important part of Shanghai's efforts to accelerate its progress towards a modern socialist international metropolis with global influence. Cosmopolitan cities such as London, New York and Singapore are also internationally renowned port cities. In the process of accelerating the construction of a socialist modern international metropolis with global influence, Shanghai has set the international shipping center as an important goal. As the largest city of China, Shanghai is also one of the largest port cities in the world. The Port of Shanghai has ranked first in the world for several consecutive years in terms of container throughput, and its foreign trade container throughput is over a quarter of China's total. The international shipping center has become an indispensable function of Shanghai as a global city. Then here are some questions: Why should Shanghai work to become an international shipping center in addition to its efforts to become an international economic and financial center? Why should Shanghai focus on port construction and decide to build itself into a transportation hub connecting China with the world?

II. Yangshan Deep-water Port: A highlight in the construction of an international transportation hub

More than a century ago, Dr. Sun Yat-sen, advocate and leader of the modern Chinese revolution, had proposed to build three major ports in China. Shanghai, known as the largest city in East Asia at that time, was considered as an ideal candidate. After the founding of the People's Republic of China, Shanghai grew fast as a window to the outside world and its

foreign trade surged. At that time, however, Shanghai had no deep-water berth for heavy-load vessels to dock at. Therefore, building a deep-water port in Shanghai was imperative. The completion of Yangshan Deep-water Port injected a strong impetus into the development of Shanghai as a port city and contributed to the fulfillment of Shanghai's goal to become an international shipping center.

1. Yangshan Deep-water Port, a new pillar of the Port of Shanghai

Shanghai Yangshan Deep-water Port is the first port in China ever built on small islands, and the port can operate 24 hours a day. In 2021, the throughput of Yangshan Deep-water Port exceeded 22.8 million TEUs, approximately 48% of the annual throughput of the Port of Shanghai (47 million TEUs) in the same year. In recent years, although the international shipping industry has faced many challenges, Yangshan Deep-water Port's throughput continues to grow, laying a solid foundation for the steady growth of the capacity of the Port of Shanghai.

The construction of Yangshan Deep-water Port was considered as part of the development and opening-up of Pudong. In late 1995, to support this, the central government made a strategic decision to build Shanghai into an international shipping center, which created unprecedented opportunities for the Port of Shanghai. As international container ships became ever larger, building a deep-water port became a top priority in Shanghai's blueprint for future development. The site of this new deep-water port is about 30 kilometers southeast of Luchao Port in Shanghai, comprising several small islands including Dayangshan and Xiaoyangshan Islands in the north of the Qiqu archipelago in Shengsi County, Zhoushan City, Zhejiang Province. In June 2002, the construction of Yangshan Deep-water Port officially started. Engineers expanded these small islands and combined them, using soil collected from the seabed nearby. In that area, the average water depth is 20 meters. Hence, the required volume of the soil was incredibly huge. The soil used for this construction project can be stacked to the height of a seven-floor building on a ground covering the space of 1,000 football fields - a marvelous achievement. On December 10, 2005, the first phase

Night scene of the Yangshan Deep-water Port (Photo by Huang Weiguo/ IP SHANGHAI)

Fully automated terminal of the Phase IV of the Yangshan Deep-water Port (Photo by Huang Huaying/ IP SHANGHAI)

Cargo ship in the Yangshan Deep-water Port

of the port was put into use, becoming the largest container terminal and deep-water port in China. Later, the second, third and fourth phases of the Yangshan Deep-water Port were completed and put into use successively.

2. Intelligent ports increasing the international influence of the Port of Shanghai

In recent years, China has continued to make breakthroughs in infrastructure development. Building on this momentum, the fourth phase of Yangshan Deep-water Port has installed automated loading and unloading facilities solely designed and manufactured domestically. As part of its fully automatic system, the fourth phase of the Yangshan Deep-water Port chose to use automated guided vehicles, which would shuttle back and forth in the port area to provide container services. This automatic system would raise the efficiency of port operations, bringing a disruptive change to the shipping industry. In the era of artificial intelligence, digital technologies have been widely used in large-scale infrastructure projects. Shanghai has seized the opportunity of digital transformation to accelerate the construction of intelligent ports. In December 2017, the fourth phase of the Yangshan Deep-water Port became operational. As the world's largest automated container terminal, this port boasts the highest level of automation in the world. Standing on the 2,350-meter-long wharf of the fourth phase of the Yangshan Deep-water Port, you can observe beautiful sights of nature and a bustling scene of the port area. As the world's largest container terminal with the highest level of automation, the fourth phase of the Yangshan Deep-water Port has seen continuous growth in port throughput since it entered into operation. On May 3, 2022, it set a new record in the efficiency of automated terminal operations, with a single machine loading and unloading 58.95 units per hour, which reveals the technological sophistication[1] of an unmanned terminal and demonstrates the

---

[1] Cargo Ships no longer have to Wait: The Fourth Phase of the Shanghai Yangshan Deep-water Port is Automatically Running at Full Capacity [EB/OL]. China Media Group Shanghai Bureau, https://sh.cctv. com/2022/06/25/ARTIBBVHR7gK4jqg5bWWQmLQ220625.shtml.

resilience of China's economy to the world.

While China works to promote independent scientific and technological innovation, it uses its own technological achievements to promote common development of the world. The technologies adopted in the fourth phase of the Yangshan Deep-water Port have been widely applied in other parts of the world, proving that the technological development of China benefits the world. In 2015, Shanghai International Port (Group) Co., Ltd. (SIPG) outperformed multiple international competitors and obtained the operation rights for the Haifa Bay Port Terminal of Israel. The terminal began construction in 2018 and started operation on September 1, 2021, becoming the first new port in Israel in 60 years. The Haifa terminal is equipped with the technologies already used and proven in the fourth phase of Yangshan Deep-water Port. It is the first real case of China's readiness to export its advanced intelligent port technologies and management expertise to developed countries. It is also a witness to Shanghai's firm steps to promote high-quality cooperation in technology and infrastructure development.

3. Resources agglomeration based on Yangshan Deep-water Port

Yangshan Deep-water Port gathers resources from Shanghai, the Yangtze River Delta, and other parts of the wider Yangtze River Basin, enabling the Port of Shanghai to become a showcase of China's high-level opening-up. The agglomeration effect of the Yangshan Deep-water Port is manifest in the increased cooperation among the ports in Shanghai, the accelerated construction of the Yangtze River Delta port cluster and the coordinated development of the Yangtze River Basin, etc.

First, as an important constituent of the Port of Shanghai, Yangshan Deep-water Port advances cooperation among ports in Shanghai and contributes to the establishment of an international transit port in Shanghai. Located at the Yangtze River Estuary, Shanghai has numerous river ports and seaports. Since its completion, Yangshan Deep-water Port has boosted the agglomeration of cargo resources, formed close links between ports in Shanghai, and joined other ports in Shanghai in building the city into an international shipping center.

Moreover, Shanghai has implemented a pilot project for cargo relay [1], allowing international container companies to operate coastal shipping in Yangshan Port Area and use the Yangshan Deep-water Port as a transportation hub. Shanghai has also fostered a complementary relationship between Waigaoqiao Port and Yangshan Deep-water Port, two major parts of the Port of Shanghai. This has laid a solid foundation for the Port of Shanghai to work as a hub for freight consolidation and international transshipment. Cooperation among major ports in Shanghai has advanced the integration of cargo resources and routes and captured more market share in freight consolidation and international transshipment. Subsequently, the efficiency of transshipment services provided by the Port of Shanghai increases, further cementing Shanghai's status as an international shipping center.

Second, the construction and completion of the Yangshan Deep-water Port leads to coordinated development and the emergence of a world-class port cluster in the Yangtze River Delta. The Yangshan Deep-water Port was established based on the cooperation between Shanghai and Zhejiang Province. In fact, as a part of the Port of Shanghai, this port is located in Zhoushan City, Zhejiang Province. Based on local conditions, the Port of Shanghai has fostered a cooperative relationship with the Port of Ningbo and the Port of Zhoushan, both among the top ten ports in the world, with an agreement signed to further promote the comprehensive development and cooperation of Xiaoyangshan Island area. This is a new model of cooperation across provinces, facilitating the formation of a world-class port cluster and a new model of integrating ports in the Yangtze River Delta. Moreover, Shanghai has forged closer connections with Zhejiang in foreign trade, contributing to the integrated and high-quality development of the Yangtze River Delta. An integrated regulatory model has been developed to govern Yangshan Deep-water Port and other regional ports in Zhejiang. Likewise, inland ports can be regarded as extensions of the Port of Shanghai. This holistic regulatory model has reduced water transportation

---

[1] Cargo relay refers to the practice of coastal relay of international cargo by a foreign carrier in China's port areas.

costs and streamlined customs clearance procedures. These measures have promoted the coordinated development of logistics and transportation sectors in the Yangtze River Delta. In collaboration with Jiangsu and Zhejiang Provinces, Shanghai has developed a joint maritime supervision mechanism for the Yangshan Deep-water Port Area. The Shanghai Maritime Safety Administration has developed an implementation plan for the integrated development of the Yangtze River Delta. These measures are designed to achieve integration in port supervision, traffic organization, ship inspection and safety management, meet the need of ship companies for joint maritime supervision in the Yangshan Deep-water Port Area and surrounding waters, and boost the integrated administration of maritime affairs in the Yangtze River Delta.

Third, the Yangshan Deep-water Port has expanded the hinterland of the Port of Shanghai from the Yangtze River Delta to the entire Yangtze River Basin. Utilizing the supporting role of the Yangshan Deep-water Port, the Port of Shanghai integrates logistics channels such as waterways, highways, and railways, aiming to promote all-round integration of ports and logistics services in the Yangtze River Delta, and serve as an inland container hub. Besides, the completion of Yangshan Deep-water Port has driven the development of integrated river-ocean transportation and maritime transportation network in the Yangtze River Basin. The transit function of the Port of Shanghai has been strengthened by the Yangshan Deep-water Port, as more goods from the Yangtze River Basin are transported to the world from here. The Yangshan Deep-water Port indirectly boosts the construction of port facilities along the Yangtze River, facilitating the expansion of foreign trade in the Yangtze River Basin, reaching the upper reaches of the Yangtze River in western China. As a cargo-gathering hub and transit port, the Yangshan Deep-water Port has optimized the port structure of the Yangtze River Basin, highlighting the advantage of the Yangtze River as a golden waterway, and promoting the development of an outward-oriented economy in this region. It can be said that, as regards the logistics chain, the Yangshan Deep-water Port is an important link in China's new development pattern with domestic circulation as the mainstay, and domestic and international circulations enhancing

one another.

This agglomeration of resources contributes to the fulfillment of Shanghai's goal of building itself into an international shipping center, enables the Port of Shanghai to win the competition to become a global shipping hub, and makes important contributions to the economic development of Shanghai, Zhejiang, the wider Yangtze River Delta, and even the entire Yangtze River Basin. This strongly supports China's opening-up and builds a strategic fulcrum for China's successful participation in international competition and global collaboration.

4. Yangshan Deep-water Port: A highlight in the development of free trade areas

As Shanghai's function as a bonded area continues to improve, development opportunities for the Yangshan Deep-water Port are becoming increasingly exciting. With the inclusion of Xiaoyangshan Island (where the Yangshan Deepwater Port is located) into the Lingang Special Area of SFTZ established on August 6, 2019, the Yangshan Deep-water Port has become a global hub port, and efforts have been made to encourage coastal transportation, international ship registration, and opening of international navigation rights. As its capacity to attract and allocate cargo resources improves, the Yangshan Deep-water Port has also become a critical node in the international shipping route network. The exciting opportunities have attracted many leading domestic and foreign businesses such as Tesla to build factories in the Lingang Special Area of SFTZ, since they can leverage the convenience offered by the free trade zone to facilitate the shipment of their products within China and to other parts of the world.

In May 2020, the Yangshan Special Comprehensive Bonded Area was established, which is currently the only special comprehensive bonded area in China's customs special supervision zones, playing an important role as a major driver of domestic economic growth and a strategically significant link for domestic and international economic circulations. The establishment of this bonded area also highlights China's institutional and policy

strengths as it pursues higher quality and efficiency in an accelerated high-standard opening-up process. The Yangshan Special Comprehensive Bonded Area also has instituted mechanisms for higher-level trade liberalization and facilitation, including special models for declaration, trade control, and the administration of bonded areas, statistics, information and collaboration respectively. As a result, it will become a demonstration area for new-type trade facilitation and a new global shipping hub where innovative business operations are encouraged. Specifically, it aims to establish an internationally recognized and most competitive framework for free trade by 2025, with significantly improved economic quality and efficiency, integrated innovative bonded businesses, and improved resource allocation capabilities. In other words, it is striving to become a showcase of China's dual economic circulations, domestic and international. Looking ahead to 2035, the Yangshan Special Comprehensive Bonded Area will strive to become a major center for ten purposes, including international transit and distribution, international distribution and delivery, international order placement and settlement, global sales and services, and cross-border digital trade. Owing to the high-level opening-up in both the Lingang Special Area and the Yangshan Special Comprehensive Bonded Area, the Lingang Industrial Zone in Shanghai, launched as a "national foreign trade transformation and upgrading base", has experienced tremendous high-quality development. It is home to many global suppliers of automobiles and components which have generated a total output value of nearly 200 billion yuan. In 2022, the Lingang Industrial Zone exported half of China's total new energy vehicles, with total exports and imports exceeding 10 billion US dollars. The prosperity of the automotive industry in the Lingang Industrial Zone has attracted leading international automotive manufacturers such as Tesla, BMW, Mercedes Benz, Volkswagen, Porsche, Volvo, and Chrysler to establish their regional headquarters there, while domestic auto companies such as SAIC Motor have been encouraged to expand their global marketing platforms in the zone. In this sense, the Lingang Industrial Zone has become a magnet for foreign companies while also serving as a springboard for domestic ones to go global. These efforts have provided a strong institutional guarantee for Shanghai to become one of the world's leading shipping centers in

the future.

From Phase I to Phase IV of the Yangshan Deep-water Port to the establishment of the Yangshan Special Comprehensive Bonded Area, the Port of Shanghai has relied on the Yangshan Deep- water Port as a large-scale advanced infrastructure to increase its cargo handling capacity, so this facility marks a significant breakthrough in Shanghai's infrastructure construction to become an international shipping center. On May 15, 2017, Kitack Lim, Secretary General of the International Maritime Organization (IMO), said during a meeting with Ying Yong, then Mayor of Shanghai, that the city has already grown into a world-class shipping center in terms of both hardware and software. Despite these great achievements, however, Shanghai still has a lot to do on the road towards cementing its position as an international shipping center which has broad development prospects in the future.

The broad development prospects are attributed to two major endeavors of Shanghai. The first is that the city embraces digital technologies such as the Internet, cloud computing, big data, and blockchain. By applying these technologies to the shipping industry, Shanghai is committed to promoting the digital transformation of its shipping services as an international shipping center. In the future, the shipping center will become more digital and efficient in its operations, thus increasing the global influence of its shipping services. Second, improving shipping services has been made a top priority in the overall development. Shanghai will provide high-end services such as shipping finance and insurance, shipping brokerage and arbitration, as well as maritime consulting services. To this end, the city is working to attract shipping-related functional institutions at all levels to Shanghai and accelerate the digital transformation of traditional shipping services. These efforts will enhance Shanghai's ability as a shipping center to provide better services to the world.

III. Conclusion

Facing the negative impacts of growing reverse globalization and anti-globalization thinking, as some major countries resort to trade protectionism and erect trade barriers,

China has remained firmly committed to multilateralism and globalization, adhering to a policy of high-level opening-up and peaceful development. While China enters into many multilateral trade agreements such as the Regional Comprehensive Economic Partnership (RCEP), the construction of new land-sea channels continues to advance. The development of shipping infrastructure helps drive regional economic integration and increases logistics demand significantly. This is of great significance for China to promote high-quality development and ensure global supply chain security and stability.

In the era of globalization, Chinese modernization plays a critical role in the world economy. China's strengthened connection with the outside world is closely related to the development of international trade from port to port. China is a major maritime country and a leading player in the shipping and shipbuilding industries. It tops the world in major areas including water-borne transportation, shipbuilding, fishing, and crew strength, and boasts numerous maritime routes and expanding service networks worldwide. Boasting access to the most container routes and the densest flights, or the most extensive transportation network in the world, Shanghai has become a leading international sea and air hub city in the mainland of China and even globally. The city has basically completed the construction of the international shipping center. Based on its high-quality shipping infrastructure, this international shipping center consolidates Shanghai's leading position in China's foreign trade and enables it to draw quality resources to the Yangtze River Delta and even east China as a whole. It also helps China play an important role in global supply chains and industrial chains, and contributes to economic globalization while promoting Chinese modernization.

The construction of the international shipping center is also a major project under the Belt and Road Initiative, which has become an important global public good. In 2023, while marking the 10th anniversary of this Initiative, China is working with other countries to achieve mutual prosperity, which demonstrates China's strong commitment to peaceful development and modernization. Shanghai has proactively promoted high-quality development of the shipping industry under the Belt and Road Initiative and as part of its efforts to build itself into an international shipping center. Following the new

trend of eco-friendly, low-carbon and smart development, Shanghai has also driven the integrated development of ports, bonded areas, and free trade areas to achieve coordinated development in the Yangtze River Delta. Besides, Shanghai is utilizing emerging digital technologies to improve the efficiency of the shipping industry and is attempting to break through institutional constraints over shipping trade through institutional opening-up, coordination of various departments to create an efficient port system for trade facilitation, while also gathering more high-quality high-level elements to fuel the transformation of the shipping industry and applying international rules and standards.

Outstanding achievements made in international shipping center construction are also breakthroughs of Chinese modernization in the new era. China, relying on its own industrial strengths and resource endowment, has accelerated the construction of shipping infrastructure, improved its shipping capacity, and upgraded shipping service standards, promoting the steady growth of international trade and the prosperity of the world economy, and making a great contribution to the improvement of global wellbeing, which is part of its efforts to build a community with a shared future for mankind.

High-level opening-up to promote global prosperity

I. Introduction

International cooperation is an important driver for the progress of human civilization and a necessary path towards global prosperity. To create mutual benefits, China has continued to promote export and import cooperation through opening-up, which has aided in enhancing the development momentum of other countries while pushing forward economic globalization. Over the past 40 years of reform and opening-up, China has achieved remarkable progress. From 2012 to 2021, China's average contribution to global economic growth reached 38.6%, making it the primary driving force behind the world's economic expansion. China's total retail sales of consumer goods have grown at an average rate of 8.8%, making it the second-largest consumer market for commodities worldwide. The proportion of China's manufacturing value-added to the global total has increased from 22.3% to nearly 29.8%, continuously maintaining its position as the world's leading manufacturing powerhouse.

Traditional development economists believe that developing countries pay more attention to exports and less to imports in their development strategies. The reason is that greater exports can expand employment and drive economic growth, while more imports will reduce savings and even open the domestic market to external competition. In recent years, however, China has implemented a new round of high-level opening-up and further

deepened the import cooperation. Why should China, as a developing country, further deepen its import cooperation? What are its key measures to advance import cooperation? How effective are these measures? How can overseas entities participate in this process, seize the market opportunities China offers, and share in the country's development achievements? These four questions boil down to China's strategy in the new round of high-level opening-up and they will be answered by presenting some typical cases. CIIE is the world's first national-level exhibition focusing on imports. We will analyze it through the vivid case of China's deepening deployment of import cooperation in promoting a new round of high-level opening-up: CIIE. Supporting and participating in this process, Shanghai has fully played its role as a pioneer of China's reform and opening-up and innovation-driven development, which is why it is the host city and an important organizer of CIIE.

II. CIIE: The world's first national-level exhibition focusing on imports

CIIE, first held in 2018, runs from November 5 to 10 each year at the National Exhibition and Convention Center in Shanghai (NECC Shanghai). It is an extraordinary exhibition for several reasons. First, the event focuses exclusively on imports, unlike other exhibitions that feature export or import-export themes. Second, CIIE, proposed by Chinese President Xi Jinping, is the first national-level import exhibition worldwide, which is set apart from exhibitions organized by provinces, cities, or individual enterprises. Third, while other exhibitions solely focus on products, CIIE attaches importance to promoting international exchanges and mutual interest by organizing the Hongqiao International Economic Forum. Fourth, while other exhibitions highlight the products and concepts of businesses, CIIE also includes both displays of products and national comprehensive strengths. The scale of participation in CIIE is amazing. The 5th CIIE welcomed the participation of 145 countries, regions, and international organizations, as well as 284

Fortune 500 companies and industry captains who came for the commercial exhibition. CIIE has also garnered worldwide attention. According to the Report on the Media Coverage and Influence of the 5th China International Import Expo, the total media exposure of the 5th CIIE exceeded 5.6 billion times, bringing the total exposure of CIIE to 10 billion times over the past five years.

South square of the venue of 5th CIIE (Photo by Zhu Weihui/ IP SHANGHAI)

1. Background of CIIE

Speaking at the opening ceremony of the first CIIE, Chinese President Xi Jinping explained the background of the event. As he said, the world is going through a new round of major development, transformation and adjustment. The economic and social well-being of countries in the world is increasingly interconnected. The reform of the global governance system and the international order is picking up speed. On the other hand, the world economy is going through profound adjustment, and protectionism and unilateralism

are resurging. Economic globalization faces headwinds, and multilateralism and the system of free trade are under threat. Uncertainties and instabilities still abound, and risks and challenges are growing. Living in such a complex world, we need to see the underlying, bolster confidence in our future through opening-up and cooperation and work together to cope with risks and challenges. It was against this backdrop that China decided to host CIIE to promote global trade and investment liberalization and facilitation, to maintain the multilateral trading system, to promote regional economic integration, and to expand the convergence of interests with other countries.

China recognizes that greater openness is key to spurring high-quality development, which is a major motivation for CIIE. On one hand, domestic demand and consumption are important drivers for China's economic growth. According to data released by the National Bureau of Statistics, consumption has contributed an average of 58.1% to China's economic growth, making it the primary driver of China's development. Over the past decade, the annual average contribution of domestic demand to China's economic growth has exceeded 100%, reaching 105.7%. Therefore, expanding domestic demand holds great significance to the growth of the Chinese economy. In this case, domestic demand refers to people's need for quality consumer goods and services. When the domestic supply of goods and services fails to meet the demand for consumption upgrading, it becomes necessary to ensure that import channels are smooth. On the other hand, CIIE plays a crucial role in upgrading industry, consumption and trade, and would create opportunities for consumers, enterprises, local communities, and overall economic growth in China. China hopes to use CIIE as a window to bring in advanced technologies, standards, and management expertise to enhance the innovation and development of domestic market entities. Products imported through this mechanism can also help Chinese enterprises enhance their competitive advantages by reducing costs, improving processes, and updating the application of technologies. Furthermore, expanding imports through CIIE serves other essential purposes. First, it helps resolve the principal contradiction between unbalanced and inadequate development and the people's ever-growing needs for a better life. Second, it addresses the mismatch between

supply-side and demand-side factors. Finally, it helps address the structural imbalance of surplus supply at the low end and relatively insufficient supply at the middle and high-ends.

Shanghai was chosen as the host city for CIIE for good reasons. First, Shanghai is blessed with favorable geographical advantages and other endowments. The Port of Shanghai has topped the world in container throughput for seven consecutive years, which underscores the city's exceptional import and export transportation capabilities. Shanghai's location at the mid-point of China's coastal line enables it to effectively harness spillover effects. Second, Shanghai boasts a highly developed MICE industry. The success of APEC China 2001 in Shanghai earned the city the fame as "the safest city in the world". The success of Expo 2010 Shanghai China brought new opportunities for Shanghai's MICE industry, further elevating the industry's internationalization, branding, specialization, and marketization efforts. Third, Shanghai provides a first-class business environment. It offers a fair and competitive market environment, efficient government services, an independent and convenient investment climate, and an open and inclusive atmosphere for foreign businesses. The favorable business environment has benefited and drawn overseas enterprises, such as Tesla. In 2019, Tesla completed the construction of its Gigafactory in Shanghai (Tesla Giga Shanghai) at an amazing pace; in 2021, Tesla Giga Shanghai produced over 480,000 vehicles, surpassing Tesla Fremont Factory, the North American champion, which produced approximately 450,000 vehicles. Tesla CEO Elon Musk attributed the impressive speed to the joint efforts between the Shanghai Municipal People's Government and the Tesla team. Fourth, Shanghai boasts a great record of opening-up to the world. It is a pioneer in China's reform and opening-up, as well as a trailblazer in China's innovation-driven development. Shanghai has gained a wealth of experience from building SFTZ, which has been promoted nationwide.

2. CIIE enriching and improving people's lives

Import of goods and services is a key purpose of CIIE and an important part of China's attempt to promote international cooperation. Over the past five years, evolving and upgrading consumer needs in China have been very well met, which has allowed

people to live a better life. It is clear enough that the import of high-tech products from overseas through CIIE directly improves people's lives. Classic vintage cars and Metaverse technologies were displayed at the event side by side, showing an amazing collision and fusion between retro and futurism; from French cheese, Zimbabwean coffees, to naan pizzas, CIIE has a display of delicious foods; and green technology was everywhere, showcasing that fashion personalization has come true at CIIE. In short, CIIE shows an image of a desired life. For example, Alfred Kärcher SE & Co. KG utilizes advanced intelligent cleaning technologies to meet the demands of Chinese consumers. The company collaborates with China's top R&D teams to build visual navigation systems and create a cutting-edge AI commercial cleaning product with local intelligence. Inspired by China's cleaning market, this intelligent cleaning tool has been developed exclusively for Chinese consumers.

The benefits that CIIE brings to people are realized by the huge number of import transactions. The total volumes of intended transactions reached at the event during the past five years were 57.83 billion US dollars, 71.13 billion US dollars, 72.62 billion US dollars, 70.72 billion US dollars, and 73.53 billion US dollars, respectively. According to a report on the media coverage and influence of the 5th CIIE, "carbon-neutral milk" became a buzzword, and Theland was a Top 2 brand in media exposure and influence. Yan Zhijun, marketing director of Theland, said that this new product was first launched at the 5th CIIE, and registered a year-on-year sales growth of 225% after this exhibition, showing the event's strong influence. Besides, all products displayed there can be bought throughout the year. CIIE has set up a "6+365 days" (6 days of CIIE plus a regular year of 365 days) exhibition platform which also allows sellers to meet and trade with buyers anytime. At the first four CIIEs, this platform attracted 502, 888, 866, and 920 overseas exhibitors respectively, with import transactions worth 66.35 billion yuan, 80.12 billion yuan, 78.66 billion yuan, and 82 billion yuan, respectively. To convert imported exhibits into bonded goods and facilitate bonded cross-border e-commerce trade for qualified goods, CIIE has built a bonded logistics center. These measures have prolonged the period open to purchase and maximized the

influence of CIIE.

Import transaction services have been upgraded at CIIE, which has paved a more convenient and economical way for consumers to buy overseas goods. Customs clearance and financial services have also played an important role in establishing a smooth, efficient, and well-regulated procurement process. For example, transportation tools including ships that deliver CIIE exhibits have access to convenient and preferential services, including port services, traffic organization, and information services. In a media interview, a respondent said, "Thanks to CIIE, now we can buy fresher and less expensive Thai durians." Meanwhile, the Shanghai Branch of China Construction Bank has set up a temporary office at CIIE venue to provide on-site professional services. In response to buyers' large-scale purchasing intentions and their temporary financing needs, it has established a green channel to realize rapid financing and has developed exclusive products to provide efficient and high-quality financial services for enterprises, facilitating the import procurement and the transformation of "exhibits" into "import goods".

Procurement channels have been increased at CIIE, so the needs of more consumers can be better met. A typical example is the introduction of popular and efficient sales channels among local people such as live-streaming e-commerce. In China, live-streaming e-commerce, a new type of online trading, has quickly emerged in recent years. Livestream anchors would present products online and interact with potential customers, and customers would then complete their purchase by clicking relevant links. To facilitate and realize this new model of e-commerce, many well-known anchors familiar to Chinese customers would be invited to CIIE, and a way has been created for Chinese anchors to sell products through livestreaming together with exhibitor teams. This model has achieved good results. At the 5th CIIE, high-quality exotic products such as Malaysian coffee, Thai young coconut, and Japanese and Korean beauty products were sold online, with the total sales revenue reaching 132 million yuan in just 6 hours, and 120,000 cans of hand-peeled pine nuts from Afghanistan were sold out within just 14 seconds. In short, CIIE has utilized various sales channels such as live-streaming e-commerce to realize the

transformation of "exhibits" into "imported goods".

3. Enhancement of cooperation between enterprises

CIIE has not only promoted import procurement but also foreign investment and investment cooperation between exhibitors. Over the past five years, many businesses have strengthened their cooperation with their partners through CIIE, some finding new partners, and some deepening their cooperation with existing partners. For example, Panasonic Group has participated in the event for five consecutive years and has entered into partnerships with many other enterprises. At the 4th CIIE, Panasonic signed a memorandum of understanding with CIMC Enric Holdings Limited and its subsidiaries to jointly develop integrated hydrogen-electric products using its hydrogen/electricity co-generation module and technology. In addition, after signing strategic cooperation agreements with China Pacific Insurance Co., Ltd. (CPIC) and Mitsui Sumitomo Insurance (China) Co., Ltd. (MSI China) in 2020, Panasonic also signed an agreement with CPIC's elderly care division to create a smart elderly care laboratory. The three parties have also established their cooperation in the field of electric vehicles and signed a cooperation agreement on providing new insurance services and developing new businesses. Tetsuro Homma, executive vice president of Panasonic Corporation, said,

"We have been in the Chinese market for many years, and our traditional products sell very well here. However, CIIE has become a driving force for us to further increase our sales. Orders we receive at CIIE outnumber the same period in previous years, and the volume of the entire year has also increased remarkably."

Trade and investment matchmaking fairs held during CIIE have benefited more than 3,800 exhibitors and 7,800 purchasers from over 100 countries and regions over the past four years, and more than 4,500 cooperation intents have been reached. Organizing investment matchmaking fairs is the largest and longest sideline activity at CIIE. In addition to those that take place during exhibitions, there are also many pre-exhibition meetings. The organizer brings exhibitors and purchasers together at the NECC (Shanghai) to facilitate

negotiations and match investment supply with demand. Exhibitors said it was "unexpected" and "very surprising" to participate in such investment matchmaking fairs. For example, Bai Daping, general manager of Jungheinrich China, said, "Previously, most of our customers in China were foreign companies running factories in China. This matchmaking fair allows us to meet many Chinese State-owned enterprises, which is very surprising." Song Chao, network promoting manager of Omron Health Medical (China) Co., Ltd., said that they had only been familiar with medical markets in the first and second-tier cities of China and had no knowledge of the third or fourth tier cities before, but investment meetings helped them easily find potential customers in those smaller cities which used to cost a lot to connect. BioMérieux, a world leader in the field of in vitro diagnostics, has participated in CIIE every year since 2019 and displayed their newly developed products for COVID-19 testing and diagnostics, solutions for microbiology lab automation, and cutting-edge antimicrobial stewardship (AMS) solutions. "Through CIIE, BioMérieux has showcased our latest products and technologies to the world. At the fourth CIIE, we held 8 signing ceremonies and attended 10 large forums and promotion meetings. Over 90 delegations including purchasing teams visited our stand. CIIE has created excellent opportunities for international exchange and cooperation."

Shanghai has worked to optimize its investment environment and facilitate the entry of foreign investors in order to promote cooperation. The city has built trade facilitation platforms such as the Hongqiao Overseas Trade Center, demonstration zones for promotion of import trade, and the Import and Export Commodity Distribution Center. Recently, more than 30 trade service institutions including the Silk Road Chamber of International Commerce (SRCIC), Shanghai Association for Foreign Cultural Exchange Hongqiao Overseas Academy, Singapore Enterprise Center (SEC), Swiss China Center (SCC), Cámara de Comercio e Inversiones de China en España (CCINCE), Maycham China, the Japanese Chamber of Commerce and Industry in China, Centre des Entreprises Françaises, Shanghai Taiwan Investors Association, Croatian Chamber of Economy (CCE), Brazil's Invest SP, European Business and Innovation Centre Network (EBN), and the Thailand Cultural

and Economic Association have settled in the Hongqiao Overseas Trade Center. Through these trade service and facilitation institutions, Shanghai connects with over 150 trade and investment promotion institutions worldwide. For example, the Singapore Enterprise Center (SEC) has brought 18 Singaporean companies to the Yangtze River Delta within two years.

4. International cooperation empowered by institutional opening-up

Institutional opening-up increases the mobility of goods and elements by unifying rules and mechanisms and enhancing the transparency and stability of international exchanges. As President Xi Jinping said at the opening ceremony of the 5th CIIE,

"China will work with all countries and all parties to share the opportunities from its institutional opening-up. We will steadily expand institutional opening-up with regard to rules, regulations, management and standards, put into full effect the new Catalogue of Encouraged Industries for Foreign Investment, and further develop the national integrated demonstration zone for greater openness in the service sector. We will implement the strategy to upgrade pilot free trade areas, accelerate the Hainan Free Trade Port development, and tap into their role as pilot platforms for comprehensive reform and opening-up."

Important issues such as trade and investment facilitation, intellectual property protection, and business environment improvement have been embedded into the institutional opening-up drive of CIIE. Over the past five years, measures of opening-up such as reducing tariffs, easing market access, deepened implementation of pre-entry national treatment, and negative list administration, as well as support for the deepening of reform and innovation in the SFTZ, have been basically put into action, which has strongly facilitated international cooperation. Many foreign companies such as Moh Kee Enterprise from Malaysia have benefited from this. An executive of Moh Kee said:

"As few people knew about our products before, it was very difficult to export them. By collaborating with Chinese companies and allowing Chinese agents to showcase our products at CIIE, we've given purchasers and consumers a more direct idea of our products. Through exhibition and promotion at CIIE, our sales have significantly increased. For us,

CIIE is a great opportunity to enter the Chinese and the global markets."

Shanghai is proactively promoting institutional opening-up and issued the Regulations on Shanghai Serving CIIE on the eve of the 5th CIIE, mainly to optimize the business environment. This was the first time that the Chinese government had legislated for an exhibition. It was a concrete manifestation of China's commitment to integrate with the world. It also served to highlight Shanghai's determination to take actions based on order and rules, build a law-based environment for investors and traders from all over the world, and demonstrate the significance and practical value of the rule of law.

On November 5, 2022, the Minhang Trading Branch of the 5th CIIE signed a centralized procurement contract at Building A of Hongqiao Pinhui (Photo by Minhang District Information Office × IP SHANGHAI)

Government departments will be the main targets of regulation while they work to organize and support CIIE. They are obliged to comply with laws and regulations to set an example for other participants. In other words, a law-based government is a prerequisite for law-based CIIEs. The effectiveness of a law-based government is shown in two aspects. First, as scientific concepts are incorporated into laws and regulations, governments will properly steer participation in CIIE, establishing high standards and enhancing exhibition quality. These concepts, including those proposed by President Xi Jinping, including an open, innovative, coordinated as well as green and sustainable development, are all pillars supporting the success of CIIE. Legislating scientific concepts also demonstrates China's responsiveness to international trends and its national consensus on the development of the MICE industry. Following rules and regulations that encourage environment-friendly, technology-intensive and collaborative exhibitions, the government would lead and inspire other entities involved to open wider to the world. Second, the Regulations have been drawn up based on the past experience of governments in organizing CIIE, especially on how to interact with the market and perform their respective roles and responsibilities. This ensures an effective coordination between governments and the market in making the event a success. CIIE is a high-level exhibition organized by the Chinese government rather than any business entity, while the success of such an exhibition and the MICE industry is a symbol of the vitality of China's socialist market economy and highlights the decisive role of the market in resource allocation. By coordinating government macro-control and market dynamics, China is putting its economy on the track towards Pareto optimality. The government's primary duties for CIIE are to provide support for exhibition organizers and services for exhibitors, while creating positive ripple effects in related industries and regions. This is also part of the government's efforts to become more service oriented. Focused on the government's functions, the Regulations include three chapters as follows: "Support for Exhibition and Conference Organization", "Services and Guarantee", and "Comprehensive Effects". The legalization of effective experience enables the government to continue to serve as a good example for market entities.

Shanghai has made significant achievements in advancing institutional opening- up and creating positive spillover effects in multiple dimensions to enhance international cooperation. The first is the time dimension. Shanghai has created a never-ending CIIE. How has this been achieved? The answer can be found in the Regulations, which dictates how exhibits can be transformed into bonded goods and traded via cross-border e-commerce after the exhibition. Furthermore, as per the Regulations, the Hongqiao International Open Hub has set up such year-round and around-the-clock platforms as the "6+365 days" platform, the display and trading center for imported goods, and the bonded logistics center. The second dimension is space. The Regulations clearly dictate how to unleash or capture the spillover effects of CIIE in a broader area, such as the Yangtze River Delta, the whole of China, and the Asia-Pacific region. The third is the industrial dimension. Boasting agglomeration effects, the MICE industry can drive the coordinated growth of upstream and downstream industries, deepen the division of labor, optimize resource allocation, reduce search costs, and promote industrial upgrading. Therefore, the Regulations require governments to formulate measures and develop proper mechanisms for resource sharing, thus facilitating the growth of CIIE-related industries like commerce, tourism, culture, and sports.

III. Conclusion

Open cooperation means that countries and regions enhance each other while working together. It can boost total global demand and create momentum for global economic growth. The key to open cooperation lies in the interplay between domestic and international markets and resources. After more than 40 years of reform and opening-up, China can now meet the basic needs of its people. As people seek a better life, the demand for consumption upgrade becomes obvious. However, domestic producers still fail to satisfy all demands for high-quality goods and services. Therefore, China needs to bring in more quality goods and services, advanced technologies, standards, and management expertise from overseas to promote consumption, trade, and industrial upgrading. At the same time, increasing imports

can also stimulate total global demand and economic recovery. As the world's second largest consumer market and the largest trader in goods, China has a huge potential demand to satisfy. By expanding imports to meet the demand, China can not only promote its own economic growth, but also bring prosperity to the rest of world.

Recognizing the importance of imports, China has developed effective approaches to promote open cooperation. First, China will promote institutional opening-up and advance law-based governance. It will align with international rules, enhancing transparency and stability in international interactions and facilitating the flows of goods and factors of production. Second, it will also advance innovation governance by, for example, integrating national exhibitions with commercial ones, and organizing forums during exhibitions. Third, the nation will highlight collective power through investment and trade matchmaking events and group procurement. Finally, China will create spillover effects of good governance. Take for example its efforts to create and capture ripple effects of open cooperation in CIIE from the dimensions of time, space, and industry. China can fully leverage the effective governance of Shanghai, the host city, to increase the effectiveness of State governance.

Opening-up helps China overcome difficulties in development, drive cooperation and innovation, and contribute to prosperity. It facilitates economic globalization, injects impetus into the growth of various other countries and regions, and makes the fruits of growth benefit people around the world. By opening-up, China can work together with other economies to make the global economic pie ever larger, and eventually build a community with a shared future for mankind.

Epilogue

The city of Shanghai, backed by the Yangtze River Basin and facing the Pacific Ocean, has long led China in opening to the outside world. It is a city full of charm, so it is hailed as a "Magic City" around the world. In this book, Shanghai is taken as a sample for studying the Chinese path to modernization, not only because today's Shanghai is accelerating its efforts to become a modern socialist international metropolis with global influence, but also because of its special history: it was once humiliated as it was forced open in the past but is now confident and proactive in opening up to the outside world. The logic behind this dramatic change is inspiring.

We've decided to publish this book entitled "Why Shanghai? —The Stories of Chinese Modernization" because we hope that readers around the world can better understand the past, present and future of Shanghai, and hence the characteristics and bright prospects of Chinese modernization.

There are innumerable enlightening stories of Chinese modernization, but the cases selected in this book are limited and may not fully and accurately represent the latest practice and achievements of China in pursuing modernization. Due to the unique readership of this book, we've focused on the interest of our readers in the development of megacities. We hope to create a basis for dialogue about urban development and thus contribute Chinese wisdom and Shanghai experience to help improve urban development and governance around the world.

This book is written by the young faculty of Shanghai Party Institute of CPC (Shanghai Administration Institute). This writing project was completed within around half a year,

after a lot of research was done in the early preparatory stages. The fast speed has been made possible by the fact that these young scholars have participated in both online and offline international exchange programs in recent years. Some cases have been taken from the recorded online courses or on-site visit materials. This writing project was planned and organized by Prof. Luo Feng, Provost of Shanghai Party Institute of CPC (Shanghai Administration Institute), and for the purpose of this project, Prof. Luo has convened and chaired multiple expert meetings to determine the writing requirements, including the style and structure, of this book. He has also written the preface for this book. The division of duty for each chapter is as follows: Chapter 1 was written by Wang Yao, Gan Meixia, and Zhao Enguo; Chapter 2 was written by Zhou Jing, Xin Yaoyao, and Han Xu; Chapter 3 was written by Hu Jirong, Yu Jianning, and Chen Yuting; Chapter 4 was written by Sun Lingxue, Ye Lan, and Wang Zhongqi; and Chapter 5 was written by Ding Changyan, Geng Zhao, and Xu Yulu. Thank you all for your hard work.

Xu Jiangang, Executive Vice President of Shanghai Party Institute of CPC (Shanghai Administration Institute), has shown great interest in this writing project and remained personally involved from beginning to end. Thanks also go to many other experts and scholars including: Sha Hailin, former Deputy Director of the Standing Committee of the Shanghai Municipal People's Congress, Wang Weisong, Secretary of the Party Leadership Group and Full-time Vice Chairman of Shanghai Federation of Social Sciences Associations, Liu Genfa, Director of the Department of Foreign Exchange, Training and Development of China Executive Leadership Academy Pudong, Chen Yiqun, Deputy Director of the International Publicity Office of the CPC Shanghai Municipal Committee and the Information Office of the Shanghai Municipal People's Government, Zhu Feng, Director of the News and Culture Department of Shanghai Municipal Foreign Affairs Office, Zhou Zhiqiang, former Deputy Secretary of the CPC Committee of Jiefang Daily, Shen Guilong, Research Professor and Director of the Institute of China Studies of the Shanghai Academy of Social Sciences, Wu Xueming, Director of the Publicity Department of the CPC Committee of the Shanghai Academy of Social Sciences, Prof. Wen Jun, Dean of the School

of Social Development of East China Normal University, Prof. Huang Xiaochun, Dean of the School of Sociology and Political Science of Shanghai University, Prof. Zhao Meijuan, Secretary of the CPC Committee of the Graduate Institute of Interpretation and Translation of Shanghai International Studies University, Prof. Zhao Gangyin, Director of Department of Party Building of Shanghai Party Institute of CPC (Shanghai Administration Institute), Wang Zhen, Editor-in-chief of Jiefang Daily Theory Studio and Wu Ting, Editor-in-chief of the international edition (Sixth Tone) of The Paper, who have participated in the writing project from preparing the outline to the review of drafts of this book, and have provided many valuable suggestions. Thank you for your generous support.

The Civil Servant Training Department of Shanghai Party Institute of CPC (Shanghai Administration Institute) has set up an ad hoc team in charge of the writing project, consisting of Zhao Wen, Hu Jingbo, Ouyang Chengyi, Cao Jing, Xu Hui, Zhang Yuan, Yu Jinjin, and Han Shengyi who have done a great organizing and coordinating job. Last but not least, I would like to thank editors of the National Academy of Governance Press and the translation team from Shanghai International Studies University as this book is published in both Chinese and English.

This is the first attempt of Shanghai Party Institute of CPC (Shanghai Administration Institute) to publish a bilingual reader. Due to limited experience, as well as the shortage of time, mistakes may exist. Please kindly let us know if you have found any.

Editorial Board

September 2023

汉字与大千世界

汉字与书写

汉字与书法艺术

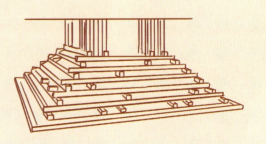